D0842888

LHASA LORE

THE COMPLETE LHASA APSO HANDBOOK

Sally Ann Vervaeke-Helf

1992

Rainbow Olympia Publishers
P.O. Box 1545
Poughkeepsie, NY 12601

Design and layout by Joan Harris

International Standard Book Number 0-931866-12-X

Printed in the United States of America.

In Memory of

Kachina Beryl Shalimar
1976–1978

KACHINA

She was as free as a butterfly
    On the wings of the breeze;
Joyful as a daffodil
    Shining in the sun;
Deep as a silver mysty shadow
    On a moon-lit night;
She waltzed into my life
    And out again . . .
Leaving behind good memories
    And a very small legacy.
                 –S. V.-H.

TABLE OF CONTENTS

PREFACE

This book is an expression of love and dedication for the Lhasa Apsos which are a part of my life. When Kachina, my first Lhasa, came into my life, she opened a Pandora's Box. Ever since that time I have studied and listened and learned. This book represents the questions I have sought answers for throughout the years, what I have learned, and the questions which new owners now ask me. Hopefully it will make your quest for knowledge and understanding of our breed a little easier.

There is so very much to learn, all of which takes more time than I have, and I shall never know all. As for what I have shared, there will be those who agree with me, and some who will disagree. There may be errors in these pages, albeit the effort has been made to avoid them. Though it has not been easy to assimilate some of the facts nor to spell them out for others, I have tried my best to clearly state matters as I understand them.

Some of the facts have been found in special places, such as history items in the Rare Books Library at Rochester Institute of Technology. Other facts were located at the AKC Library with the help of Roberta Vesley. Every book, magazine, newsletter, and bulletin about Lhasas which I have been able to obtain has been perused over and over. Robert Sharp lent me everything in his library, including valuable old books. Mary Smart Carter sent me treasure boxes of materials, including her scrapbooks, some of which I could get nowhere else, from her library in Texas. I cannot thank these two enough.

Many facts were shared with me by friends like Ruth Smith, Pat Chenoweth, and Ann-Marie Adderly. Others shared so much with me through demonstration, discussion, and letters. These included Dr. Ellen Brown, Betty Anne Joseph, Bonnie Sellner, Noel Benson, Dorothy Wilson, Jane Browning, Annette Lurton, Jean Kausch, Harriet Silverman, Nancy Coglianese, Elizabeth Faust, and many others. Barbara and Charles Steele sent materials which included the skeletal rendition of the Lhasa Apso and the materials for the chapter on wills and disposition of Lhasas.

The many discussions which Shirley Lennox and I held as she worked on the line drawings certainly clarified my understanding of the structure of our Lhasas. Then there was the knowledge, expertise, and materials about breeding shared with me by Jon Rawleigh and Jerry Watson.

Then, too, there were colleagues at Brockport High School who helped me. David Kelly, who instructs biology, aided much with helping me to understand and to write about genetics. James Godshall, instructor of photography, not only took some of the photos and prepared them, but also taught me how to develop, print, and reproduce photos. Their help was invaluable.

The members of our specialty club, the Canal Country Lhasa Apso Club, have also shared information with me. They include the Mauros, the Scheelers, and the Murphys. Karen Elibol took the whelping pictures I needed. Above all, there have been the Lhasas whom I have observed and with whom I have worked. There are those who co-own Lhasas with me—Joyce and Bill Spence, Karen Elibol, and Donna and Elizabeth Mauro.

Comments which have been made to me have been considered. You know, I shall never forget Maria Aspuru saying to me as I came out of a ring in North Carolina with Rumpie: "That is a beautiful dog. Put him with a handler." Of course, she did not know that that decision had already been made and that was why I was there. Although she didn't do much for my already shaky self-confidence in the ring, she did stimulate me to attend handling classes. Above all else, Maria Aspuru gave me confidence in my judgment.

I attended handling classes under Nancy McGarvey, John Fabian, Jon Rawleigh, and Betty Austin. I learned from all. Then, too, I was lucky to get advice from one of the best Lhasa handlers of all time, Robert Sharp.

As I extend my thanks to all of these people, I must also express my appreciation for the editing of Betty McKinney, without whom this book might not be a reality. I must also thank my family—my mom, my dad, my son Curt, my daughter Althea, and my Auntie Beryl—who never doubted that I would complete the job I had set out to do.

I am a teacher by vocation, and as a teacher I have tried to share with you what I have learned. I am also a breeder of Lhasa Apsos, and as a breeder I have tried to share with you the knowledge I have accumulated thus far. I am an exhibitor of Lhasa Apsos, and as an exhibitor I have tried to share what knowledge I have gained with you. I am a "lover" of Lhasas and a recipient of the love of Lhasas. I hope that love is apparent, too.

Sally Ann Vervaeke-Helf
April 1982

FOREWORD

Lhasas are gaining in popularity every year. Thus, it is essential that people be informed about the breed. Sally Ann Helf has done the job.

Sally has followed a family tradition of involvement in purebred dogs. She has memories of her grandmother going to shows in the 1920's. As a child she started breeding Toy Fox Terriers. Later she expanded her interest to Miniature Poodles, and in 1976 Lhasas came into her life.

The thrust of Sally's breeding program has been to maintain a sound temperament along with a sound body in the Lhasa. Her concern and emphasis on temperament and behavior led her to write many magazine articles before undertaking this book. Sally has consistently defended the Lhasa from people who claim that it is no longer a suitable pet because of an unstable personality.

This new book has been written to aid the novice pet owner as well as the more experienced show breeder. Everyone can benefit from it.

Jane Browning

A curious four-month-old sired by Ch. Innsbrook's Patrician O'Sulan. Courtesy of Sulan Lhasas.

TO OWN A LHASA APSO

The Lhasa Apso is one of the most adaptable breeds of dogs. They are companion dogs, show dogs, obedience dogs, and hearing aid dogs. They are beautiful, intelligent, and loyal. They offer love, devotion, mobility, and watchdog characteristics all in one relatively small package.

Lhasas can be raised almost anywhere. They are bred and raised in city apartments, suburban homes, and rural kennels. They usually travel well and make delightful traveling companions. They are small enough to fit in a small spot, but big enough to offer protection and companionship. They often open doors for conversation because people—even connoisseurs of the large or terrier breeds—are curious about them.

One very interesting Lhasa is Ch. Potala Keke's Fraser, who acts as a hearing dog for his young mistress, Sherry Baxley. Fraser, who announces when the telephone rings and when the doorbell sounds, is a very typical Lhasa, as the breed is noted for its hearing ability. Sherry, quite a young girl at the time, trained and showed Fraser to his championship. According to Sherry's mother, the day they achieved that championship there was not a dry eye around the ring.

There are many special Lhasas like Fraser who offer so much to their owners. Marion Knowlton of Knolwood Lhasa Apsos, remarked: "As one elderly lady put it, 'I can share a close friendship with my Lhasa not hindered by my lack of achievement by the world's standards. Now, I am not alone; there is always someone who cares and will listen and, without talking, seems to understand when there are problems. He makes my days shorter and happier—he has so much love for me.'"

Marion went on to say that "some of my Lhasas have been therapy for elderly owners. I have placed puppies with people in nursing homes who felt they had nothing to live for—nobody needed them. Now they get up early to fix breakfast for a loving friend. The Lhasa is always

glad to see them, and lets them know it with a friendly wag of the tail."

These proud dogs normally have no bad personality traits and usually have an even, obliging disposition. They are wary of strangers and, like many other breeds, do not like people "moving in on them" too quickly. The Lhasa Apso is a beautiful, graceful animal, and because of this, it often "stops traffic."

Lhasas have always been special to their owners. When people were escaping from Iran in 1981, the newspapers reported that one couple refused to fly out because they could not take their pets, including a Lhasa, on the plane. Instead they made a hazardous trip to the seacoast, escaped by boat, and ultimately returned home to the United States. Today's owners appear to experience the same feelings about the dogs as did those who possessed them in the land of their origin.

The Lhasa Apso is one of the oldest breeds in the world, dating back to over a thousand years ago in Tibet, its country of origin. The dogs were unknown to the outside world for a long time because of their isolation in Tibet and, it is said, because they belonged only to the Dalai Lama, rulers of other monasteries, or other aristocrats. Considered sacred little dogs, they were kept hidden and were well protected from strangers, seen only by the privileged few.

The Lhasa Apsos were the inside watchdogs at the Potala Palace of the Dalai Lama. They were trained to be warning dogs and were taught to distinguish between residents and strangers. By nature these dogs are especially well equipped for the job, as they possess a keen sense of hearing (perhaps the best among all breeds of dogs), an innate intelligence, and, although they are an obedience-type dog, an independent mind. For these reasons they continue to make excellent house dogs.

The Lhasa Apsos were always raised as indoor dogs. To some people they were known as the "Holy Dogs of Asia," and they often kept the monks company in their lonely cells. From the sixteenth to the twentieth centuries, the Lhasa Apsos were used to pay tribute to members of the Chinese Royal Family—the Manchu Dynasty. Pairs of the dogs were sent to the Chinese as tribute. Tradition states that Lhasa Apsos bring good luck and happiness to their new owners; thus, the ancient Chinese treasured them.

After the fall of the Manchu Dynasty, Lhasas began to make rare appearances in the Western World. Although the dogs had been depicted in earlier art works, indicating some knowledge of Lhasas, the first recorded Lhasas in the Western World were taken to England around 1900 by Colonel R. C. Duncan when he returned from service in India. Just before World War II sufficient numbers appeared in the United States for the Lhasa Apso to be recognized as a breed by the American Kennel Club, as was true in other world areas.

Ch. Hamilton Katha at age nine. Katha was bred by C. Suydam Cutting. A lovely lion gold color, she stood nine inches tall and weighed fourteen pounds.
Sired by Ch. Hamilton Tatsienlu ex Hamilton Docheno. Owner, Pat Chenoweth.

C. Suydam Cutting received credit for the prestige of the Lhasa Apso in the United States. It was through his friendship with the thirteenth Dalai Lama that the Cuttings obtained their Lhasa Apsos. In 1933, the Dalai Lama sent a pair to the Cuttings. The male, Taikoo, was a black-and-white parti color, while the female, Dinkai, was a pale gold. In all, the Cuttings received a total of seven Lhasa Apsos from Tibet, and with them they started their world famous kennel, Hamilton Farms, in Gladstone, New Jersey.

If we may stop for a minute and consider the name of these dogs, Lhasa Apso, we may realize some things about their appropriate breed name. Lhasa is the capital city of Tibet, and it also means Place of the Gods. Apso is a corruption of the Tibetan word *rapso,* which means shaggy or goatlike. Thus, the name depicts both its country of origin and its characteristics. A Lhasa Apso is a shaggy dog in that it has long hair, which we in the Western World often groom to perfection. As one watches a Lhasa Apso at play, one can observe its goatlike characteristics as it leaps from one object to another if the opportunity is provided. The surefootedness and the ability to leap justify the use of *rapso,* or apso.

The Lhasa Apso has also been known as Apso Seng Kye (Bark Sentinel Dog) and as the Little Lion Dog. When one looks at a typical Lhasa, one can see why they were known as the Lion Dog, for a typical Lhasa resembles a small lion. It should be pointed out, however, that the Tibetan lion was a mythical snow lion—white with a blue mane. There are no white Lhasas with blue manes. While the lion colors have been popular—fads do affect color preferences—the breed standard accepts all colors. I have been told that the black Lhasas were considered sacred by the Dalai Lama, and thus were rarely seen even in Tibet. However, no corroborating evidence has been found to date.

Because it comes in a wide variety of colors, the Lhasa Apso is sometimes called the "Jelly Bean Dog." It can be found in solid, blended, parti, or brindle mixtures of golds, reds, grays, whites, blacks, browns, and blues.

The face of the Lhasa is usually covered by a dense growth of hair, which includes a beard. The hair on the ears is long and blends into the coat. The eyes are hidden by a head fall, which most owners today pin or fasten back to reveal the beauty of the eyes (but not in the show or obedience ring). The tail of the adult dog is so well feathered that it tends to blend in with the coat.

One of the most famous Lhasa Apsos is Best in Show American Canadian Bermudian Mexican International Champion Kyi-Chu Friar Tuck, bred by Ruth Smith and Jay Amanns and owned and campaigned by Bob Sharp to thirteen Best in Show awards (still the record for parti colors) and innumerable Best of Breed and Group placings.

Best in Show International Champion Kyi-Chu Friar Tuck ROM winning the Group at Harrisburg, 1970. Photo by Shafer.

3

Tuck's last ring appearance was April 30, 1977, at the American Lhasa Apso Club (ALAC) Eastern Specialty at Syracuse, where he placed first in the Veteran Dog class. When Bob entered the ring with Tuck, Tuck was given a standing ovation by the crowd packed in around the ring and caused many of their eyes to fill with tears. Tuck was an outstanding champion, and he sired fourteen champions including one Best in Show champion.

PURCHASING A LHASA APSO

Now that you have decided that the dog of your dreams is a Lhasa Apso, you wish to purchase one. When you decide to purchase a Lhasa as a companion, you need to seriously consider the reasons for obtaining him, his suitability, and your involvement with him.

At this point it would seem pertinent to note that sex makes no real difference in your choice of a companion Lhasa. Lhasas are what are called "people dogs" in that they tend to own you, rather than vice versa. Either sex has a tremendous loyalty to its owner, and the personality traits appear to be much the same. Having had both sexes as companion Lhasas, my advice would be to opt for the Lhasa Apso with the temperament and other attributes which you desire and to forget about sex.

Your first step is to determine why you want a Lhasa and then to consider your life-style.

A Lhasa Apso makes an excellent companion dog as it is a good house dog and a good traveler. Since Lhasas are usually not noisy dogs, they fit into an apartment or town house situation as well as they do in a private home. The Lhasas will tend to adapt to and to reflect their families' life-styles. Because they have such keen senses of hearing, they will make excellent watchdogs, and also for this reason they make excellent companions for those persons living alone.

While Lhasas need and love human companionship, as all dogs do, they can be alone for periods during the day, such as when one is working or shopping, providing that preparation is made for such periods.

Their long coats will need some care. Thus, another factor for your consideration will be your personal schedule. You must determine if you will care for the coat yourself. This could be time consuming, as it could mean ten minutes daily or several half-hour sessions a week with about a three-hour session every week or two for bathing and complete grooming for a puppy or young Lhasa. Adult Lhasa coats do not need excessive grooming if properly cared for, but they will require a good combing and brushing not less than once a week and shampooing when necessary. The need for shampooing will depend on the Lhasa's activities. One which plays outside quite often will probably need shampooing more often than one which is usually indoors.

If you determine that you do not have the time and will instead take your Lhasa to a groomer experienced with Lhasa coats, you must also be aware of the costs involved. The prices which groomers charge vary in different areas of the country.

It is fun to get a tiny ball of fur, a Lhasa puppy, but for your purposes an older puppy, young dog, or even an older dog might be more suitable. Under any circumstances, do not buy a puppy less than eight weeks old, and remember that when you buy a very young puppy, you must do all the training. If you do not want the hassle of training, opt for an older Lhasa. Remember, however, that the older Lhasa may need a longer adjustment period before it totally settles into your routine and life-style. Just as we just adjust to new locations, so must your new Lhasa. This adjustment will vary from Lhasa to Lhasa. Some adjust in a matter of hours; others may take several days, a few weeks, or even a month or two. However, it is rare that a Lhasa fails to adjust.

Sometimes a breeder would like to find a good home for an older Lhasa who just didn't like being shown, but who would make an excellent companion dog. My own experiences have proven this to be true. Thus, if the situation warrants it, or if such an opportunity is presented to you, do not avoid taking the older dog.

Any Lhasa Apso, regardless of age, will need both an adjustment period and socialization. Consequently, you should establish your frame of reference before you purchase your Lhasa: "Lhasa attributes × Your need × Your life-style × Lhasa cost in care and time."

Questions to Consider

Before you purchase your Lhasa, consider the information about the dog which is important to you. Have your questions ready before you go to shop for a Lhasa and do not be afraid to ask them. Your choice of places to purchase your Lhasa will be limited only by your area and whether or not there are breeders available. Thus, your first questions will be for the seller.

Is the seller the breeder of this Lhasa? Are the dam and possibly the sire available for seeing? If the sire is not available, is there a picture of him which can be viewed? As a breeder, does the seller exhibit his/her Lhasas in American Kennel Club (AKC) or Canadian Kennel Club (CKC) sanctioned shows?

These facts may provide you with an inkling as to whether or not this is a "professional" breeder. A professional breeder usually does not breed excessive numbers of Lhasas, but rather breeds for himself or herself to provide a good Lhasa for either the show ring or for breeding because this person loves the breed. A professional breeder does not run a "puppy mill" where dogs are bred just for monetary recompense.

Is the puppy from a litter registered with the AKC or CKC and thus eligible for individual registration? The answer should be yes. Are the papers available? If not, when will they be? Will the breeder provide a pedigree?

Has the puppy received its shots—canine distemper, hepatitis, parainfluenza, leptospira bacterin, parvo virus—and has it been wormed or had a worm check? Usually after purchase a reputable breeder will allow you to take your puppy to your vet for a health check. Simply ask how long you have to get the puppy checked by your vet. Most breeders will say 24, 32, 48, or 72 hours or even a week, as I do. If they do not, go elsewhere for your puppy.

If the breeder is placing any restrictions on the purchase, such as neutering or spaying, this will be stated. You will usually be asked to have this done when the puppy is about six months old. Ask for assurance of registration papers when the requirements are met.

Will the breeder be available for advice and for help with your Lhasa? Most breeders want to know how the puppies they have placed are doing, and rather than have you run into problems with grooming and training, will help with advice. Some breeders, as I do, provide small pamphlets with information and advice.

If you desire a nice companion Lhasa, you will have more options than if you desire a brood bitch, a stud dog, or a show-quality Lhasa. Discussion concerning the purchase of these will take place in a later chapter. In addition to having more options, your companion Lhasa will usually cost less.

Remember that the costs for breeding purebred puppies are affected by inflation just as are all other costs. Food prices have risen by 50 percent and more in the past three years, and veterinary costs have increased correspondingly. Owners of studs are increasing stud fees. Transportation costs have risen. The costs to show outstanding dogs have risen. Thus it is costing more to produce puppies.

Meili Jin Shaunya and her basketful of Christmas puppies. Photo by Jamison.

A breeder simply cannot keep all the puppies which result from a planned litter, unless it is very small. The stock behind such a puppy will usually be good, and the puppy not intended for show or breeding will be sold as a companion Lhasa.

Perhaps the most important factor in a companion dog is its temperament, which should be pleasant. You will have to decide whether or not you want a bouncy, outgoing pup or a quiet one. Choose a puppy that is not overly frightened nor overly aggresssive. Even at eight weeks, temperament differences between littermates are apparent.

Contrary to the advice of some, I do not think it necessary to visit numerous breeders to select a companion dog, especially if you have done your homework. If the breeder has a good reputation and the puppies are clean and healthy looking, do not be afraid to take the puppy with which you fall in love.

Health Checkup

It is your responsibility to take your Lhasa to your vet for its health check within the time allowed by the seller. Your vet will check the puppy's heart and respiration, ears, eyes, and teeth. He will also look for umbilical hernias, and check the male puppy for two testicles.

Be sure to take a stool sample to be examined for the presence of worms, and a record of any immunizations the pup has received. Puppies receive antibodies for various canine diseases from their dam at birth. These same antibodies are known to prevent successful immunization from vaccinations until the level of maternal antibodies declines. It is the antibody titer (level) of the bitch which determines when the puppies can be successfully vaccinated. This is why it is best to take the record of

Best in Show Am. Can. Ch. Anbara's Hobgoblin was number one Lhasa, all systems, for 1980 and 81. He was also number eight Non-Sporting dog in 1980. Sired by Ch. Tabu's King of Hearts ROM ex Am. Can. Ch. Anbara's Abra-Ka-Dabra ROM. Owner, Betty Bowman. Photo by Ashbey.

any shots the pup has had, and any information you have about the dam's immunity, to your veterinarian and follow his recommendations concerning a vaccination schedule for your puppy. He will recommend a series of shots two to four weeks apart, which should include immunization for canine distemper, hepatitis, leptospirosis, parainfluenza, and parvo virus.

Registration Papers

Be sure that the registration papers for your puppy are available or that you get a receipt or sales contract stating when you will receive them. You should also request that the registration numbers of the sire and the dam be included on the evidence of sale. Sometimes litter registration papers are delayed, and the owner may not have them at purchase time. For instance, litter registrations must be signed by both owners—that of the sire or representative handling the breeding and that of the bitch—before the owner of the bitch can forward them to the AKC. Should you pay for your Lhasa by personal check, the breeder may forward the papers to you after your check has cleared the bank.

When you receive your signed registration papers, fill in the required information and mail with the appropriate fee to the AKC or CKC. Do this promptly. It might be wise to copy the form before mailing so as to have a copy for your records. It will take from a month to six weeks for the form to be processed. If you do not receive the registration papers in a reasonable time, write to the AKC or CKC, giving all the pertinent information, and request that your application be checked.

Champion Krisna Likala Kar-Dan (Ch. Chen Krisna Nor X Krisna Kusuma). Breeder-owner-handler Wendi Harper. Co-breeder Lila Kaiser. Co-owner Vera Snow Reid.

An eight-week-old Lhasa puppy and a seven-week-old German Shepherd puppy were playmates at Llenroc Farm. Photo by Shafer.

2

THE HOMECOMING

If we could put outselves in the place of a Lhasa Apso, we would find our "little" self in the world of giants. But never let it be said that a Lhasa considers himself to be little, for he does not.

Our new Lhasa comes into very strange surroundings. He has left all his companions and his dam and is now on his own. Thus he needs time for adjusting.

Now, if you are like the rest of us, you want to show off your beautiful new companion. It would be wise, however, to limit company at least during the first week or ten days so that you new Lhasa can get used to his new surroundings and his new family.

Your Lhasa puppy needs a sense of security in his new home. One method, and a good one, to provide this security is to purchase an air crate in which a puppy may sleep or to which he may go to escape. Put a piece of blanket or sherpa in the crate, and place newspapers under the floor. Do not isolate your puppy. Block off a corner of the kitchen or family room and place the air crate in that area. Be sure that the area chosen is one from which the puppy can observe his family and in which the family can observe and talk to the puppy. You can make a small pen, or you can purchase a wire pen. Put plenty of papers on the floor, water, toys, and chew sticks in the area. Prop the door of the air crate open, or even remove it while the crate is used in the pen.

To prevent the puppy from feeling lonely while you might be away from home, turn on the radio.

FEEDING YOUR LHASA PUPPY

Be sure to inquire about the diet of your new Lhasa Apso puppy. Keep it on the same diet. If you wish to change the type of food or the brand, do so gradually.

My puppies start on puppy chow and by eight weeks of age they are eating four meals a day— ⅓ to ½ cup dry chow softened with water at each meal. A little dry puppy chow is kept in a bowl so the puppies can exercise their teeth. Also, small puppy biscuits are supplied to aid teething.

At about three months of age, cut your Lhasa puppy back to three meals daily. During the fourth month, the puppy may be cut back to two meals daily. Remember, when you cut back one meal, increase the portions of the others. It has been my experience that during the fourth month the Lhasa puppies tire of puppy chow. When this occurs, good results can be had by switching them to a quality dry dog food supplemented by a tablespoon of cottage cheese.

Your puppy should be on one meal a day at about six months. The Lhasa will usually let you know by just not eating one of the meals. Depending on the puppy, from 1 cup to 1½ cups of adult meal will be sufficient. Add a tablespoon or two of canned ration or of cooked and chopped chicken gizzards and hearts at this point. Also add 1 teaspoon of brewer's yeast each meal.

Do not give your Lhasa an excess of milk or milk products. Some dogs, like some humans, cannot tolerate too much milk. If you are giving the dog milk or milk products and the Lhasa's stool exhibits mucous, cut back the milk or milk product.

Should your Lhasa become ill or develop diarrhea substitute at least one-half of the dog chow with either cooked rice or cooked barley. The Lhasa can also be given all cooked rice or cooked barley—1 cup or so—plus about 2 tablespoons of broiled drained ground beef. Save the broth from the cooked barley and give it to the Lhasa for drinking water.

NEW LHASA APSO CARE

When you take your Lhasa puppy or adult home, make its first days as free from stress as you can. Avoid excessive company for a few days until your Lhasa adjusts. Remember that his fears probably compare to that of a child's. No one should tease or play roughly with the Lhasa puppy or older dog. Your new Lhasa will probably try very hard to please you. Praise him when he does so, and allow no one to strike him if he commits an error.

Ch. Cameo's Khor-Ke San O'Honeydew, BOB Westminster 1981 (by Ch. Donicia's Chim El-Torro out of Honeydew's Kissi Lu). Owner, Joyce Hadden. Photo by Ashbey.

Provide your Lhasa with a spot to call his own. One good idea is to have an air crate available for your Lhasa. It can serve as his bed at home and when traveling will provide your Lhasa with a sense of security.

Remember that Lhasas have very sensitive hearing. For this reason your Lhasa may not tolerate excessively loud noises. Because of this hearing ability, though, your Lhasa should make a good watchdog for you, warning you of the approach of strangers.

Most Lhasas are not "barky" dogs. If they do bark annoyingly for you, tell them "No," and then crate them. Never for any reason strike a Lhasa on the head or face. Such a blow could easily fracture facial bones, even crushing the sinus passages. Use your Lhasa's crate judiciously for correction.

Treat your Lhasa in a firm and quiet manner and you will have a lifelong friend, one who lives to a good age. The average life span is around fifteen years. One Lhasa has been recorded to have lived to within one week of thirty years.

Moreover, according to the Tibetans and the Chinese, Lhasas will bring good luck to your home. They will certainly add interest to your life.

Play with your Lhasa puppy, but do not allow anyone to tease him. Teasing any dog can damage his personality.

There are many toys available today. Do not get too large a toy for your puppy, but remember that too small a toy can be dangerous. Soft latex squeaky toys are good. Latex balls and tennis balls also are effective playthings. The cardboard cores from paper towels or toilet paper also make good inexpensive toys. Knot old socks, nylons, or panty hose; the pup will tug on these. Toys will help prevent boredom, mischief, and a tendency to chew on paws.

Cuddle your Lhasa puppy and express your love for it. The more attention and stimulation the young puppy receives, the more his personality will be developed.

HOUSE TRAINING

Whether it is a young puppy or older dog, crating and restricting your Lhasa are the best methods for house training it. Except when family members are with the puppy, limit your Lhasa's freedom until house trained.

Am. Can. Ch. Regal Reginald of Lori Shan, a multiple group winner from the classes whose entire show career lasted ten weeks.

Take your puppy outside to a designated exercise area very shortly after he eats, upon arising in the morning, frequently in between, and just before going to bed. Praise the Lhasa when he does what is expected. Soon he will ask to go out. Watch for this asking, as it may be a sign rather than a bark. Never allow your puppy to run freely in an unfenced area. Use a lead.

Should your puppy have an accident, or start to make a mistake, issue a stern vocal command and either take him outside to the designated area or put him in the restricted area. *Do not* rub the puppy's nose in the error. *Do not* correct unless you catch in the act. Merely pick the puppy up and return to its confined arca. Deodorize the area on which the puppy made the error.

Use a positive approach. Praise your Lhasa puppy for going on the papers or outside. Make him know that he has done the right thing.

WALKING YOUR LHASA

Walking is good exercise for your Lhasa and for you. When walking a young Lhasa, it may be wise to start with a small figure-eight harness and lead. My experience has been that my best results in lead training were when I started in this manner. Some puppies are frightened by collars around their necks and thus become very resistant to walking on lead. The harness prevents this problem.

By the time the puppy outgrows the harness and graduates to a simple show lead—collar and lead in one—he has accepted control. A show lead of cordahyde is a good one because it does not tangle the hair. It is not a good idea to keep a collar

Use a figure-eight harness to eliminate strain on the neck when training the young puppy. Trainer wears light colored shoes which are easy for the puppy to see.

on a Lhasa at all times. The collar will wear down and tangle the hair.

TRAVEL

You can travel everywhere with your Lhasa. The #100 or #200 air crate which you purchased for home can be used. If space in your vehicle is at a premium, use a #100 air crate, which may be safer in case of accident as there is less room for bouncing the dog around. All but the biggest Lhasas will fit into a #100. The crates fit easily into cars and can be used while riding and at motels or friends' homes for sleeping and confining. These crates are the safest method for traveling and are required when flying.

I have also used a dog car seat. This works well for a Lhasa which may experience motion sickness. Usually within a short time the Lhasa will adjust to the motion and be able to ride in his crate.

Moreover, a Lhasa in its car seat may be protection for you when riding alone. It may also provide some stories for you. Once when I was crossing the border on my way to a show in Ontario with Rumpie in the car seat, the custom's officer, seeing only Rumpie's golden-red hair past my shoulder, asked me rather impatiently where my friend was born. Then, at the fee collection booth the attendant asked me for an extra dime for my passenger. Rumpie thought he was a person before that experience, but after. . . .

Lhasas do make good traveling companions and are welcomed at many motels. But be sure to have a crate in which to confine your Lhasa and carry a box of baggies and paper towels with which to clean up after you exercise your Lhasa. Turn a baggie inside out over your hand and pick up any droppings. As you invert and close the bag, the droppings are contained cleanly inside.

GROOMING YOUR PUPPY

A few minutes brushing or combing each day helps to get the Lhasa used to the grooming procedure. Thoroughly brush or comb your puppy not less than once a week. At first hold the puppy securely on your lap and run the comb or brush through its coat. Roll the puppy over on its back and play gently with it in order to accustom it to this position. Comb and brush its tummy and the insides of its legs, its chest, and under its chin.

When your puppy is used to being combed and brushed, place it on a sturdy table and start training it to lay on its side while being groomed. Be gentle but firm. Training a young puppy to accept grooming will greatly facilitate this act later.

There is no set time for giving your Lhasa puppy a bath, except that if its coat is dirty, it needs a bath. Your Lhasa puppy will already have had experience with baths. You should wash the puppy at least once a month. If your puppy plays outside, you may want to wash it once a week.

Be sure to spray the coat lightly with water or a water with creme rinse mixture and to comb thoroughly before washing. All mats should be removed before shampooing, as water tends to set the mats.

EXERCISE PENS

It is recommended that your Lhasa be exercised in a fenced-in area. If your own yard is not encircled by permanent fencing, there are several other solutions. If you have an area approximately 4 × 10 feet, you can purchase or build your own run. Very fine stone, pea gravel, or cement (roughened) makes a good base. Cement, however, can be very hard on a Lhasa's coat. Since Lhasas are house dogs rather than outside dogs, you may not wish to invest in a permanent run.

Portable exercise pens (x-pens) can be purchased. A 36–40-inch-high pen is recommended for the Lhasa who will be in the pen unattended for a period. Although Lhasas are small dogs, some will have extensive jumping or climbing abilities. If someone will be with the Lhasa, a 24- or 30-inch pen will do. This size is easier to take on trips.

A pen can be created of ⅜-inch pegboard. This pen is useful for a puppy, an old dog, a bitch in heat, or a dog who doesn't jump. The pegboard also protects against the wind. Cut a 4 × 8-foot sheet into four 2 × 4-foot sections. Join sections together in a square using 1-inch notebook rings or small ties (such as garbage bag twists), or lace the corners together with cord. This pen will be 4 feet square and 2 feet high. You can easily lift your Lhasa over the side.

You can purchase 3-foot or 4-foot-square exercise pens with raised floors. These pens are sani-

tary and can be used for the dog's lifetime, either indoors or out. These pens are an excellent investment if you intend to show your Lhasa. Other pens from 24 to 40 inches high, without floors and which fold up, can also be purchased for use indoors or out.

Another solution is to sink pipe into the ground in the appropriate places. Fasten wire fencing to stakes which will fit into the pipe. These fence sections can then be lifted to mow the lawn. The fence can also be adjusted to the shape of the area available, whether it be an oblong, a square, or a hectagon. If you make your sections more than 24 inches high, allow for a gate. The joints can be held together with hook-and-eye fasteners. This can be very practical and can be used within an already fenced yard to create a run.

Clean, fresh water should be available to your Lhasa at all times. Shade must be provided during hot weather. If natural shade is not available, shade can be created by placing a mosquito net screen or a plastic or cloth "blanket" over the top of the pen and fastening it on the side with snaps or clothespins. Leave the sides open for ventilation.

Providing your Lhasa with a safe place to exercise, an area to call his own within the house, good care, and much love should help to make him feel secure, happy, and contented.

An exercise pen gives puppies play room when you do not have a fenced yard.

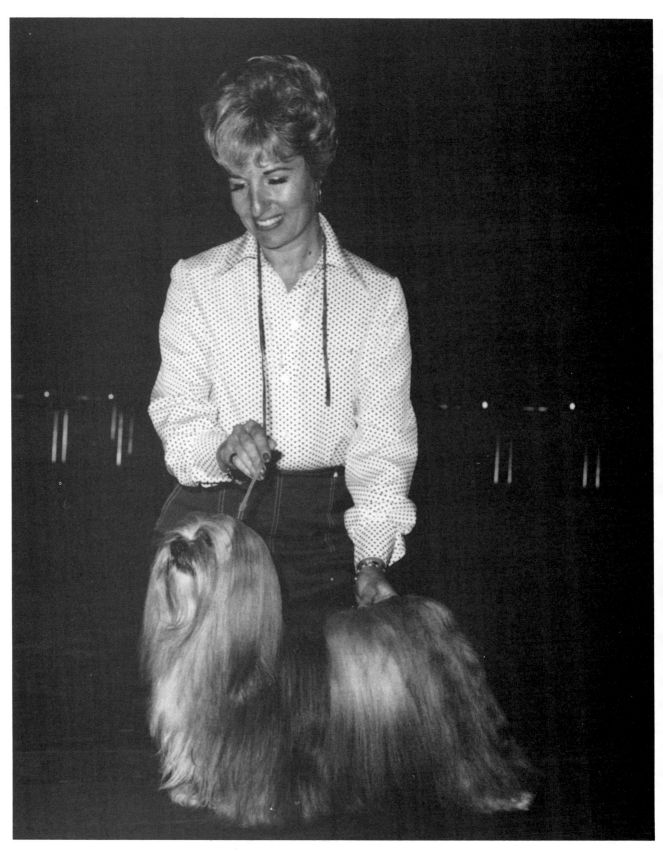

Am. Can. Ch. Chen Krisna Nor's last ring appearance at age twelve, winning Best of Breed and Group third. Owners, Wendy Harper and Patricia Chenoweth. Photo by Langdon.

14

3

IDEALS AND INTERPRETATIONS

INTERPRETING THE STANDARD

Each national kennel club which registers dogs establishes a standard which portrays a concept of the ideal dog for a particular breed. This standard, it must be remembered, does not represent a particular dog, but rather is a conception by which we judge members of that breed.

The Lhasa Apso Standards for various countries differ. The standard with which we are most familiar is that established by the American Kennel Club. This standard was originally established in 1935 and was amended in 1979. While in many ways this standard is similar, it differs in wording when compared to the Canadian Kennel Club Standard, the English Standard, the Indian Standard, and the English Standard originally written in 1901.

Not only do the standards differ in some aspects from country to country, but so also can the *interpretations* of each given standard differ within a country. Thus, those factors which could be acceptable to one, may not be to another. Too often differences of opinion are caused by word meanings. Throughout this chapter, therefore, in interpreting the AKC Standard for the Lhasa Apso, emphasis is placed on the denotative, or dictionary, meaning for those words which encourage differences of opinion.

The purpose of the Lhasa Apso Standard is to provide a guideline for evaluating our Lhasas. It provides a model to which the breeder can strive; an essential unity of type within a framework broad enough to allow personal interpretation.

THE AKC STANDARD

CHARACTER: *Gay and assertive, but chary of strangers.*

The meanings of gay, assertive, and chary are those which cause confusion at this point. Probably chary is the least understood.

According to dictionary definitions, a "gay" Lhasa would be one who is full of life and high spirits. He would be assertive in that he would present a positive attitude, but he would also be "chary" (careful or cautious of strangers).

It is important that the definition of chary be understood. Lhasas should not be vicious in any sense, as sparing might suggest to some. A Lhasa will be careful of risk, mistrustful, and alert for danger. Thus, a Lhasa may not greet strangers joyfully, but rather in a reserved and watchful manner. Moreover, a Lhasa who moves jauntily and gayly around the ring may also be very reserved with the unknown judge who examines him. And it is this chary quality that makes a Lhasa a good inner watchdog.

By dictionary definition, a Lhasa is on the one hand free from care and full of life, joy, and high spirits, and is positive and forward with those he knows well. On the other hand, reflecting his heritage as an inner "guard" dog who could discriminate between friend and enemy, the Lhasa is on his guard against danger and deception and thus is cautious, even suspicious, of strangers.

But chary by no means excuses any form of viciousness, such as biting, unless the circumstances warrant it—circumstances such as an owner being attacked. In the ring the biting Lhasa cannot be said to be chary. Neither the Lhasa nor his owner are being attacked; therefore, the judge should excuse any Lhasa that attempts to bite.

A Lhasa should be full of life, outgoing, and positive with owners and friends, but he may be quite cautious with those he does not know.

SIZE: *Variable, but about 10 inches or 11 inches at shoulder for dogs, bitches slightly smaller.*

The Lhasa is a rather small dog; its height would be at the lower end of the standard for the Miniature Poodle, and this factor should be kept in mind when breeding and showing a Lhasa Apso.

The key word is *about*, which is often loosely interpreted. The general denotation of "about" is: somewhere near; close to; not far from; nearly; approximately. I interpret this to mean that a dog in the show ring should not be less than 9½ inches nor more than 11½ inches. Slight means not much or trivial. This denotation, at least to me, means that bitches should be between 9 and 11 inches.

If the Standard is to mean anything, then breeders must stick to it, as must the judges. Overstandard Lhasas are too close to the heights of the Tibetan Terriers—14–16 inches. When these over-

BIS Ch. Potala Keke's Candy Bar, a multiple BIS winner. Owners, Keke Blumberg and Janet and Marv Whitman. Photo by Ashbey.

16

standard Lhasas are accepted in the ring and for breeding, the uniqueness of the Lhasa is being changed. Recently, a judge sitting at ringside during the Non-Sporting Group was overheard making a comment about the length of coat on the "Tibetan Terrier." What he thought to be a Tibetan Terrier was really a Lhasa Apso.

When a breeder is involved in an extensive breeding program, accurate measurements can be a good tool. For instance, growth patterns on different lines can vary. For example, bitch C and stud R produce puppies that attain their full growth before eight months; but bitch M and stud R produce male puppies that have their growth at eight months, but females that grow until eighteen months. Within each of these litters there may be early indicators of the final heights. By keeping growth charts, one can come close to determining the final height of a given puppy and can use this factor when culling litters. Consequently, an inexpensive, accurate measuring device is a valuable tool in determining a Lhasa's height potential. Measuring standards such as the one pictured are readily available.

Here in the United States we have a tendency to equate bigness or tallness with better, or straightness with better, and to feel that first is everything. We must always perfect everything to fit our conception. The original Lhasa Apso was not a large dog nor did it have long legs. The

Lhasa's broad chest does not permit straight legs nor long legs such as those expected on a Brittany Spaniel or similarly built breeds. Yet some have attempted to mold these unnatural qualities into our Lhasas. Their STANDARD size provides a dog which can fit in an apartment or in a compact car, but which is not lost in a mansion nor a Chrysler Imperial. Such a dog can curl up on your lap or accompany you jogging or walking. Let us develop the *best* that we can, then, *within* our Standard.

A Lhasa Apso fitting the Standard for height can do well in the Group ring also. Two of the greatest "show" Lhasas measured 10½ and 10⅝ inches. They were: BIS Am. Can. Bda. Mex. Int. Ch. Kyi-Chu Friar Tuck and Bis Am. Bda. Mex. Col. Ch. Chen Korum-Ti. A Lhasa doesn't have to be tall or big to do well in the Group.

COLORS: *All colors equally acceptable with or without dark tips to ears and beard.*

Lhasas come in a wide variety of colors, a fact which explains one nickname – jelly bean dog. Prior to 1978 there was a color preference, now deleted, in the Standard. Today, whatever preference you have, you can find that color eventually. There are golds (including apricots), sand, honey, and red shades; there are slate, smoke, grey, pewter, blue, black, white, or brown; there are brindles, grizzles, and salt and peppers; there are parti-colors, which are at least 50 percent white plus another color.

The solid shades are the easiest to define, although individuals may differ in their perceptions of gold, apricot, sand, etc. The salt and pepper, of which few are seen, has a top coat with a relatively even distribution of white and black hairs.

A brindle, per the AKC, is "a fine mixture of black with hairs of a lighter color, usually tan, brown, or gray." The dictionary defines it as gray, tan, or tawny with darker streaks or spots. A good brindle Lhasa coat, to me, should have an even mixture of colors which somewhat blend together and which are evenly distributed.

Left:
Top: Am. Can. Ch. Sharpette's Rumpie Dil Dox, a true apricot. True apricots have no black roots. Note also the white marking on the forehead. Photo by Stonham.
Center: Ch. Taikoo of Shukti Lingka, "TK," an evenly marked parti-color. Owner, Harriet Silverman. Photo by Ashbey.
Bottom: Lori Shan Ms. Mariah, a cream with black tippings owned by Lorraine Shannon. Photo by Langdon.

Right:
Top: A promising six-week-old Irish Setter red bred by J. Holsapple.
Bottom: Ch. Tiffany's Yolanda La-Tsu ROM, a rare blue Lhasa. A blue is a very dark grey, not quite black, with a definite blue cast. Owners, Barbara Peterson and Marilyn Campbell.

A blue is a very dark grey, not quite black, blended with lighter hairs to give a definite blue cast. Pups are born glue-grey in color.

A grizzle, per the AKC, is a bluish grey. The dictionary defines grizzle as a gray hair or gray animal.

Often a Lhasa is described as having a grizzle overlay; i.e., the top coat is grey over another colored undercoat (usually lighter).

Any color is acceptable, but that color should not be doctored or changed by artificial means.

Top left:
BIS Ch. Keke's Yum Yum won over one hundred Best of Breeds, plus one All-Breed and two National Specialty Best in Show Awards. In 1976 she won both the Eastern and Western Specialty Shows at age seven. Breeder-owner, Keke Blumberg. Photo by Petrulis.

Bottom Left:
Ch. Taglha Dum Cho, a grizzle, is the dam of numerous outstanding Lhasas. Breeder-owner Jane Browning.

Right:
Ch. Suntory Affirmative Action, a black. Note how breeder-owner Cassandra de la Rosa's lavender dress provides a soft background to accent his stunning appearance. Photo by Ludwig.

BODY SHAPE: *The length from the point of shoulders to point of buttocks longer than height at wither, well ribbed up, strong loin, well-developed quarters and thighs.*

One fact is apparent from this description; a Lhasa Apso should not give a square appearance. Its structure is that of a rectangle.

The Lhasa Apso Club of Northern California (LACNC) stud issue for 1972 presented the body lengths for nineteen of the advertised dogs. (See Chart 1.) The longest of these dogs were 16½ inches and the shortest 12 inches. By comparison, the tallest was 12 inches and the shortest 9½ inches. The heaviest were 21 pounds and the lightest 13. According to Pat Chenoweth, owner of Chen Lhasa Apsos and long-time breeder, height and length are more important than weight, as weight is affected by bone density.

In considering the height of these 1972 dogs as a group, the mean is 10.5 inches, the median 10.5 inches, and the mode 10 inches. Unfortunately, such figures are not available today, but a conjecture might place the mean closer to 11 inches.

When the length is examined, the mean is 15.1 inches, the median 15, and the mode 15.

The mean for weight is 17.4 pounds, the median 17.5 pounds, and the mode is either 16 or 18 pounds.

Therefore, an average-size Lhasa in 1972 was 10.6 inches tall, 15.1 inches long, and weighed 17.4 pounds.

Of those kennels which submitted this same information to me in 1979, the average dog was about 10.7 inches tall, 17.6 inches long, and weighed 17.5 pounds. However, the number who were willing to participate was insufficient to get a meaningful average. For instance, many dogs appear to be much more "square" than these figures indicate.

CHART 1. Size Comparison of Lhasa Apso Sires, 1972.

	DOG	HEIGHT	LENGTH	WEIGHT
(1)	Ch. Pandan Tsar-Ba-T-M	10"	15"	16 lbs.
(2)	Pandan Can Sa Ster Ling	11"	16"	16 lbs.
(3)	Ch. Zijuh Seng-Tru	10"	15"	16 lbs.
(4)	Ch. Kimmi's Shan Ser	12"	16"	20 lbs.
(5)	Ch. Pandan Ka-Tando-Tu	10"	13"	13 lbs.
(6)	Shalu's Marba Rjebo	10"	15"	18 lbs.
(7)	Ch. On-Ba Yasha Khan of Sharbo	10 3/4"	16"	19 lbs.
(8)	Ch. Cordova Tom-Tru	9½"	15"	16 lbs.
(9)	Sharbo Mondo Khan of Ramarka	10½"	15½"	16 lbs.
(10)	Ch. Sharpette's Gaylord	11"	15 3/4"	21 lbs.
(11)	Ch. Sharpette's Number One Son	11"	15¼"	21 lbs.
(12)	Ch. Milbryan Kim Ly Shim	10½"	15½"	17½ lbs.
(13)	Ch. Lingkhor Bhu of Norbulingka	11"	16½"	18 lbs.
(14)	Migou's Sonan of Shalu	10 3/4"	15"	18 lbs.
(15)	Ch. Geradene's Mon-Po-Chia-Py	10"	15"	14 lbs.
(16)	Ch. Licos Gebuk La	10½"	14½"	17 lbs.
(17)	Ch. On-Ba Jes-Su Khan	10 3/4"	15"	18 lbs.
(18)	San Jo's Corgi	11"	16½"	18 lbs.
(19)	Ch. Ferseyn of Zorosha	10"	12"	15 lbs.

*This information was found in the ads for the 19 Lhasa Apsos listed, LACNC Stud Issue 1972.

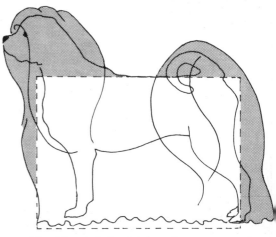

The Lhasa's body structure forms a rectangle.

The parts of the dog. Drawing by McGuire.

1 - Muzzle
2 - Forehead
3 - Occiput
4 - Neckline
5 - Topline
6 - Withers
7 - Croupline
8 - Loin
9 - Croup
10 - Tail
11 - Buttocks
12 - Hip Bone, Pelvis
13 - Upper Thigh
14 - Second Thigh or Gaskin
15 - Point of Hock
16 - Rear Pastern, Metatarsal
17 - Hind Foot or Paw
18 - Pad
19 - Hock Joint or Tarsal
20 - Stifle or Knee
21 - Patella
22 - Abdomen
23 - Brisket or Lower Chest
24 - Elbow
25 - Forearm
26 - Front Pastern, Metacarpal
27 - Forefoot or Paw
28 - Carpal Joint, Wrist
     (also called pastern joint or "knee")
29 - Forechest
30 - Point of Shoulder, Shoulder joint
31 - Scapula or Shoulder Blade
32 - Humerus
33 - Dorsal Bones
34 - Lumbar Bones
35 - Sacrum
36 - Femur
37 - Tibia
38 - Ulna
39 - Elbow

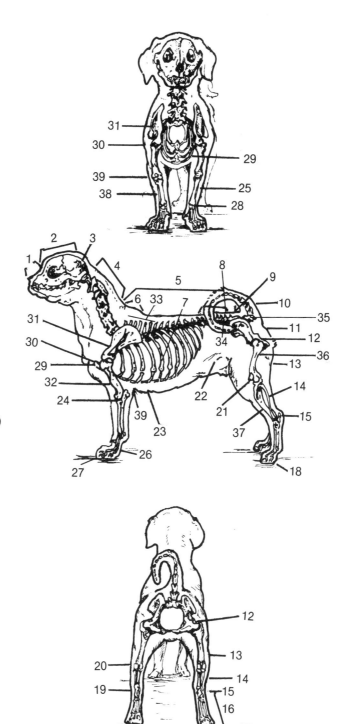

BONE AND MUSCLE: *Well ribbed up, a strong loin, well-developed quarters, and thighs.*

This describes a dog of good bone density. The bone, however, cannot be so massive as to restrict the movement of the Lhasa. The Standard indicates that a Lhasa should be of good sturdy bone structure. A fine-boned dog would not be likely to be sturdy enough to easily exist in a mountainous land.

In addition to good bone, the Lhasa should also possess good muscle. Well-developed muscles indicate strength and good bone.

Weight

The AKC Standard does not mention weight. A Lhasa true to its heritage should not be overweight or even pleasantly plump. For those judges who prefer "fat" dogs, this aspect can be a disturbing factor. It should be noted, also, that extra weight can be reflected in the topline, legs, and gait. However, when a Lhasa is picked up, it should seem surprisingly heavy because of its bone density.

Rib Cage

The rib cage on the Lhasa frame should be well sprung and should extend back along the body. Since the Lhasa should not have a barrel-shaped chest, the first four ribs should be relatively flat. The spring of the ribs starts with the fifth rib. To tell whether or not the spring of the ribs is correct, run your hand between the dog's front legs. You should be able to put four fingers through, indicating a space of 3½ to 4 inches.

The lung expansion of the Lhasa is extensive for a dog of its size. Thus, a good chest (rib development) is necessary.

Thoracic Region

Ninety percent of front-end faults occur in the thoracic region. The thirteen thoracic vertebrae correspond with the thirteen ribs, the last two being floating ribs. These vertebrae are characterized by high spines.

The first eight vertebrae constitute the wither. The next three—9, 10, and 11—almost fuse together and form a kind of point.

Wither

There are several factors about the wither of which we should be aware. A high wither indicates more flexibility in the shoulder muscles as there is both more movement and more length of muscle. The wither controls the dog's center of gravity which, if the wither is correct, will be located just behind the shoulders.

Should the wither be a flat, mutton type, the head will drop. There will be a definite relationship here: a flat wither and a short shoulder blade.

A disproportional length of shoulder blade (a front fault) is often indicated by restricted forward movement.

Neck

There should be a nice arch to the neck. The lack of neck arch may be caused by insufficient muscle, which relates to a skeletal problem—lack of enough substance in the vertebral bone for muscles to form. The two major muscles which run from the skull to the upper arm and pectoral muscles are very important in movement. Muscles hold the head firmly: "nervous" muscles cause movement; that is, motor nerves convey impulses from the brain to the muscles, thus producing motion. Length of neck is also an indicator of a dog's reach. A good neck length suggests good shoulder layback and therefore a good reach.

Lay On

The term "lay on" is defined as the closeness of the tips of the shoulder blades to the midline. For a Lhasa, about one finger width (perhaps ½ inch) seems to be about the right separation. Too wide a lay on, i.e., too wide a distance between the shoulder blades, could result in loaded or over-muscled shoulders and in the dog becoming muscle bound, which would be revealed in a "restricted" front movement, sometimes indicated by an inability to jump. On the other hand, the shoulders may be loose with "joints" showing. In this situation there is a lack of muscle development. This could result from either too-straight shoulders or too "slender" bones.

Back

The back is the area between the withers and the loin. It is the length of the total back area which often makes a Lhasa seem short or long backed. The length should be approximately one-half the distance of the loin to the croup, the start of which is located by the "hole" in the sacrum. The length in the total back area which makes a Lhasa seem "short backed" or "long backed" is found in this section. This area is termed "coupling," or as Dr. Quentin LaHam calls it, "kineck."

Loin or Lumbar

The loin is the area between the last rib and the sacrum or croup. It is composed of seven lumbar vertebrae which are shorter, thicker, and coarser than the thoracic vertebrae and which have two articulations, one on each side. There should be a slight arch over the loin.

Unlike the horse, the dog is held together by muscle. Ninety-nine percent muscle holds the shoulder or the loin, and a lack of muscle causes a bend in the back.

It may be an optical illusion that a dog is long in loin. Close examination will usually reveal that he is actually long in the middle piece of the back, or "coupling." This was clearly demonstrated by Dr. Quentin LaHam during a seminar I attended on "Anatomy of Movement." When we examined those dogs which appeared to be long in loin, we found that the dogs in question were often long in the back section.

Dogs can appear to be long because they are not "all together," i.e., a compact moving unit. Perhaps the best way to express it is that the Lhasas are not "collected." To be collected, the Lhasa uses its muscles to get its hind feet underneath it. This in turn forces the head up, and thus the Lhasa has an overall balanced, collected look.

Sacrum

This is the only part of the back where the vertebrae are fused, i.e., the lumbar vertebrae. The sacrum is a mass of three lumbar vertebrae which have a concave inner surface and a convex outer surface. An arched sacrum which tilts the tail down causes the misnamed low tail set. There is actually no low or high tail set. The so-called high tail set indicates a flat sacrum and flat croup.

Croup

The set of the croup is determined by the set of the sacrum, and is affected by both the development of bone and the muscle tone. To determine the croup, stick your index finger in the sacrum hole, lift up the tail, and notice the space. The croup is also partly formed by the first tail vertebra, a fact which creates an optical illusion.

There should be a slight slope to the croup. Both a steep croup and an extremely flat croup will interfere with movement.

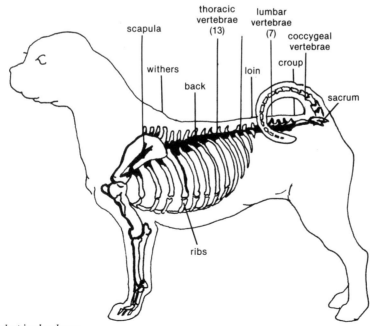

The back assembly and spinal column.

Topline

In the Lhasa a relatively level topline can be expected. Toplines so level as to hold a small glass of liquid are rare in the ring. The topline should, however, give a level appearance.

It is also true that a level topline may not stay level or firm. It may soften. This softening can be the result of age, pregnancy, weight, or lack of muscle toning. A poor topline can be caused by dipping shoulders or a roach back. Some Lhasas are slighty higher in the rear. This gives the effect of a sloping topline. Although this can be caused by longer rear legs, it is usually caused by a lack of sufficient angulation in the rear.

Further discussion of body structure will be included under angulation and movement.

COAT: *Heavy, straight, hard, not wooly nor silky, of good length and very dense.*

The Lhasa Apso is actually a double-coated breed. Part of the density of its coat lies in its undercoat. This undercoat should be present on the dog entering the show ring, although on many companion dogs much of it may be removed to facilitate easier grooming.

A hard coat is solid and firm to the touch, not soft. The outer coat or top coat should have this characteristic. The undercoat usually tends to be of a softer variety. Lucky is the owner whose Lhasa has a relatively hard undercoat.

Wooly refers to fine, soft, curly hair such as that which forms the fleece on sheep, goats, and alpaca, and is characterized by felting. A Lhasa's top coat should not be wooly.

To describe silk as soft, which the Standard infers, seems to be a misnomer. Silk material is lustrous and strong, but not soft in the same sense that wool is. Silk thread is exceptionally strong and difficult to break with one's hands. When knitting socks, if one runs a silk thread along with the yarn when knitting a heel or toe, that heel or toe is virtually indestructible. Consequently, for a Lhasa's coat to be described as not silky is questionable to me.

Nothing is mentioned in the Standard about the fineness or coarseness of a Lhasa's hair. The fine, hard coat is just as proper as the coarse, hard coat. However, the fine coat can be more difficult to control.

24

MOUTH AND MUZZLE: *The preferred bite is either level or slightly to undershot. Muzzle of medium length; a square mouth is objectionable.*

Prior to the 1978 revision, the Standard stated that the muzzle was to be about 1½ inches long. This control could be important because it differentiated the Lhasas from other oriental breeds. Inasmuch as a longer or shorter muzzle changes the mien of the Lhasa, it is important to maintain some size reference. The longer the muzzle, the less the oriental look is preserved, and the more the Lhasa resembles the Tibetan Terrier. The shorter, pushed-in muzzle, more like that of the Shih Tzu, also loses the unique quality of the Lhasa head.

On the other hand, a Lhasa's overall head should be in proportion to the Lhasa's size. A 1½-inch muzzle might be very appropriate to an average or small Lhasa, but it might be a bit short on a bigger Lhasa.

Thus, a one-third to two-third proportion, keeping the 1½-inch perspective as a guide, should provide a good maxim for the proper Lhasa muzzle.

Bites

A level bite is self explanatory in that the incisors meet in a level manner. Slightly undershot is really a reverse scissors bite in which the upper incisors touch the inside of the lower incisors.

The 1902 British Standard and the standard for India state that the mouth should have a scissors bite, but that an undershot jaw is permissible. Certainly a scissors bite should be preferable to undershot or excessive undershot or overshot. A scissors

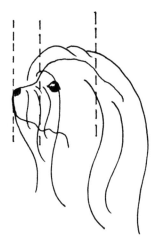

The correct proportions of the Lhasa head are one-third muzzle to two-thirds backskull.

bite is that in which the lower incisors touch the inside of the upper incisors. In a scale of points, an undershot jaw would be preferable to an overshot one, which should be severely faulted.

Nothing is said in the Standard about the teeth nor their line-up. Breeders prefer to see incisors in a straight line, not jumbled. A Collie-type jaw, rounded at the front, is incorrect.

The preference is for full dentition; however, a good bite with reduced dentition, in my mind, should not be penalized. These factors are more thoroughly discussed under dentition.

HEAD: *Heavy head furnishings with good fall over the eyes, good whiskers and beard; skull narrow, falling away behind the eyes in a marked degree, not quite flat, but not domed or apple shaped; straight foreface of fair length. Nose black, the length from tip of nose to eye to be roughly about one-third of the total length from nose to back of skull.*

A Lhasa Apso should have a lovely head, one not too refined, but also not coarse. The head furnishings should be heavy, and often they may be so heavy that they hang over the eyes, making a Lhasa

ring blind. Coping with this problem will be mentioned under grooming.

Whiskers, beard, and head furnishings blend into the rest of the coat to some extent. These may be short on the young dog but easily reach to the elbows on some mature dogs. The ear fringe should be long, and may be close to the length of the dog's coat.

The head should look proportionate to the rest of the body. It should be neither too broad nor too coarse, nor too narrow nor snipey. The muzzle should neither be overlong nor pushed in. The length of this muzzle is one-third of that of the whole head. The nose should be black, as a self-colored nose is no longer acceptable in the ring.

At this point it perhaps should be mentioned that among the early Lhasas there were brown noses and that good Lhasas with brown noses did achieve their championships. Those which were mentioned were Hamilton-line dogs. Moreover, there were many discussions held among ALAC members over the acceptance of this characteristic in the Standard. The "black noses" won the day.

A "Dudley nose," a term not so well known any more, is defined by the AKC as a flesh-colored

The curved Collie-type jaw is incorrect in a Lhasa.

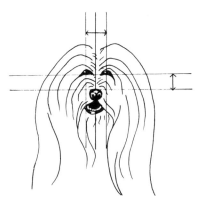

An incorrect head—too narrow between the eyes; muzzle too long.

The correct Lhasa jaw is flattened in front, with the incisors in a straighter line.

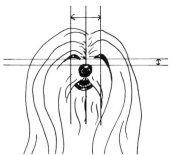

The correct head proportion—short muzzle, proportionately greater width between the eyes.

25

nose. The term developed in the late 1800s (about 1877) and was then defined as a brown or flesh-colored nose. Dogs who possessed this characteristic often had eye rims of the same shade and light-colored eyes.

The AKC defines a "Butterfly nose" as a particolored nose, or one which is dark and spotted with flesh color. This, too, occurs in Lhasas.

Another factor should be mentioned. Sometimes a black nose will fade during the winter, causing the so-called "winter nose." This will occur in dogs with excellent black pigment. One reason given is the lack of sun during the winter in the north. This may occur one winter and not the next. In the hot summer I have sometimes noticed Lhasas with

On the correct Lhasa head the muzzle is straight and level with the lower eyelids; ⅓ to ⅔ head proportion. Nose, eyelid, mouth have black pigment. Bite, six incisors in a straight line; white teeth. Eyes, dark and almond shaped. Backskull falls away behind eyes as specified by Standard; is neither high nor apple domed. Headfall arched over eyes; long and full. Coat texture hard, straight, and of good thickness. Photo by Clark.

26

much sun exposure whose noses appear to have a rusty cast.

EYES: *Dark brown, neither very large and full, nor very small and sunk.*

The Lhasa eye should be almond shaped, giving a somewhat oriental look.

The acceptable color is a dark brown. However, there are degrees of dark brown, and the shades of brown may vary. According to several sources, there are some Lhasas with very light brown eyes, but the darker shades are preferred.

Blue eyes, however pretty, are not acceptable in a Lhasa to be shown or used in breeding. Nor are one blue eye and one brown eye acceptable.

It should be pointed out that any Lhasa may carry this blue-eye gene, which has been traced back to some of the early Lhasas used extensively at stud. It takes many generations to weed out this fault, as it is probably a genetic recessive trait.

The factor I question at this writing is whether or not such a Lhasa should be completely eliminated from a breeding program. No Lhasa is perfect. One must consider a balance between structure and eye or dental defects. A very straight front or faulty hocks are just as, and perhaps more, difficult to eliminate, but some people do not seem to question these faults as seriously and continue to use such stock when breeding. Consequently, if a Lhasa is structurally considered excellent—angulation, body, tail set, balance—but has a blue eye, then the breeder must make his or her own judgment. Old-time breeders tell me that they have eliminated the blue eye from their lines. By judicious breeding, others may also.

One factor of which the owner should be aware is that a Lhasa whose eyes are irritated for some reason (such as an allergy to grass or hair spray used at shows) will tend to have eyes which may appear at times to be enlarged. Because of the shape of the Lhasa's eyeballs—slightly rounded—lack of tearing can be a minor problem. The use of a sterile eye wash can help temporarily; a chronic problem should be checked by a veterinarian.

Eye level for the Lhasa is the widest part of the head as the bony structure rising from the jaw level distinctly curves under the eye toward the back of the head. The eyes are somewhat frontally placed because of this curve.

EARS: *Pendant, heavily feathered.*

The Standard makes no mention of the placement of the ears. The ears should be level with the eyes, a little below the topline of the skull. The ear leather hangs close to the head and reaches the level of the lower jaw in the adult Lhasa.

The hair furnishings of the ear should be abundant and should give the ear a longer look. In the younger Lhasa this hair should reach below the shoulder, and as the Lhasa matures may reach to the elbow and may be as long as the coat. It also should be mentioned that in the adult Lhasa the head hair blends in with the ear furnishings giving an overall smooth look and making the top of the ear indistinguishable to the eye. One must part the hair to find the top of the ear. Both head hair and ear furnishings blend together to frame the Lhasa's face.

LEGS: *Forelegs straight; both forelegs and hindlegs heavily furnished with hair.*

The forelegs should not be bowed. From the front the legs should appear straight and parallel when the dog is standing. Actually, the upper arm may have a slight allowance for spring of rib.

The front shoulder bone connects with the upper leg. There should be a slight break at the elbow, with the legs dropping straight down. Sans coat, the Lhasa front should give a clean appearance.

There should be a balance in the leg. This can be determined by feeling the notch in the scapula and by running your hand up that ridge. The shoulder blade should balance the humerous bone in length.

Front Faults

Fiddle Front: Too much curve to the bones in the upper arm is usually genetic. But remember, on a Lhasa there must be some curve to allow for a proper chest or rib expansion. Curved bones in lower legs could be caused by several factors such as genetics, rickets, etc. When a fiddle front is apparent, a dog usually throws its elbows. The elbows come out because of lack of angulation.

On a Lhasa, one cannot make this judgment on coat movement. One must actually feel or actually see the bone structure.

Angulation Too Straight: Shoulder blades which are too straight, that is, which have insufficient angulation from the horizontal, definitely affect gait. To me, the Lhasas with too-straight shoulder blades tend to have the gait of Terriers. Since Lhasas are "mountain dogs," it is conceivable that a Lhasa with too-straight shoulders would have difficulty in maneuvering. The best-moving Lhasas are moderately angulated. Proper angulation for the Lhasa, a rectangular dog, would be about 39 degrees.

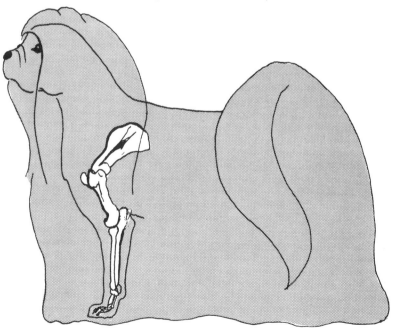

The correct shoulder angulation in a Lhasa is approximately 39 degrees.

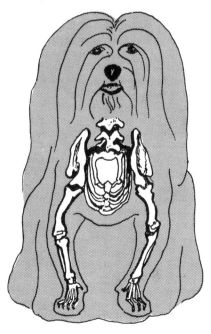

The bones of the fiddle front are curved.

27

Rear

The Standard mentions little about the rear legs except that the thighs should be well-developed and the legs should be heavily furnished with hair.

Examination – Look for the bend of the stifle. The hock should not be extended beyond the perpendicular to the ground. A long femur and a short tibia indicates underangulation. An overangulated hock is the worst fault. In this case the lower hock is longer than the upper thigh.

View – The hocks should, then, appear strong and parallel when viewed from behind. When moving, the hocks should go neither in nor out. When there is a seemingly short distance between the hock joint and the ground, it is termed a well-let-down hock. This type of hock reduces fatigue as it lessens leverage on the Achilles tendon.

Thighs – The thighs should be well muscled, as indicated in the ability of the Lhasa to spring and to climb. My own Kachina, a small Lhasa about 9½ inches tall, could jump 6 feet with ease, could climb anything, and could wiggle through a hole seemingly smaller than her body. It looks as though her granddaughter Shali is following in her paw-steps; she jumps and crawls and climbs and leaps. Both Pat Chenoweth and Bob Sharp have told me of Kori's (BIS Am. Bda. Mex. Col. Ch. Chen Korum-Ti ROM) escapades with 7-foot fences and gates. It would be natural for a breed developed in a mountainous area to have well-developed thighs.

Angulation – The Lhasa Apso should have good rear angulation. This angulation will be sharper than that of a terrier who gives a straighter, more upright appearance and whose rear legs give a somewhat mechanical appearance when moving, rather like a modified goose-step. Instead, the Lhasa should give a fluid appearance. This fluidity is caused by the sharper, but not exaggerated, angles created by the thigh bone at the hip joint and stifle. In no case should the angulation be exaggerated, as is the German Shepherd's.

Furnishings – That the legs should be well furnished with hair is really self-explanatory. This hair will usually be similar to that of the undercoat and will be covered by the top coat dropping over. To me, the well-furnished leg can be likened to that of a girl's in pantaloons. A lack of leg furnishings would be a serious fault in coat.

Rear Faults

Cowhocked – The hocks turn in and the stifle turns out. A dog may possibly stand somewhat in this manner, but not move in the manner of a well-angulated dog. Of course, a full coat on a Lhasa may hide this fault. Movement from the rear, then, should be noted because "cowhocked" may indicate a hip-joint problem. The Lhasa should not move with the hocks turned in and the stifles out.

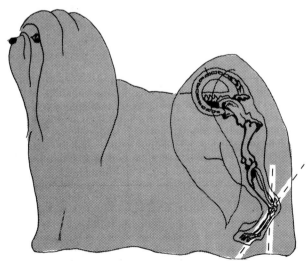

The sickle hock angles forward instead of standing perpendicular to the ground.

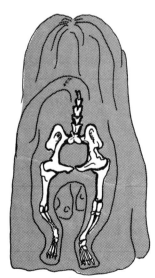

Cowhocks are a common fault.

Sicklehocked – These hocks can be compared to a farmer's sickle, with a rigidity apparent in the hock and with pasterns angling forward. In this case the hock cannot be fully extended, there is no follow through in gait, and there is a choppy dig.

FEET: *Well-feathered; should be round and catlike with good pads.*

The AKC defines a cat-foot as one which is short, round, and compact like that of a cat. It is a foot with short third digits.

The pads appear somewhat rounded. Between the pads on a Lhasa's foot there will be hair, which should be kept trimmed level with the pads.

Although the Standard mentions no color, the pads should be black, although occasionally a white or light-colored dog may lack this dark pigment, which is not a fault. The nails also should be black, except that a white or light-colored dog may have light-colored nails. The dew claws may be left on or taken off the front feet. There should be no dew claws on the hind feet.

TAIL AND CARRIAGE: *Well feathered, should be carried well over back in a screw; there may be a kink at the end. A low carriage of stern is a serious fault.*

The tail is formed of wormlike muscles which go up over the vertebrae into the tail. Tail carriage depends on equal muscle length and the tightness of muscle.

A Lhasa's tail is long and, if extended outward, should continue the line of the back and should not give the appearance of a pothook, as mentioned in the English Standard. The pothook appearance is caused by the tail being at right angles to the back, which perhaps could be caused by a very steep croup. The tail is carried over the back in a curl.

Then there is that characteristic, unique to the breed, of the kink in the end of the tail. Many Lhasas do not possess it. One person told me that the Lhasa born with the kink was an especially lucky one. This idea would, of course, go with its heritage of bringing good luck to a home. Consequently, I am alert for it with each new litter.

My own experience shows that it happens only occasionally but seems to repeat in certain matings. Rarely has there been more than one in a litter. Some matings do not produce this unique quality.

The kink, of course, makes it impossible for such a Lhasa to completely straighten his tail.

Stern

The last line of the Standard seems ambiguous, as it can be interpreted several ways. The AKC Glossary defines stern as the tail of a sporting dog or a hound. Of course, the Lhasa Apso belongs to neither group, but rather to the Non-Sporting Group. Even so, a Lhasa which carries its tail in a low manner, i.e., drags it or carries it at "half mast" rather than carrying it over its back, is exhibiting a "serious" fault. This could also mean a rather flat carriage of the tail over the back instead of with sufficient height to balance the head, which to me is more serious.

Dragging the tail behind is a "fault" which usually is an expression of feelings or attitude at a particular time. In the show ring it could mean apprehensiveness, a lack of confidence, or a sense of unhappiness on that particular day. A bitch coming in or in season will often react in this manner. A frightening experience while in the ring could also be a cause. While one of my bitches was performing beautifully with her handler, someone just beside the ring taking pictures had a flashbulb explode just as she went by. Needless to say, just as we were startled, so was she and badly frightened to boot by the gunfire sound. The drooping tail could also be a symbol of a Lhasa's cautiousness, much like a cat checking the situation over.

Since a Lhasa is expected to be gay and jaunty in movement, its tail is expected to reflect this by being over its back in the ring.

A very flat carriage of tail over the back does not provide a proper silhouette for a Lhasa. Most, and probably all, of the great Lhasas, such as BIS Am. Bda. Col. Mex. Ch. Chen Korum-Ti ROM, exhibited this balance of tail and head.

Feathering

The tail is well feathered, and this feathering may fall to either side of the body. I have noticed, too, that an especially well-furnished tail may tend to separate, with half the hair falling to each side of its own accord and when allowed its own expression.

The tail hair may grow so long that it trails on the ground alongside the body. It should be noted that a low carriage of tail over the back, one tight to the back, could create the illusion of longer tail hair in comparison with a proper high carriage of tail, one balancing the head, with hair of equal length.

The goal for those of us who breed is to find among our puppies that potential Best-In-Show dog or bitch. When mature, this dog would have a heavily feathered tail with a high tail set (level croup) and with excellent carriage.

The young dog pictured possesses a nice high tail set and the tail has good carriage. The feathering should develop with maturity. These two figures show what we aim for in breeding.

The Lhasa with too low or too flat tail carriage is seen very often in the ring today. This is faulty. The tail should balance the head.

Likewise, the tail can be carried too high. Sometimes this is a fault which cannot be corrected. Other times the dog may simply be expressing happiness, or apprehension may make the dog straighten the tail rather than allowing it to curl naturally. Sometimes the tail is late coming down into position. As the Lhasa puppy grows older, feathering will help bring the tail down.

Corrective grooming may help balance head and tail carriage.

The mature Lhasa has a high tail set, fully feathered, with excellent carriage.

Lhasa with "too low" or "too flat" tail carriage. This tail, which is often seen, does not balance the head.

The desired high tail set and good carriage in a young Lhasa.

A potential "gay" tail. This tail may feather out heavily, causing it to come down.

Movement

The tail does not influence movement much, but it may signal a shift of weight. However, a happy, excited dog furiously wagging a heavily feathered tail can affect his rear movement, albeit he will usually be standing in such tail-wagging situations.

Tails are marvelous things, as they are important both as a signal of social order and as a directional signal.

Kaleko's Kristiana of Kamala winning best Junior Puppy at a match. Owner, Debbie Burke.

CANADIAN KENNEL ASSOCIATION
STANDARD FOR THE LHASA APSO
Effective: January 1, 1981

Origin and Purpose – Beyond the northern boundary of India, where Mt. Everest stands like a guardian sentinel is the land of Tibet. A country of huge mountains, deep valleys, windswept plateaus, warm summers and cold winters, it is the home of the Lhasa Apso. It is an ancient breed and genealogical tables show them to be in existence as far back as 800 B.C. Having been bred for centuries as a special indoor sentinel, the Lhasa Apso has never lost his characteristic of keen watchfulness.

General Appearance – The Lhasa Apso is a medium small, exotic, very hardy breed with a well developed body, strong loins, good quarters and thighs. The long, straight, hard, dense coat enhances the beauty of the breed and completely covers the dog.

Temperament – Gay and assertive but chary of strangers.

Size – Ideal size for dogs is between 10 and 11″ (when breed standards are converted to metric, the figures 25 cm to 28 cm should be used) with up to 11½″ permissible (when breed standards are converted to metric, the figure 30 cm should be used). Bitches should be slightly smaller. Lhasa Apsos over 11½ (when breed standards are converted to metric, the figure 30 cm should be used) are to be disqualified. Body length from the point of the shoulder to the point of the buttocks should be slightly longer than the height at the withers. A well balanced type is to be preferred.

Coat and Color

(a) Coat – The adult coat is heavy, straight, hard, not wooly or silky, of good length and dense. The coat should be parted from the nose to the root of the tail.

(b) Head – The head should have heavy furnishings with a good fall over the eyes. Good whiskers and beard. In Obedience the hair may be tied back from the eyes.

(c) Ears – Should be heavily furnished.

(d) Legs – Should be well furnished.

(e) Tail – Should be well furnished.

(f) Feet – Should be surrounded with hair. The pads have hair between them which may be trimmed.

(g) Forequarters, Hindquarters, and neck – are heavily furnished.

(h) Colours – All colours and mixtures of colours considered equal.

Head

(a) Skull – Narrow, falling away from behind the eyebrow ridge to a marked degree. Cranium – Almost flat, not domed or apple-shaped. Viewed from the front, the top of the cranium is narrower than the width at the level of the eyes. The foreface is straight.

(b) Muzzle – The length from the tip of the nose to the inside corner of the eye to be roughly 1½″ (when breed standards are converted to metric, the figure 4 cm should be used) or the length from the tip of the nose to the inside corner of the eye to be roughly one-third of the total length from the tip of the nose to the back of the skull. A square muzzle is objectionable.

(c) Nose – Black. The tip of the nose is level with or very slightly below the lower eye rim when viewed from the front.

(d) Mouth – Bite – Reverse scissors (upper incisors just touching the inner face of the lower incisors).

Full Dentition – Incisors (6) to be in a straight line.

Acceptable bite – Level (the front incisors of the upper and lower jaw meeting edge to edge).

Undesirable bite – Overshot. Excessively undershot (more than ⅛″) (when breed standard converts to metric, the figure .3 cm should be used). The teeth must not show when the mouth is closed.

Lips – Black.

(e) Eyes – Dark Brown. Not large and full or small or sunken. The Iris should be of reasonable size, no white showing at the base or top of the eye. The eyes are frontally placed in an oval shaped black rim.

(f) Ears—Pendant. The ears should be well set back on the skull at eye level (not level with the topline of the skull). The leather should hang close to the head and in an adult dog should reach the level of the lower jaw.

Neck—Well set on to the shoulders. Long enough to carry the head well creating an impression of elegance. Slightly arched.

Forequarters

(a) Shoulders—Strong, muscular, well laid back.

(b) Upper arm—The upper arm should not be "Terrier straight" allowing for the desired width and depth of the chest.

(c) Lower arm—The forelegs should not be bowed. From the front when the dog is standing, the legs should be straight parallel, elbows well under the body. The forelimbs support a good share of the body weight when the dog is standing or moving at a slow pace.

(d) Pasterns—The pasterns should be straight and firm when viewed from the front. Slight deviation from the perpendicular when viewed from the side.

(e) Feet—Short, round and compact with good pads turning neither in nor out. Nails—Ideally black. In parti-coloured or light coloured coats light nails and pads are permitted. Dew claws permissable.

Body

(a) Topline—level.

(b) Chest—Well ribbed up, i.e. the ribs should extend well back along the body. The slightly curved ribs should not extend below the elbows.

(c) Loin—Too long a loin adds excess length to the back and results in a loss of strength to the forepart of the body. If the loin is too short there will be a loss of flexibility. The loin should be firmly muscled.

(d) Croup—The angle formed by the pelvis and the backbone should not be more than 30 degrees from the horizontal. This angulation gives power for the forward propulsion.

(e) Abdomen—Tucked up to a shallower depth at the loin.

THE ENGLISH STANDARD FOR THE LHASA APSO

Effective 1973

Characteristics—The Apso should give the appearance of a well-balanced, solid dog. Gay and assertive, but chary of strangers. Free and jaunty in movement.

Size—Ideal height—10 inches at shoulder for dogs; bitches slightly smaller.

Colours—Golden, sandy, honey, dark grizzle, slate, smoke, parti-colour, black, white, or brown.

Body—The length from point of shoulders to point of buttocks greater than height at withers. Well ribbed up. Level topline. Strong loin. Well balanced and compact.

Coat—Top coat heavy, straight and hard, not wooly or silky, of good length. Dense undercoat.

Mouth—Upper incisors should close just inside the lower, i.e., a reverse scissors bite. Incisors should be "nearly" in a straight line. Full dentition is desirable.

Hindquarters—Strongly muscled and in balance with the forequarters.

(a) Hocks—When viewed from the rear at a stance the hocks should be strong, straight and parallel, turning neither in nor out. When viewed from the side, they should be perpendicular to the ground and not stretched out beyond the rump of the dog.

(b) Stifle Bend—The stifle is moderately bent.

(c) Feet—Same as in forequarters.

Tail—Set high. Carried forward close to the back with the tip draped on either side of the body. The tail should not rise vertically. A kink in the end is permissible A low carriage of tail is a serious fault.

Gait—An easy moving free flowing trot is the normal pace of the Lhasa Apso. This trot shows the character of his movement at its best and is what is aimed for. The pads should be seen as the dog moves away indicating a strong hind drive which is balanced by a good reach of the forelegs. Moving too quickly in the ring throws the dog off gait and should be avoided.

Disqualifications – Lhasa Apsos over 11½″ (30 cm) are to be disqualified.

Head and Skull – Heavy head furnishings with good fall over the eyes, good whiskers and beard. Skull moderately narrow, falling away behind the eyes in a marked degree; not quite flat, but not domed or apple shaped. Straight foreface, with medium stop. Nose black. Muzzle about 1½ inches long, but not square; the length from tip of nose to be roughly one-third the total length from nose to back of skull.

Neck – Strong, well covered with a dense mane which is more pronounced in dogs than in bitches.

Eyes – Dark, medium sized, eyes to be frontally placed, not large or full, or small or sunk. No white showing at base or top of eye.

Ears – Pendant, heavily feathered. Dark tips an asset.

Forequarters – Shoulders should be well laid back. Forelegs straight, heavily furnished with hair.

Hindquarters – Well developed with good muscle. Good angulation. Heavily furnished. The hocks when viewed from behind should be parallel and not too close together.

Feet – Round and cat-like, with good pads. Well feathered.

Tail – High set, carried well over back and not like a pot hook. There is often a kink at the end. Well feathered.

Note – Male animals should have two apparently normal testicles fully descended into the scrotum.

THE LHASA APSO STANDARD
INDIAN KENNEL CLUB

Appearance – A small, short-legged, shaggy dog with pendent ears and curled tail. Height for dogs 10 to 11 inches; bitches being smaller.

Head – Narrow, the skull being neither flat nor domed nor apple-headed, but conical. Stop well defined. Muzzle of medium length of skull as 1:3. Mouth with scissors bite, but undershot jaw is permissable. Eyes dark brown, of medium size and not sunken. Nose black. Ears pendant and well feathered. The head fringe falling over the eyes, and the moustache and beard making the muzzle appear longer than it actually is. Neck of medium length.

Body – Longer than high, well ribbed up and with straight back. Loins strong and straight, croup not falling away. For and hind-limbs short and straight; well covered with hair and feathered.

Tail – Carried over the back – never down – and covered with long hair.

Feet – Round, with strong pads and plenty of feather.

Coat – Hard and straight, neither wooly nor silky; of good length and very thick.

Colour – Golden, sandy, or honey, with dark points to the hairs on the muzzle and ears preferred. May also be dark grey, slate-grey, smoke grey, or white pied with black or brown.

1901 Description

Lhassa Terrier, an interesting little breed formerly found under the inappropriate name of Bhuteer Terrier.

Head – Distinctly Terrier-like. Skull narrow, falling away behind the eyes in a marked degree, not quite flat, but not domed or apple-shaped. Fore face of fair length, strong in front of the eyes, the nose, large, prominent and pointed, not depressed; a square muzzle is objectionable. The stop, size for size, about that of a Skye Terrier. Mouth quite level, but of the two a slightly overshot mouth is preferable to an undershot one. The teeth are somewhat smaller than would be expected in a Terrier of the size. In this respect, the breed seems to suffer to an extraordinary degree from cankered teeth. I have never yet seen an imported specimen with a sound mouth.

Ears – Set on low, and carried close to the cheeks, similar to the ears of a drop-eared Skye.

Eyes – Neither very large and full nor very small and sunk, dark brown in colour.

Legs and Feet – The fore legs should be straight. In all short-legged breeds there is a tendency to crookedness, but the straighter the legs the better. There should be good bone. Owing to the heavy coat the legs look, and should look, very heavy in bone, but in reality, the bone is not heavy. It should be round and of good strength right down to the toes, the less ankle the better. The hocks should be particularly well let down. Feet should be round and cat-like, with good pads.

Body – There is a tendency in England to look for a level top and a short back. All the best specimens have a slight arch at the loin and the back should not be too short; it should be considerably longer than height at the withers (note the measurements given of the Bitch Marni*). The dog should be well ribbed-up, with a strong loin and well developed quarters and thighs.

Stern – Should be carried well over the back after the manner of the tail of the Chow. All Thibetan (sic) dogs carry their tails in this way, and a low carriage of stern is a sign of impure blood.

Coat – Should be heavy, of good length and very dense. There should be a strong growth on the skull, falling on both sides. The legs should be well clothed right down to the toes. On the body, the hair should not reach to the ground, as in a show Yorkshire; there should be a certain amount of daylight. In general appearance the hair should convey the idea of being much harder to the eyes than it is to the touch. It should look hard, straight and strong, when to the touch it is soft, but not silky. The hair should be straight with no tendency to curl.

Colour – Black, dark grizzle, slate, sandy, or an admixture of these colours with white.

Size – About 10 in. or 11 in. height at shoulder for dogs, and 9 in or 10 in. for bitches.

*Note – No picture of Marni was given, but her measurements are listed as follows: "Length of head 6¼ in. Height at shoulder 10 in. Length of back 19 in. Length of ear 2¼ in."[1]

---

[1]*ONBA OPUS* No. 2; Original source: W. D. Drury, *British Dogs,* Vol. 1, The Various Breeds, 3rd Edition.

Ch. Licos Kula La was a top winning Lhasa in the early 60s. Bred and owner-handled by Grace Licos, Kula won five BIS awards. He is found in many pedigrees.

Head study of Ch. Dell's Regal Gable of Lori Shan. Compare with illustration of correct head on page 25. Owner, Judy O'Dell.

36

LET'S TROT

In the show ring, dogs are judged at a trot as a means of assessing correct structure. A dog with faulty conformation usually cannot move as fluently and correctly as one with correct structure. The Lhasa Apso should exhibit a balanced trot that is smooth and effortless. There should be a sense of "spring," giving the impression that the Lhasa could drive forward if necessary.

The Lhasas' gorgeous coats prevent us from easily analyzing angulation and movement. When they are in their gait parade in the ring, they present a beautiful picture, but those profuse coats may cover faults, or the movement of the coat may give the illusion of faults that do not exist. This is especially true on the very heavily coated dog whose legs have extremely full "pantaloons." The thick undercoat may cause the coat to bounce and to part in the leg areas.

Coat color is another cause of faulty illusion. When the top coat of a heavily coated Lhasa is slightly darker than the undercoat, an optical illusion in movement can be created. A clean, untreated coat will tend to move when the Lhasa is gaited, causing the darker top coat to split and reveal the lighter undercoat. This can create the optical illusion that the dog is out at the elbows. It takes a discriminating eye to determine if there is really a fault or only an illusion. To really know what is under that coat, a physical examination is necessary.

STRUCTURE AS RELATED TO GAIT

The Neck

Elegance in a Lhasa Apso demands a good length of neck. This length of neck is indicative of the length of reach when the Lhasa is gaiting.

The neck should have a nice arch to it. A lack of arch indicates a lack of muscle, which forms on the bone. Thus, a lack of muscle could indicate insufficient bone substance.

Muscle formation is very important in movement. Two major muscles run from the skull to the upper arm and to the pectoral muscle. When the Lhasa levels his head when gaiting, he is putting maximum tension (a contraction up to fifty to sixty-five percent can be accomplished) in order to get maximum traction on the muscles for forward movement.

The length of neck can be as apparent in natural movement as when a dog is in show pose; in fact, it may be more so. It is natural for a Lhasa to level his head out when gaiting, just as a runner tends to hold his head forward rather than directly upright. A Lhasa moving in the yard will carry his head in a comfortable position. In the ring, however, the Lhasa's head is expected to be held high, to give a perfect silhouette, and is often held in this position when gaiting.

A handler often creates an illusion of good neck by stringing up the dog on a tight lead, but this can destroy good natural movement. Another method used is to "sculpture" the coat to create this illusion. There should be a good fall of hair from the head, which will come down over the shoulders.

When evaluating movement, look at neck length as an indicator of reach and observe the natural carriage of the head. Reach of neck and good head carriage indicates the proper placement of the scapula. A physical examination by touch reveals adequate muscle formation.

Shoulder

The best lay-back for the shoulder blade (i.e., the degree from horizontal), of a rectangular dog such as a Lhasa Apso is about 39 degrees. This shoulder angulation is important in movement.

The muscle development in this area is also very important, as the front assembly is not attached in any way except by these muscles. Good muscle development aids in front thrust.

The uniqueness of the Lhasa Apso movement results from this shoulder formation, from which comes the sprightliness and the jauntiness. A good spread of muscles indicates proper slant to the shoulder bone.

A Lhasa with a "straight" front (i.e., with shoulder blades too upright) indicates that the size and the slant of the bones are reduced, which in turn reduces the area for muscle attachment. A dog with a straight front may have poor muscle development. Such a Lhasa could be said to lack substance. Straight or steep shoulders also tend to make the neck appear short.

In a "touch" observation the leg rectangle, as measured from the shoulder blade ends to the ground, will be broader for the proper shoulder than that of the straight shoulder.

Good shoulders, good angulation usually indicate a good mover.

BIS Am. Can. Bda. Ch. Bihar's Revenger of Sammi Raja, "Tux," exhibits the tremendous reach and drive that made him a top winner in '80 and '81. Owner, Carol Strong. Photo by Moore.

38

Pastern

There is a parallel between pasterns and fronts. A moderately sloping pastern usually accompanies good front angulation. An upright pastern causes a hard contact with the ground. A pastern with too much slope will be weak. Either will affect gait.

Forelegs

The forelegs should be straight and parallel with each other. There should be a slight "break" at the elbow, which should be relatively tight to the body.

The legs should be extended forward when gaiting. The pads will not show; however, in spite of the long coat, the flicked action of the pads as the leg stretches forward should be visible from the side. The pictures of Chaos, Krissi, Rumpy, and Tux reveal this. Should the Lhasa have proper lay-back but not extend the legs when gaiting, exercise which extends the dorsal muscle will help.

Front Faults

East-West Front – Also known as toeing out. Your Lhasa may toe out *slightly* when standing at rest, but let's emphasize the slight. A pronounced east-west front is caused by weak carpal joints and is a serious fault. A Lhasa should not gait with the toes turning out.

Elbows out – When a dog's elbows turn out when he moves, the problem may be caused by one of the following: a fiddle front, a lack of angulation, or barrel ribs. With a Lhasa be sure this is not an optical illusion caused by parting of the coat.

When this problem is pronounced, the elbows will turn out when the dog is standing.

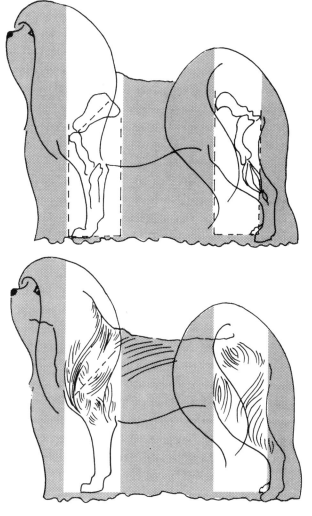

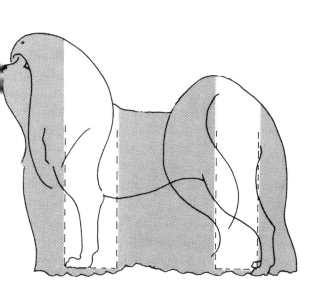

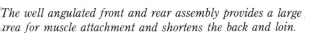

The well angulated front and rear assembly provides a large area for muscle attachment and shortens the back and loin.

REAR QUARTERS

Observe the angulation of the thigh and pelvis. Again, a proper slant gives more area for muscle development and subsequently indicates better movement. Here again, the width of that area indicates potential of movement. To measure this area width, drop figurative lines from the front of the pelvis and the rear of the buttocks.

Hocks

The hock needs to be supple and flexible. To determine a proper hock, tuck the leg snuggly to the belly. The hock should be flush with the pelvic bone, and it should be short in proportion to the leg bones. The hock should drop down perpendicular to the pelvis. It should not extend beyond the pelvic bone. In stance, the hocks should appear straight and parallel from the back, and from the side the hock joint should point rearward.

The short hock indicates endurance, and a need for less energy to move; a high hock, on the other hand, is indicative of speed.

Rear Faults

Cowhocks – A Lhasa that is "cowhocked" will stand with its hocks turned in and its stifles out. Standing slightly cowhocked is not a major fault; some of the best-angulated dogs may stand in this manner. However, moving in a cowhocked manner does affect rear thrust and is a serious fault.

Sickle Hock – If you have seen a farm sickle, you can picture this fault. The "sickle hocked" Lhasa stands with his hocks down and his pasterns angled slightly forward. He is unable to fully extend the hock. When the leg is drawn up, the hock will not drop perpendicularly.

This dog will need to make a functional adjustment in gait and will therefore exhibit a choppy

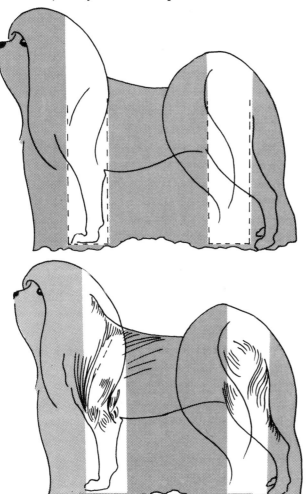

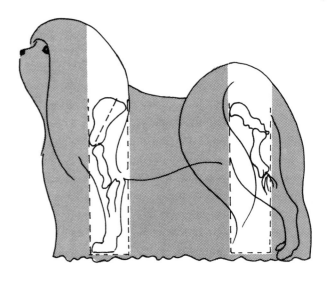

Straight shoulder and/or rear angulation reduces the area for muscle attachment and creates a long loin and a short, obliquely set on neck.

"dig" and no follow-through. The gait will tend to be stiff, almost shuffling, with limited forward propulsion.

Hocking out – In this case the hocks turn out, and regardless of the severity, cause the feet to toe in. Hocking out sometimes occurs in conjunction with front feet that cross over when the Lhasa is gaited.

LHASA GAIT

Ideal Lhasa gait at a trot is smooth, balanced, and effortless. This usually occurs when the structure of the dog is in good proportion. Sometimes, however, a well-proportioned Lhasa will not move well, while a less-well-structured dog will have excellent gait. It is difficult to account for these variations.

In order for movement to be "balanced," the dog must have similar angulation both front and rear. A Lhasa with good shoulder layback but a straight rear will not have a balanced gait when viewed from the side. Neither will the dog with a straight shoulder and excellent rear angulation.

A Lhasa has four very distinct gaits – the walk, trot, amble, and gallop. Movement varies considerably depending upon the gait and the speed the dog is traveling. In the show ring, the gait normally judged is the trot. It may be helpful to have someone else move your dog so you can observe the trotting speed which shows your dog's gait to the best advantage.

The Walk

Young people with farm experience have described the Lhasas' slow walk as that of a duck. They do rather waddle at this speed. The reason is, of course, that while three feet are on the ground, one leg is moving, and the pelvic end of the Lhasa seems to do its own thing. This is the most awkward gait for the Lhasa, and, if you observe other rectangular dogs not possessing long legs, this type of walk seems to be normal. The Lhasa that doesn't perform a slow walk in this manner probably does not possess true Lhasa proportions; i.e., it is either too square, too high on leg, or has faulty structure.

One wonders what a judge is looking for in the Lhasa ring when he requests Lhasas to be walked, rather than to be trotted, which is their best gait.

Amble

Sometimes the Lhasas move at a pace, or amble. In this case the legs on either side move almost together. As the weight switches from side to side, there appears to be a roll to the hips. This rolling is not abnormal. It has to do with the speed at which the Lhasa is moving. This gait is not desired in the show ring.

Trot

There is a definite two-beat rhythm to this gait. Two feet are on the ground at a time; i.e., the left hind foot with the right front foot; the right hind foot with the left front. A good trotting Lhasa will please a horse fancier because the Lhasa in this case moves much like a trotting horse – smoothly, easily, gracefully, and effortlessly. The trot is the correct gait for the ring.

At a trot, a Lhasa comes close to single-tracking, which is when a dog places his feet as nearly as possible under the center of his body and the hind footprints cover the front footprints. Because of broader rib spring and shorter legs, a Lhasa will not achieve a complete single-track as will a taller dog such as a Brittany Spaniel. The feet should come down in a regularly spaced pattern, however.

This tracking can be tested, I am told, by spreading a length of white paper out (say, about 15 feet of shelving paper), coloring the dog's paws with chalk or ink, placing the Lhasa on the paper, and then gaiting him. The resulting marks should be informative.

Single-tracking usually produces a smoother and more efficient movement.

When a Lhasa is tracking correctly, the inside edge of the pads converge on a center line.

Right:
Note the tremendous reach of Am. Can. Ch. Kyi-Chu Chaos. Owner, Ruth Smith. Photo by Callea.

Bottom Left:
Another dog with good reach and drive is Am. Can. Ch. Chen Krisna Nor. Owner, Wendy Harper. Photo by Callea.

Bottom Right:
His beautiful movement helped make BIS Am. Can. Ch. Rimar's Rumpelstiltskin number one in 1978. Owner, Betty Bowman. Photo by Callea.

The Gallop

This is not a speed at which we often see a Lhasa, but some can gallop and cover a great deal of ground in so doing. It is the fastest gait and one which has a four-beat rhythm. At times the Lhasa seems to have all four feet off the ground. He extends his front legs with power to their maximum reach, and then brings the rear legs forward with strength for that propulsion stroke. For a Lhasa to gallop, he must have good shoulders, good thighs, good legs, a good chest indicated by good rib spring, a strong heart, and a love for moving with the wind.

One thing that I have noticed is that those Lhasas who can gallop with ease over an acre of ground also have a smooth, sparkling trot.

Faulty Movement

There are numerous kinds of faulty movements including close movement, parallel movement, exaggerated rear action, and restricted rear movement.

Hackney Gait – Occasionally you will see a Lhasa moving in a very flashy manner, which is a variation of a trot and is called a hackney gait. While proper for a toy breed such as a Min Pin, it is not proper for a Lhasa Apso. In this case there is a high flashy action caused by an exaggerated flexing of the joints in the style of a hackney pony. There is a sense of stiffness and of the mechanical in movement.

The hind legs of this dog will probably be well under the body with little bend at the hocks.

The Close Mover – The close mover often appears to be moving properly; however, his elbow is flexing and bringing the forearm inward; the carpal joint of the front legs and the rear pastern also bend in order that the pad is placed on the "center line." There will tend to be a parallel line from hock to pad, and the pasterns or legs may actually strike together when moving. From a rear view, the hocks will tend to turn in and the pasterns drop straight to the ground. In movement the stifle may be thrown out of line.

The only clue that I can accept for closeness in a moving Lhasa is that the hocks actually rub together. I believe that some dogs are actually falsely accused of this because of their efforts to single-track.

Exaggerated Rear Action – Exaggerated rear action indicates several faults: the rear limbs cannot be fully extended as the pad hits the ground before the extension occurs, and the hock must rise high in the air to clear the ground; the hip rotation is completed while the leg is in the air.

The lack of extension indicates a lack of front angulation which may inhibit rear movement, or an overangulated rear which must restrict its movement or tangle legs. The hip rotation problem may be caused by too flat a croup which would limit rear reach. Usually the legs of this dog will extend well to the rear.

Restricted rear movement, when the rear legs do not easily extend, can be caused by inadequate rear angulation, a short back, a steep croup, or a joint disease such as arthritis. The limitations of rear movement are indicated by legs moving very quickly while conversely covering very little ground.

Elbows in or Paddling – Indications of this fault are the rocking of the body and a lack of "single" tracking. This is a serious defect as it severely restricts movement. The front legs tend to swing stiffly out because not only do the elbows move too tightly to the body, but so also do the shoulder joints. The effect is that of paddling a kayak.

Tight Lead – Using a tight lead in the show ring can "cause" faults which do not exist. Stringing a dog up can, of course, cause a dog to choke (although there may be other reasons) and to act badly. It can also cause a dog to pull to one side, to cross its front legs when gaited, to twist the feet outward (winging), or even to toe in.

There are noticeable differences between a loose lead, a firm lead, and a tight lead or stringing up. Careful use of the lead can avoid the appearance of a fault not there.

Parallel Movement – The legs move in a parallel manner with no effort toward single-tracking. If I consider the Lhasa in comparison with people I know who walk in this manner, I would suspect a weight problem. If I consider a Lhasa's structure, I would suspect a barrel chest in which the first four ribs are sprung.

Ch. Sulan's Gregorian Chant. Breeder-owners Suzette Michele and Marlene D. Kimbrel. Handled by Emily Gunning. Photo by Ashbey.

44

5

LHASA DENTITION

Perhaps no one has stated more succinctly for me her feelings about the bites of Lhasa Apsos than breeder-judge Ruth Smith of Kyi-Chu Lhasas:

> About bites. At one time almost no attention was given bites, but recently I feel the pendulum has swung too far in the opposite direction. I have heard more than one judge . . . put great emphasis on bites. . . .
>
> I sincerely believe we need to get back to the middle of the road, and before letting the bite be a deciding factor (either way), we need to step back and look at OVERALL EXPRESSION. A scissors bite usually gives an "Andy Gumpish" look—as can a level bite. A severely undershot bite can give a gargoylish look. I think when expression is distorted both bites should be penalized. If the expression, regardless of degree of under, or level, or even scissors, has a sweet, alert look then never mind how the teeth are lined up. A scrambled bite should be penalized, regardless, SINCE THIS LEADS TO EARLY LOSS OF TEETH—IT IS INHERENTLY TO THE DETRIMENT OF THE DOG'S DENTAL HEALTH. Like anyone else who has bred any length of time (it is inevitable in this breed), I have had every kind of bite imaginable. . . . I think that we need to look at the strength of the jaw, the number of teeth (and size) in evaluating a mouth because these factors definitely affect expression, more than level, scissors or reverse or whatever.[1]

As Ruth indicated, a wide variety of dental patterns can be found among the Lhasa Apsos. These various patterns—undershot, reverse scissors, level, scissors, overbite, full dentition, reduced dentition, scrambled dentition—result from a variety of causes. There are those who say variety in dentition is caused because Lhasa Apsos are a brachycephalic, or short-headed, breed. By definition a brachycephalic head is one which is short and broad, with a breadth of scull at least four-fifths as great as the length from front to back.

The foreshortening involved in developing this head type may cause a mismatch of bones. The maxillary (the upper jaw or its bones

---

[1]Ruth Smith, Letter to Helf, March 24, 1978.

containing the upper teeth, nasal cavity, and bottom part of the eye socket) can thus be longer than, shorter than, or even with the mandibular bone (the lower jaw).

The question remains: Can a Lhasa head be defined as a brachycephalic head? In my opinion, the definition of the brachycephalic head does not describe the Lhasa head. However, there may be some other reasons for the variety in dental patterns. For instance, evidence indicates that the process of evolution may be reducing the numbers of teeth. This reduction of teeth, such as the elimination of premolars and some incisors, is occurring in the oldest breeds and may soon occur in others. The Lhasa Apsos are among the oldest breeds.

The Lhasa Apso Standard states that both the level and the slightly undershot mouth types are acceptable. The fact is, however, that scissors, level, and reverse scissors bites are prevalent in the breed. In addition, the new Canadian Standard emphasizes full dentition. This stipulation, as well as the occlusion stipulation, should be seriously considered in the light of evolutionary evidence.

PROBLEMS

Malocclusion

The undershot and overshot occlusions vary widely. In breeding, care should be exercised in choice of breeding specimens. A dog or bitch with an excessive malocclusion should not be used for breeding if the problem is such that it both interferes with the dog's eating abilities and/or can be inherited. The extreme underbite, or "shovel jaw," which hinders a dog's eating or carrying objects can be eliminated, as can the severely overshot mouth, also known as the Mendallion recessive, the "Andy Gump," or the "shark face." The cause of this latter condition is a mandibular bone, or lower jaw bone, which does not grow to match that of the maxillary, or upper jaw, and the rest of the skull.

Tooth Reduction

The reduction of number of teeth is another dental variation found in Lhasas. The absence or presence of any tooth may be genetically determined. Stanley Salthe tells us, "it may be noted that if the presence or absence of this molar is directly genetically determined, it could be in terms of small differences in a codon or so at a single locus. Suppose that the absence of this tooth derived from the inactivation of a crucial enzyme. This would actually mean that in the environmental conditions present at this particular anlage, the altered enzyme has an activity so low as to inhibit a crucial

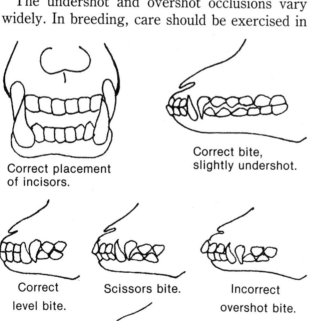

Correct placement of incisors.

Correct bite, slightly undershot.

Correct level bite.

Scissors bite.

Incorrect overshot bite.

Incorrect undershot bite.

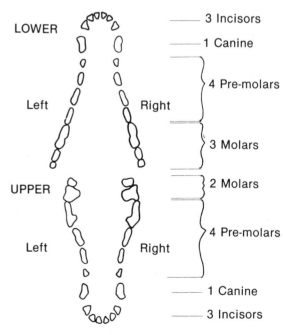

LOWER

Left

Right

UPPER

Left

Right

3 Incisors

1 Canine

4 Pre-molars

3 Molars

2 Molars

4 Pre-molars

1 Canine

3 Incisors

Permanent teeth of the dog.

pathway (which might remain active at the other anlagen, because the environments there are not inhibitory to it), so that no extra molar is formed."[2]

It is possible for a molar cusp or incisor to reappear. For example, in a recent set of breedings a stud with an excellent bite and full dentition was used with two bitches, both with an underbite and four incisors. All the male offspring inherited six incisors, but the females inherited only five incisors, an increase of one over the dam's. The bites for all the males were very good. Only one female inherited the undershot bite, albeit with five incisors. Salthe points out "that the return of a small morphological trait, such as a molar cusp, after it had disappeared from some lineage could easily occur without there having been any actual evolutionary reversal at the genetic level, even if the trait in question is directly coded for genotype.[3] It is possible, then, for a prepotent stud to increase the number of incisors. Conversely, both the stud and the bitch may have full dentition and not produce the same. Therefore, if it is indeed true that the incisors as well as the premolars, no longer useful in a dog's present environment, are in the process of being eliminated by evolution, these teeth may well be in the process of permanent reduction.

Others have said that the reduction in tooth number is also due to brachychepoly. In addition to the reduction, the teeth are often placed in different positions. The most noticeable variations in number are found with the incisors, the upper jaw having a full complement of six, but the lower jaw revealing only four or five. Xrays in such cases reveal no roots for the missing teeth. Usually when the lower incisors are reduced to four or five, there is also an obvious narrowing of the mandibular bone, the lower jaw.

Less noticeable are missing molars. Premolars I and/or II are the ones which may not appear, and very occasionally upper molar II and lower molar III may be missing. Some place the cause as genetic, but it also may be the process of evolution.

S. W. Williston formulated "the principle that, during the evolution of a lineage, serially homologous parts tend to become fewer and increasingly differential."[4] Spaeth goes farther to state that "each part becomes more specialized in function."[5] This appears to be true for incisors and molars. As environmental conditions have changed for our Lhasa Apsos through the years, so have their specific dental needs changed. Consequently, if Lhasas are in an evolutionary tooth reduction process (as in other older breeds), it is possible that some of the dentition problems stem from attempting to maintain so-called full dentition in mouths which no longer need all of the teeth. This could account, then, in some manner for jumbled tooth eruption.

Misplacement

One condition resulting from missing teeth which may not be so apparent, especially on a dog exhibiting a level bite, is the misplacement of the canine teeth in the lower jaw. These tend to be forward, perhaps in place of the missing incisors, instead of in proper alignment with the upper jaw canines. When this is true, there may be a noticeable gap between the canines and premolar I, a gap which may be only a few centimeters or as much as 12 centimeters or more.

Another dental variation, unique to Lhasa Apsos, is the set of the incisors of the lower jaw and occasionally the upper. The widths of the jaw may not be complementary. Should the lower jaw be narrow, and perhaps pinched, the normal placement of incisors is impossible. If the number of incisors has not been reduced and all six are present, the teeth may well be out of line, causing a jumbled mouth.

The lower canines in a too-narrow jaw may also cause the displacement of upper incisors by either separating the upper canines or pushing them into improper positions.

Mis-shaped Jaws

The too-narrow jaw occurs for several reasons. For instance, the effort to obtain the so-called perfect or level bite may influence the jaw width. Often, in order to get such a bite, a longer muzzle is the result. This correspondingly longer muzzle also appears to be narrower. "Suppose that the

---

[2]Stanley N. Salthe, *Evolutionary Biology,* New York, 1972, pp. 146–147.

[3]*Ibid.*
[4]Salthe, p. 148.
[5]*Ibid.,* p. 150.

tendency in this lineage to increasing the length of the jaws was the major factor in eliminating the influence of mammalian tooth fields. Suppose that this lengthening of jaws was a genuine evolutionary change involving the replacement of many alleles by others in a number of genetic loci."[6] Thus, if we breed for the longer muzzle and level bite, are we then breeding an evolutionary change, i.e., forcing one? This could be true if we are not selective about breeding practices.

There are, if we examine numerous Lhasa bites, a variety of jaw shapes. Ruth Smith tells us that "Everyone raves about . . .'s bite because the teeth are even and it was level. However, the lower teeth were rounded and actually he has a 'collie' bite, not a true Lhasa bite where the teeth should go straight across, not in a curve."[7]

Lhasa breeders should therefore keep in mind the true shape of a Lhasa's bite when breeding. The longer muzzle and the Collie bite certainly would change the proper expression of a Lhasa's face.

In addition to the narrow mouth and the Collie-type jaw, a Lhasa may have a wry mouth, one for which the jaws do not align properly, may have very small teeth, or may exhibit a very slow eruption of teeth, all aspects which many breeders have experienced.

One breeder suggests that one of the reasons such problems have arisen was the crossing of various lines, e.g., Lhasas with shorter muzzles with Lhasas having longer muzzles. From such crosses came extreme underbites or overbites, mismatched jaw widths, and jumbled teeth. Consequently, dentition problems may have arisen because of indiscriminate breeding practices.

Retained Teeth

Not all Lhasa dental problems are inherited. As in other small breeds, retained primary (puppy) teeth present a problem, and that problem can be disastrous for a Lhasa which is otherwise of show quality.

A Lhasa puppy's mouth should be checked every two weeks from four through six months of age and those primary teeth which interfere with erupt-

ing permanent teeth should be carefully removed. These offending teeth should not be just "yanked out," as such action could cause the roots to break off, which will not eliminate the cause of the problem. To remove the teeth a curved tool, such as #46R by Norton Star, should be used to penetrate the area around the tooth, cutting any tendons, until the tooth (with root intact) can be lifted out. Removal of the primary teeth would allow the jaw to grow in its normal manner and the permanent teeth to erupt in their normal pattern.

Primary teeth which do not fall out on schedule can cause an undershot or awry jaw. Excessive pressure from the two sets of teeth can damage the jaws by preventing the eruption of permanent teeth in the proper places. Thus, a section of jaw could be pushed out of its normal alignment, either preventing the normal extension of the jaw or causing a distortion in the jawline—an awry mouth.

PUPPY TEETH

There is a simple ratio for proper dentition:

Primary:	Incisors	Canine	Premolar	Molar
upper	3	1	3	0
lower	3	1	3	0
Permanent:				
upper	3	1	4	2
lower	3	1	4	3

It is difficult to examine some active, wiggly puppies' mouths, but it is important that their mouths

Puppy with an underbite, which may correct as the pup grows. Only five puppy incisors are visible; there should be six. Note that the incisors are correctly placed in a straight line.

[6]Salthe, p. 145.
[7]Smith, ltr. 3–24–78.

be examined regularly. In training your puppy to open its mouth for a judge's examination, Bonnie Sellner suggests rubbing its lips with gravy, then opening gently to look. Use some similar method to examine your puppy's mouth.

The problems are easy to discover when incisors are involved, but more difficult with premolars. Consequently, it is a good idea to have your vet thoroughly check the puppy's mouth during teething. Prompt attention could prevent dental problems. Permanent incisors are usually in by four months of age. At four to five months the baby canines should have erupted. Permanent canines come in at approximately six months. Adult molars usually begin to come in at six to eight months.

Preventative Dentistry

As we do with people, we can also practice preventative dentistry with dogs. In addition to preventing dentition problems caused during the replacement of teeth, problems such as tooth decay can also be avoided with judicious care. Diet is important. A good dry dog food which gives the dog much chewing action can prevent the buildup of tartar on the teeth. Remember that soft foods and the sugar and/or fat content of some dry dog foods can cause tartar and decay. In addition to a good diet, brushing the dog's teeth can also prevent tartar and decay. If tartar does build up, it can be removed by a veterinarian.

Tooth Repair

It would be wise to have a diseased tooth taken care of promptly. Such a tooth does not have to be extracted. In fact, in some cases it would be better to repair a tooth rather than to extract it, as when the removal would cause a jaw distortion or allow other teeth to shift position. Such dental work as filling teeth and root canal surgery is being done. Just as a diseased tooth can cause pain in a human, so too can it in a dog. But the dog, like a small child, cannot tell us the problem. Thus, if a dog seems "off his food," unusually cross and out-of-sorts, or paws at his mouth, it would be wise to have your veterinarian give the dog a thorough checkover, including a dental examination.

CONCLUSION

In summary, many dentition problems can be eliminated by wise, careful breeding practices. Other dentition problems can be prevented by timely care and proper diet.

We must keep in mind that the environment changes gradually and continually and that natural selection works in connection with existing conditions. Since evolution is slowly taking place, the trend toward lesser dentition should not be underestimated. "Individuals do not evolve; alleles do not evolve; gene frequencies, and therefore, the phenotype characteristics of individuals in populations, and ultimately, species do evolve," according to Salthe. "Structures such as a tooth . . . pattern . . . are multigenetic traits, because they are the results of the interaction of a large number of different primary gene products acting in concert and sequentially."[8] It is important to remember that "gene mutation is the fundamental source of all biological variability."[9]

There are no definite conclusions to be drawn which would apply to all dental situations found in Lhasa Apsos. The wide variety of dental patterns result from head type; from breeding practices, that mix head types indiscriminantly; and from the evolution pattern, reducing unneeded teeth. Other dental problems evolve from the retention of primary teeth and from either tooth decay or tooth breakage.

Thus, the breeder must keep in mind the dental backgrounds of studs and bitches. Breeders and owners need to practice preventative dentistry where Lhasas are concerned. On the other hand, judges should keep in mind the evolutionary factor and should place dentition in its proper perspective. It should be remembered that it is the overall expression of the face which is most important, and dentition problems affecting correct expression should be penalized.

---

[8]Salthe, p. 183, 209.
[9]*Ibid.*, p. 210.

Show coat or leisure suit? Pictured with Dr. Janine Charboneau are Am. Can. Ch. Hell's A Blazen Billy the Kid in full coat and Ch. Rito's Maggie Mai of Ming Toy in a leisure cut.

50

6

TO LOVE AND TO CHERISH

Your Lhasa Apso should live a long, happy life if kept in good physical condition. Physical condition results from good health, feeding, and exercise practices. Even a good coat is reflective of physical condition.

Namgyl Tsering commented on the diets of the Tibetan Lhasas when asked about their teeth. "He said that his family and the monks who bred true did not [have trouble with teeth]. . . . He explained that Tibetans did have very good teeth. He put this down to a high protein diet coupled with herbs, minerals and the water. He said that this diet combined with the strenuous exercise made men and dogs strong and hard."[1]

LHASA NUTRITION

Nutrition plays an integral part in the overall condition of any Lhasa. Therefore, a well-balanced diet is important. The base of that diet should be a high-quality dry kibble, of which there are many kinds available. This dry kibble not only gives the Lhasa a good balanced diet, but it also helps with dentition as it aids in removing tartar from the teeth and in keeping them clean. This is important with a Lhasa.

You will have to experiment with the various dry foods to find the one best for your Lhasas. Some of the brands, those sprayed or soaked in fats, have both given my Lhasas diarrhea and yellowed their teeth. Others do not have sufficient protein, which seems to be important for good coats. One brand which all of my Lhasas can eat without adverse results is *Purina Hi-Protein.* This food has its advantages: high quality control maintains the uniformity of every bag; availability makes it easy to purchase wherever you are; small-size pieces seem

[1]Fred (Joan Beard), "Tibetan Meets Tibetan," *Northern California Lhasa Apso Club Bulletin,* 1974.

just right for Lhasas who do not like the large kibble. The Lhasas that eat this seem to have tighter, firmer stools than Lhasas fed some other products.

The amount of kibble which your Lhasa will eat will probably depend upon his size. A very small dog will eat from ½ to 1 cup, and an average-sized Lhasa will eat 1 to 1½ cups of good-quality kibble per day. I supplement the kibble for variety, using a tablespoon or two of good canned dog food, cottage cheese, or oriental-style vegetables. I also add 1 teaspoon of brewer's yeast daily to aid coat growth and prevent fleas. (Even though some tests say this is not effective, I find that feeding yeast in combination with dipping works better than dipping alone.) Scrambled eggs can be added to the kibble. We can buy eggs for dogs very inexpensively from the egg farm. Another variation would be about ½ teaspoon of powdered cottage cheese.

An inexpensive dietary treat is chopped chicken gizzards and hearts. Simmer them until tender, cool, and chop into small pieces. Feed about 2 tablespoons at a time. Lhasas like some liquid – warm water, gravy, or broth – with their kibble; therefore, use broth from the gizzards and hearts in place of water to moisten the kibble. A good ratio is 1 tablespoon per ¼ cup kibble. Sometimes as a variation, or if the Lhasas are off their food, give them cooked rice or barley in place of the kibble. Rice and barley are staples in Tibet, which is the world's largest producer of barley. My Lhasas really love Chinese food. When I go to Chinese restaurants, I always ask for a "doggie bag" for that which I cannot eat. When I prepare Chinese dishes at home, I always prepare some extra for them.

Feeding Schedule

Adult Lhasas should be fed once a day unless ill, pregnant, or caring for puppies; two or three meals might be more appropriate at these times. Do not overfeed your Lhasas. Excess weight can affect their legs as well as hearts and other organs, and could even shorten their lives. Usually the Lhasas' feeding time will fit into your schedule. Some people like to feed in the mornings, while some prefer evenings.

Lhasas may cut back on their consumption of food during warm weather, and they may increase their consumption slightly during very cold weather. Occasionally they will, like humans, just not be hungry at a given meal. Bitches, for instance, may eat less when in heat. Usually, a stud may eat less if there is a bitch in heat on the premises.

To prevent possible motion sickness, my Lhasas are not fed just before traveling, but do eat on arrival at our destination.

MAINTAINING WEIGHT

A Lhasa is in correct weight when there is enough flesh to cover the ribs, but not enough that you can pinch a half-inch of fat between thumb and forefinger in the rib area.

Whenever a Lhasa needs more weight, as a show dog may, add some rice or barley to his diet. Showing places a great deal of stress on a dog. One thing that I have found to attract them when nothing else will is Chinese food – vegetables with or without meat and rice.

I have not as yet found it necessary to force feed a Lhasa, nor have I seen others do it, albeit some may. I prefer to let nature take its course.

Do not allow your Lhasa to get overweight. This will definitely affect his movement. Simply control the amount which he eats.

LHASA COAT CONDITIONING

Good health and a good diet are reflected in a Lhasa's coat. The true sheen of good care cannot be sprayed from a can. Thus, a balanced diet is important. Of course, inheritance plays a part in the texture, thickness, length, and rate of growth of a Lhasa's coat.

There are other things which you can do to enhance the coat. Spraying the coat lightly with water before and while brushing will help. For a coat which tends to be dry, make up the following: one part *Clairol Hair-So-New* to eight parts of water, plus one capful *Alpha-Keri* oil. Spray lightly on coat while brushing.

Human products seem to work better on Lhasa coats than dog products. However, never use neutral henna, or any other henna of any type or in any product. A coat cared for with henna products will burn, break, and dry in the sun.

Some Lhasa coats will "burn" if the Lhasa gets too much sun. A black coat, for instance, will take on a rusty cast. The burning may cause the hair to split and to give a fuzzy appearance to the coat. Drying a Lhasa coat under too hot a heat will also burn it. Complete care of a Lhasa's coat is discussed in the chapter on grooming.

TEMPERATURES AND YOUR LHASA

You will have to determine what effect heat and cold have on your Lhasa. The double coat does act as an insulator against both heat and cold. However, high heat plus extreme humidity may take its toll.

If your Lhasa pants and drools on a hot, humid day, keep an eye on him and keep him in a cool, shady place. There are several things which you can do to protect him. For instance, do not take him outside during the middle of the day when temperatures are soaring, and never go away and leave your Lhasa outside while you are gone. Your Lhasa will be better off if kept inside in a cool spot with an adequate water supply. If you must take your Lhasa out keep him in the shade as much as possible. Never leave your Lhasa in a closed car on a warm summer day.

If you are at a show or are traveling, place a frozen ice container under the false floor of the air crate. I have found some about 10 inches by 10 inches by 1¼ inches which work very well. Freeze the containers before starting. They will still be effective when thawed but still cool. The cap can be opened and ice added if necessary. Also, a small pouch ice bag, such as used for a headache, with

Sabu gets a hug. Owner, Karen Elibol.

ice or cold water in it and held against the tummy of the Lhasa will help. The ice packets that come with vaccines may also serve either way. Be sure that water is available.

Gatorade is another help to prevent dehydration. It comes in packages to which water is added and thus can be stored easily and even carried in a tack box.

DO NOT shave your Lhasa down during the summer. Its double coat is nature's method of protecting him. Shaving can be a very traumatic experience for a Lhasa. (See chapter on grooming.)

Most Lhasas tolerate normal cold quite easily. They love to play in the snow, romping and rolling in it, filling their coats with small ice balls. Often they will be reluctant to return inside. Remember that the ice balls can be damaging to their coats and that a wet coat must be dried. If your Lhasa is being shown, a romp in the snow is not recommended because of the potential coat damage. A Lhasa with an injury probably should not be outside for long in extreme cold, nor should an old Lhasa, nor one with arthritis.

A good maintenance temperature for their living area in the winter would be 50–65° F. Therefore, my home is kept quite cool, helpful with oil bills. In addition, should you have forced-air heat, consider using a humidifier to maintain adequate humidity in the air in order to prevent coat damage.

EXERCISE

Lhasas in exercise pens with wire bottoms get better conditioning than is expected due to the isometric effects. One of the best-conditioned Lhasas I know of spent much time in his exercise pen during the day. However, when he went to a new home where he became a house dog and had the freedom of the yard to run and to exercise, his tight muscling relaxed.

A romping area for your Lhasa is good. A 35-foot by 35-foot area will provide room for running, playing, and investigating. The area should be fenced and will have to be kept free from coat-damaging materials.

Road work can also be done. This should be restricted to trotting or a fast walk. Choose a level area with a smooth dirt or sand surface if possible. You usually can road work a Lhasa on foot if you are physically fit. Start at about one-half mile a day and gradually increase to a mile (or more). Do not exercise a lame, an injured, or a tired Lhasa. If your Lhasa pants excessively, take the exercise in smaller segments and gradually lengthen the distance. Continuous daily road work for three to four weeks will tone up the Lhasa; thereafter, once or twice a week will maintain that conditioning. During the summer exercise during the early morning or late evening to avoid extreme heat. However, if you are showing your Lhasa during the summer, brief exercise excursions in the heat, carefully supervised, might better condition your Lhasa for hot summer rings.

Walking a pregnant bitch will help tone up her muscles for whelping. The distance should be reasonable. Start with an eighth, then a quarter, and then one-half mile once or twice daily during the morning or evening.

GERIATRICS

Our Lhasas give us so much that we owe it to them to keep them comfortable in their old age. Avoid expressing resentment or impatience with them. My experience has been that when their time comes to die, they seem to know. If you are truly close to your beloved pets, you will also sense this. Somehow it makes the acceptance of their demise a bit easier, if that is possible.

The first thing to do is to keep your dog as healthy as possible. The Lhasa which has been healthy during his young years may begin to show some signs of age by the time he is five to seven years old. The signs of which you should be aware are: an obvious decrease in energy and a lack of interest in his surroundings, a tendency toward "fussy" eating, a development of sensitivity to temperatures, a lack of attentiveness, a change in awake/nap habits, urinary incontinence, changes in eyes, loss of hearing, gum problems, obesity, labored breathing, cysts or tumors, expressions of pain, decreased amounts of urine, jaundice, staggering, weakness, uncoordination. Periodic checks by your veterinarian, at about six-month intervals, will help prevent problems, as will your awareness and giving prompt care when symptoms become apparent.

A good diet is essential for the maintenance of your older dog. Overfeeding is a common problem, and today's dog has no need to store fats. Your older Lhasa will need fewer calories to give him energy. Therefore, it is necessary to keep your older Lhasa on a well-balanced diet which includes a good kibble to aid in preventing dental problems.

Kibble and a chew toy, perhaps a rawhide bone, encourage chewing which aids in removing the food particles which catch between teeth. There are brushes and tooth paste on the market for cleaning teeth. A soft brush to avoid damage to the gums is important. For an older dog you may need to resort to baking soda and your finger. Keeping the teeth and gums healthy is important because peridontal disease can lead to kidney disease.[2]

Adapting diets to changing physical conditions will be important. A Lhasa that loses his teeth can no longer chew dry kibble. A dog with a physical condition affecting kidneys or other glands may need a special diet prescribed by your veterinarian. For kidney diseases, "eggs, lean meats, cottage cheese, and chicken are good sources of high biological value protein. Good carbohydrates and fats include spaghetti and noodles, rice, cake, cream cheese, ice cream, vegetable oil, and bread. Your veterinarian will help you select the right amounts of each food to be included in the diet every day; these should not be changed except at his instruction."[3]

In cases of diabetes mellitus high-protein, low-carbohydrate dog foods may be required. Your veterinarian will prescribe the proper diet. There are special canned foods for special dietary requirements which can be purchased. However, your Lhasa may not like them, a fact which will necessitate your preparing the special diet.

Reproductive problems may occur in your older Lhasa. The dogs' testicles will normally shrink and be less firm. The three problems which may occur are: inflammation and swelling of the testicles, growths on one or both testicles, and enlarged prostate. Needless to say, all require veterinarian care. The most common problem in older bitches is pyrometra, discussed in chapter 18. Cysts and tumors may occur near ovaries or on breasts. Mammary tumors are commonly found in unspayed older females. Aging bitches are targets for pyrometra and other disorders affecting the reproductive

[2]Jan L. Seager, "The Geriatric Dog," *Pure-Bred Dogs American Kennel Gazette* (97, 5), May, 1980, pp. 22–30.

[3]*Ibid.*, (97, 6), June, 1980, p. 48.

system. These problems do require a veterinarian's care. Check with your vet about spaying any bitch over eight years old. Preventative practices may prolong their sojourns with you.

Cancer does occur in dogs; about "one in four will develop some form of cancer in his lifetime."[4] Internal cancers, which you cannot detect yourself, have been successfully treated in many older dogs. Any unusual growths should, of course, be reported to your veterinarian immediately. Diagnosis and prompt care are important. Lhasas with cancer do survive surgery, and with it can live comfortably for some time.

Although heart attacks are uncommon, an older Lhasa may develop some type of heart abnormality by the age of ten.[5] Early detection and treatment can prolong the Lhasa's life and make it possible for him to live in relative comfort for many years. A wise regimen of diet, medication, and exercise are important aspects in the treatment of heart ailments.

Accept the physical disabilities of your Lhasa with grace and learn to cope with them. A Lhasa which loses its sight will learn where furniture and doorways are. A deaf Lhasa too will cope. Of course, neither can meander freely in an unrestricted area. Those with arthritis can be kept comfortable, but long walks and stairs may have to be avoided.

There are various exercises which you can encourage your aging Lhasa to do to help keep him fit. To keep the abdominal muscles and hindquarters firm, use sitting exercises. This exercise can be varied to suit your needs. Command the dog to sit each time you fill the washer or open or close a door. Combine sitting and heeling by having your dog walk at your side. As you walk with your Lhasa, periodically command him to sit. Push-ups can be accomplished within one room. "Walk around the perimeter of a nine foot by twelve foot rug stopping at each piece of furniture in the room: the dog will have walked forty-two feet and done several pushups." The fourth exercise is retrieving. Use a 10-foot throw, but limit retrieves to three.[6]

Adjust some things to help your dogs, especially the aging: ramps for easy access in and out, a comfortable place to sleep (mine like to pillow their heads), proper diets, a place to curl up and sleep in

[4]*Ibid.*, p. 47.   [5]*Ibid.*, p. 45.   [6]*Ibid.*, p. 52.

Ch. Ginseng Yoshi Su relaxes on a picnic bench. Owner, Joan Paul.

the yard. Cater to their idiosyncracies: use their favorite bowls, allow them to sleep in a favorite place, even trim their long coats into a leisure suit. Never shave an older Lhasa down. I have seen even young Lhasas hide when shaved. Lhasas seem to have a sense of vanity and love to look "pretty." Clip hair above eyes into bangs. Trim down pantaloons and cut side coat and chest coat shorter.

Like many old folks, our older Lhasas prefer routines which are followed relatively strictly. If you are to be away and are unable to take the Lhasa with you or he is unable to go, it would be better to have a dog sitter, preferably someone the Lhasa knows, than to put him in a boarding situation. He likes to be with you and often would prefer to travel with you rather than to stay home.

The Lhasa who will wish to travel with you most will probably be your retired show dog. Being groomed, traveling, and performing were important parts of his life. Retirement removes this need. It is vital that the older dog still have a sense of importance. If the dog is physically capable, obedience may be one answer. Showing the Lhasa in occasional Veterans' classes will help his esteem. The twelve-and-one-half-year-old Ch. Chen Krisna Nor ROM took the Breed and a Group III from Veterans Dog class, and Ch. Everglo Flair took Best of Opposite Sex from the Veterans Bitch class at age thirteen.

Create activities of interest which your Lhasas will enjoy and in which they can participate. These activities may include a ride to the store, a walk in the park or garden, some extra special grooming, a special rug, and your attention and time.

Give your older Lhasas loving attention, use common sense with them, keep them in relative good health, have regular physicals, and enjoy each day with them. They have earned these good years.

Euthanasia

Euthanasia is an easy, painless death. It is practiced when animals have incurable, distressing, painful diseases or handicaps, and is often called mercy killing.

There are, of course, two sides to every problem. It is to be abhorred that people use euthanasia as a means of disposing of an unwanted animal which has long given them love and loyalty, but which can no longer be a productive stud or bitch, or which has an ailment or handicap which is an annoyance to his owner. Such situations are a reflection on society. Dogs are not stock in the sense of other domesticated animals such as cows and hogs. They are and always have been man's companion.

When we are faced with the reality that our beloved pets have a serious problem, we have difficult decisions to make. Ralph Reid perhaps states the situation best: "No creature wants to [not] go on living, hopeless though it may be. Some day you will know, from personal experience, how true this is. You, too, will be old and useless, perhaps helpless, and you will need love and care, not a euthanizing needle."[7] Our dogs have given so much

[7]Ralph B. Reid, "The Handicapped Canine," *Dog World*, February 1978, p. 140.

Mei Tzu Man-Di. Owner, Carol Stauffer.

to us. Now they need us as loving and caring persons. We must respond to that and provide for their needs.

When the time comes when there is no hope—when the physical suffering is so great, when there is no end to pain—we must make the heartrending decision to mercifully end a life. Be prepared for an extremely bereft feeling, an emptiness, but time eventually assuages those loss feelings.

Burial

The disposition of a beloved pet's body will be determined by circumstances, by personal preference, and by area codes. Your veterinarian will take care of disposal for you if you prefer. There are pet cemeteries in many areas where you can have your pet buried. Pet cemeteries do require the purchase of a lot and payment for upkeep. They also have requirements as to caskets. Zoning codes will dictate whether or not you can bury your pet on your own property. You may wish to do this. The final choice is yours.

REPLACEMENT

Michael McDowell says "then find another lively, healthy puppy; for a dog is the only living creature that can bring out the best qualities of his master and forget the others."[8]

The time element in replacing a beloved dog can be very important. My personal feeling is that the replacement should be made within a reasonable length of time, a week to a month later, unless your Lhasa died of a contagious disease and your veterinarian advises otherwise. A new healthy puppy can certainly temper the grief that you feel, but will not lessen the love for the lost Lhasa, which will always have a special place in your heart. The timing for purchasing a new puppy would only be dictated by the circumstances surrounding the death of your older dog and by the availability of a puppy in your choice of breed. My preference is to purchase the puppy some time before you lose the older dog.

When you are searching for a new Lhasa, do not seek to replace your Lhasa with a replica of the one which you lost. Do not attempt to replace your Lhasa only with one the color, markings, or sex of the previous Lhasa. The important aspect is only that it is a healthy puppy.

Each Lhasa Apso will have his own personality; thus each will make his own spot in your life.

---

[8]Michael R. McDowell, "From Puppyhood to Old Age," *Dog World,* November, 1979, p. 87.

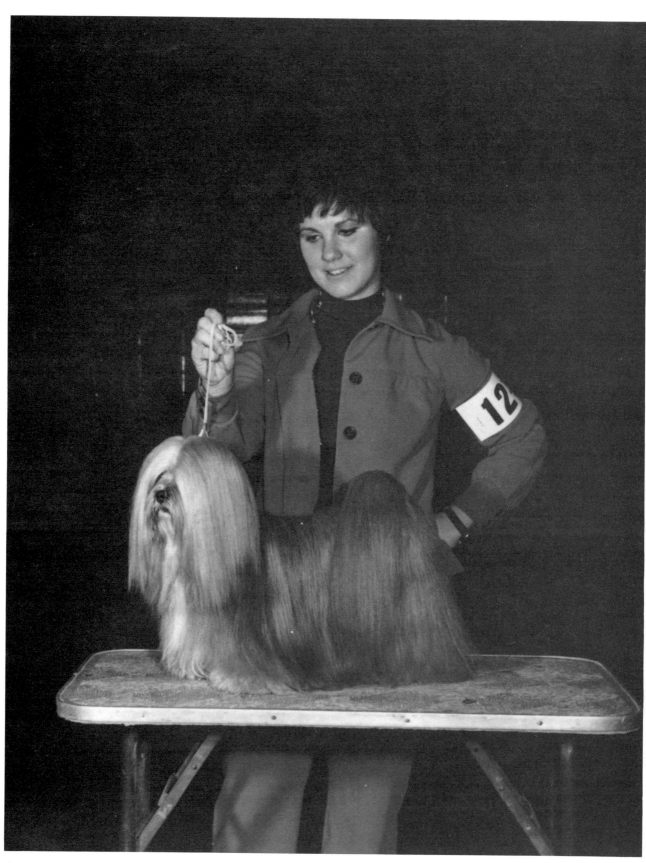

Am. Can. Ch. Rondelay Red Lucy of Llenroc, foundation bitch for Llenroc. Owner, Noel Benson. Photo by Olson.

58

IN SICKNESS AND IN HEALTH

Most Lhasa Apsos are healthy canines. Their coats have a lovely natural sheen and bounce, their eyes are clear, they are alert to noises, and they move like a sailing ship on a smooth sea with a gentle breeze. Your mental awareness of your Lhasa can aid you in an instinctive daily health check. As you comb the headfall, eyes and nose can easily be checked: no inflammation and no draining from the eyes and a cool, slightly damp nose are good signs. The rear "skirts" also can be checked to be sure they are clear of fecal matter. Since most Lhasas are "kissers," you can easily be aware of their breaths. During grooming sessions, ears should be checked for signs of problems such as excessive brown or black matter or red marks.

If there appear to be indications of illness, take the Lhasa's temperature. Use an infant's rectal thermometer which has been sterilized with alcohol or peroxide. Shake the thermometer down until it registers just below 96° F. Coat the bulb end with vaseline or KY jelly and insert into anal opening. It will take from three to five minutes for a proper registration of the dog's temperature on a manual thermometer. Normal temperature is between 100 and 102° F. If the Lhasa is running a temperature, check other vital signs before calling your veterinarian.

There are many health problems which can affect your Lhasa Apso, from flu to cancer. The most common shall be touched upon. Parasites, often sources of health problems, must be controlled.

These subjects are written about in light of presently available research and facts. However, even as this is written, new research is under way and new findings are being made. Each of us must keep abreast of newly published information.

Learn to recognize your dog's normal behavior and appearance, then you can more easily spot signs of illness. If you watch your Lhasa carefully, you will know when he is not feeling well or is not behaving normally. Then you can begin to look for more specific symptoms.

A sick dog may first appear listless or tired, or he may only whine. He may show more serious signs such as vomiting, diarrhea, coughing, or limping. The first thing you should do is just observe. Check his eyes and nose for discharge. Check the gums to see if the color is normal. Take his temperature. Try to determine if he is constipated, has diarrhea, or whether he is urinating more or less frequently than usual. Watch for signs of soreness or lameness. Check his quarters for signs of poisonous or harmful substances which he could have swallowed.

If you can rule out the possibility of poisoning and the condition doesn't seem serious, keep your Lhasa quiet and just observe him for twelve to twenty-four hours. If he has not improved by the following day, take him to your veterinarian.

However, if high temperature, labored breathing, continuous vomiting, convulsions, or other acute symptoms appear, or if the dog loses interest in what is going on and tries to hide, do not hesitate—take him to the veterinary hospital immediately.

FIRST AID

Every dog owner, like every mother, soon learns how to administer first aid and basic medical care.

Set up a supply area near your Lhasa's quarters and stock it with the basic items listed below. Then, learn the basic first aid procedures that follow.

Taking Pulse

A dog's pulse can easily be determined by feeling for the throbbing of the femoral artery. This artery can be located by placing your index finger inside the hind leg as far up against the body as possible. In a healthy animal the pulsing artery is easy to locate. Another method of checking the pulse is to place your fingers over the heart itself.

Count the number of beats per minute. The average is 90 to 100 beats per minute. They should be rhythmical and steady, although slight arythmia is not uncommon.

Muzzling

A dog in pain may bite at anyone who tries to handle him. To prevent this, tie the mouth of the frightened Lhasa shut with an old nylon stocking or a strip of soft cloth. Make two wraps around the muzzle and tie under the chin in a hard knot. Then bring the ends of the cloth behind the ears and tie in a bow.

The Medicine Chest

Your medicine chest should include these items:
- A rectal thermometer. Same as for humans and obtainable at any drugstore or pet supply store.
- A good antiseptic liquid soap
- Q-TIPS cotton swabs
- Peroxide
- Cotton balls
- Gauze pads and bandage wrap
- Alcohol
- Antiseptic spray for minor wounds
- Clean towels
- A blunt-nosed scissors for cutting hair around wounds, cutting bandages, etc.
- Styptic powder or silver nitrate to control bleeding of minor cuts and bites. (Note: Silver nitrate is poisonous if swallowed and will stain anything it touches black.)

- An old nylon stocking to use as a muzzle
- KAOPECTATE for diarrhea
- MILK OF MAGNESIA tablets for a laxative
- ARTIFICIAL TEARS for washing out eyes. You may also want to keep a product like GARAMYCIN (available from your veterinarian) for mild eye inflammations
- A general purpose dip for fleas, ticks, mange, eczema, etc.
- PANALOG or TOPTIC ointment for skin inflammation, mild skin infections, cuts, and scratches
- A medication for ear mites if you live in an area where they are a problem
- Something for motion sickness. DRAMAMINE for humans is fine, ¼ tablet
- A product such as BITTER APPLE to prevent chewing
- Activated charcoal as universal antidote for poison

Artificial Respiration

An unconscious dog that is not breathing but has a heartbeat may need only artificial respiration to revive him. Place the dog on his right side with head and neck extended so the windpipe is in a straight line. Pull the tongue forward and out. With the heels of your hands, press the chest moderately hard just behind the dog's shoulder blade, forcing air out of the lungs. Relax the pressure, count to five, and repeat. It is important that the rhythm be smooth and regular.

Continue until the dog is breathing smoothly on his own. Then treat for shock.

A dog's normal respiration rate is 15 to 20 times per minute.

Giving Medication

Administer pills by grasping the Lhasa's muzzle with your palm over his top jaw. Tilt his head back. Squeeze the lips against the teeth at the back of his mouth, forcing the mouth open. With your other hand, place the pill as far back on the Lhasa's tongue as you can reach. Remove your hand and quickly close the dog's mouth. Hold his jaws shut while you stroke his throat until he swallows. Greasing the pill with butter will help it to go down easier.

To give liquid medication, place your Lhasa in a sitting position. Pull the corner of the lower lip outward and upward, forming a small pocket. Pour the liquid into this pocket, a little at a time. Raise the dog's head slightly as you pour, causing the medication to run down into his mouth and throat. Again, hold his jaw closed until he swallows.

An alternative method of giving liquid medicine is to inject it into the back of the mouth with a hypodermic syringe which has had the needle removed.

It is important to give only the exact amount specified by your prescription at the time interval specified. Liquid medication may be drawn into a plastic syringe for easier measurement. You can convert to the cc's marked on the syringe as follows:

16 drops	= 1 cc or ¼ teaspoon
5 cc	= 1 teaspoon
15 cc	= 1 tablespoon
½ oz.	= 1 tablespoon or 15 cc
1 oz.	= 2 tablespoons or 30 cc
8 oz.	= 1 cup
1 liter	= 1 qt or 4 cups

Treating for Shock

Shock is an overresponse of the dog's system to trauma, injury, or stress. A dog in shock has pale mucous membranes and a weak, but rapid, pulse. He may shiver and feel cold to the touch. Breathing is slow and the eyes are glazed. Keep him warm by wrapping him in towels or blankets. Get him to a veterinarian immediately.

It is generally best to withhold liquids, although a tablespoon of whiskey may help revive a dazed dog.

Hold the Lhasa's mouth open with one hand while you insert the pill as far down his throat as possible.

Hold the mouth closed and stroke the dog's throat to induce him to swallow.

Transporting an Injured Lhasa

If no bones appear to be broken, carry the injured dog under one arm with your forearm supporting his weight and your hand under his chest. Use the other hand to steady his head.

If your Lhasa is badly injured or appears to have broken bones, back or neck injuries, place him gently on a stretcher made from a sheet, towel, or board. The bottom board from a crate also works very well. Lacking any of these, place two sticks through the sleeves of a jacket or shirt to form a stretcher. Try to disturb the dog's position as little as possible.

External Heart Massage

If your dog's heart has stopped, combine artificial respiration with external cardiac massage.

With the dog on his back, legs in the air, put the palms of your hands on the sternum, with your fingers on one side of the chest and your thumb on the other. Alternately compress and release the chest. Compress the chest strongly between your thumb and fingers, pressing the ribs together and at the same time pressing the sternum down toward the spine. (Do not press hard enough to fracture the ribs of a puppy.) Release the pressure suddenly. Repeat at the rate of 70 times per minute for up to three minutes.

COMMON PROBLEMS

Car Sickness

Puppies are easily prone to motion sickness. Most of them will outgrow it by one year of age.

Help puppies enjoy traveling by taking them on very short rides to a place where they can have fun. Take them to the park or the country for a romp, then back home for feeding. Some breeders train their show puppies to eat in a crate in the car at home so that traveling to shows will not throw them off feed so easily.

You can help prevent motion sickness by withholding food and water for four hours before a trip. Give only small amounts of water while traveling. Wait until you reach your destination before feed-

ing. Motion sickness pills like *Bonine* or *Dramamine* given at the rate of 0.5 mg per pound (¼ to ½ tablet for a Lhasa) are helpful. Do not use tranquilizers unless prescribed by a veterinarian, and do not use them at all when traveling to a show or class. Plan to arrive at least an hour prior to a show so your dog has time to recuperate.

Constipation, Diarrhea, and Vomiting

Diarrhea, constipation, and vomiting can be either temporary problems or a symptom of something more serious. For instance, a change in diet could be the cause of any of the three. Also, especially during the spring and early summer, Lhasas delight in eating fresh, tender pieces of grass which will often cause them to vomit. Then, too, when you travel, the different water may affect your Lhasa; to prevent that, carry drinking water for the Lhasas with you.

Should the problem result from motion sickness, your veterinarian will prescribe an appropriate medication.

Note the color of any excreted matter. Should it contain blood or be of an unusual color, contact your veterinarian immediately for advice. You should be able to cope with a mild upset and not have to make an unnecessary trip to the clinic.

For each of the problems, substitute one-half or all of the kibble in the diet with rice or barley. Barley water may also be substituted for drinking water. *Kaopectate* may help the diarrhea. A drop of vegetable oil or vitamin E oil will help the constipated Lhasa.

Constipation can result from fecal impaction due to overly long confinement, such as while traveling, from improper diet, tumors, internal parasites, abscessed anal sacs, or old age, among other causes. A tablespoon of *Milk of Magnesia* may relieve the condition. If not, try a human rectal suppository.

Diarrhea can indicate a disease or infection, but often it results simply from overeating, eating spoiled food, change of diet, too much excitement, parasites, or other upsets of the digestive tract. It is common in puppies. If no other symptoms are present and no blood is in the stool, a few doses of *Kaopectate* may clear up the problem. Give two or three tablespoons every four hours for an adult Lhasa.

If you raise puppies, ask your vet for a stronger medication which you can keep on hand for emergencies. Be careful of diarrhea medication sold through vet supply houses. Some are very strong and if used improperly can cause a blockage or intestinal torsion.

If your Lhasa has acute diarrhea, discontinue food for 12 to 24 hours, then put the dog back on food slowly with a diet high in rice, cottage cheese, or cooked eggs, and low in kibble. Avoid milk in the diet.

Unchecked diarrhea will result in dehydration. Puppies can dehydrate in a surprisingly short time unless fluids are administered subcutaneously. Always contact your vet if diarrhea persists, if blood is present, if the diarrhea has an extremely foul odor, or if the problem is abnormally acute.

Eye Irritations and Inflammations

Dust, pollen, or foreign objects often cause a Lhasa's eyes to tear. Wash the eye area with a cotton ball dipped in warm water or a mild salt-water solution (1 teaspoon salt in 1 cup of water).

Recurring surface irritation may be soothed by using artificial tears sold for contact lens wearers. If red or irritated eyes do not clear up within a few days, take your Lhasa to the veterinarian.

Irritation of the eye can result in conjunctivitis, an inflammation of the thin, transparent mucous membrane lining the inner surface of the eyelids and the front of the eye. The eyes will water and the membranes in the corner of the eye will become inflamed. Conjunctivitis may be caused by dust, or from a viral or bacterial infection. A culture is required. Treatment varies depending upon the cause. Infective forms can be contagious. Continued irritation of the eye which is not treated can result in scarring of the cornea, corneal opacity, or other problems.

Do not leave persistent eye inflammation untreated. Conversely, do not try to treat eye problems yourself, or use eye medication given for one problem to treat a later problem. Eye medication is very specific. Using the wrong medication can cause severe problems.

Celebrating the holidays.

Tonsillitis; Chronic Coughing

Dogs have tonsils, too. Open your Lhasa's mouth wide and you may be able to see them. If the tonsils are red and swollen, or if your Lhasa seems to have trouble swallowing, refuses to eat, gags, or vomits while eating, and if he has a slight temperature, the problem is often tonsillitis. Show dogs exposed to rapidly changing weather conditions are especially susceptible.

Antibiotics are usually effective against the infection. Some dogs have recurrent problems and should have their tonsils surgically removed.

However, a chronic-type cough may be experienced. The causes for the cough may be head type, hair balls, or allergies. A simple cure may be the daily addition of one-eighth teaspoon ascorbic acid to the Lhasa's food.

Anal Glands

A Lhasa's anal glands can become clogged or even impacted. These glands are found on either side of the anus. Their purpose is to supply a lubricant which aids the dog in expelling feces.

The usual symptom is the dog's scootching along the floor as he attempts to relieve the intense discomfort these glands may cause. However, some dogs do not react in this way, and the only sign may be a howl or scream of agony when their tails or buttocks are touched. There may or may not be an odor exuding.

If the glands are clogged, the dog may need help in expelling them. To do this (and it is best to do it in the tub if possible), hold a wad of cotton or a tissue loosely covering the anal opening with your left hand, and using your right hand with the thumb on one side and the forefinger on the other, feel the nodules, which are the glands. Exert pressure and pull toward you slightly as you do so. The secretion will usually shoot out suddenly as a boil will when squeezed and should be brownish in color. If there is either blood or pus present, infection is indicated and a trip to the veterinarian for antibiotic treatment will be necessary.

Occasionally you will not be able to express the anal glands because they are impacted. This, too, means a trip to the veterinarian for removal of the secretion, which will be quite solid. After treating impacted or infected anal glands, the veterinarian then will usually insert some type of antibiotic jell into the glands, where it remains for about three weeks.

Repeated attacks of this nature may necessitate the removal of these glands.

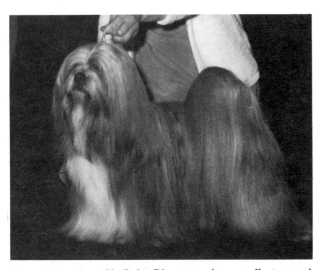

"Ringo," Am. Can. Ch. Dolsa Ringmaster is an excellent example of the breeding program at Dolsa. Breeder, Jean Kausch.

Am. Can. Ch. Tob Ci of Shukti Lingka, foundation bitch for Harriet and Kenneth Silverman.

Tumors

All breeds of dogs are subject to developing tumors, but Lhasas seem much less subject to them than many other breeds. Tumors are more common as the dog ages.

All tumors, benign or malignant, must be diagnosed and treated by your veterinarian, and biopsies must be sent to laboratories for accurate diagnosis. Surgery, chemical therapy, X-ray therapy, and immunotherapy are the normal methods of treatment. Early detection is the first step in any treatment. Thus, since our Lhasas are long-coated dogs, our fingers must routinely examine them as we fondle, play, or groom them. Any significant abnormality including ulcerations, swellings, lameness, prolonged illness, bad odors, bleeding, discharge, unhealed sores, pigment change, fatigue, weight loss, and difficulty in eating and drinking should be brought to the attention of your veterinarian.

There are many types of cancerous and benign tumors which include oral, nasal, mammary, skin, bone, and lymphosarcoma. Some types are much more prevalent in certain breeds other than Lhasa Apsos.

Mammary gland tumors are mentioned in Chapter 6. This type is the most common type for bitches and is usually found in bitches over six, and in Lhasas, usually eight years of age. Many breeders have their brood bitches spayed at age eight in order to prevent this type of tumor. These tumors are usually found in the glands lying between the rear legs, and most often there is more than one. The percentage of these tumors that are benign is more than 50 percent, but biopsies must be made to determine this. Any abnormal glandular breast lumps should be given immediate attention.

Skin tumors are usually benign; moreover, Lhasas are not one of the breeds which experiences a notable incidence of these types of tumors, which include: glandular benign tumors on the head, especially the muzzle and eyelids; histiocytoma, a benign tumor afflicting young dogs and common on the head, neck, and legs; cysts and dermal tumors from glands and hair follicles; squamous cell carcinomas found on heads and bellies of sun-loving dogs; perianal adenoma, a benign anal tumor; the rare perianal adenocarcinoma, malignant; papillomas or true warts; and TVT, transmissable venereal tumor. Remember that these types are not prevalent in Lhasas.

Oral tumors can be determined by repeatedly checking the inside of the dog's mouth. Early discovery is important, as this type of tumor often grows to the point of making surgery difficult. The Lhasa owner should be aware of gagging, coughing, excessive swallowing, and eating problems.

Nasal cavity tumors affect the nose, windpipe, and lungs; they are relatively unknown among dogs, but, if found, they are usually cancerous. Symptoms include a thick, white, bloody mucous from the nostrils, sneezing, and breathing difficulties.

Bone tumors are most often malignant, but are also usually found in large breeds of dogs and not Lhasas. The tumors are most often found on the long bones of the legs. Persistent lameness and abnormal swelling could be signs of this type.

Lymphosarcoma is a malignant cancer which affects the lymphocite, a white cell, and affects the lymph glands in all areas of the body. The most specific symptom, enlarged lymph nodes, may be accompanied by depression, loss of appetite, weight loss, vomiting, diarrhea, increased thirst, increased urine volume, coughing, and labored breathing.

Warts – Warts, I am told, are caused by a virus which spreads from one animal to another. Occasionally a Lhasa will get warts, which can cause grooming problems. Consequently, the warts must be removed by the veterinarian with an electric needle. Do not try to remove warts yourself. Some warts are slow growing, while others seem to grow with astounding rapidity. These latter need to be removed very promptly. The smaller the wart is, the easier it is to remove.

Recently, an item about garlic and warts caught my eye. It seems a veterinarian in Texas discovered that giving cattle afflicted with warts a daily ration of garlic cured the warts when nothing else would.[1] It might be worthwhile to try giving an afflicted Lhasa garlic on a regular basis to see if it would help, especially since warts seem to reoccur in a different spot on Lhasas even after the originals are removed.

---

[1]"Garlic, an ancient and valuable food," *Today's Living* (13, 2), Feb. 1982, New York, p. 28.

Corona Virus – This virus is a hemorrhagic gastroentritic and can be, as it was in 1978, very virulent. The incubation period for the disease can be as short as three days and as long as two weeks. Symptoms include a loss of appetite and lethargy, followed by a sudden onset of diarrhea and vomiting, both of which exude a very foul odor. The stools may be orangish in color and may develop a bloody aspect.

Warmth, a lack of stress, and *very prompt* veterinarian care are essential for recovery. The convalescent period will be quiet and extensive as relapses, causing death, have occurred from one to two weeks after the dogs seem to have recovered.

There is no preventative for corona as yet, and there is no one cure. Good sanitary measures such as cleaning with 1:30 *Clorox* water and isolating Lhasas upon return from shows, matches, and clinics may help.

Distemper – This is a common virus-caused disease which affects young dogs, especially those unvaccinated. This virulent disease has been known throughout the ages, and it was only in 1904 that Louís Carré determined the virus which caused it. The disease is usually airborne, but may be transmitted from dog to dog or by contaminated environment.

The general symptoms include a loss of appetite, chills, fever, reddened eyes, and a dry muzzle. Specific symptoms indicate the area of infection. A mucous discharge, cough, and heavy breathing indicate infection in the lungs; frothy, bloody diarrhea designates infection in the intestines; convulsions denote infection of the nervous system, which could cause death or muscular twitching, chorea. The virus multiplies in lymphatic tissues.

Vaccination is the major preventative and is essential. A distemper-measles vaccine can be given young puppies from two weeks of age, and it must be followed by a regular distemper vaccine covering distemper, parainfluenza, and leptospira; it may be given either subcutaneously or intramuscularly, and it must be repeated in four weeks. Two doses are suggested to give the greatest immunity. Thereafter, annual boosters are required.

Infectious Canine Hepatitis (ICH) – This is a very contagious viral disease which affects the liver, the kidneys, and the linings of the blood vessels. At the onset of the disease the afflicted dogs shed the virus in stools, in saliva, and in urine. Moreover, these same dogs may continue to shed the virus in their urine during their convalescence and for many months after recovery.

The dog's symptoms may be as mild as reddened eyes and a temperature, or the dog may develop diarrhea, become very ill, and die suddenly. When the infection is severe, the Lhasa will refuse to eat and may become comatose. After a period of six to ten days, the dog either recovers quickly or dies.

The virus which causes ICH is CAV-1, or Canine Adenovirus type 1. *Vaccination is used to prevent the disease, and annual boosters are necessary.*

Leptospirosis – This is an infectious bacterial disease, with numerous strains worldwide, caused by leptospira, a bacteria located by microscopic examination. Three varieties affect dogs in the United States: L. icterohemmorrhagiae, which causes jaundice and eye disturbances in dogs, but which is found only occasionally in dogs; L. pomona, which has been found in dogs which have associated with other infected animals and which is rare; L. canicola, which is the strain primarily found in dogs, which is spread by infected urine, and which causes nephritis in dogs.

Susceptible animals must make actual contact with leptospira, which is a very aggressive bacteria. The disease attacks suddenly with symptoms such as lack of appetite, vomiting, high temperatures, and an accumulation of mucous and/or blood in the eyeball. The dogs experience severe abdominal pain and are therefore hesitant about moving. During this very ill period the dogs will pass little or no feces and will have a deep-colored urine. The recovery prognosis is very good, usually about 90 percent. Fatalities occur within five to ten days after the symptoms appear. As in the other viruses and bacterial diseases, the young dogs have a lower resistance to the disease.

Leptospirosis may also be a chronic illness, which is more common and which causes progressive damage to the kidneys. These infections, whether acute or chronic, do respond very well to antibiotic therapy. *Vaccination is required for prevention.* For dogs that are being shown in areas where the disease is common, boosters every six months may be advisable.

Parvo Virus – In 1978 the first canine parvoviral infections were recognized. It is now known that many dogs over six months old have experienced mild infections which required no special care. It has also become apparent that there are two known forms: enteritis in dogs of any age and myocardis in young puppies.

The onset of a virulent enteritis is usually sudden and violent. The symptoms are similar to those of other viruses: decrease in appetite, depression, vomiting, diarrhea, fever. The diarrhea is usually a light tan or a greyish color, is quite watery, and exudes a foul odor. Vomit may be of the same color, and both may exhibit blood, which has been found in about 50 percent of the cases. The Lhasa's temperature may range from 104 to 107° F; thus dehydration may be a problem. To determine parvo, a blood analysis, revealing leukopenia or lowered white-cell count, must be accomplished.

Puppies less than twelve weeks old may be infected with the uncommon form, acute parvoviral myocardis. This form of the disease attacks and progresses rapidly. Sometimes the finding of a dead pup may be the first warning that a litter has been exposed. Puppies may die shortly after starting to breathe laboriously, to cry, and to retch. It occurs without enteritis in puppies three to seven weeks old and may kill more than half of the litter. Autopsies of the dead puppies will reveal damage to the tissue in the heart.

Treatment includes medication to control vomiting and diarrhea and intensive fluid intake to ward off dehydration. In addition, antibiotics will be given to ward off bacterial infections. *Vaccines have been developed for prevention of parvo;* thus vaccination would be a primary step.

An important source of the virus is the feces of infected dogs, from which there is extensive viral shed. It has been found that the virus does not exist after three weeks in the feces of the infected dog; thus, a Lhasa would not be infectious after three weeks from the onset of the disease. However, from feces eliminated during the contagious cycles, infectious virus has been recovered as much as six months later when the feces were kept at room temperature.

Consequently, the environment plays an important part. Clean up and disposal in outside areas could be vital. Grounds can be treated with *Clorox* and water (1:30). Cleaning and disinfecting the Lhasa's living areas, linoleum, and tile floors with a water-soap combination which includes *Clorox* 1:30 will also aid in prevention. Also, I firmly believe in the use of raised exercise pens as a preventative with Lhasas.

Tracheobronchitis – This disease often affects dogs in kennels and strikes dogs more often in hot and humid weather, but it is not adverse to cold and to damp weather. There are several types of canine respiratory diseases, but one which presents special problems is Infectious Canine Tracheobronchitis (ICT). The disease can spread rapidly throughout a kennel or during a show circuit.

Usually this will be a mild respiratory disease symptomized by spells of dry hacking coughing after exercise. There may be some sneezing. The symptoms can be alleviated with medication supplied by your veterinarian. A lack of appetite and lethargy, plus the cough and discharge from nose and eyes and a low-grade fever, may indicate a more serious form. Pneumonia and other complications may occur in severe cases.

The major causes of ICT are parainfluenza, adenoviruses types 1 and 2, and Bordetella bronchisepticas. Vaccines such as canine parainfluenza are effective against ICT. The vaccine is included with distemper, leptospirosis and hepatitis vaccines. *Vaccination, starting during puppyhood and followed by annual innoculations, is the best preventative.* Other preventative measures include sanitation and air exchange systems.

KIDNEY DISEASES AND URINARY PROBLEMS

The signs of chronic kidney disease include: marked increase in the volume of urine, systematic vomiting, loss of appetite, weight loss, possible fever, depression, diarrhea, coma. Tests can be accomplished to determine kidney damage and include collecting and analyzing urine samples.

Lower urinary tract diseases are symptomized by increased attempts to urinate, a decrease in the volume of urine, and blood in the urine. The urinary tract may become obstructed, as by stones, which could cause uremic poisoning. Prompt treatment is required. Chronic obstruction could cause the kidneys to enlarge and become nonfunctional. In all cases the stones must be analyzed as the type determines the treatment.

Urate stones require uric acid control, which can be accomplished by a vegetable diet and elimination of liver. For crystine uroliths, bicarbonate may be added to the diet or d-penicillamine may be prescribed.

Chronic nephritis in a Lhasa Apso may have one of two causes. It may be a congenital, hereditary type of progressive kidney disease, or it could start as an acute infection in the kidneys.

Urinary problems and kidney diseases require the expert help of your veterinarian. One of the tests which he may perform is the BUN, or a serum creatinine test. My veterinarian has warned that these tests should be interpreted by an experienced veterinarian or technician and that diagnosis should not be based on just one test. If there is kidney disease present, the test results will be elevated.

Kidney disease may be found in some young Lhasas from four to six months old. The causes may be either a severe infection which affects the kidneys, or it could be inherited. Viremia and other diseases could affect the kidneys. So jumping to conclusions and blaming the sire and the dam, spaying or castrating them, may be a foolish and unnecessary action. Such drastic measures should be taken only with more than sufficient proof.

For instance, a few years ago a Best in Show Lhasa was performing poorly in the ring and I was told that he had developed a severe kidney problem involving kidney stones. The Lhasa ultimately died, probably from uremic poisoning. However, that Lhasa had lived a very strenuous life for a number of years. Stress and diet could play a very important part in this disease.

At least one form of kidney disease is said to be inherited. But, before any drastic steps are taken, all aspects from environment and diet to illnesses and ancestors should be examined. Kidney damage or disease may also result from heartworm infestations or from toxic reactions to certain drugs such as arsenic, which is often used for treatment of heartworm and which, according to many reports, is being used by some handlers and breeders to promote coat growth in long-coated breeds.

SKIN PROBLEMS

Hot Spots – Some Lhasas are known to have hot spots, which usually erupt very suddenly. One factor which seems to stimulate them is hormonal change, as when a bitch comes in heat. Another is stress. The spots develop quickly and become covered with an oozing pus. The situation must be quickly cleared up or there may be permanent hair loss.

Emergency treatment on discovery can help. We have found that a good washing of that area with one part *Clorox* to eight parts water really helps. This is repeated four to six times daily. We have followed the *Clorox* and water with vitamin E oil and furacin ointment, or vitamin E in wheat germ oil ointment. Cover the area thoroughly. This is vital. Usually you will see a marked improvement within twenty-four to forty-eight hours. It usually is not necessary to shave the coat in that area, and especially not on a show Lhasa.

If your Lhasa has repeated attacks, or if the spot does not clear up promptly, a trip to your veterinarian is in order. He may treat your Lhasa with steroids and/or antibiotics.

Allergies – Allergic reactions, whatever the symptoms, can be very frustrating, especially when searching for causes. Like humans, our Lhasas may also react to irritants in their environments or in their diets. The symptoms may be skin rashes, flea allergy dermatitis, hives, upset digestive system, coughs, irritated eyes, mucous-coated stools, and an unhappy dog.

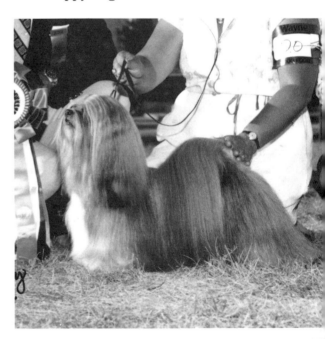

BIS Ch. Sho Tru's the Main Event is making his presence felt on the West Coast. Owner, Pat Keen.

Research is being done. For instance, the RAST test, developed by Dr. Richard Halliwell and Dr. Gail Kunkle, is used in the measurement of antibodies in the blood, which are an accurate gauge of an animal's sensitivity to allergens. But testing for allergic responses can be time consuming, frustrating, expensive, and perhaps fruitless.

Having suffered from allergies most of my life, I really do sympathize with afflicted animals. Medication, when it works, is only good so long before it no longer gives relief. Some medication the body will not tolerate. After years of daily medication (I am allergic to something every season), I bless the Bichon lady from Atlanta who suggested I try pantothenic acid (vitamin B5) when I accidently left my allergy pills home. It is so much easier to take a vitamin without reactions than all the different drugs I had been given for years. Hopefully it will continue to work. Even with all the tests, some allergies are still found only after trial and error. Therefore, unless the allergic reaction is very severe, as it may be with bee stings, home treatments with common sense can be effective for your Lhasa.

One method is avoidance. If your Lhasa is allergic to fleas, to foods, to shampoos, to laundry soaps, or even to some weeds and grasses, avoid them whenever possible.

For fleas, take preventative grooming procedures. Use dips, shampoos, and creolin when bathing. Flea sprays and powders do not seem to be especially effective for Lhasas and tend to damage coats. Your yard may be sprayed with a yard and kennel spray to eliminate fleas in the grass. Your house can be treated with a flea bomb to eliminate any there.

Hives, skin rashes, and the so-called "tummy spots" — small, rather dark reddish-brown spots — may be symptoms of many different allergens, as can digestive upsets, mucous stools, and irritated eyes. Let's consider the causes.

Shampoos, rinses, laundry soaps, and fabric softeners may be major causes. Consider first the rugs, bedding, and towels with which your Lhasa comes in contact. Anything that is unusually harsh can cause a reaction. Perfumed products can also be a source of irritation. The itching which causes your Lhasa to scratch can be helped by coating a rash with vitamin E and wheat germ oil ointment or by giving an infant-size antihistamine. Include vitamin C and vitamin E in the diet. Another source of relief could be 100 units of pantothenic acid (vitamin B5) which may relieve allergic symptoms.

Foods also are sources of allergens. One of my Lhasas reacts with violent digestive upset to pasteurized cheese, which he loves. Other milk products also can stimulate allergic reactions such as mucous in stools, running noses or eyes, and even sneezing. For instance, Lhasas given a teaspoon daily of dried, powdered cheese started to have these reactions after a week to ten days. Removing it from their diets produced a discontinuance of all symptoms within twenty-four hours. They will tolerate ½ teaspoonful in their food once or twice a week without discomfort.

If your Lhasa is exhibiting these symptoms, review his diet, and if anything new has been added, eliminate it. When all the symptoms have disappeared, try it again. If the symptoms return, you know the culprit is within that item.

Perhaps the most difficult symptoms to eradicate are those caused by weeds or grasses. These often cause eyes to tear, and that discharge often stains the coat and makes the coat sticky, which in turn collects dirt, may give the facial coat a musty odor, and can cause the eyes to look enlarged and swollen. Recently I decided to try pantothenic acid on one Lhasa exhibiting some of those symptoms. One 100 mg pill was given. Within twenty-four hours all symptoms were gone. Repeat dosages are given only when symptoms return. No adverse effects are apparent. On the contrary, the Lhasa is more full of energy and life than ever, even when the grass is being cut.

Some veterinarians have been doing research concerning vitamins. A deficiency in pantothenic acid is said to cause not only greying hair or discoloration of hair, but also gastroenteritis, a fatty liver, a poor appetite, and retarded growth. So it is probable that no harm can come from using it to remove allergic symptoms. In the Southwest some breeders are experimenting with it to help with their coat problems there. It is certainly worth a try.

If all else fails, all sorts of tests must be tried until the culprit or culprits are located.

Bee, Hornet, and Wasp Stings – These stings may be very toxic to your Lhasa. My first Lhasa was attacked by wasps at eight weeks. Within a short time she was swelling and having breathing difficulties. She had to be rushed to the veterinarian for emergency treatment, a cortisone shot, and removal of the stingers through her thick coat. Since the wasps had caught in the coat, most of the stingers were found relatively easily. For a while I had to carry antihistamine medication in case she was stung again.

In the last few years several of my Lhasas have been stung about the head. It has been necessary to remove the stingers and cover the area with a soothing salve. One of the bitches was badly stung on her muzzle, and she was in considerable pain for a short period. The area scabbed over badly even though she was covered with salve. Eventually she lost considerable muzzle hair, and for a while her facial furnishings were sparse. All of that hair grew back in.

Do beware of stings and watch your Lhasas closely. Often bees, hornets, or wasps will get caught in their coats so that you can tell what kind of a sting it is. If there is swelling or shortness of breath, get your Lhasa quickly to a veterinarian. For a minor sting, baking soda and water paste will remove the pain. If nothing else is available, make a mud pack. Or use an infant-size antihistamine.

STRUCTURAL PROBLEMS

Patella-Stifle Problems – Lately there have been scattered reports of "stifle" problems among Lhasas. Just how extensive the problem is is questionable. In addition, the definition of this problem seems somewhat ambiguous in that many different responses were given. The problem appears in the area about the patella, a very vulnerable area because of the construction and the placement involved. The patella lies between the femur and the tibia. The whole structure is somewhat like two chopsticks held end to end by rubberbands. Two crescent-shaped pieces of cartilage, miniscuses, prevent the two bones from grinding together, and ligaments stabilize the joint. In front of this joint is the patella, a small bone which is attached to the front thigh muscles by a tendon and to the tibia by a ligament.

If it is suspected that a Lhasa is experiencing pain and/or movement problems, a visit to a veterinarian is in order. It probably would be best that the Lhasa be withdrawn from the show ring temporarily. Un-

til the Lhasa can be examined by the veterinarian, he should be kept quiet and not be allowed to jump. The causes for injury or problems in that area surrounding the patella may be several: breeding practices, environment, accident, and degeneration.

Breeding practices are one probable cause of the increase in patella-stifle problems. As some breeders attempt to deviate from the rectangular Lhasa and to put more leg on the Lhasa while shortening his back, they may be developing problems. In changing the build, the result could be a patella which does not properly track in its groove, thus causing a "slipped patella" and ultimately damage of the patellar cartilage. In addition, breeding practices could change the balance of the leg bones; i.e., either the tibia or femur could become longer than the other, which would cause muscles and tendons to develop in a pattern not conducive to proper movement. The muscles or tendons could be elongated, thus being more prone to injury, or they could be compacted, therefore restricting movement. The straighter the angulation, the more stress can be put on the joint. That stress can cause problems.

Environment, too, may add to the problems. The floor or ground on which the Lhasas move could be vital. Cement, for instance, is a hard surface which causes a constant shock to joints, especially weight-bearing joints such as the patella. Our Lhasas, like basketball players, experience a constant impact on this joint. A constant repetition of this impact could, it would seem, cause repeated microtrauma which could lead to stress injuries, to arthritis, and perhaps to degeneration of the joint. A gravel or wood surface would provide better footing than cement.

Another type of flooring which would be bad for the active Lhasa would be a linoleum or other slippery surface. Slipping on the floor could cause bones to dislocate, muscles and ligaments to be stretched or torn, sprains, and even fractures.

Injuries may result from many causes: blows, sudden starts and stops, sudden turns, falls, and jumping. One must be careful when handling a Lhasa so that he is not dropped, nor pushed with extra force into crates, nor handled in a rough manner. This area is also subject to reinjury.

There are several types of injuries. Just as a human may have a trick knee, so may a Lhasa have a trick patella when the bones slip out of line and either dislocate or pinch the cartilage. The cartilage, tendons, and muscles may be torn. Just slipping may cause this type of injury. Ligaments have only so much elasticity, and stretch beyond that will cause a tear, which occurs when a ligament is strained.

Degeneration of the patella and surrounding area could occur because of repeated extensive stress or injury. Repeated tearing of the cartilage, for instance, could cause it to fray much like an old rug. In addition, the Lhasa could suffer from a type of traumatic arthritis as a result of injuries.

Since our Lhasas cannot vocalize their pain and trauma, we must be aware of other signs of the problem, such as reluctance to traverse a very few steps, a favoring of a leg, a limp, or a cry of pain. Some Lhasas are very stoic, and thus you may only sense an injury by an unfamiliar feel to the lead.

The patella, suspended between the femur and the tibia, is more than a simple hinge. With each step it goes up and down and from side to side as it rolls, glides, rotates, or angulates. It is a very vulnerable area. The cartilage may degenerate, twist, or tear, tendons may become inflamed, and ligaments and muscles can tear or stretch. It is important to the well-being of our Lhasas that we are aware of potential trauma and take necessary precautionary methods.

Canine Intervertebral Disc Disease – "A survey of 8,117 cases of intervertebral disc disease reported by 13 veterinary colleges and reported by W. A. Priester in the scientific journal, *Theriogenology*, indicates a significantly increased risk in the Dachshund, Pekingese, Beagle, Welsh Corgi, Lhasa Apso and Shi Tzu."[2]

This disease has three forms: herniated disc, degenerated disc, and calcified cartilage. The herniated disc is sometimes described as an exploding disc. What happens is, just as in a hernia, a portion of the inner soft portion of the disc protrudes through a crack in the fibrous outer cover of the disc. Ninety percent of those afflicted have an involvement of the IV disc and the IV cartilage.[3]

This disease is not new but has been known in Lhasa Apsos at least thirty years. Ch. Ming Tongo, owned by Dr. Frank T. Lloyd, Jr., suffered an in-

jured disc in his spine just following the completion of his championship. After seeking much medical care with no positive results for Tongo, his case was given up as hopeless. Solomon, Lloyd's kennel manager, asked if he could try. He gave Tongo much companionship and love as he patiently and faithfully massaged and exercised Tongo, who finally regained the use of his legs. Two years later he debuted as a Special with a Best of Breed win.

The 1977 report stated that there were twenty-three cases per thousand dogs per year. Also, the chondrodystrophic, or long-backed and short-legged, dogs often show no symptoms of this disease which indicates other factors are involved. For instance, there is a greater risk for spayed females and intact males. Dr. Priester suggested that "young dogs in high-risk categories should avoid undue stress and rough play."[4]

Among the few Lhasas suffering this syndrome of whom I have heard, one factor stood out: owners stated that these Lhasas were finer boned than other Lhasas they owned. This, of course, may just have been coincidence. Dr. Priester did mention that breeding practices should be examined in these cases.

Massage, exercise, love, support, and understanding are important for recovery. Some people have had good results by using water therapy. Perhaps the keys are patience and faithful routine practiced with love and understanding.

---

[4]*Ibid.*

PARASITES

Roundworm – Your Lhasa can come in contact with roundworms through contaminated soil or fecal matter, by consuming small rodents or small vermin as transport hosts, or in areas to which the embryonated eggs were carried by water bugs. The cycle for these worms is as follows: undeveloped eggs are passed in the fecal matter from an infected dog; the eggs develop further in the soil and are picked up in some manner and ingested by the dog; the embryonic roundworms are in the ingested eggs; these worms hatch in the host's small intestine; in larval stage, worms migrate through the liver and the heart to the lungs; they are coughed

---

[2]"Canine Intervertebral Disc Disease," *Dog World* (62, 11), November 1977, p. 16.
[3]*Ibid.*

up from the lungs, are swallowed, and reinfest the intestinal tract; there they mature and lay eggs, completing the life cycle.

Symptoms for roundworm are: abdominal enlargement, cough, nasal discharge, weight loss, reduced growth rate, diarrhea, vomit, digestive disturbances.

A brood bitch may have dormant roundworms in the muscle tissues; the larvae will be activated by the hormonal changes of pregnancy and will migrate to the developing fetuses. Worming for roundworms in the brood bitch should be done before breeding. Roundworms may be present in very young puppies, which should only be wormed under a veterinarian's supervision.

Otherwise, any infected Lhasa over six weeks of age should be wormed. For proof that a Lhasa has roundworms, a stool check can be done by your vet or you can learn to do the checks yourself. Your veterinarian can prescribe medication, but there are products readily available which you can purchase. My preference is for medication which expels the roundworms, such as *Piperazine Citrate,* rather than medication which causes the worms to disintegrate. Do not use too harsh a medication with your Lhasa, as some cannot tolerate them.

Medications for other types of worms or for a combination of several worms are harsher than piperazine and should be used only when necessary and then under veterinary supervision.

Hookworm – These tiny, hairlike parasites attach themselves to the lining of the intestine by their hooklike mouths. The symptoms which may indicate your Lhasa is infected are a dark diarrhea-type stool (which may reveal blood), loss of weight, and poor coat.

Hookworm can be contracted through infested soil, in barnyards or in horse barns, and may be passed to puppies before birth. If suspected, stool checks should be made. Your veterinarian will prescribe the proper medication, which should be given under his supervision. A seriously infected dog may need blood transfusions.

Tapeworm – The usual carrier for tapeworm is the flea, which the Lhasa must ingest to become infected. The signs of tapeworm are segments found in the stool, around the anus, or on the rear hairs of the dog's coat. These segments look like pieces of rice.

The tapeworm is the one flat worm which dogs get. Within the segments which break off are the

Sherry Baxley with Ch. Potala Keke's Frazer, her beloved hearing-aid dog. Photo by Gilbert.

72

eggs. This parasite attaches itself to the lining of the intestine by its scolex, or head. New segments are produced at the scolex, and the tapeworm becomes longer and longer and, like a kite's tail, floats into the lumen of the intestine.

To remove tapeworms, special vermicides must be used. Pills such as *Scolaban* or *Yomesan* may be used, and for Lhasas which either have difficulty swallowing the pills or do not tolerate oral medications, one shot of *Droncit* may be used. Treatment for tapeworm should be carried out under the guidance of a veterinarian.

Whipworm – Like roundworm, whipworm can be found in all parts of the United States. The worms are grayish-white, and the adult may reach 2 to 3 inches in length. The eggs of these worms are difficult to eradicate from the soil.

Affected dogs may have an unhealthy appearance, may perform poorly, may lose weight, may be nervous, could be dehydrated, have bloody diarrhea, or have anemia. A severely infected dog could develop either colitis or typhlitis.

The cycle of whipworms begins with the ingestion of the eggs; the larvae hatch in the small intestine and then penetrate the inner lining, remaining there for eight to ten days; then they migrate to the colon or cecum where they go into the lining and remain for two to three months while developing to maturity; once mature, the eggs are passed through the fecal matter; within twenty-four to thirty hours the eggs begin embryonation, and within two to four weeks reach the infective larval stage, in which they remain active up to several years.

Diagnosis of whipworm should be made by your veterinarian, and prescriptions for medications should also come from him. Some Lhasas may have toxic reactions to the drugs used to treat them for parasites.

To control this parasite, good sanitary practices are vital. Favorable temperatures and humidity may keep the infected eggs alive. A dry summer and exposure to the sun helps to destroy the eggs. Prompt removal and disposal of fecal wastes and a thorough cleaning of exercise areas will help.

Heartworm – Mosquitoes are the intermediate hosts for heartworm, and they should therefore be controlled. First they bite an infected dog. The microfilariae which the mosquitoes ingest incubate for a period of ten to thirty days, and then the infective larvae enter the mosquitoes' saliva. The mosquitoes transmit the larvae to the dogs with their "bites," after which the larvae develop for three to four months, moving as they do so toward the large veins near the hearts of the dogs, making their final stops either in the pulmonic vessels or in the right ventricles of the hearts.

Most Lhasas, like other breeds, will not show signs of the disease until it is well advanced. The best means of detecting it is a blood test, which is positive if microfilariae are found, and which is then confirmed by X-ray studies of the heart and the lungs. Other tests involving kidneys, liver, and blood are also completed and are used to determine the proper treatment. When the infection is serious, symptoms may include a constant soft cough, a shortness of breath, a lack of stamina, nervousness, weakness, and listlessness.

A Lhasa in good physical condition whose infestation is detected early may be successfully treated. This treatment must be accomplished under the guidance of your veterinarian and consists of an arsenical drug to eliminate the adult heartworms first. This treatment must be constantly monitored by using laboratory tests. Once the adult worms are destroyed, medication can be started three to six weeks later to eliminate the microfilariae.

Veterinarian supervision is absolutely necessary in order to detect any adverse reactions so that

Ch. Red Boy's Alla Baba of Al-Mar, foundation stud at Tashi. Owner, Jeanne Holsapple.

prompt treatment can be given. The drugs used in this portion of the treatment are also toxic and may cause kidney damage. If the drugs cannot be used because of advanced kidney or liver disease, or because of a toxic reaction to the drugs, heart surgery for the removal of the worms may be necessary.

At this point I have heard of no Lhasa who has experienced heartworm. However, one of the most distinguished Brittany Spaniel champions and field trial champions experienced heartworm at about two years of age. After being treated for a serious infection, he went on to enhance his fame for ten years and to sire many good Brittanies.

Mosquito prevention is one method of control to prevent this disease. Another method is *preventa-tive medication initiated after the negative blood test and used daily throughout the mosquito season.* The decision of whether or not to use heartworm medication should be based on the incidence of heartworm in your area and should be made in consultation with your veterinarian.

Coccidiosis – This protozoan infection may be stress related. It is caused by a protozoan parasite which lives in the intestinal tract. Transmission is by ingestion. The dogs may seem very normal while the parasite develops in the intestinal tract for from seven to twelve days. The symptom of the disease is persistent diarrhea, which may be bloody. The disease is usually determined by fecal exam. Prompt care may be very important, especially in puppies.

Ch. Kaleko's Gyn Rhumi. Owner, Debbie Burke.

PHYSICAL ENVIRONMENT

One of the major areas of concern in eliminating causes of health problems is the physical environment. There are numerous things which you can do.

To control fleas and ticks, you can spray the outside areas where your Lhasas exercise with a yard spray; and you can also "bomb" your house with a fogger, which also will help to eliminate other insects such as spiders and flies. Do not forget your Lhasa's sleeping area. It too should be cleaned and sprayed. Should you live in an area where hookworm is prevalent, a hookworm spray for yards and kennels is available. Follow directions on the labels for any of these products carefully. To help in preventing viruses, veterinarians recommend the use of *Clorox* in your yard in about a 1:30 mixture. It can be sprayed, sprinkled, or used in a hose sprayer. Saturate the area quite thoroughly, as it will not hurt either the grass or the shrubs.

If you are showing your Lhasa, a good investment is a raised-floor exercise pen and/or a raised-floor crate. One of the nice benefits is that our Lhasas appear to avoid picking up parasites. It may also help your Lhasa to avoid contact with viruses which could be in the urine or fecal matter in public exercise pens or on the grounds. And, of course, the Lhasa's coat will be kept cleaner and drier when using the pen.

The use of a 4-foot-square exercise pen with puppies makes clean-up easier and more sanitary conditions available. This could prevent opportunities for young puppies picking up parasites or even coccidiosis. The pen can continue to be used with older puppies and with adults, as well. These pens also aid in the control of those viruses which are transmitted through feces.

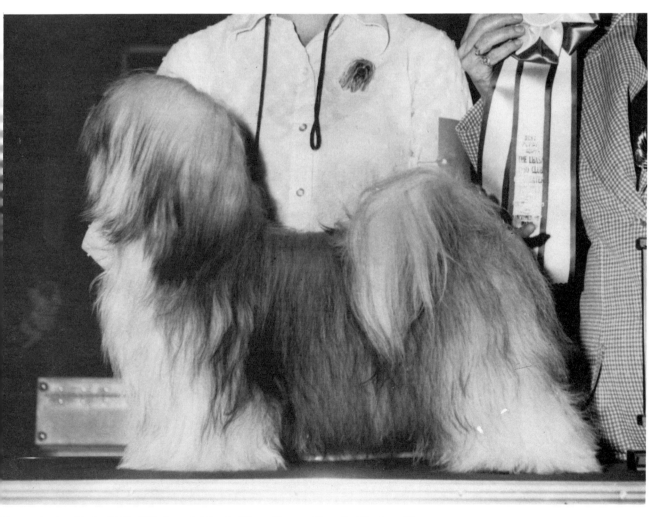

Top-producing bitch, 1979, Windsong's Xanda Shan. Owner, Tom C. Meador, Ginseng.

75

Foundation stud for Seng Kye, Ch. Dolsa Tsin Ah Mhun, sire of World Ch. Dolsa Red Alert (sired by Ch. Zijuh Don- Na Tsamten ROM out of Cordova Sin-Sa ROM). Breeder, Jean Kausch. Owners, Susan Session Yuncer and Jean Kausch.

76

EYE PROBLEMS

The swelling red gland can be shocking. Excessive tearing can be annoying. Lack of tearing can be dangerous. Lack of pigmentation can be hazardous. Some of these conditions have names which sound threatening and confusing: keratoconjunctivitis; follicular conjunctivitis; Harder's gland; prolapse of the gland of the third eyelid; dysfunction of lacrimal ducts. Each will be discussed.

LACK OF PIGMENTATION

Perhaps a most obvious condition found in puppies is a lack of pigmentation of the third eyelid. In our Lhasa Apsos, and in many other breeds, the third eyelid is expected to show black pigmentation. However, hair coat color characteristics may influence the pigment of the third eyelid. Thus, for example, white-coated dogs may lack the black "eye" pigment. This lack of pigment may be found in other light-colored Lhasas as well. The black pigment actually provides protection from solar rays. Therefore, the nonpigmented eye would be more subject to solar irritation. A dog lacking the black "eye" pigment would probably have to avoid excessive exposure to the sun and have its eyes checked by its owner on a regular basis. If irritation appears, the dog should have a check-up by a veterinarian.

Many breeders maintain that the best method for preventing pigment problems is to periodically use a black Lhasa in a breeding program, especially one which concentrates on light-colored Lhasas. Some say that a black should be used every third or fourth generation.

EXCESSIVE TEARING

Tear staining is a common affliction of the long-haired breeds regardless of coat color. The characteristics are hair staining and a thick discharge. The hair just below the inside corner of the eye will be stained from a bright rust to a deep brown. If there is a thick discharge, the discharge will vary in color from a light grey to a dark brown, and it will have a foul odor. The causes of tear staining are excessive tearing and an abnormal condition of the eye.

In the normal eye the lacrimal gland produces tears which bathe the eye and then evaporate. Excess tearing would drain from the lacrimal duct into the lacrimal sac, then into the naso-lacrimal duct into the nasal cavity, and then either appears from the nose or goes down the back of the throat. (See Figure 1.)

There are numerous causes for abnormal tearing. First is the overproduction of tears by the lacrimal gland. A second cause could be a double set of eyelashes which could cause severe irritation to the corneas and thus result in excessive tearing. Entropin, the inturning of the eyelid, is another cause. In this case the rubbing of the eyelashes on the cornea produces excessive tears.

The cure for both the double set of eyelashes and entropin is surgery. However, since both of these conditions are hereditary, very serious consideration should be given to the breeding of dogs with these disorders. Unless special circumstances exist, such dogs probably should be withdrawn from a breeding program. My research did not reveal whether or not this was a dominant or recessive trait, a fact which might influence breeding decisions.

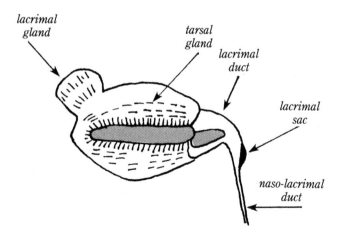

The normal lacrimal gland. This gland produces tears which bathe the eye and then evaporate. Excessive tearing drains from the duct into the nasal cavity.

78

Another cause of excessive tearing would be the dysfunction of the lacrimal ducts. When the ducts are plugged, excessive tears overflow onto the skin, causing stains and discharges. The causes for this condition are numerous: infections; conjunctiva (swelling and inflammation); dirt or dust; foreign substances such as hair sprays, shampoos, or rinses; cysts; other growths. The cure for dysfunctioning or plugged lacrimal ducts would be surgery.

Thus, any dog exhibiting excessive tearing should visit a veterinarian for a thorough ophthalmological check.

FOLLICULAR CONJUNCTIVITIS

Follicular conjunctivitis is another eye problem common in dogs. In this case the follicles (small cavities, sacs, or glands) develop not on the third eyelid, but elsewhere on the conjunctiva, the mucous membrane which covers the front of the eyeball and the inner surface of the eyelids. Signs of this problem are persistent mucoid discharge. Behind the posterior surface of the third eyelid will be found hyperplastic (having to do with an abnormal multiplication of elements) follicles which are red and roughened in appearance. For a mild case, the cleansing of the eyes each morning, and for the more severe cases several times daily, with a preparation suggested by your vet is recommended.

THE PROLAPSE OF THE GLAND OF THE THIRD EYELID

The prolapse of the gland of the third eyelid, often called "cherry eye" by the breeders, can be very frightening to the uninitiated. This problem is now seen frequently in dogs, and no longer seems to be restricted to a few breeds.

The signs of the "cherry eye" are easily visible (Figures 2 and 3). The gland protrudes above the free border of the third eyelid, usually near the inner corner of the eye, and becomes inflamed and then enlarged. After it protrudes, it becomes red, from which derives the name cherry eye. Also, secondary epiphora and conjunctivitis may occur.

The development of the disease is as follows. The normal gland of the third eyelid has connective tissue bands anchoring it to surrounding eye tissues. If these bands should not develop properly, postorbital fat can cause the gland to prolapse (to slip out of place) when the eye is retracted into the orbit by the extrinsic, or external, muscles. The eye may be stimulated to retract into the orbit by any superficial irritation such as conjunctivitis, a scratch, or even an insect bite. As soon as the gland is prolapsed (out of place), the gland develops inflammation and hypertrophy (enlargement).

There are two major causes for prolapsing glands. First, there can be a congenital lack of tissue band for fastening the gland tightly to the periorbital or surrounding tissues. This congenital lack possesses the probability of being inherited and is most often seen in Beagles, Cocker Spaniels, and Pekingese. The second major cause is post traumatic, resulting from a wound either to the orbit or to the third eyelid.

The treatments for this prolapse vary. The common procedure is to remove the gland under a topical anesthesia, possibly followed by the use of opthalmic ointments. It is, in reality, a minor operation with no post-operative problems.

One of my Lhasas was stung on the lower eyelid by a blackfly while at an outdoor show, which caused a prolapse of the gland of the third eyelid. He experienced several things. First, a veterinarian was not readily located. There was little handy to reduce the inflammation. An old wives' cure for inflammation in a human eye is a wet tea bag. The tea contains tannic acid which reportedly provides relief from inflammation. So, while we waited, a wet tea bag was held onto the eye. The tea bag became very warm from the contact and dried out. A second one was used. These poultices seemed to control the inflammation and even to reduce it. The veterinarian finally arrived and ordered Gentocin drops to be used several times daily and an ointment also to be used several times daily. Within three days the situation had cleared up. Although the veterinarian advised that the gland probably would eventually have to be removed, there has been as yet no serious recurrence of the problem.

HARDER'S GLAND

The Harder's gland, or harderian gland, is located in the base of the third eyelid or in the inferior orbit. It is a separate and a different gland from the gland of the third eyelid. This gland alone can be infected. But such an infection could be traumatic and thus cause the prolapse of the gland of the third eyelid. In either case the infection would need to be diagnosed and treated by a vet.

KERATOCONJUNCTIVITIS

Keratoconjunctivitis, or dry eye, is a chronic disease which involves the cornea and the conjunctiva and which results from inadequate tear production. This is very common in dogs.

The clinical signs of this disease aid in diagnosis. The first is pain, indicated by signs of discomfort or by increased blinking. A decreased tear film is

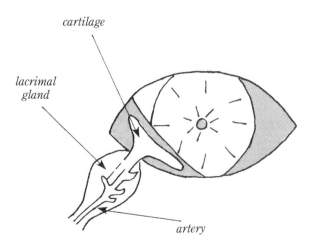
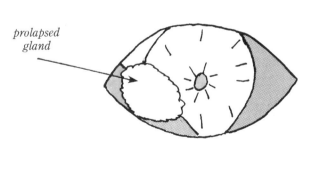

The prolapsed gland of the third eyelid. The lacrimal gland protrudes from the border of the third eyelid, becomes inflamed, and then enlarged.

79

noticeable. Obvious changes in the mucous thread can be observed and include an increase in the size of the thread, a color change from clear to yellow or yellow-green, and an adherence to the conjunctiva.

Additional clinical signs include excessive ocular discharge. There can be corneal changes such as ulcers, opacity, vascularization (having to do with blood vessels), pigmentation, or keratinization (a changing or hardening). These corneal changes would need to be discovered during examination. Another sign would be inflamed and thick conjunctiva, which would also give a dry appearance. The last clinical sign would be the nostrils, which could be either normal or dry.

A veterinarian uses the clinical signs and the Schirmer tear test in making his diagnosis of keratoconjunctivitis. The Schirmer tear test, which appears to be relatively simple, was performed for me by Dr. F. Charles Mohr, D. V. M. In doing this test, which is a measure of corneal sensitivity and the dog's ability to produce tears, neither anesthesia nor drops are used. A small amount of distilled water is dropped into the eye to stimulate tearing. Then the end of a strip of filter paper, about ¼ × 1½ inches, is placed in the inferior cul-de-sac, i.e.,

Ch. Norbulingka's Crazy Daisy, fourth generation for breeder-owner Phyllis Marcy. Photo by Tatham.

below the lower lid with the lids held in a closed position, for one minute. The amount of wetting is then measured in millimeters; the normal amount would be from 10 to 25 mm in one minute. Values of less than 10 mm in one minute, especially under 5 mm, when combined with the clinical signs of keratoconjunctivitis, indicate keratoconjunctivitis or "dry eye." Dr. Mohr pointed out that both eyes must be tested and that the difference between those readings is also important and aids in diagnosing such eye problems. He also emphasized that the readings can vary from day to day, as the Schirmer test values can be affected by humidity.

There are two primary causes for keratoconjunctivitis. One is a lacrimal activity which is caused either by a lack of glands or a lack of nervous stimulation. The second primary cause is spontaneous atrophy (senile).

Numerous secondary causes exist for dry eye. For instance, it can occur during or following systemic diseases such as canine distemper, under acute hypotensive conditions caused by shock or Addisonian crisis (characterized by anemia), or as a result of allergy. Chronic ocular infections can cause dry eye.

There could be a toxic reason such as caused by sulfadiazine and phenazopyridine when given for chronic therapy. In such cases the dry eye condition is usually reversible with the discontinued use of the drugs.

Older dogs can experience temporary hyposecretion following surgery. Surgical removal of the gland of the third eyelid when there is decreased lacrimal gland activity can also cause the condition.

Finally, in many cases, the causes can never be determined.

INHERITED EYE DEFECTS

Lhasa Apsos are not among the breeds listed by Charles W. Foley as susceptible to inheriting either any eye defects or deafness.[1] Both cataracts and superficial ulcers on the cornea are inheritable and do occasionally occur in Lhasa Apsos.

---

[1]Charles W. Foley, Ph.D., "Genetic Defects in the Dog," *Pure Bred Dogs American Kennel Gazette* (97, 5), May 1980, pp. 81–82.

A cataract affects the lens of the eye, which becomes cloudy, and consequently destroys vision in the eye. It is actually the loss of the crystalline lens. Skillful surgery can remove the cataract and restore a good percentage of the vision. Cataracts are often associated with old age. Lhasa Apsos are not among the sixteen breeds who are susceptible to either dominant or recessive inheritance of this disease. However, cataracts are occasionally found on Lhasas' eyes.

Moreover, superficial ulcers of the cornea also occur once in a while. When these occur, surgery is indicated.

CONCLUSION

Certain eye problems are inherited, and the breeding of dogs with these problems is discouraged. As far as my research went, there was no mention of serious eye problems among Lhasa Apsos, although like other breeds Lhasas may develop cataracts which would require skilled care. If common sense is used in protecting our Lhasas from unnecessary exposure to irritants, if we seek expert advice when signs of eye "infections" are apparent to us, if we avoid breeding where hereditary problems are apparent, we will be doing the best we can for our Lhasas. If any of the conditions discussed appear to exist, seek the advice of a qualified veterinarian.

My thanks go to the personnel of the Barre Animal Hospital, Barre Center, New York: Dr. Ronald Harling, D. V. M., Dr. F. Charles Mohr, D. V. M., and Nancy Blank, Veterinarian Technician. They provided resources and explanations.

SOURCES

Kirk, Robert W., B. S., D. V. M. and Stephen I. Bistner, B. S., D. V. M., *Handbook of Veterinary Procedures and Emergency Treatment.* Philadelphia, 1975.

Severin, Glen A., D. V. M, M. S., *Veterinary Opthalmology Notes.* Fort Collins, Colorado, 1976.

Tomlinson, B. L. "Tear Staining." *Lhasa Tales,* December 1977.

9

THE BEAUTY PARLOR

A good coat is usually the result of good health and of good grooming practices. Basic grooming for show and companion Lhasas is generally the same; it is the degree of grooming which makes the difference. Neither coat texture nor coat color seems to require any major differences in grooming techniques.

A shaft of hair is basically made of scales which overlap like roof shingles. Harsh shampoos, improper rinses, and excessive heat cause the scales to lift up. It is this lifting up of the scales on the hair shafts that gives a Lhasa's coat a dry, rough look which lacks sheen. When the scales are tight and firm, the light reflects off the hair, giving a healthy sheen.

SHAMPOOS AND RINSES

Lhasa Apsos, unlike most breeds, have hair like human hair with a pH balance between 4.5–5.5, which is acidic. Therefore, human products give best results. Most dog products are alkaline, which means they are stronger and harsher, open the scales of the hair shaft, and make the hair feel dry and brittle. Though it may seem strange, baby shampoos also fall in this category. Alkaline shampoos can cause a dandruff-type result also, in which small scales of skin appear under the hair shafts.

The pH range is 0–14; 7 is neutral, as is distilled water. Above 7 is alkaline and below is acidic. However, because a shampoo has a low pH does not make it good for a Lhasa coat. Many over-the-counter products may be low in pH, and may leave the coat feeling smooth, but these products do not do the best possible job on a Lhasa's coat as they do not do anything to restructure the coat. Rather, these products have a basic parafin wax base which covers up the hair shaft rather than restructuring, or rebuilding.

At present there are only a few shampoos and conditioners on the market which comply with a Lhasa's coat requirements, and most of these products are made by Nucleic A, Langé, Redkin, Jhirmack, and Nexis. These products contain panthenol, or pantothenic acid (vitamin B5). Your choice should make the Lhasa's hair feel stronger and better and should restructure the hair. Protein is essential for this purpose; however, the animal proteins used in most shampoos and rinses are not compatible with hair because the molecules are too large. The above-mentioned products hydrolize the animal protein to break down the molecules, a process which makes it possible for the Lhasa's hair to absorb the protein. The hydrolizing process enables the animal protein to be broken down by interaction with water.

Protein is essential for a good coat. In addition to using low pH shampoos with panthenol, diet can also aid the development of a good coat. Add brewers' yeast, pantothenic acid, or other B vitamins.

An acid-balanced shampoo, which must be in the 4.5–5.5 pH range, does an excellent job of cleaning Lhasas' coats. Choose a good creme conditioner, such as Nucleic A *Seal 'N Protect* or *Langé Panthenol Conditioning Rinse,* which will do an excellent job of keeping the coat easy to handle and of protecting against a tendency to mat. If the coat has not been left without grooming for long (several weeks), mats will slide right out.

For frizzy, dry, brittle, or damaged coats use a moisturizer creme rinse. It is essential for the restructuring of the hair that the product used contain hydrolized animal proteins, such as Nucleic A *Phlexhair,* Langé *Panthenol Treatment,* or *Infusion 23.* The dry or damaged hair shaft must be restructured and protected. Usually these products are left on the coat for up to fifteen minutes before rinsing.

In order to prevent a frizzy appearance, lightly spray each layer of coat when grooming. Use plain water, a mixture of one part Miss Clairol *Hair-So-New* to eight parts water plus one cap of *Alpha Keri Oil,* a 1:8 mixture of *Infusion 23* and water, or Langé *Panthenol Treatment.* The purpose for spraying the coat is to prevent damage, and it also helps control static electricity.

Do not use any product which contains henna – neutral henna or otherwise. The Lhasa coat exposed to the sun, to a hot drier, or to hot lights after treatment with henna, however properly, may burn, may dry out, may become brittle, and may break off in a constant flurry of hair. To me, coats thus treated present a dull, dry, fuzzy look. It may take a year or more to correct the damage. Beauticians have advised me that they are warned not to use henna on strawberry blonde (apricot), light grey, or white hair.

Other products necessary for grooming include a good flea shampoo, a product for removing and preventing ticks and fleas, latex orthodontic bands, antibiotic ear powder for dogs, vitamin E oil, baking soda, cornstarch, and brewers' yeast.

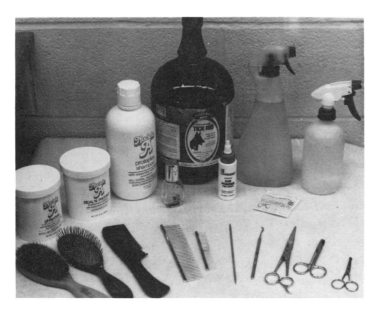

Grooming tools and supplies. Back row, l to r: conditioner, creme rinse, shampoo, tick and flea rid, spray bottles containing water and with water plus creme rinse and oil mixture.
Middle row: Vitamin E oil, ear powder, latex bands.
Front: bristle brush with nylon pins, pin brush, wide tooth plastic comb, large metal comb, "mustache" comb, knitting needle, tooth scaler, straight scissors, nail clippers, blunt end scissors. (Missing items that you also need are: curved blade scissors and hair pulling forceps.) Photo by Godshall.

GROOMING TOOLS

Your choices of combs and brushes are important. Your tools must do the jobs for which they are designated without damaging the coats. Therefore, brushes should have ends which are neither sharp nor "catchy." My preference is for ball-point ends and pin flexibility for pin brushes. Such a brush does not rip out coat. Another type of brush which I like is a combination bristle brush with nylon pins, which can be used on the coat having a tendency to wave. A good bristle brush, one not exceptionally stiff, is also a good investment.

I use two metal combs chosen because they also have ball-point ends. The larger comb is 6½ inches long with 1¼-inch-long teeth set with a ⅛-inch space between teeth. The smaller-type comb, sometimes called a mustache comb, is about 4½ inches long and has teeth about ⅝-inch long, but the teeth are set differently, one-half being spaced at about 1/16 inch and the other half at about 1/32 inch. The comb used on wet coats is a wide-toothed plastic comb, such as that made by Ace, which can be purchased at a drug store. The metal combs must be purchased from a pet supply house.

Scissors also play an important part in grooming. I use baby nail scissors with rounded ends for trimming between the pads. This type can be purchased at a drug store. The other types usually must be purchased from a pet supply house. These include: a good 5-inch straight scissors; a curved-blade scissors with blunted ends; a single-blade 30-tooth thinning sheers; and a nail scissors. It is not necessary to buy the most expensive, but do not buy the cheapest, either. Try to protect the scissors from rusting and have them sharpened periodically.

For parting I use a number 6 aluminum double-pointed knitting needle.

There really is no point in economizing on your grooming tools, as with care they will last a long time. I do not recommend using household scissors on your Lhasas, and your Lhasa scissors should be kept for that use and NEVER used for household chores or art projects or children's projects. They need to be kept sharp and nick free. Other tools also should be used exclusively for the Lhasas, including your pin brushes which some teenagers think make nice hair brushes.

APPLIANCES

A good sturdy grooming table is essential. If space is at a premium, the 18 × 24-inch size is plenty large. Or the next size, 24 × 30 inches, is more than adequate for Lhasas.

You will need a tub selected with Lhasas in mind. It need not be large, but should be about 14 inches deep. A simple spray attachment for the faucet, a 4-cup plastic measuring cup, and a 1- or 2-cup plastic measuring cup are also needed.

The purchase of a large professional hair drier seems expensive, but it can be effectively used for human hair as well as for your Lhasa's coat. If you do not own a large professional drier, a blow drier (used on medium or low heat, never on hot) will do. In order to free both hands for brushing and grooming, hang the drier in some manner over your grooming table. I have placed my grooming table under a clothes line in the utility room. The drier was hung from the line by a hook and a clothes hanger, or some sort of wall hook could be used.

FACIAL HAIR STAIN

Breeders, owners, and handlers have always been concerned with removing stains from Lhasa facial hair. They have, I am sure, tried many things. Several have told me that a major problem with products used to remove stains, especially from light coats, was that some seemed to affect the coat color or even add a color cast to the coat. The method described here appears to be one of the safest.

To clean up staining, make a paste of hydrogen peroxide (local antiseptic type) and cornstarch. Mix the paste in small amounts at a time because the paste tends to harden in a dish rather quickly. Work this paste heavily into the stained area and allow to dry. Be sure that you do not get the paste in the Lhasa's eyes. When dry, brush or comb the cornstarch out and then wash the facial hair during the bath.

A preventative for tearing which appears to be caused by allergy is pantothenic acid (vitamin B5). The 100-mg size pill will be adequate as it reduces tearing from one to several days and consequently also relieves the swelling, itching, and redness which accompany allergy attacks. Do not repeat until symptoms return.

HEAD TRIM

Very little trimming is done about the head. Sometimes a very thin line is clipped from the corner of one eye to the corner of the other. A variation of this would be a small triangle clipped at the inner corners of the eyes. This trimming must be done with great care and should never be obvious.

One purpose for this is to emphasize the muzzle by creating an optical illusion of length, and another is to remove a bit of excess facial hair which may be getting in your Lhasa's eyes. There is a drawback. You must either keep up the trimming once trimmed, or go through an awkward period of regrowth.

TRIMMING PAWS AND COAT

It is better to trim a Lhasa's coat before washing because the coat tends to stretch when washed and may be trimmed too short.

Working with the paw turned up, part the hair at the ankle and comb toward the pads. Hold the hair in place with the thumb and forefinger. With your 5-inch shears, clip the hair so that it is flat to the pad. Comb another ½-inch layer of hair down and repeat. Continue in this manner on leg coat only. Do not trim the guard or top coat. Repeat this trimming on all four paws.

Brush the coat down into position. Now stand the Lhasa with his front legs at the front edge of the table and one rear leg at the side edge. Using the

Train your Lhasa to lie quietly on the grooming table.

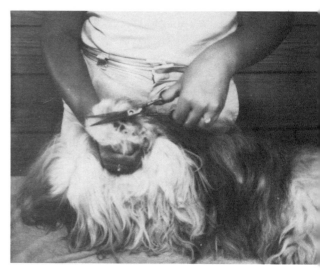

Trim hair flat to bottom of pad.

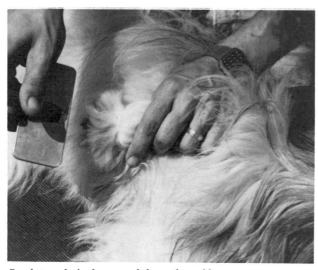

Comb paw hair downward from the ankle.

Trim the hair between the pads.

86

table as a guide, trim the coat level with the table from one side of one front paw, across the front, to the side of the other front paw. The curved scissors usually work best for this type of trimming, which is important because too long a coat in this area distorts the Lhasa's gait.

Repeat the trim with the rear feet at the table edge. The amount of trimming on the side coat is optional. When trimming the side coat, rather than using the edge of the table as your guide, trim at the bottom edge of the metal strip encircling the table. You should trim the sides if it either affects the gait or if it is uneven. If you prefer the coat to be long on the sides, at least trim it so that it looks even and neat by eliminating any jagged edges.

Trim the area around the anal opening by clipping the hair short for a small space. The purpose is to keep the area cleaner. Do not exaggerate the trim here, as it will look ugly. However, some people trim the area an exaggerated amount to establish the illusion of a high tail set.

Comb the matted area gently. Start at the outer edge of the area and comb a small amount of hair at a time.

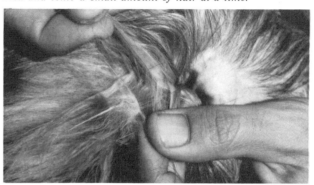

Pull the matted hair apart gently. Remove mat.

Small mats can be separated with your fingers.

Thoroughly comb the paws and legs. Remove any mats.

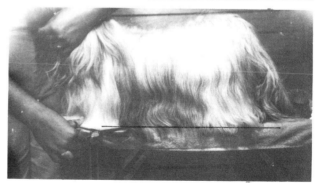

Part the Lhasa's coat and brush it down. Stand the dog at the table edge, both front and side. Use the scissors with the curved blade to trim the coat across the front and around the pads, using the lower edge of the table as a guide. Continue trimming down the side, then turn the dog and trim around the back legs and the opposite side (see line in photos).

87

THE BATH

Once the coat is brushed, the mats are removed, and all the trimming is done, the Lhasa is ready to be washed. Check his ears and "puff" in ear powder, using the special container it comes in and squeezing it, which will help prevent moisture from getting into the ears and also, heaven forbid, prevent fleas from hiding there. You can, if you like, put a drop of mineral oil into each eye to protect the eyes from shampoo.

Prepare the shampoo before washing. Into a large plastic measuring cup pour about two tablespoons of shampoo, plus one capful of flea shampoo, and one capful of flea and tick preventative. Fill the cup with lukewarm water and mix.

Prepare the tub. Fill with at least 6 inches of water (except for small puppies) or water enough to go well up the Lhasa's sides, and drop in two capsful of a flea and tick preventative. The water should always be tepid or lukewarm.

Immerse your Lhasa in the bathwater. Use the small cup to thoroughly douse the coat, being care-ful not to get the flea and tick preventative in your Lhasa's eyes. Spray the head with clear water until thoroughly soaked.

Empty the tub and refill. Pour one-half of the diluted shampoo mixture, about two cups, over the Lhasa. Dip water from the tub with the cup and pour over and through the coat repeatedly. To prevent matting, do not rub or scrub the coat.

Wet a small washcloth, dip into the shampoo, and wash the face thoroughly. You may use diluted shampoo for this purpose.

Rinse the coat of the Lhasa thoroughly while emptying the tub; repeat shampooing, and rinse again.

Then take the creme rinse on your hands and rub over the coat thoroughly, being sure to cover those areas well where your Lhasa may mat: feet, legs, and ears. Then rinse with tepid water. If you are using a creme-rinse treatment, allow it to remain on the coat for fifteen minutes before rinsing.

Allow your Lhasa to drip in the tub for a few minutes.

Carefully brush the hair around the ears and on the head.

Comb facial hair, removing any food or debris.

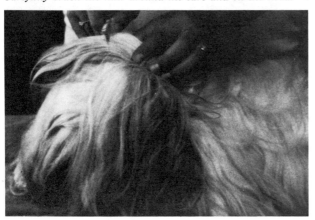

Comb thoroughly the hair under and over the ear.

Ear powder will help keep moisture out of the ear canal.

88

DRYING

Place a towel on your grooming table; position the drier and set the temperature on medium or low (too high a heat dries and burns Lhasa coats). Put the Lhasa on the towel under the drier. For the first half hour, if a thick coat (or fifteen minutes if a thinner coat), allow the dog to drip and periodically comb through the coat with the wide-toothed plastic comb.

The use of human hair products such as Nucleic A *Seal 'N Protect* or *Phlexhair* seems to have an advantage over other products which I have tried in that they cut drying time for most Lhasa coats except on humid days. The length of time it takes to properly dry your Lhasa's coat will depend on its texture and its thickness. Also, the daily humidity will affect this drying time.

When the towel under the Lhasa is soaked, replace it with a dry one. Roll your Lhasa on his back. Comb through the undercoat with the wide-toothed plastic comb; then start brushing gently with the pin brush, directing the drier onto the hair being brushed. Brush the area as thoroughly as possible while it dries. Be sure to do the chest and under the chin area as well as the belly and the legs.

This coat may dry in the first session, but if your Lhasa has an exceptionally thick coat, it may take two or three sessions to dry this underhair.

Turn the Lhasa over; brush the coat up, and then brush down in thin layers with the drier directed on the area which you are brushing. Always do the right side (the side away from the judge) first, and the left, or judge's, side last. Be sure to dry the head area thoroughly, especially around the ears and under the chin. You may discover that with your Lhasa a comb will work better than the pin brush when drying the head area. But always use the comb in a gentle manner; never force or tear through the hair.

Repeat brushing and combing every area of the coat, including the tail, until all is thoroughly dry. Remember, the key word with both comb and brush is gentleness.

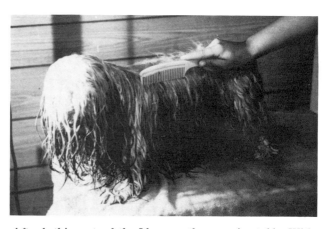

After bathing, stand the Lhasa on the grooming table. With the drier set on medium heat, gently comb through the wet coat with the wide-tooth plastic comb.

Brush the top coat gently with the pin brush until dry. Brushing the coat while it dries will prevent waves from forming.

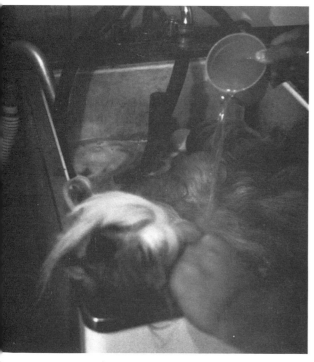

Pour half the shampoo mixture over the coat. Use a cup to dip and pour the shampoo water through the coat.

89

EARS

The hair inside the ears should be removed. When washing the Lhasas or during very humid weather, this hair tends to become damp and may cause an ear problem. For this reason it is suggested that ear powder be "puffed" into the ear as a protective device before washing.

Once the Lhasa is dry, pull the ear hair out with your fingers or use tweezers to pull it out. The Lhasa feels no discomfort when you remove this hair.

Once the hair is removed, take a swab, dip it into vitamin E oil, and clean the ear thoroughly. Some years ago I received a Lhasa bitch whom I was told had a chronic ear problem—that goopy black stuff which indicates an ear infection—which had to be treated repeatedly. I started cleaning her ears with the vitamin E oil, and now it is very rare that she has any ear problems. I believe in preventative care when it is possible.

TEETH

Bath time is a good time to check teeth. Brush them if you like, using a dog toothpaste and a soft toothbrush (so as not to injure the gum). You may also remove tartar with a scaler. Should there by decay or excessive tartar, a trip to your veterinarian for dental care is in order. For dental care, your own veterinarian may refer you to a veterinarian dental specialist. All types of dental repair are being accomplished, albeit this work may be being done in specialized clinics.

TOENAILS

If you haven't already done so, now is the time to clip the nails. Clip back to just before the vein. One way to do this is to place the scissors against the pad and to clip cleanly. This method usually finds the cut made just before the vein. It can be difficult to locate the vein on a black toenail. The vein can be determined by what seems to be a dark line, easily seen on a light-colored toenail. Clip between the end of that vein and the end of the toenail. Always clip so that the cut angles from bottom to top; that is, the cut is deeper at the top of the nail.

Since even the best of groomers sometimes clip a nail too close, causing it to bleed, it is a good idea to have a styptic powder such as *KWIK-STOP* on hand to stop bleeding. If you have nothing else, use cornstarch.

Another method of doing nails is to use a grinder. The grinder actually grinds the nail down to the vein. Grinders are available through pet supply houses. Be careful to keep hair away from the grinder. One professional groomer recommends pulling the nails through an old nylon stocking to protect the hair on the feet of long-coated breeds.

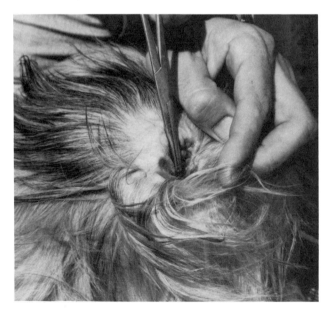 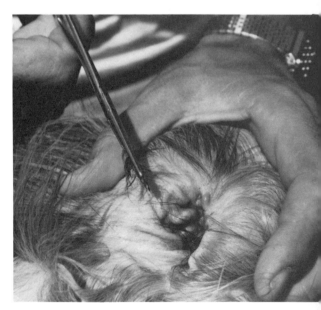

Use a hair pulling forceps, tweezers, or your fingers to remove as much hair as possible from the ear canal and outer ear. This hair forms a trap for dirt and water, which cause infections and other problems.

PADS

Check to be sure that the hair between the pads has been clipped flush with the pads. You may need to trim it again. Your little metal comb comes in handy to comb through this hair, and it also helps to remove any debris caught there. Do not leave any lumps of debris, as they may cause the Lhasa to limp. Sometimes the hair mats into balls between the pads. Use your small comb to be sure that this hasn't occurred.

An untrimmed nail that is too long. Long nails cause splayed feet, interfere with correct movement, and can snag in carpeting. Note that the nails are below the base of the pad.

Use the nail clippers to trim off the curved tip. A gilloutine clippers is shown, but the scissors-type clipper is preferred by many owners.

The correctly trimmed nail does not protrude as far as the base of the pad (see line).

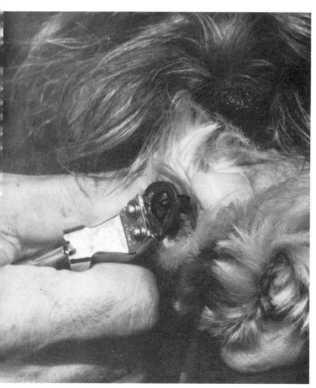

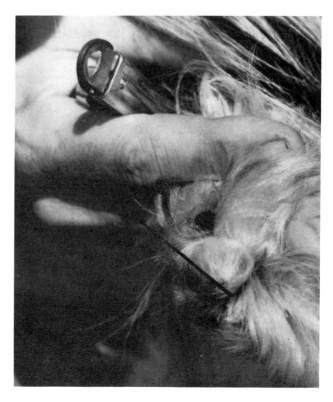

BRUSHING AND PARTING

Now rebrush the coat from the underside up. If necessary, spray lightly with water. Once the coat is hanging neatly, it is time to part it.

A number 6 knitting needle works well. The hair is parted from the nose to the tail. Starting at the nose, go up over the bridge, up over the head to the withers. There you will feel two small vertebrae; go between them and continue down the spine. Make the part as straight as possible. It will probably take practice to part the coat quickly and easily.

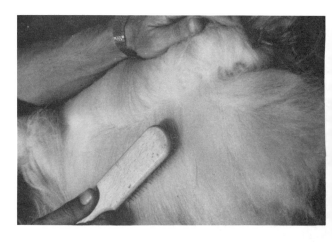

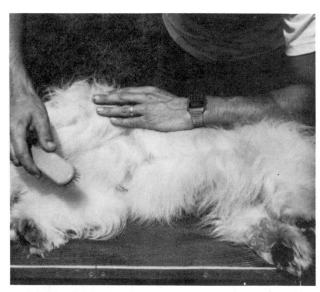

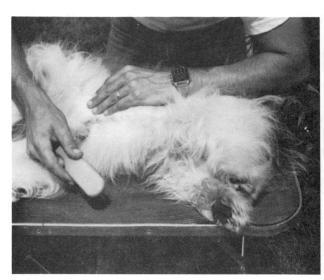

The hair should be combed or brushed in layers. First, brush all hair up toward the part. Then, starting with the belly coat, brush down in thin layers until the part is reached. Always do the judge's (left) side last.

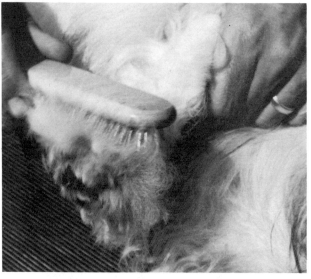

In the final brushing, every hair must lie straight and flat. Begin brushing the legs at the feet and work up, brushing the hair down toward the pads.

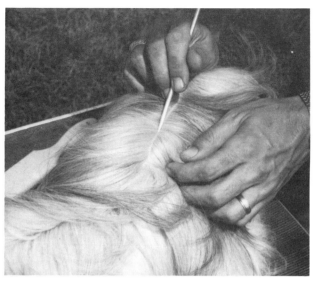

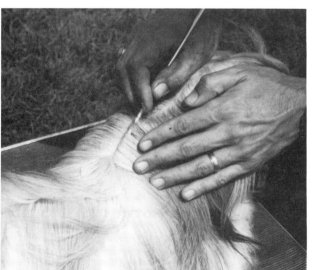

To part the Lhasa's coat, start at the nose, go between the eyes, up and over the head, and down the tail to the back. Use a knitting needle to separate the hair. Use your pin brush to smooth the coat down and spray lightly with water as you go.

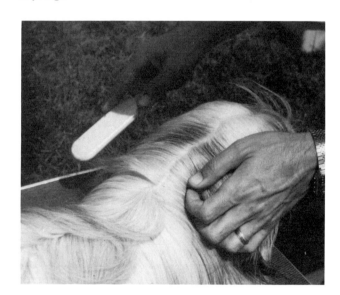

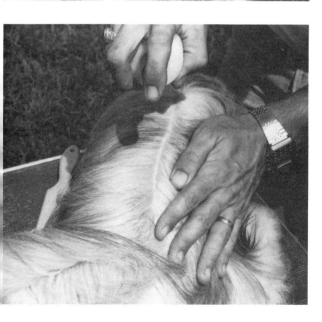

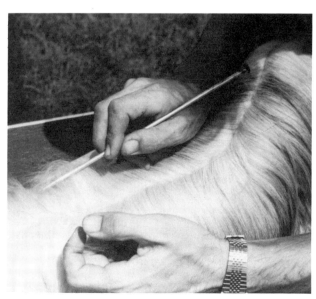

SUBSEQUENT BRUSHINGS

Each time you brush the coat between bathings, spray the coat lightly with either water or a creme-rinse mixture, as described earlier in this chapter. The creme rinse spray is better for the coat which tends to be dry. Always brush from under to top coat in layers. This method will give the smoothest look.

Brushing is essential for a very beautiful coat. Professional handlers spend hours brushing. Proper brushing tends to make the coat lay neatly and to look especially beautiful. The amount of brushing depends upon the individual Lhasa's coat. Some will need daily brushing, some less.

THE LEISURE CUT

Your Lhasa can be given an attractive trim if you do not wish to keep him in full coat. A preferred method is the leisure cut rather than cutting the coat down to the skin. The leisure cut can be given about twice a year and will cut down on matting and on bathing time.

First, pin the top coat up (pinch-type clothespins will work). Brush the legs thoroughly. Trim the foot as previously described. Then scissor, going down the leg much as a Bichon's leg is trimmed. Shape the leg to give a trim pantaloon effect. Do all four legs.

Let the top coat down. Decide on the desired length and trim the coat bluntly at that length. Brush the coat. Then, holding the scissors straight down (or a #4 or #5 blade on a clippers), gradually shape the coat to the body. The chest coat and belly coat may be trimmed and shaped close to the body in the same manner. This trim would be somewhat similar to the Town and Country cut used on Miniature Poodles.

Do not cut facial and ear trimmings unnecessarily short as these maintain the Lhasa appearance. Trim the ears to about shoulder length, and trim the beard and facial hair to about 1 inch below the chin. The head fall can be kept back in barrettes, or it may be cut into bangs over the eyes if you prefer. The tail should be left at full length to maintain the Lhasa quality unless it is unusually long. In that case, see the picture of BIS Ch. Rimar's Rumpelstiltskin in his leisure suit for an idea of the length to trim the tail. Comb the tail and trim to blend in with the balance of the coat.

SPOT CLEANING

For emergency cleaning, *Self-Rinse Plus* or a similar product should be kept on hand. This product can be used alone or with cornstarch. Dilute the rinse about half and half with water and put in an adjustable spray bottle. Spray on the coat in a fine mist and brush dry; or brush dry using a

Ch. Rimar's Rumpelstiltskin in his leisure trim the day after he retired from the ring. Cutting the coat in this manner makes coat care easier and is attractive on the Lhasa. It also prevents the Lhasa from being mistaken for some other breed such as when the coat is clipped in a poodle clip.

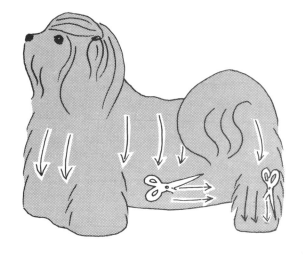

This sketch shows areas and direction for cutting the coat into a leisure suit.

drier; or work cornstarch into the sprayed, dampened coat, and brush out. This latter method works well for removing any stains such as a urine spot on the undercoat, dirt on any part of the coat, or vomit or diarrhea stains.

SHAVING A LHASA

In my book, shaving a Lhasa is a "no-no." Reasonable care should prevent any necessity for it. The fact that the Lhasa is heavy coated does not make it necessary either. The double coat acts as an insulator in both summer and winter. Moreover, most Lhasas who are shaved are traumatized by the experience and may react psychologically, thus affecting their personalities.

BLOWING COAT

A Lhasa Apso will blow coat – either summer or winter coat – during the seasonal changes. Periods of rapidly changing weather, from hot to cold, tend to encourage blowing coat. It is the undercoat which is blown, and this undercoat will usually catch in the top coat. During these periods your Lhasa's coat will need to be combed more often to remove this loosened coat and to prevent matting.

STRIPPING COAT

Should you desire to remove hair from a Lhasa's coat, take your largest metal comb and use it perpendicular to the dog's skin. Draw it down through the dog's coat. This will remove any loose coat and will thin the coat on a very heavily coated dog. Sometimes it is necessary to remove excess coat to provide a smooth silhouette or a balanced look.

FLEA AND TICK CONTROL

Some grooming tricks can help to control fleas and ticks, but even the best tricks may not always prevent the problem. I use a combination attack: yeast internally and dip externally. My Lhasas receive a teaspoonful of brewers' yeast daily in their food.

When the Lhasas are bathed, they are always dipped first. The tub is filled with lukewarm water into which is mixed two capsful of a flea and tick preventative. First I puff ear powder into their ears to help prevent fleas from hiding there. The dog is then immersed in the tub of prepared water, all except his head. Then you have two choices. You may cover the dog's eyes to protect them from the dip and immerse the head under the solution; or you may "hose" the head with the sprayer. Either way, you must soak the head thoroughly.

Also, put a capful of good flea shampoo and a capful of flea and tick preventative into the shampoo mixture as directed on the product.

An old method which not only helps but which also seems to enhance the Lhasa's coat is to use *Creolin,* a type of coal-tar oil, as a dip. *Creolin* can be obtained at your local drug store. For a long time it was one of the few products available for killing fleas. When using *Creolin* as a flea dip, fill the tub as usual and pour in either one or two capsful, enough to make the water milky. It can also be used in the water used to scrub floors in your dog room or kennel. One kennel club in Eastern Canada used it to scrub down the show floor between shows in order to prevent an influx of fleas.

OILING A LHASA'S COAT

Some people oil a Lhasa's coat between shows. Those who do so usually brush the coat at least every other day, adding conditioning oil as they brush to remove any mats or tangles. These Lhasas are usually washed at least every two weeks, and then the process is repeated. Those people who have success with this method are very methodical about the care given the coats. Perhaps some coats are more receptive to this method than others. It could also be that this method works in some areas better than others.

My experience with oil was not impressive; therefore, I do not oil the coats of my Lhasas. One reason is that dirt seems to collect on the coats, and dirt can cause breakage. There is no escaping the "dirt" in the air here, especially when one of the farmers plows a nearby field on a windy day. Removing the oil was a problem, as my skin would not tolerate the shampoo which would work on removing the oil. Moreover, since the oil must be removed with a harsh alkaline shampoo, that seems to defeat its purpose. Remember, too, that a Lhasa may not be shown with any oil in its coat.

There are several other oil treatments which can be used: olive oil, other cooking oils, and mayonnaise. The hot-oil treatment works as follows. First, the Lhasa's coat should be shampooed and allowed to drip off. Warm the olive oil. Part the Lhasa's hair as you do when brushing and apply the oil at the roots; work it thoroughly through the hair, being sure to saturate the ends. Make a hole for the dog's head in a small garbage bag. Put the bag over the dog, and then place the dog under a drier for about ten minutes. Shampoo the Lhasa's coat again. Be very careful about using this method during hot weather as your Lhasa might experience heat prostration, and never use the method with a pregnant bitch.

If you prefer to use corn oil, safflour oil, or sunflower oil, the application method is as above. However, in this case cover the coat with a hot wet towel covered by a dry towel and/or a piece of plastic. The dryer may or may not be focused on the coat for a few minutes. Shampoo and rinse.

Since mayonnaise contains a considerable amount of protein, it can be used on your Lhasa's coat. Apply it to the coat just as clear oil is applied. Then follow with the hot towels as you did with the cooking oils, leaving the towels on up to one-half hour. Shampoo and rinse.

As a precaution, always remember that it is the coat all over the Lhasa's body which is treated. Excessive heat could cause dehydration, could affect body functions, and could cause heat prostration.

WRAPPING COATS

There are a few exhibitors who wrap Lhasa coats much as Yorkie coats are wrapped. Tissues are used in the manner that rags were once used for curling a woman's hair. There are some drawbacks in that the coat must be taken down, brushed, and rewrapped not less than every other day. This can be tedious and time consuming, especially on a very heavy-coated Lhasa.

Another problem is that wrapping tends to crimp the hair, which requires brushing to smooth. In addition, the Lhasa must be continually observed to be sure that neither the wrapped Lhasa nor another chews on the wrappers. A chewed wrapper could result in the loss of a section of coat.

This method has been used by breeder-exhibitors to preserve coats on bitches they have been showing, but which also have been bred. At least one I know who tried it said the puppies chewed on the wrappers and her bitch lost several sections of coat on the judge's side. Some exhibitors use it to prevent urine stain on the coat. In any case, you have to be careful not to pull the hair too tightly so as to irritate the Lhasa's skin, as he will dig and chew at the offender himself.

Very few exhibitors use this method at present.

HEAD FALLS

At home it is a good idea to fasten the Lhasa's head fall back to prevent eye irritation. There are several ways in which this can be done. The simplest method is to pull the coat back on each side of the part and fasten it with *all-plastic* barrettes or latex bands (the small ones used with braces on teeth). Sometimes little bows can be placed on the hair of the bitches.

Some people braid the hair on either side of the head. Others draw the hair into one topknot, like a Shih Tzu's or a Yorkie's. Some oil this facial hair and wrap a single or double topknot in plastic, handiwrap, wax paper, or art foam and then fasten with latex bands.

To braid the topknot hair, first make the center part; then on each side, part the hair from the

Using two barrets is an attractive and easy way to fasten the head fall back at home.

96

corner of the eye to the ear, divide that hair into three parts, and braid as for a child's. Fasten the ends of the braids with latex bands.

The method used is a matter of personal choice. I find that braids take more time and tend to crimp the hair; therefore, I prefer to use barrettes or latex bands.

Some Lhasas have such heavy head falls that they are what we call "ring blind." The head fall prevents them from seeing adequately, and if it is allowed to fall over the eyes, they may actually walk into things. To resolve this problem, a small amount of hair at the top of the eye from about halfway over to the outside corner is drawn back and fastened with a very small latex band.

The balance of the head fall is shaped around the eyes.

After parting the hair, with your hands arch the hair around the eyes so as to frame them. To keep this hair in place while training, rub a small amount

Ch. Chen Korum Ti exhibits the length and thickness of the headfall on a show dog. Kori and his handler, Bob Sharp, were a well-known ring duo in the early 1970's. Owner, Pat Chenoweth.

of a product similar to Wella *Kolestral* between your thumb and forefinger, then rub gently on the "arched" hair. The *Kolestral* must be combed out before taking the Lhasa into the ring, but the effects will last. It will take daily training over a period of weeks to achieve the desired effect on the young Lhasa's coat, especially one with a very heavy head fall.

COAT CONDITIONING THROUGH DIET

Protein is important for hair growth. This protein comes from the food which your Lhasa eats. The body of the Lhasa will draw off the portions it needs, and the balance is available for coat growth. Remember, it is purine, not protein, which causes kidney problems. A Lhasa should have a long coat with a healthy sheen; a dry, scruffy, brittle coat may well be the result of insufficient protein. To retain its natural beauty is essential because the damaged coat takes a long time to restore. The coat which is receiving protein naturally will have a beautiful sheen to it. To me, this is important, as a healthy coat indicates a healthy dog.

The hydrolized animal protein shampoos and rinses with panthenol will protect the hair shaft on the outside. Hair growth is stimulated by proteins and B vitamins from the inside. There are protein supplements such as powdered cheese and oils which are added to food for coat conditioning. Oils were the supplements which I used with my Poodles; however, when I used them with the Lhasas, they developed diarrhea, which is a handicap with long-coated breeds. A daily use of powdered cheese caused the Lhasas to develop mucous in their stools, but by giving about ½ to 1 teaspoon of the cheese once or twice a week, this problem was eliminated. The solution was to feed high protein in the kibble which they received daily.

In the Southwest, pantothenic acid (vitamin B5) tablets are used to encourage coat growth and to enhance coats. One teaspoon of brewers' yeast daily also aids in coat growth and beauty. Vitamin E oil, about one drop daily, also helps in developing a beautiful long coat, and it is said that ascorbic acid, about ⅛ teaspoon daily, should be used in conjunction with vitamin E to maximize results.

Consequently, use protein inside and out, plus vitamins B (especially B5), C, and E, for a beautiful, long, healthy coat.

97

Kin Koe Ganje, owned by Steve and Cherie Newell, practices a Sit-Stay. Photo by Newell.

10

OFF TO SCHOOL

The Lhasa Apso is a very intelligent breed. Most of them not only have the ability to learn, but use that knowledge in different situations. From their beginnings in Tibet, Lhasas have been inner watchdogs with the ability to judge human beings and to determine friend from foe. This act went beyond training. Lhasas apply what they know and manipulate their environments. Just as a child will do certain things to get your attention, so too will a Lhasa in order to change a situation.

Lhasas comprehend to a certain still unmeasurable degree and often reveal a shrewdness. Thus it is that attempts often fail when one desires to form a Lhasa Apso, as in obedience, by instruction, discipline, or drill. One outstanding Lhasa, BIS Kyi-Chu Friar Tuck ROM, was trained for the obedience ring by Ruth Smith. Ruth tells of the time they were in the ring, had started the long sits and downs, when the rain started to fall in torrents. Tuck looked around, got up, and walked from the ring to the judge's tent, where he got himself out of the rain. He could see the obedience ring easily, and when he figured that it was almost time for the long sits and downs to be over, he returned to his place in the line-up. Tuck's reaction to the rainstorm gives evidence of his intelligence and reveals why some Lhasas may not do well in the obedience ring. However, with perseverence and patience they can achieve the Companion Dog (CD) title and perhaps other degrees, and may do quite well in the obedience ring.

Often the meaning of intelligence is confused with that of either to train or to teach. When one teaches another, one is aiding the student to accustom himself to either an action or an attitude. The teacher trains the dog by instruction, discipline, or drill to prepare him for a test of skill and to make him qualified for that skill. Thus, repetition of a drill is a means of teaching a skill. It is the performance of that skill which is important in the obedience ring and also in the conformation ring, in addition to other aspects. Some dogs, like some humans, will respond

well to routine, and some will not. However, the ability to perform a routine procedure does not indicate either intelligence or the lack of it.

Intelligence is comprehension and the ability to apply knowledge to change or to manipulate one's environment. As an example of this intelligence in Lhasas may I present Rumpie and two litters of puppies—eight in all. The puppies were romping on the kitchen floor when one had a small "accident." Rumpie made a special sound in his throat, not a growl, and while I watched he herded the puppies, all eight, to the utility room, where there were papers spread on the floor. He looked somewhat like a mother hen herding her chicks. But the end result was that not one of those puppies had an accident in the kitchen again. All used the papers in the utility room if they were not either in their puppy exercise room or in the fenced-in yard, and all easily house trained at their new homes.

Intelligence does not mean that a Lhasa, or any dog, will do well in obedience training. The Lhasa could become bored with either the obedience ring or the breed ring and will commit some act out of that boredom. Thus, when training your Lhasa, you must convince him that this is what he wants to do. Most Lhasas will participate if only to have your undivided attention.

AGE FOR BEGINNING

Basic lead training is covered in Chapter 18. Here we are concerned with training for the breed ring or the obedience ring, which at the beginning are basically the same. There is one thing to remember and that is that individual Lhasas differ as to the age at which they are willing to conform and the degree to which they will conform.

The period from four to twelve months of age is a difficult time for some puppies. First, they lose their primary teeth and cut their permanent teeth. Should their little jaws be quite tender, they may resist anything around their heads, even leads on their necks. At teething time it probably would be best to avoid excessive lead training. It might even be wise to pass up a match or a handling clinic if they seem excessively tender.

Then, as the Lhasa puppies mature, hormone changes occur. Young bitches experience their first heats between five and nine months of age. The young Lhasa bitch may react to this by dropping her tail, especially in the ring. Young males mature and may even sire litters during this period. This aspect of growing maturity may present a problem in the ring for the young stud when he is confronted with either the odor of or the bitch in heat. He may preen or act up in an effort to attract the bitch's attention, thus destroying his ring image. Another factor that occurs is that suddenly older Lhasas may not accept the younger ones, and may even intimidate them. All of these factors add stress to puppies' lives and are important both in training and in ring deportment.

One puppy bitch of which I know took well to lead training and by the age of two months walked over a mile a day on lead, and was performing well in early matches. However, when she comes in heat, there is no touching her tail nor her rear legs or buttocks. At other times she shows extremely well. Other puppies will not lead train at a young age. I had one that would not walk on lead until she was nine months old, when we accidently discovered that she would walk on a very loose lead, so loose that the lead touched the floor. So puppies differ no matter how enjoyable the training period is.

If some sort of crisis happens while the puppy is on lead, such as his balking or twirling or getting caught in the lead, do not panic or pick up and cuddle the puppy. You may only be rewarding his bad behavior. Be firm with the puppy. Try not to be anxious about the puppy's behavior because your feelings transfer down the lead to the puppy, and later to the adult Lhasa. Try to be positive and go on to another activity.

Some puppies grow up without trauma. They lead train with no problem whatsoever. These puppies enjoy the time which they spend with you. They truly love going to the shows, and unless the unexpected happens, will continue to do so. It is important to make their first matches and shows as enjoyable and trouble free as possible.

The career of one young Lhasa started with a blue ribbon at his first show, Winners Dog and the points at his second, a blue ribbon at his third, and then at his fourth a traumatic experience. Since there was a night guard, he, along with numerous others, was left in a securely fastened crate inside the show building on a stormy winter night. There was a disturbance and the guard left the room for a short time to check out the cause. When he returned, the dogs were in an uproar; he noticed an open crate, and he then discovered a very frightened young Lhasa puppy. What happened is not known, but the puppy experienced both an upset stomach and diarrhea the next morning. Thereafter the ring was not his favorite place to be, although every so often he would again exhibit his early showmanship. It took over a year of patience and understanding to retrain this valuable young Lhasa.

Just as temperament varies from person to person, so does it vary from Lhasa to Lhasa. Each of them is quite independent, and each will react in his own way. If a Lhasa dislikes any part of his training, he will become most resistant. This resistance may be in the form of sitting on his haunches, and no amount of dragging will make him do differently. A very unhappy Lhasa may only indicate this by dragging his tail.

Lhasas are known to do some other weird independent acts. For instance, at least two I know of will give the judge big sloppy kisses if he gets his face too close. Then there is the elegant Lhasa who on occasion refuses to perform by rolling over on her back and kicking her feet in the air.

There is another factor to keep in mind—the judge under which you show your young Lhasa Apso. Many judges are very good with puppies, some are exceptionally good, but some are heavy handed or a bit rough. If you don't know about the judge, find out, and avoid those who are heavy handed to prevent opportunities for trauma with your young Lhasa.

Do not rush your puppy. Make the show or match as pleasant an experience as you can.

SHOW TRAINING

At this point we assume that your puppy is lead trained and is familiar with a grooming table. In preparation for the ring, always reinforce positive behavior. Introduce new aspects gradually. Make the training sessions short. Be careful not to bait excessively. Undertrain rather than overtrain. (Sometimes it seems to me that we practice excessively not for the dog, but for ourselves and for our own confidence.)

As you walk your Lhasa on lead, use proper posture and practice accordingly. Loop your lead neatly as you would in preparation for making a bow, and hold the loop in your left hand. Your upper left arm should be close to your body; at the elbow, bend your arm out at about a ninety-degree angle; hold the lead in your left hand directly above the dog. This method allows your elbow to be the lever which controls the lead. Do not string your dog up. Keep the Lhasa as happy as possible. If he is a driver who thrusts his head forward with movement, remember that this is normal. You will need to gradually train the young dog to carry his head higher by giving short, quick upward jerks on the lead. Should you string the dog up so that the lead is actually lifting the dog up, he will have an abnormal gait.

Your Lhasas should move at a brisk trot. He should not run, as he is not in a race. On the other hand, he should not move too slowly, either. In fact, the Lhasa Apso which moves too slowly indicates that he does not possess the proper drive, and moreover, that slow Lhasa can hamper well-moving Lhasas behind him in line.

Training to stack on a table can start at five weeks.

Thus, as you train your Lhasa, note whether he prefers a firm or a loose lead and encourage him to move at the proper brisk trot. When you are practicing, do not merely move your Lhasa in a rectangle or a square; also practice in the L, the T, or the triangle.

Another aspect to consider is the stop. Learn to judge just how much space your Lhasa needs in which to come to a proper stop (which means that he stands for the judge's observation on returning from an independent gait). For some Lhasas this means that the handler is slightly in front, perhaps with a piece of bait. Some Lhasas will stop in stride beside the handler. You must practice this stop in order to find the one most advantageous to your Lhasa and most comfortable for you. Try to avoid teaching your dog to sit when you stop, especially if you are taking your Lhasa to obedience classes while he is showing in the conformation ring. Sometimes a Lhasa may automatically sit when you stop. Should this happen in the ring, try getting the Lhasa to take a few steps in order to keep him in stance, or drop to your knees and put the Lhasa in show stance.

The first match. Notice how the tail is held in position and fingers under the chin steady the head.

Show training should be fun. It is not always necessary to stack on a table.

As you practice with your Lhasa, carefully observe the length of time which your young dog is willing to participate. The first sessions should be short, perhaps only five minutes, and then gradually lengthened. Remember that the length of time which your Lhasa will be in the ring will be approximately two minutes per dog in the class. Thus, if there are four puppies entered, your Lhasa will have to perform for eight to ten minutes. As you train your Lhasa, start with five minutes, work up to ten, and then later to perhaps twenty minutes. This training time includes gaiting around the ring, the table examination, show stance, and the individual gait pattern.

The table examination includes stacking your Lhasa on a table and the Lhasa's examination by the judge. Simulate this by having a family member or friend examine the Lhasa. Also, if you have an opportunity to attend a handling clinic, give your Lhasa that experience. The opportunity to work with other Lhasas and other dogs can be invaluable.

When you are training your Lhasa to maintain a show stance, use a large mirror or a reflection in a glass door to check the picture which you and

your Lhasa are presenting. Note whether your Lhasa looks best presenting a full silhouette or with his front angled slightly toward the judge. Check the arch of the tail. Practice keeping the tail in place with your hand on the off side and as out of sight as possible. Make sure that you are not hovering over your Lhasa, but that you are presenting him as an exhibit. The Lhasa should be at almost arm's length from you. Practice controlling the lead in such a way that the Lhasa's head is up, but that he is not uncomfortable. One way to do this, especially when training, is to put the lead around your neck from left to right and to use your right hand under the Lhasa's chin with the middle finger in the indentation there.

One thing to remember is that you cannot force a Lhasa Apso to do anything. Your Lhasa must want to do it.

HANDLING CLASSES

Handling classes are usually sponsored by either an all-breed or specialty club. The purpose is both to help the inexperienced handler and/or the inexperienced dog and to make extra funds to be used for club projects. Handling classes are usually directed by a professional handler with a wide variety of experience. There is almost always some fee involved.

The duration of these classes varies. For instance, some handling classes are two-day clinics. At one I attended the instructor spent the morning and afternoon sessions of the first day on basic handling. The second day was spent on fine points and problems. The experience was valuable and confidence inspiring.

The second handling class that I attended was held one evening a week for four weeks. Again, class started with basics and continued through to skills. The use of video tapes enhanced these classes in that we were able to see ourselves as we improved. Knowing that we were making adequate presentations gave us added confidence.

Specialty clubs, such as Lhasa Apso clubs, often run one-session clinics or matches. Our first venture was an evening session for twenty-five people under the direction of a professional handler. It allowed the human participants to gain some basic

While the judge examines the body, steady the dog's head with the lead and your free hand. Talk softly to a puppy while he is being examined to instill confidence.

Place the index or third finger of your right hand into the cleft under the dog's chin. Teach the pup to keep its head high with the neck arched.

knowledge and the Lhasas to gain show experience.

Another venture involved an AKC judge and a professional handler. In this case the judge explained what she was looking for and gave all the different ring directions. The handler demonstrated with a Lhasa in response to the judge's requests and commented on what he was doing and why. After this very valuable exhibition, the club members practiced in a "fun match."

Thus, there are various ways by which to gain beginning experience. Hopefully, you will find a means of gaining this experience in your area. If not, gather some interested people together, get a professional handler, a judge, or some other experienced person to help you, and have your own informal session.

OBEDIENCE TRAINING

If you are interested in obedience, you will usually find obedience classes available. In our area several handlers regularly hold classes, and some classes are even held during adult education sessions at the high schools. These six to nine-week sessions are usually the best way to train both you and your Lhasa for the obedience ring.

Basic obedience training starts with teaching your Lhasa to heel, just as the basic gait for conformation. The best approach is the positive one, according to Miriam Crum, who tells us that a Lhasa may need more than average time and patience in order to convince him to like this experience. She also points out the Lhasa's advantages when it comes to training. The Lhasa strives to please his people, is smart, learns fast and well, and possesses sensitivity.

The Lhasa must know that he is doing what you want, and you must enthusiastically praise all he does correctly. But keep the training sessions short; because he is intelligent, he becomes easily bored.[1] When taking Lhasas to obedience classes, it might be good to have an understanding with the instructor about short sessions for your Lhasa. When one of my Lhasas was in a class, he became bored with the constant heeling exercise. Looking back, I would say that after the third round, perfectly executed, he had had it. He did the sits and downs well the first time or two, then wanted no more. So short sessions are probably the answer.

_____

[1]Miriam S. Krum, "Lhasas in Obedience," _The Lhasa Apso Reporter_ (8, 4) December–January, 1982, p. 56.

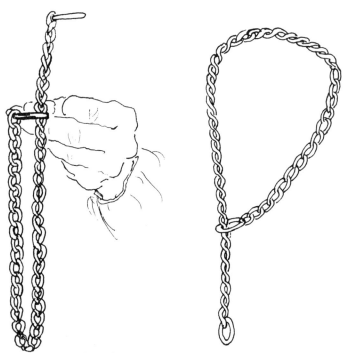

Drop one end of the chain through the ring in the other end to make a loop. Form a "P" with the collar.

Brush the hair back and slide the choke collar over the Lhasa's head. The leash must be on the dog's right with the end to which the leash is attached coming over the neck and hanging down on the right.

Much of what occurs in the obedience ring depends upon many variables: time of day, weather, other dogs, and how your Lhasa feels. Like any athlete, the Lhasa will have good and bad days. His performance is really no reflection on his handler or his training.

Obedience training can start quite early, at about four months of age. The supplies which you will need are a ¼- to ⅜-inch braided nylon choke collar and a matching 6-foot lead. The nylon choke collar is better than the usual chain-link collars as it doesn't tend to catch in the Lhasa's coat. This collar and lead are used only for obedience training sessions or performing.

While basic training can be done individually, your Lhasa will need a group experience. This can be done with a small group or a large group. Young puppies are better off in a small kindergarten group. An older Lhasa can cope with a larger class, but not so large that your Lhasa feels overwhelmed. Instructors at training classes will work with you and your Lhasa on the correct way to heel, sit, stay, down, come, and stand.

Caren Curtiss, professional trainer, is presently training a young Lhasa for the obedience ring. As a four- to five-month-old puppy, he was taught to sit and to stay. Gradually his training has been ex-tended to include all aspects. Caren says the most important thing is to keep the Lhasa puppy happy, to make the training sessions enjoyable. Once he has mastered the various skills, he can then participate at matches by starting in Beginners on Lead or Pre-Novice. The handler and the Lhasa can use the matches to gain experience as a team.

The following skills are those which you and your Lhasa must learn.

Heel – Hold the lead loosely in your left hand and place your Lhasa at your left side close to your leg. Allow your arm to hang loosely at your side and keep your lead slack. Step forward with your left foot, and at the same time say: (Your dog's name), Heel. Give the lead a crisp jerk forward and keep moving. Walk briskly in a natural stride unless you have very long legs, in which case you should shorten your stride. Talk to your Lhasa constantly, praise him, and be careful not to step on him.

To keep the Lhasa's interest, make right and left turns as you go along. Keep your lead sufficiently loose so that you can jerk it after making the turn. Every so often command his name followed by "heel," and praise him for staying in position. To make an about turn, pivot to your right, step forward with your left foot (this time in the opposite direction), and jerk the lead forward after you have

When he is heeling, the Lhasa's shoulder should stay even with the handler's left leg.

turned. Never jerk the lead up; always jerk forward and parallel with the ground.

Do not allow the Lhasa to forge ahead or lag behind you. Encourage him to stay beside you on a relatively loose lead. Do not allow your dog to sniff during practice, because sniffing will cost him points at a trial. Constantly encourage and praise the Lhasa by telling him how good he is, and when the opportunity avails itself, pat him. Never be negative.

When you stop, your Lhasa should sit squarely close to your heel. Say "Sit" at each halt, and encourage him to sit properly. Remember to praise him at the end of each exercise.

Sit – In preparation for this step, take the lead in your right hand and keep it taut. As you say "Sit," jerk the lead up and back with your right hand while pressing down on the dog's haunches with your left. When he sits, loosen the lead promptly, and praise him. Be sure that he sits straight, correcting him if he does not. Return the lead to your left hand and repeat the heel exercise.

Sit-Stay – Hold the loops of the lead in your right hand, with the lead running through your left. The Lhasa will be sitting in heel position. With your left hand held in front of the Lhasa's head, palm toward the Lhasa's nose and fingers to the ground, command "stay." Move very slowly to a short distance in front of the dog; repeat "Stay" only if the Lhasa moves. During different practice periods go farther from the Lhasa until you are at the end of the lead. Also, gradually extend the time he sits. To return to your dog, circle to your right and the Lhasa's left, walk behind him, and move into position at his side. Praise the Lhasa quietly.

Figure Eight – This exercise is required in obedience competition. Two stewards (posts) stand 8 feet apart. You and your Lhasa gait in heel position around them in elongated circles. To prepare for this, walk your Lhasa in circles, which should be done in both directions. Then practice doing the figure eight. Use posts, rocks, or chairs as your posts for this exercise at first, and when your Lhasa becomes proficient at the exercise, substitute people for the inanimate objects.

To start the exercise, stand midway between the two posts, but on a line about 2 feet behind them, with your Lhasa in heel position. Start off in either direction. As you go to the right, stay close to the post. As you go to the left, leave plenty of room between you and the post. Your Lhasa must have sufficient room so that he touches neither you nor the post, and you must not touch him. You should stand straight, schooling yourself not to watch your Lhasa, and walk forward with confidence.

Do not spend more than fifteen minutes on this exercise, nor practice more than three times a week, as your Lhasa will become bored.

Lhasas in Novice obedience class perform the Long Down. They must remain in position without moving for three minutes.

Come Fore – Although this exercise is not required in competition, it is a good base for other exercises. Hold the lead as you did for "Sit-Stay." As you and your Lhasa are walking in heel position, give the command "Come Fore," and walk backwards several steps, keeping your hands in a low position. When the Lhasa hears the word "Come" and sees you moving from him, he should turn and follow you. After the Lhasa turns and is facing you, stop, keep the lead taut, and say "sit." Your Lhasa should sit facing you, close to but not on your feet. You then pivot on your left foot and go into heel position. Praise him verbally and give him a nice pat. Then proceed with the heeling exercise.

Going to Heel – When the judge says "Exercise finished" at the trial, you then order your Lhasa to heel, which he must now learn to do on his own.

With your Lhasa sitting facing you in a fore position, hold your lead in both hands; say "heel" and walk forward to your right and the Lhasa's left. Go past him. He will swing around to go with you and therefore come into heel position. You halt immediately and say "Sit-Stay," and give him the signal to stay. Be sure to praise him.

Do not try to teach all the exercises at one time. Add a new exercise gradually as your Lhasa successfully completes the one on which you are working. Make your exercise periods short. Remember to praise lavishly for correct behavior.

Obedience classes and obedience training for your Lhasas offer many rewards. It is a chance for the two of you to be together in a rewarding experience. Even if you do not plan to show in obedience competition, the classes provide opportunities for socialization. Choose your class and your instructors with discretion. Obedience training for Lhasas should be done with firmness, but not with roughness. Love, patience, and firmness can make obedience training and competition a very rewarding experience for both of you.

Left:
Green Ponds Bow Bay CDX performs the Broad Jump in Open class. Owner, Miriam Krum. Photo by Newell.

Below:
Green Ponds A Golden Glow CDX is completing the Open exercise "Retrieve on the Flat." The handler tossed the dumbbell and the Lhasa went out on command, picked up the dumbbell, and here he has returned to a sit in front. Photo by Newell.

Ch. Lei Roi Sung Chu is an example of the potential which may be recognized in a young Lhasa. Shown at just over a year taking Best of Winners under Anna K. Nichols. He went on to finish his championship at age two. Owner, Elizabeth Faust. Handler, Michael Kemp. Photo by Petrulis.

108

CHOOSING
A SHOW PROSPECT

There is no sure method for choosing a show prospect. If there were, top quality Lhasas would not end up neutered in companion homes, and some less than perfect ones would not be promoted as the elite of Lhasas. Moreover, many things can happen to prevent even the best of Lhasas from doing well in the ring.

Most breeders have difficulty in selecting the puppy with the greatest potential at a young age. Very occasionally a puppy is born which seems extra special to a breeder, but the older any puppy is, the more its potential is revealed. A breeder will have more assurance about a given puppy when he is about a year old. But some are question marks even then. A Lhasa can change from disaster to triumph, and vice versa, in a matter of days or weeks.

An eight-week-old puppy should not be sold as a show prospect. If the puppy appears to have no obvious faults, and if it has an excellent linebred pedigree, the puppy might be said to have show potential, but his price should be about the same as that of a good companion Lhasa.

Buying a show prospect at less than four to five months of age is chancey. No miracles produce a champion. If you are a beginner, you will be learning with this Lhasa, and there is much to learn. That could be a hindrance in finishing the dog unless you are both exceptional and lucky. Therefore, even though having a puppy is fun, if it is a show dog you want, remember that the cute two-month-old may not turn out to be a show dog. A breeder really can guarantee only that the puppy has show potential unless the puppy is a proven, pointed Lhasa.

I prefer not to ship a show potential Lhasa before he is four months old. The Lhasa puppy's second teeth will be erupting at four months of age. If you are very committed about showing, then wait at least until the puppy is four months old and has his permanent teeth. Final size will be more apparent at six to seven months. Although some puppies may have their full growth by then, some with a slower growth

pattern keep growing taller until they are twelve to fourteen months old. The Standard indicates that the maximum height should be 11 inches; therefore, be sure that the Lhasa you choose will be under 11½ inches when fully grown. Knowing something about the growth of the Lhasas in his pedigree may help with this decision.

One thing must be understood and that is that a perfect Lhasa Apso has yet to be born. On the other hand, *some obvious faults should not be found in the show prospect:* crooked or bowed legs; obviously deformed bite—excessively overshot or undershot; blue eyes; liver-colored nose; the smooth coat of a Prapso; a lack of either leg or facial furnishings. The Lhasa must also be free of any negative or congenital conditions: heart, kidney, etc. A male must have two testicles.

HOW DO I DECIDE

Study is your first step. Study the books and breed magazines which concern Lhasas. Peruse the breed Standard. If at all possible, get to a sanctioned show and see Lhasas in the ring. Check with your nearest kennel club for either a reputable breeder or knowledgeable person with whom you could talk.

As you study, make notes about those factors and blood lines which impress you. Collect all the information you can. Even collect pedigrees. Then write or call reputable breeders. Be precise. Tell them as precisely as you can what you want in a show prospect (age, color, bite, sex). Underscore that you wish a show prospect and advise if you will be handling the Lhasa yourself or placing it with a handler. If the latter, advise which handler you are considering. If the former, advise what experience you have had with dogs. Also, enclose a self-addressed stamped envelope. Should the breeder send you pictures, remember that these are to be returned to the breeder as soon as you make a decision.

Another method of finding a show prospect would be to have a professional handler locate several prospects for you and aid you in your final selection. If you choose the right handler, he or she will have contacts to aid you in finding a good Lhasa Apso. After all, if he is to handle the Lhasa, he will want the best available prospect. Moreover, many breeders will not sell their best show prospects to a novice. When the breeders are also exhibitors, they may sell the Lhasa with the proviso that either they or a specific handler shows the dog. Owners will be enthusiastic about good handlers. Also, contact the handlers for rate cards and, if possible, visit their facilities. Be sure that the handler

Sixteen-month-old Kar-Lees Golden Bandit, bred and owned by Carol and Wes Rose. A young bitch with potential. Photo by Joe C.

110

you choose is not only familiar with the care of the Lhasa's coat, but is also gentle but firm.

Finding a reputable Lhasa Apso handler is important. When you visit the shows, note those who are listed as handling Lhasa Apsos (usually indicated in the catalog by the Lhasa's name) and add these names to a list for later consideration. Note the condition of the Lhasa and the handler's methods: smoothness of presentation, sportsmanship, manners in and out of ring, and treatment of the dogs when outside the ring. When the handler is not busy, obtain his address and telephone number. Examine Lhasa specialty and all-breed magazines and note those handlers pictured. Add their names and, if possible, their addresses and telephone numbers to your list.

Next start a process of elimination. Question the owners of handled Lhasas and other exhibitors about the handler. Listen carefully. Should there be a hesitancy in polite response or a careful choice of words, make note of it. These may be warnings.

Since the rates for handlers vary, since those fees are changing at present to incorporate inflation, and since rates may vary per area, it is difficult to state a figure. However, most handlers have a base rate for class dogs, a higher rate for specials, and some even charge additional fees per group placing or for BIS awards. Be sure that all aspects of a handler's fee are clearly stated and understood.

QUALITIES FOR CONSIDERATION

The Lhasa Apso which you choose should be typey; he should fit the breed Standard. His overall conformation should be good. He should have relatively straight legs, a nice shoulder lay-back, a reasonably level topline, a head in a one-third to two-thirds proportion, a decent bite, and a nice tail

Chen Tai-Chi Rani made his mark on the match show scene at only ten weeks. His sire is Am. Can. Ch. Chen Krisna Nor ROM. Owner, Marcia Roth. Photo by Fox.

Bottom
This appealing Lhasa puppy grew up to be BIS Ch. Rimar's Rumpelstiltskin. Head quality, expression, and elegance are apparent.

set. Avoid as a ring prospect the Lhasa that is either cowhocked or sicklehocked. The Lhasa should give no evidence of physical problems when gaiting – an effortless movement is desired.

Temperament is also important. While an outgoing Lhasa may seem to be best for the ring, some of the very best showmen are quiet and may even be aloof! Two of the top all-time Lhasas – Ch. Kyi-Chu Friar Tuck and Ch. Chen Korum-Ti – would be excellent examples of this. The "no-no" factor for temperament is nastiness – particularly biting tendencies.

Color is not of prime importance unless you have a specific color preference. If you choose a parti color, he should be symmetrically marked so that he gives a balanced look. The quality of the coat is more vital than the color, but remember that some Lhasas grow coat more slowly than others. Whether fine or coarse, the top coat should have a hard quality. The older a Lhasa is, the more you can tell about coat.

When a breeder is planning to keep a Lhasa for showing, he or she culls a litter as the puppies grow. Once a breeder knows his or her line well, certain signs will signal the potential of a puppy. For instance, when Lhasa puppies are born, structure is viewable. The lay-back and angulation are apparent, although it must be remembered that this is a tiny puppy. So some tentative choices can be made.

By six weeks, litters can start to be culled for bites. If there is an apparent poor bite, that puppy can be eliminated from the show list. I should underscore that a breeder must gain experience with his or her line to know how much any bite may change. What may be bad for one line may not be for another because of the variables. Experience helps. The second cull for bites may be made at the eruption of second teeth. An overbite or an excessive underbite would be eliminated from the potential show list. The bites the breeder desires are the tight reverse scissors or the level bite. However, remember that these bites may change, that they may still become undershot, until the Lhasas are about eight months old. There may be further change in an adult Lhasa after three years of age; again, the lower jaw may move slightly out.

The breeder may also view tail set, and if a tail is obviously improper, that puppy too may be culled. A gay or loose tail, however, is not reason for culling as this situation can correct itself with hair growth and maturity. Remember that a crook in the end of the tail is not a fault, but rather is a quirk of this breed.

Balance and coat growth will depend on the lines involved. As Lhasas tend to grow at different rates, this fact must definitely be taken into consideration where overall balance is concerned. Coat maturity must be considered in this same manner. Thus a

Misti Acres Gin Jo at four months. Owner, Joan Paul.

breeder's experience with his or her line is invaluable here. (See illustrations in Chapter 18.)

Pedigrees

Pedigrees can be most valuable in selecting a Lhasa Apso, especially if the champions listed are well known. The Lhasas behind the sire and the dam can reveal a great deal: size, silhouette, head, tail set, bite, dentition, color, and gait. Knowledge of the grandparents and great-grandparents may indicate the potential of a Lhasa puppy. (See illustration, linebreeding, Chapter 14).

Pedigrees are relatively easy to read. The name of the Lhasa in question will be located at the left center line of the pedigree. The Lhasas listed above this point will be paternal relatives, and those below will be maternal. This pattern holds true throughout. The male Lhasa is always the top name in a given bracket, and the female is always the lower name.

It may also help to know something about littermates of ancestors. Consequently, the pedigrees can be used as a starting point for the utilization of old magazines and bulletins which may well give you other information.

Faults

No Lhasa Apso has been perfectly conceived. Some fault may be apparent in the show prospect Lhasa Apso which you choose. The degree of the fault is what is important. That fault must be balanced with the overall Lhasa. Some faults you can live with and eliminate through your breeding program.

Head faults are usually the easiest and quickest to eliminate. My personal preference is for a beautiful, well-balanced head, with eyes set to the side

Destined to become a champion! Ch. Joyslyn's Clown Prince, owned by Joyce and Lynn Johanson. Top left, nine weeks. Top right, receiving table training at fourteen weeks. Bottom left, seven months. Bottom right, at three years a finished champion in full coat.

of the facial plane as required by the Standard. The very narrow head is not for me, and neither is the very broad head. But the narrow head bred into some lines will produce a more balanced head. It is this knowledge which is essential in making judgments.

A good bite is also my preference. Mouths are an unstable quality, as two good bites can produce one poor; conversely, two poor can produce good. In breeding, my feeling is that at least one of the pair should have a good bite. The shape of the jaw and the overall expression are more important. A Lhasa which is uniformly good, but which possesses a mediocre bite can finish, and many do. Unlike Miss America, our number-one Lhasa Apso is not allowed a teeth straightening job.

Body structure is another story. Upright, straight shoulders and bowed legs are more difficult to eliminate. Lhasas possessing these traits, unless they are really exceptional in some other ways, should probably neither be aimed for the show ring nor the breeding program. But such a Lhasa might do well in the obedience ring and certainly could make a good companion dog.

A loose tail (that is, a tail not yet curled down to the body) is not a serious fault. Usually with the growth of tail hair and with maturity, this tail will fall into place. And remember, a happy, outgoing Lhasa—a tail-wagging Lhasa—may give this appearance. I shall never forget one judge on hearing me tell Rumpie to keep his tail still, saying to me, "But I love a tail-wagging Lhasa!" While some tails are down over the back at three months of age—and some of these give a flat rather than a balanced appearance—others may not come completely down before a Lhasa is two years old.

A Lhasa Apso that is slow to grow coat can be a good risk, providing that you have the patience

Heritage is important. This lovely puppy became Am. Can. Ch. Kirsna Kam-Tora of Sunji. Sired by BIS Ch. Chen Korum-Ti. Owner, Wendy Harper. To get an idea of how fast the coat comes in, compare this three-month-old coat with the coat length on four-month-old Gin-Jo on page 112.

114

to wait. If you are in a hurry to get into the ring, make a different choice.

Pigment should be black on the nose. Do not accept a self-colored nose on a show prospect. This fault does not apply to the obedience ring.

Temperament

Most Lhasas can be trained to "show." But true showmanship is a very special quality. Many Lhasas have show temperaments; they are trained to perform in the ring. Handlers use all sorts of gambits to get Lhasas to use their best qualities. But showmanship is elusive. A Lhasa which has showmanship says to its audience with every move, "Look at me. I am here." That Lhasa has an electric quality. Most Lhasas, most show dogs of any breed, do not really have this quality. With clever handling some dogs appear to possess it, but true showmanship is revealed regardless of the handler's ability. The handler makes no difference.

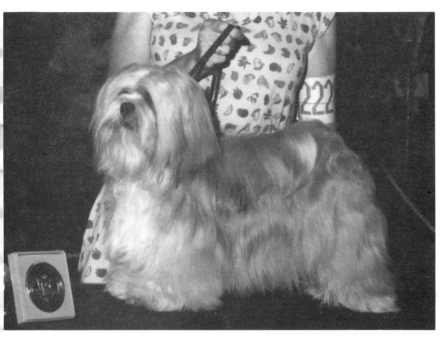

Now Ch. Marlo's I Love Lucy was Best Puppy at the 1980 ALAC Western Futurity. It was her first ring appearance. Breeder-owner, Lynn Lowy. Photo by Yuhl.

Oro's Jazzie Jamie (by BIS Ch. Potala Keke's Candy Bar ex Ch. Oro's Bani Lew) at eight months. Owners, Etta and Harold Orenstein, M.D.

115

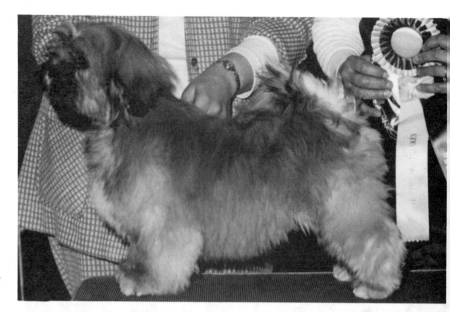

Right:

BIS Am. Can. Bda. Ch. Bihar's Revenger of Sammi Raja at fourteen weeks. Balance, angulation, and showmanship are very evident. Owner, Carol Strong.

Ch. Bihar's Revenger of Sammi Raja as an adult winning Best in Show at the Detroit Kennel Club in 1981 under judge Kay Finch. Handled by Diane Gerthoffer. Owner, Carol Strong. Photo by Booth.

Ch. Cameo's Khor-Ke San O'Honeydew at 5 weeks.

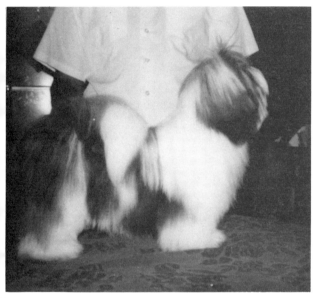

"Korky" at 10 months.

Tn Hi Pixie Minx at 6 months. Breeder-owner, Joyce Hadden.

"Korky" as a Special. He was BOB winner at Westminster in 1981. Owner, Joyce Hadden.

Pixie as an adult bitch.

117

The international show scene—Ch. Chen Korum Ti ROM is shown completing his Columbian championship. Ch. Sharpette's Cicero is second in line. Photo courtesy of Bob Sharp.

12

THE SHOW SCENE

The show bug has bitten. You have started training your Lhasa, and now you want to get involved in showing him.

Before exhibiting in a point show, make an effort to get some experience and observe several shows so that you will have a good conception of what will take place. While you are there, stop at the superintendent's table and pick up some premium lists for upcoming shows.

There are a number of good books about showing dogs written by professionals (see Appendix). Peruse them. Find out all you can from the material presented. However, book learning needs experience to make it viable. There are several pathways to experience: handling classes, club practice sessions, fun matches, sanctioned matches, and obedience classes. Once you have some experience, then brave the point shows.

HOW THE SYSTEM WORKS

Show dogs compete for points toward their championship. A dog must accumulate 15 points, including two majors (3 points or more at one show) in order to become an AKC Champion of Record. The two majors must be won under two different judges. The number of points awarded can range from zero to five, and is determined by the number of Lhasas of each sex entered that day. Points schedules (number of Lhasas required to earn one point or to earn a major) varies depending upon the region of the country. The AKC revises the number of dogs needed to make a major in any one breed on the basis of the number of dogs of that breed exhibited in a given region.

Shows may be all-breed conformation only, all-breed obedience only, all-breed conformation and obedience, or "specialty" (one breed only) shows. Most American shows are unbenched, meaning that dogs may be brought to the showgrounds just before their class and may leave

immediately after showing. A few major American shows and most European shows are "benched"; that is, all dogs entered must remain in assigned "stalls" for the entire day on which they show except for that time they are being groomed and are actually in the ring.

Each breed is judged according to the Standard of perfection for that breed. There are a minimum of five regular classes: Puppy, Novice, Bred by Exhibitor, American Bred, and Open, for each sex. All the males of a breed compete first. Then the winners of all the male (Dog) classes compete for "Winner's Dog" and "Reserve Winner's Dog." The same progression of classes then takes place with the female (Bitch) classes. Finally the Winner's Dog and Winner's Bitch compete with any champions (Specials) of the breed present for Best of Breed, Best of Opposite Sex to Best of Breed, and Best of Winners.

The dog or bitch chosen Best of Breed in every breed that composes a Group will go into the ring again at the end of the day to compete for group placements. There are seven groups: Sporting, Hound, Working, Herding, Terrier, Toy, and Non Sporting. Lhasa Apsos are a member of th Non-Sporting Group along with Bichons Frise Boston Terriers, Bulldogs, Chow Chows, Dalma tions, French Bulldogs, Keeshonden, Miniatur and Standard Poodles, Schipperkees, and Tibeta Terriers.

The seven group winners then compete for th coveted "Best in Show" title.

MATCHES

Fun matches are held by new clubs not yet sanc tioned by the AKC. Sanctioned matches are pu on by recognized clubs for the purpose of trainin club personnel in show skills. The purpose of al matches is for practice and experience. The judge are also there to learn. It is a place for the fledglin handler to learn the ropes and the opportunity fo the inexperienced Lhasa to learn what showing i all about.

Regardless of the type of match, there will b an entry fee involved. A few matches require pre

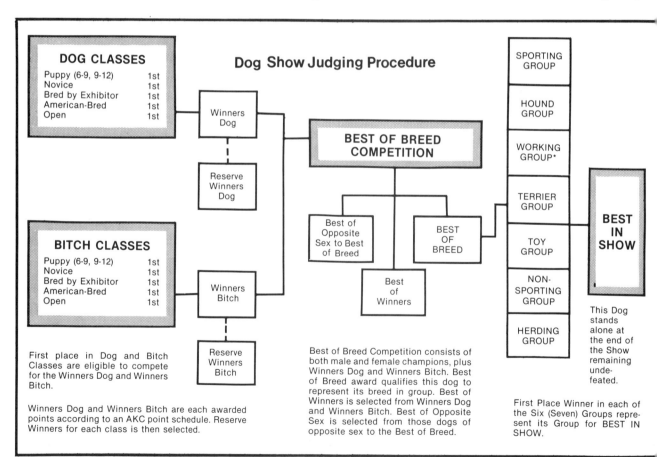

Dog Show Judging Procedure

DOG CLASSES

Puppy (6-9, 9-12)	1st
Novice	1st
Bred by Exhibitor	1st
American-Bred	1st
Open	1st

BITCH CLASSES

Puppy (6-9, 9-12)	1st
Novice	1st
Bred by Exhibitor	1st
American-Bred	1st
Open	1st

Winners Dog — Reserve Winners Dog

Winners Bitch — Reserve Winners Bitch

BEST OF BREED COMPETITION

Best of Opposite Sex to Best of Breed — BEST OF BREED

Best of Winners

SPORTING GROUP
HOUND GROUP
WORKING GROUP*
TERRIER GROUP
TOY GROUP
NON-SPORTING GROUP
HERDING GROUP

BEST IN SHOW

First place in Dog and Bitch Classes are eligible to compete for the Winners Dog and Winners Bitch.

Winners Dog and Winners Bitch are each awarded points according to an AKC point schedule. Reserve Winners for each class is then selected.

Best of Breed Competition consists of both male and female champions, plus Winners Dog and Winners Bitch. Best of Breed award qualifies this dog to represent its breed in group. Best of Winners is selected from Winners Dog and Winners Bitch. Best of Opposite Sex is selected from those dogs of opposite sex to the Best of Breed.

This Dog stands alone at the end of the Show remaining unde-feated.

First Place Winner in each of the Six (Seven) Groups repre-sent its Group for BEST IN SHOW.

entry, and some offer pre-entry to allow you more leeway in arriving, but most matches have a sign-up early on the morning of the match. Judging starts shortly thereafter.

In our area match shows are published monthly in a bulletin. This is a big help. Flyers are often mailed by match-giving clubs, or are placed for the taking at point shows or other matches. You may also find announcements in pet supply stores, or in local newspapers, or hear them announced by local radio stations. Often the news comes by word of mouth.

AKC SHOWS

For your first show it would be better to choose a smaller show as things will not be as confusing as in a larger show.

Show schedules are published well in advance in *Pure-Bred Dogs, The AKC Gazette,* and other publications. Premium lists giving the date, location, judges, entry fee, and other pertinent information are available from the show superintendent. The superintendent will be listed in the announcement, and their address also can be found in the *Gazette.* The closing date for entries to be in the superintendent's office is usually about two weeks prior to the show date. The closing date will be given on the entry form and published in the *Gazette.* Allow about five days for the mail.

Fill in the form completely (see sample). Your check or money order must accompany your entry form.

The entry confirmation and a judging schedule will be returned to you about a week before the show. (If your entry does not make the deadline, it will be returned to you about a week after closing.) Check the judging schedule for directions to the show, the ring time (time when Lhasas are due in the ring), and ring number. Also check your entry to be sure that all the information on your Lhasa is correct.

Classes

Your choice of class will depend upon your Lhasa. *Puppy* classes are for dogs at least six months old and up to one day under one year old. Any purebred puppy whelped in either the United States or Canada, who is registered by the AKC or CKC (and eligible for AKC registration) may be shown in this class as long as he is not an AKC Champion of Record. Classes are divided by sex and also by age (six to nine months and nine to twelve months of age).

Novice is for dogs six months or older that have not won more than three first in Novice, nor won an American Bred, Bred-by-Exhibitor, or Open class, nor any points toward their championship prior to the closing date for the show. This class is not often entered.

Dogs registered by the AKC and not yet champions may be entered in the *Bred by Exhibitor* Class

OFFICIAL AMERICAN KENNEL CLUB ENTRY FORM

West Texas Kennel Club
Oct. 23, 1982
El Paso, TX

I ENCLOSE $ 12 50 for entry fees
IMPORTANT: Read Carefully Instructions on Reverse Side Before Filling Out. Numbers in the boxes indicate sections of the instructions relevant to the information needed in that box. (PLEASE PRINT)

BREED Lhasa Apso	VARIETY [1]	SEX male
DOG SHOW CLASS [2] [3] Open Dog	CLASS [3] DIVISION weight color etc	
ADDITIONAL CLASSES	OBEDIENCE TRIAL CLASS	JR SHOWMANSHIP CLASS

NAME OF (See Back) JUNIOR HANDLER (if any)

FULL NAME OF DOG Charlie's Last Chance C.D.

X AKC REG. NO — Enter number here WE 836468 — DATE OF BIRTH Jan 2, 1980
☐ AKC LITTER NO
☐ I.L.P. NO — PLACE OF BIRTH ☒ U S A ☐ Canada ☐ Foreign
☐ FOREIGN REG NO & COUNTRY — Do not print the above in catalog

BREEDER Sam Superbreeder

SIRE Ch. Everybody's Love

DAM Charlie's Try Again

ACTUAL OWNER(S) Susan Showperson
(Please Print)

OWNER'S ADDRESS 100 Dogtown Rd.

CITY Anytown STATE TX ZIP 68601

NAME OF OWNER'S AGENT (IF ANY) AT THE SHOW I. Handler ID = HAN-4

I CERTIFY that I am the actual owner of the dog, or that I am the duly authorized agent of the actual owner whose name I have entered above. In consideration of the acceptance of this entry, I (we) agree to abide by the rules and regulations of The American Kennel Club in effect at the time of this show or obedience trial, and by any additional rules and regulations appearing in the premium list for this show or obedience trial or both, and further agree to be bound by the "Agreement" printed on the reverse side of this entry form. I (we) certify and represent that the dog entered is not a hazard to persons or other dogs. This entry is submitted for acceptance on the foregoing representation and agreement.
SIGNATURE of owner or his agent duly authorized to make this entry Susan Showperson
Telephone (703) 482-1186

by their breeder owner. They must be at least six months old and must be handled by their owner or an immediate family member.

American Bred is for dogs six months or older that were bred and whelped in the United States or a U.S. Territory. Some people enter inexperienced dogs which they feel are not ready for Open in this class.

All purebred dogs six months or older and registerable by the American Kennel Club are eligible for *Open* Class. This is the only class where imported dogs can be entered. Most Winners come from this class, although occasionally they will come from Bred by Exhibitor or Puppy classes. If your puppy is very mature for his age, you may want to put him in one of the other classes instead of Puppy class.

EQUIPMENT FOR MATCHES OR SHOWS

There are basic pieces of equipment which can facilitate showing your Lhasa. You will need a traveling crate. Air crates are the least expensive, are safe for travel, are easily cleaned, and store in the least space. Other crates which are available include wire crates which collapse and fold up relatively flat, metal crates, and wood crates.

You will need a grooming table. The size will be dictated by your mode of transportation and the size of your Lhasa. Since my early traveling was done in a Volkswagen Rabbit, my first table was 18 × 24 inches. I still use it. You may prefer one slightly larger than this.

You will need towels and/or a grooming table cover and small rug for ringside. A normal-sized bath towel will cover the top of a not-too-large grooming table. Place your Lhasa on it for grooming. A towel on which the Lhasa may stand or lie also can be taken to ringside. To facilitate grooming I made a cover of washable cotton for my table. A variety of pockets hold combs, brushes, and spray bottles.

For ringside a small rag throw rug is quite practical. It will lay flat and provides a clean barrier between the floor or the ground and the dog. Moreover, you can sit or kneel on the rug with your dog while you are waiting your turn. HINT: mark all your equipment and towels in some way—labels, monograms, engraving.

In addition to all else, include paper towels and plastic bags for cleaning up after your Lhasa.

SHOW DAY ARRIVES

Allow yourself plenty of time to get to the show, plan a little extra for contingencies. One exhibitor I know of missed her ring time because she was held up at a train crossing. Allow sufficient time to unpack, groom your Lhasa, and get to the ring on time. If your Lhasa tends to get carsick, be sure to allow sufficient time for him to recuperate and to relax, and also for you to dry his coat and re-groom him if necessary.

Once you are at the showgrounds, hopefully early, find a convenient spot to set up your grooming equipment. Determine where your ring is located and approximately how much time it will take

Show dogs should be trained to relax on the table. Relaxing between classes is BIS Ch. Can. Am. Bda. Ch. Krisna Hy-Lan Krissi, number two Lhasa in Canada in 1981. Owner, Colin Williams. Bred by Wendy Harper, Krissi is the foundation stud for Colin's kennel.

122

to get there. Allow yourself plenty of time to groom your Lhasa and to exercise him within an hour of going in the ring.

If your Lhasa is constipated after traveling, use a suppository (infant size) or the sulfur end of a book match to be sure that he goes. Insert the suppository or match in the anal opening, place the Lhasa in a pen, and wait for him to eliminate, which should occur in a matter of minutes. A Lhasa that has not had a bowel movement may be very uncomfortable in the ring. Moreover, should he have an accident in the ring, he may be upset or may establish a bad habit, you may feel embarrassed, and the judge may be disturbed. Be assured that even exercising the Lhasa does not always prevent accidents, but usually it will.

If it is possible, try to observe the judge's patterns before your own ring time. Also, note the classes within your own breed in the catalog.

Relax as much as you can before it is your turn. Butterflies, or even Flamingos, may be expected to be felt in your tummy. Take your Lhasa to the ring five minutes or so before Lhasas are scheduled.

If Lhasas are scheduled at 11:00 A.M., then be there between 10:45–10:55. If Lhasas are scheduled at 11:00 A.M., but after eight Bichons Frises, six Boxton Terriers, and six Keeshonden, you will have more time to get to the ring. The usual method of figuring is to allow two minutes per dog, which in this case would be forty minutes. However, there could be a few absentees.

Pick up your armband from the ring steward. In Canada all armbands are usually given out at a main location and can be picked up from just before show time onwards. At AKC shows stewards usually give out armbands shortly before various ring times.

Give your dog a last minute touch-up with the brush or comb, be sure that his lead is adjusted properly, and listen for your class to be called.

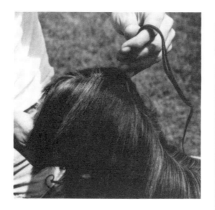

"Set" the show lead by making a part and working the lead down to the skin. Brush the hair down over the lead, making sure there are no tangles and every hair lies smoothly. Tighten the loop on the lead so it fits snuggly around the neck. Any excess lead is gathered neatly into the palm of the hand. The lead can be lengthened easily by dropping more lead, one fold at a time.

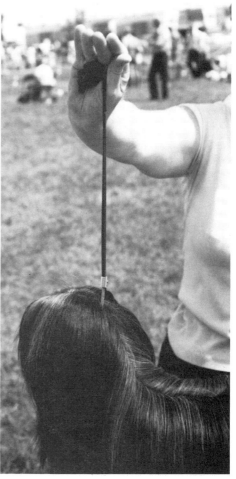

DRESSING THE PART

Whether you are exhibiting, stewarding, or judging, appropriate clothes are a must. Blue jeans—even designer jeans—and other very casual clothes are inappropriate. Excessively frilly clothes, excessively tight clothes, high heels, short skirts, sandals, scuffs, hats, shorts, or revealing tops do not belong in the ring. Also, do not wear gaudy, huge jewelry.

The clothes which you wear should be comfortable and practical. If you are a woman, avoid straight skirts which inhibit your movement in the ring. A-line, gored, or pleated skirts will be more graceful and more comfortable. A wraparound should have plenty of overlap. Remember that you will do considerable bending and kneeling and that you need a place to carry your comb, brush, or bait.

Neat pantsuits or dress slacks also are appropriate. These are especially comfortable in cool weather or in ill-heated showrooms. If you have the opportunity, however, check on your judge. There are a few who still show a preference for women in skirts. A comfortable compromise, especially in the heat of summer, and one which may be very attractive is a "skirt," or pant-skirt. Culottes and gaucho pants also look attractive in the ring.

The top which you choose should be attractive and fit comfortably. Vests and jackets should allow for easy movement. Pockets are handy.

Some women like one-piece sports dresses, which can give a very smart appearance. However, these may present a slip problem, as a slip should not show.

Shoes should be comfortable and safe. Nothing can be more out of place in the ring than improper shoes. For indoor shows consider the soles and the heels. There is nothing more disconcerting than to hear a loud clumping behind you in the ring, unless it is someone twisting an ankle and falling in front of you. Crepe, rubber, or synthetic soles on shoes are quiet and help to prevent unwanted accidents. For wet weather there are some neat shoes made by Gold Seal which take the weather well. A warm, flexible, attractive lined boot can be both comfortable and practical for cold days.

An attractive sweater or jacket for cool days is also a must. Rain gear can be vital. A rain jacket can keep you comfortable during periods of undue precipitation; a lightweight rain poncho can be most practical also. These can be purchased for about $3–$4 from camping supply companies. You can keep your Lhasa completely dry under one as you carry him to the ringside.

Male handlers should also be conscious of their attire. Neat slacks, attractive shirts, ties when appropriate, and jackets or blazers should be chosen. Plaids and stripes that are unobtrusive are acceptable for slacks and jackets. However, wildly flowered or striped pants, shirts, or jackets in loud

A trophy for a bed! BIS Ch. Kinderland's Kishri Ruff, number one by some systems in 1979, poses in his Best in Show silver platter. Owner, Faith Kirk and Ellen Lonigro. Photo by Booth.

colors tend to draw attention from the dogs to the handlers, and therefore would be in poor taste, as would blue jeans.

The male handler should wear comfortable foot attire, and he should not wear a hat. Since traditional custom indicates that a man does not wear a hat indoors and that it is removed in certain situations outdoors (impossible to do while handling a dog), the wearing of a hat in the ring is really a sign of disrespect. If the sun causes a problem, wear sunscreen to protect your skin.

Those who judge, male or female, who must wear hats in the ring for protection from the sun,

should make them as unobtrusive as possible. Also, judges should be very careful of large rings or bracelets which could catch in a Lhasa's coat.

Whether you are handling, stewarding, or judging, comfort on cold days could be most important. Keep at least one pair of well-fitting thermal underwear with your other show clothes.

Lhasa Color and Show Setting

One aspect about showing Lhasas is rarely mentioned. In fact, I often wonder how many handlers take the colors of their Lhasas into consideration

BIS Ch. BarCon's the Avenger is tied with Ch. Jo Jimbo Orion as all time top-winning Lhasas with 14 Best in Show awards. "Rastus" established the record on July 29, 1974. Owners, Connie and Barry Tomkins. Photo by Gill.

when they are planning their entries. Since I read Pat Chenoweth's comments in a magazine several years ago, I have been observing the effects of setting on color. Setting does make a difference. So be aware of your Lhasa's color and the way the setting affects it.

If your Lhasa is white, a cloudy, cool day or a dark building are good backgrounds. When the sun is very bright or the lights glare, the white coat loses distinction as everything tends to blend together, which means that the Lhasa may seem to lack character or specificity. Your clothes can help if they are pastel-colored or not too sharply contrasted with the dog's coat.

On the other hand, your black Lhasa looks best in a brightly lit building, or outside on a cloudy, cool day. Bright lighting is essential for the dark-colored Lhasas to be seen distinctly. The cloudy, cool day is preferable because the dark coat may get a burnt, rusty cast if it is in too much sun, and this same coat absorbs heat and makes heat prostration a definite possibility.

The head of a black Lhasa is the most difficult to make distinctive. An exquisite head may never really be seen because of poor lighting or glaring sun. The color of your clothing can help. Be very careful not to wear a color which "gathers in" the Lhasa; dark colors, blues, and lavender will do this. On the other hand, the color should not present too sharp a contrast because this too can defeat your purpose. Reds, soft yellows, mint greens, and pinks are usually good behind black Lhasas.

Your red Lhasas will always look good in sunlight, but beware of some fluorescent lights, which can make the reds look very drab. Your red Lhasa may allow you more leeway in choosing clothing colors, but look out for reds, magentas, and purples, which tend to "swallow" your dog.

The grey Lhasas can be shown most any place except in very dull lighting without adverse affects. However, your clothing color should present enough contrast to highlight your Lhasa. Greys, light blues, and lavenders are really not effective behind this dog. Harsh colors can also defeat your

BIS Am. Can. Ch. Sun Trader of Bihar takes Group One to finish his Canadian championship, handled by Gregory Strong. Breeder, Carol Strong. Owners, Carol Strong and Judy and Bill Famighetti. Photo by Stonham.

Multiple BIS and group winning Am. Can. Ch. San Jo's Raaga Looki Mei ROM was Canada's number four non-sporting dog in 1978. He was ALAC National Grand Futurity Winner in 1974 and National Specialty Winner in 1979. (Sired by Ch. San Jo's Tonsen Me of Sheridan ex Ch. San Jo's Lena ROM) Co-breeder, San Jo and Raaga Lhasas. Owners, San Jo and Tru Blu Lhasas. Photo by Lindemaier

126

purpose as they tend "to draw eyes away from your Lhasa."

Apricot, gold, and sandy Lhasas can be shown most any place. They can look gorgeous in the sun. Even they, however, can receive a drabbing effect from some lights. Almost any color can be worn with these Lhasas. Choose a color a shade or two darker than the Lhasa's.

Keeping records as to the lighting effects on your Lhasa can be invaluable. Why waste entry money on drab settings which detract from your Lhasa and limit your chances of winning.

JUDGING

The steward will call the classes into the ring in the following order: Puppy Dog; Novice Dog; Bred by Exhibitor Dog; American Bred Dog; Open Dog; Winners, composed of the winners from these classes; Puppy Bitch; Novice Bitch; Bred by Exhibitor Bitch; American Bred Bitch; Open Bitch; Winners, composed of winners of these classes for Winners Bitch; and Best of Breed (which includes all champions [Specials]) and the Winners Dog and Winners Bitch. From these will be chosen Best of Breed, Best of Opposite Sex, and Best of Winners.

Once a class enters the ring, the judge dictates the pattern. At times the dogs will be required to enter and line up in catalog or numerical order. The judge and steward make certain that all the dogs are present; if any are not, the judge's official record and the steward's catalog are noted for absentees. The steward will also tell the judge which numbers have not been picked up and which ones may have been reported absent. During this brief period the judge will be observing the Lhasas. Usually he will then ask that the dogs be gaited once or twice around the ring and that the first dog stop at the examining table and be set up on it. The judge will then examine the dog on the table. Usually, while the next Lhasa in line is being set up on the table, he will ask that the first be gaited individually in either an L, a T, a triangle, or just a "down and back." He will watch the Lhasa closely

Note how the contrasting color of the dress sets off the color of the Lhasa and draws attention to the head and topline. Group winning Am. Can. Ch. Anbara's Abra-Ka-Dabra ROM, dam of multiple BIS Ch. Anbara's Hobgoblin. Sired by BIS Ch. Rimar's Rumpelstiltskin ROM ex Ch. Royal Khetsa Po ROM. Breeders, Barbara Wood and Stephen Campbell. Owner, Barbara Wood. Photo by Gilbert.

One of only four bitches to attain Best in Show in the 1970's was BIS Am. Can. Ch. San Jo's Hussel Bussel ROM, ALAC top winning bitch in 1978. Breeder-owner, Marianne Nixon. Photo by Robert.

as it gaits, and he may ask you to repeat part of the formation.

When all of the Lhasas have been examined and gaited individually, they will line up again. Sometimes the judge will place them in order as he sees them, and other times he will have the Lhasas gait and signal one through four. Each of the handlers will then take his Lhasa to the number signaled, and all others will leave the ring. The judge will mark his record book and present the ribbons.

When your dog or bitch takes its class, providing there is more than one class for that sex, you

Top left:
To pick up a Lhasa, place your right hand beneath the chest.

Center:
Place your left hand between the hind legs.

Bottom left:
Lift the dog carefully and evenly.

Top right:
Steady the head with one finger between the bones at the back of the chin while you set up the back.

Bottom right:
Steady the head and hold the tail gently in position. Note the handlers hands can not be seen from the judge's side.

must remain at ringside until the Winners class is called and then reenter the ring. Courtesy and tradition dictate that the dogs line up in this manner, starting at the front of the line: Open Dog; Bred by Exhibitor; American Bred; Novice; Puppy 9–12; Puppy 6–9. Should your Lhasa be judged the

winner, you must then wait for Best of Breed judging.

If your dog or bitch places second in his or her class, you must also wait at ringside for the judging of the Reserve Winner. If the Lhasa who won your class takes Winners, you then take your dog into

A well-trained dog can be posed with the lead draped loosely over the handler's neck. Note the handler's position and the way she has a comb for last-minute touchups tucked over her armband.

Top left:
The handler steadies the dog, keeping out of the way as the judge examines the front.

Center left:
The judge examines the bite and teeth. (It is more sanitary and some judges prefer for the handler to show the bite by holding back the dog's lips and opening the mouth if requested.)

Bottom left:
Note how the tail is held.

This dog is correctly presented. Note head and tail positions.

the line up in its place and are considered for Reserve Winner. This could be important because in some rare instances the winner is found to be ineligible for some reason and the Reserve Winner picks up the point or points.

When Best of Breed judging is called, the Specials (champions) go in first. Sometimes a judge will separate these by sex also. Next in line is the Winners Dog and then the Winners Bitch. (At a specialty show other classes such as Veterans may have a Lhasa being considered also.) At the end of his judging, the judge will designate the Best of Breed winner, the Best of Winners (between Winners Dog and Winners Bitch), and the Best of Opposite Sex (to the Best of Breed).

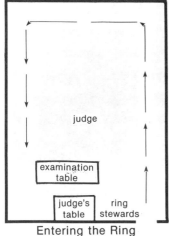

judge

examination table

judge's table   ring stewards

Entering the Ring

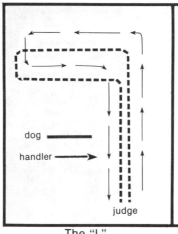

dog ——
handler ——▶

judge

The "L"

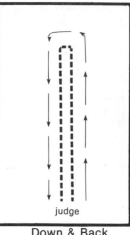

judge

Down & Back

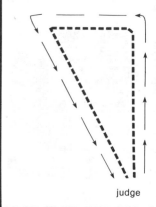

judge

The Triangle

Above:
Direction of movement for group and individual gaiting in the show ring.

Below, left to right:
Jackie Liddle with BIS Ch. ShiSedo's Mo-Li demonstrate ring procedure. During individual gaiting Mo-Li moves alongside her handler, but not too close so that handler and dog interfere with one another. Notice how the handler's body language directs attention to the dog.

A side view during individual gaiting. Leash is held moderately tight but is not putting pressure on the Lhasa's head.

130

Non-Regular Classes

Non-regular classes are usually found at specialty shows, but may be optional choices of all-breed show-giving clubs. Such classes include stud, brood, veteran, and brace classes.

Veterans Class – The Veterans class requires that your Lhasa be at least seven years old. It is open to Lhasas of either sex, and these Lhasas may or may not be champions. At specialty shows the Veterans class is judged after the Bitch classes, and its winner is eligible for the Best of Breed class. Ch. Chen Krisna Nor ROM, at age twelve-and-one-half years, placed first in his Veterans class, then took Best of Breed award, and went on to a Group III.

Stud Dog and Brood Bitch Classes – These classes, which are offered at specialty shows, are judged after Best of Breed. Judging is based on the quality of the offspring. The Stud Dog appears with two or more of his get, and the Brood Bitch appears with two or more of her get. It is not necessary that the offspring be from the same litter nor owned by the same owner. The offspring of the stud do not all need to be whelped by the same dam, nor do those of the dam have to be sired by the same sire.

Brace Class – Brace can seem a strange word, not often printed in premium lists and catalogs. The classes are often found at specialty shows, quite often in Canadian point shows, and more rarely in AKC shows. The Brace class is made up of pairs of dogs which appear to be identical twins – size, shape, color, and markings. Both must have the same owner, they can be either males or females, or one can be a male and the other a female. The odds against having a perfectly matched brace of Lhasas are great.

Let's examine the problem of matching Lhasas to form a brace. Color is the first problem. Lhasas come in many colors, many shades, and many markings. If you are lucky, you have two solid colors that match, but if you have color variety, you may have a problem. Probably parti colors are the most difficult to match.

If you are lucky enough to match colors – the reds, golds, and apricot shades being the most difficult as to shading – you must then match markings – facial, body, legs. Now the size has to be considered. If both are either males or females, the

Lhasas may be quite equal in size. But if you have one male and one female, your bitch will probably be slightly smaller, just as the Standard states. Thus size can be a problem.

There is a variety of bites in Lhasas. Thus your Lhasa may match in every other way, but not their bites.

Working a brace takes practice. The Lhasas must start simultaneously and move together as one dog, staying even, including on turns. The inside dog must learn to slow down, to mark time, while the outside dog makes the turn, and then to match pace. To be effective, a brace must stop simultaneously and the dogs must stack themselves.

Working and showing a brace is a real challenge. I give those who do it successfully real credit for their achievements. My own experience was hilarious. I had two fairly evenly marked Lhasas of equal shades and close in size. They worked quite well together here at home and in parking lots, there being no place else to get experience. They started off in the ring. Then – who knows what happened. They suddenly reversed places by one going over the back of the other. They did this several times, somehow managing not to get tangled, getting everyone – ringside spectators, judge, steward, and myself – laughing so hard we could hardly stand. Suddenly they stood stock still, looked around, got into position, took off and performed in a nearly perfect manner. The next day they performed in a very adequate manner. But I have not had the courage to take them back into the ring as a brace. Brace shows are just too infrequent.

Specialty Shows

Lhasa Apso specialty shows are put on each year by some of the larger Lhasa specialty clubs, and the American Lhasa Apso Club (ALAC) sponsors a national specialty each year. Some of the specialties are held independent of and some as part of all-breed shows. Membership in the ALAC is not a prerequisite for entering the specialty. The ALAC offers special trophies at their specialty each year, which at present is held in a different area of the country each year. At these shows a Lhasa can earn points toward his championship.

Futurities

There are usually five futurity shows each year, in the Northeast, South, Midwest, Far West, and Hawaii. These shows are usually held in conjunction with specialty shows. The judges for these shows are nominated by and voted on by the ALAC membership. Lhasa Apso litters must be nominated for the futurity within ninety days of whelping, by a breeder who is a member of the ALAC. The Lhasa must be at least six months old and not more than eighteen months on the show date. However, he need no longer be owned by the nominator of the litter, who provides the new owners with the litter's futurity registration number. This new owner may show the Lhasa in the futurity even though he is not an ALAC member. In addition to the futurity, the Lhasa must also be shown in a regular class at the associated show. In the futurity the puppies and young Lhasas are entered in class by age and sex: six to nine months, nine to twelve months, and twelve to eighteen months.

A percentage of entry money is given as prize money, and the amounts are usually published in the premium list. Futurities are judged prior to regular class judging. No championship points are awarded to futurity winners.

Canadian Puppy Classes

In Canada, puppy classes are usually designated as Junior (six to nine months) or Senior (nine to twelve months). However, in addition to the regular classes, the puppies placing first in their classes return to the ring for the choice of the Best of Breed puppy, following the breed judging for Best of Breed. The Best of Breed Lhasa Apso puppy is then shown in Group VI along with the other members of that group. The judge then chooses a Best Puppy for Group VI which must stay for Best in Show competition. Thus, in Canada, both a Best in Show and a Best Puppy in Show are chosen.

Note that in Canada if you receive a Best of Breed honor, you must participate in group classes or you forfeit any awards received. Moreover, when you receive that Group I award, you are also obligated to stay for Best in Show, even the puppy.

Show Photographs

When your dog wins, you may wish to have a photo taken to commemorate the event. Advise the steward that you would like a photo taken and ask when the judge will be allowing this (all photos are taken at the judge's discretion).

If the judge's schedule allows, the pictures may be taken at the end of your breed competition. Usually the judge asks that the pictures be taken at the end of each hour's assignment, or if he has a heavy judging schedule, at noon break for morning winners and at end of day, but before groups, for afternoon winners.

It is your responsibility to have your Lhasa all ready for the picture, his ribbons and any trophies at the ring when pictures are being taken.

Best in Show Brace. Suntory Cantata (left) and Suntory Tsoma Nor (right), litter sisters by Sinbad of Abbotsford ex Ch. Suntory Selena. Owner, Cassandra de la Rosa. Photo by Robens.

132

If possible have someone there to check your Lhasa's coat and position to be sure that all is right for the picture. Since you are behind the dog, you cannot see what the camera is seeing. Some photographers do not advise you, perhaps because they do not know your breed.

Sometimes you may need a professional photo of your Lhasa for advertising purposes. The shot does not have to include win signs, ribbons, trophies, judges, and handlers—just the Lhasa. If the professional show photographer is an exceptionally good one, he may also photograph dogs in a non-ring setting when he is not in demand elsewhere. Such shots are excellent for advertisements in stud and bitch issues of breed magazines.

Group Judging

Group judging follows the completion of the judging of the last breed in the appropriate group, which in your case would be Tibetan Terrier in Group VI, Non-Sporting Group.

At AKC shows, group participation is optional. However, unless circumstances prevent it, the appearance of your Lhasa in the group when you have won Best of Breed honors is certainly a courtesy to your Lhasa competitors.

At CKC shows, group participation is required or you lose any honors which your dog obtained, and if your Lhasa took the Breed from the classes, you also lose the points which he gained toward his championship.

BIS Ch. Shisedo's Mo-Li ranked number two Lhasa bitch in 1981 and among the top ten winning Lhasas in 1982. Breeder, Sandy Nyberg. Owners, Billie A. and Samuel L. Shaver, M.D. Photo by Graham.

Number five Lhasa in 1980 was Ch. Blahopolo's Bozo H'Bert. Owner, Tom C. Meador, Jr. Photo by Cott/Francis.

Best of Winners at the May 1981 ALAC Specialty was S. J. W. Waffle Stomper (by San Jo's Raaga Looki Mei ROM ex Ch. San Jo's Kian Kandi Kan), who went on to become one of the top ten in 1982. A sand color Lhasa with black tips, he was bred by San Jo and Wellington Lhasas. Owner, San Jo. Photo by Klein.

BIS Joi San's Happieh Go Luckieh. Owner, Joyce Stambaugh. Photo by Twomey.

133

Best in Show

The winners of each group return to the ring for Best in Show judging. The judge will gait and examine each of them before making his decision.

This is often one of the most exciting times at any show. The crowds, however, except at shows like Westminster, are often minimal. Those involved with the competitors, club members, and a very few spectators may still be around. Others not involved in these final decisions may have driven on to the next show in order to get a good parking spot or may have left for home, especially if they have come from quite a distance.

One benefit of the cluster shows is that the numbers of viewers of the Best in Show awards has greatly increased, at least at all but the last show. Cluster shows take place at one site. Two, three, or even four clubs will go together and hold their shows at one suitable location. There are numerous advantages for all involved. It usually helps to cut costs for the clubs because they can share judges, housing and traveling costs for the judges, and some other show costs, and there is less packing and moving of equipment for show superintendents. Cluster shows have increased the time available for observation, for camaraderie, and for discussion among exhibitors, owners, and breeders since participants are not always packing, rushing, and driving.

WINNING AT DOG SHOWS

Many articles have been published about the methods needed to win at dog shows. Some make it sound easy, but no foolproof method exists. If there were, you could be sure that I would use it to get a maximum return on my investment in entry fees. But I am sure, on the other hand, that a sure method would take all the fun out of it and make it a business. On that score I would want no part of it. I want to win with the best dog.

Below:
Multiple BIS Ch. Windsong's Gusto of Innsbruck is shown winning the Best in Show "blanket of roses" at the Louisville KC in 1977. Owners, Dr. and Mrs. John Lang. Photo by Booth.

Right:
Top winning Lhasa in 1982, BIS Ch. Ruffway-Patra Pololing (by Ch. Ruffway Mashaka ex Ch. Ruffway Tashi). winning the Chattanooga KC show. Handler, Jean Lade. Owners, Victor Cohen and William and Betty Bowman. Photo by Alverson.

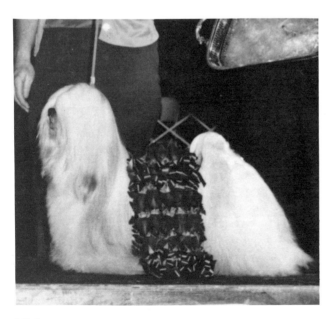

All the articles advise that you must know your dog and be aware of faults and virtues. The problem is that you may then concentrate on the faults, thus calling attention to them, rather than on the virtues. Learn to think positively about your Lhasa. Learn to emphasize these virtues and de-emphasize the faults. For example, if your Lhasa has a beautiful front, angle your dog slightly so that the front is more viewable by the judge. Some professional handlers then call attention to the front by running a hand down the front to call attention to it. Observe the professionals for their "tricks" and try to use them yourself.

Your Lhasa should be conditioned and groomed so that he presents well in the ring. Dog shows may often be noisy places. Consequently, expose your Lhasa to noise and confusion, perhaps at a shopping center.

Be aware of your competition. I know how difficult this may be for a newcomer as you have so much to remember before it becomes second nature. When you have the opportunity, study the other Lhasas. When you are not in the ring, study the other handlers and their Lhasas.

Find out something about the judges. Keep records of the color, type, and size of the Lhasas they place and put up. Also note if the Lhasa was with a handler or owner. Some judges do judge in a set pattern. Note things like: "no black Lhasas placed no matter how good; avoids placing parti colors; placed all reds; likes movement, showmanship, and disregards faults; eliminated viewable faults and placed structurally faulty dogs; impressed with coats and grooming; looks at the person at the end of the lead before looking at the Lhasa." The list is long. It is not always advantageous to know what a judge puts up in another breed because he may have very different ideas about your breed. For instance, a judge may place very small Bichons Frises and then put up huge Lhasas.

Keep records of your own experiences under various judges. Note *if there was consistency in their judging.* Keep a marked catalog with notes about dogs and handlers you competed against. The next time you go under that same judge, note the facts again and compare.

For instance, in my notes judge A likes a typey Lhasa within the height standard and with a lovely head. This judge adores puppies, likes spirit, and reveals no prejudice for color. So I choose a Lhasa to suit the judge's preferences and am conscious of head, size, and spirit.

Judge B, on the other hand, likes a well-bodied Lhasa, does not fault on bites, will even choose an overstandard, and tends to ignore smaller Lhasas. Needless to say, I do not show a small Lhasa under this judge, but instead select one which is about 11 inches.

Judge C always puts up the dog shown by a handler if the handler has an entry. Avoid judge C.

Then there is judge D. This judge takes the Standard seriously, has been known to disqualify and to withhold ribbons, looks at the Lhasas and really studies them, is serious and most professional. You should always make an effort to show a Lhasa under him that suits the Standard. Winning under this judge gives much satisfaction.

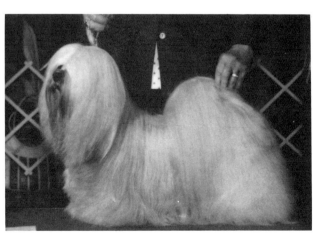

Multiple group winning Am. Can. Ch. Joyslyn's Piece of the Rock. Owners, Joyce Johanson and Ethel Hines.

Ch. Lingkhor Bhu of Norbulingka, son of Ch. Kham of Norbulingka ROM. Breeder-owner, Phyllis Marcy.

SPECIALING A CHAMPION

The dream of many breeders is to produce that Special Champion, which after achieving his championship goes on to fame in the Group and Best in Show rings. Since 1960 some outstanding Lhasas have appeared on the scene. But for every one which makes it, there are many who have that potential who are retired from the ring. One reason that some excellent Lhasas are not campaigned is the cost, which is dear. Another reason might be the lack of maturity of a Lhasa, and then the special qualities might also not be recognized.

Most of the Lhasas who place at the top of the charts are professionally handled, but that is only one aspect of the costs, which also include board, conditioning, advertising, and photos. At least one breeder told me that the cost to special her male Lhasa Apso was over $10,000 in one year. I suspect that some owners spend in the neighborhood of $20,000 on Lhasas that are in the ring every weekend and that are flown to specialties or various large shows in different parts of the country.

For example, according to my records gleaned from the *AKC Gazette,* the top Lhasa in 1980 took Best of Breed awards in seventy-six of the shows in which he was entered, and achieved thirteen Group IV awards, sixteen Group III awards, eighteen Group II awards, fifteen Group I awards, and four Best in Show awards. Through the middle of November in 1981, the top Lhasa had taken the Breed in seventy-one shows, which included ten Group IV awards, seventeen Group III awards, eleven Group II awards, thirteen Group I awards, one Best in Specialty, and two Best in Show awards. So if your aspirations are to have the number-one Lhasa, handler costs alone must be anticipated to include at least one hundred shows, group fees for fifty to sixty shows, and the special fee for Best in Show awards two to five times per year. In addition to these costs would be those for board and conditioning for the year, plus extensive advertising costs. Publicity is very important in the career of the campaigned Lhasa. Advertising is often intensified just before large or important shows.

Most breeders campaign specials on a limited basis, designating a distance radius and the amount to be spent in a given year. These breeders usually are selective as to shows entered and to judges. These Lhasas also are advertised relatively extensively.

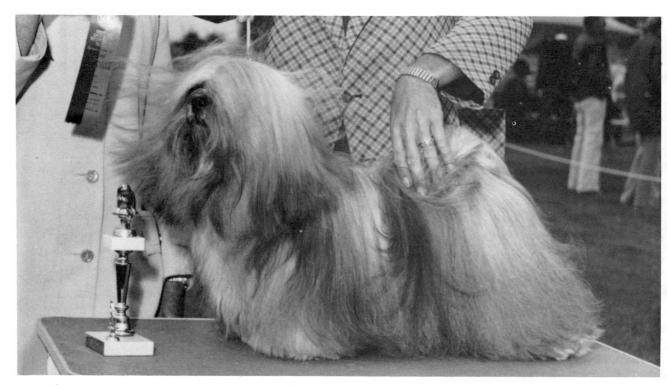

BIS Ch. Yojimbo Orion tied Ch. BarCon's the Avenger's record of fourteen Best in Show awards. Breeder-owner, Elaine Spaeth. Photo by Lindemaier.

136

Aside from the cost of specialing a Lhasa, the dog himself must be considered. He should be worthy of the time, effort, and recognition. He must have superlative health and the temperament to withstand the stress of constant traveling and showing. He should conform to the Standard in all ways, including height.

When a Lhasa finishes his championship at a young age, he often has neither the mental maturity nor the coat needed. Most of the specials seem to "hit their strides" during their third years. It is at this point that they start to make their mark in the ring. Then, if they have physical staying power, they establish a plateau of winning during their fourth and fifth years. Most top-winning Lhasas are retired about age six and return to the ring occasionally at specialties as veterans or as sires or matrons with get.

Mental and physical stamina are important for the special. It would seem, then, that the specials Lhasa would need relaxation time just as do other athletes. The show season lasts almost fifty weeks a year, and although most of the time there are two-show weekends, many times now there are three- and four-show weekends and circuits with from seven to ten shows. The sport which compares most readily with this routine and the accompanying stress would be golf. Just as the greatest golfers—the Hogans, the Palmers, and the Nicklauses—take time off from the tours, so too should our top Lhasas. Thus, plan your campaigning. If the Lhasa has a hectic schedule for the month ahead, try to see that he has plenty of rest and relaxation and perhaps forego a few shows in the previous month. Watch your Lhasa for signs of fatigue—a lack of spark in movement and expression—and, when observed, give him a rest from a few of the shows. The baseball season goes from April to October, the football season from August until December, but the dog show season goes from January through December. We do expect a great deal of our specials.

BEST IN SHOW RECORDS

Early Best in Show performers include: BIS Ch. Hamilton Torma, BIS Ch. Licos Kulu La, BIS Ch. Kham of Norbulinks ROM, BIS Ch. Karma Frosty Knight O Everglo ROM, BIS Ch. Tibet of Corn-wallis ROM, BIS Ch. San Saba Chi Chi Jimi, BIS Ch. Orlane's Good as Gold, and BIS Ch. Kili's Katara of Ketu. BIS Am. Can. Bda. Mex. Int. Ch. Kyi-Chu Friar Tuck ROM set the record of thirteen Best in Show wins before being retired. Tuck's record still holds for parti-colors. He was handled by Robert Sharp, who until the record was tied recently, was the only handler to exhibit five different Lhasas to Best in Show wins. These Lhasas, in addition to Friar Tuck, included BIS Am. Bda. Mex. Col. Ch. Chen Korum-Ti ROM, BIS Am. Bda. Ch. Kinderland's Tonka ROM (four BIS's, record for bitches), BIS Ch. Potala Keke's Zintora, and BIS Ch. Rimar's J. G. King Richard.

Friar Tuck's record was broken by BIS Ch. Bar Con's the Avenger, bred by Connie and Barry Tompkins and co-owned, handled by Dorothy Kendall, who achieved fourteen Best in Show awards. Rastus' record was tied by Orion, BIS Ch. Yojimbo Orion, owned by Elaine Spaeth.

Bob Sharp's record of handling five BIS Lhasas was tied in September 1981 by Annette Lurton. "It was a great thrill," Annette said. She has handled to Best in Show the following: BIS Ch. Joi-San's Golden Mocha of Ky, BIS Ch. Joi-San's Happieh Go Luckieh, BIS Ch. Taglha Kambu, BIS Ch. Kinderland's Kishri Ruff, and BIS Ch. Shishedo's Mo-Li.

Another Lhasa to set a record is BIS Am., BIS Can., BIS Bda. Ch. Bihar's Revenger of Sammi Raja, who is the only Lhasa at this time to have won Best in Show honors in three countries. "Tux" has three Best in Show awards in Bermuda, two in the United States, and four in Canada.

JUNIOR SHOWMANSHIP

Many Lhasa specialty clubs and Lhasa breeders are encouraging girls and boys over ten years of age and under seventeen to participate in Junior Showmanship competition. Junior Showmanship classes are additional classes held at many AKC shows, and a fee is now charged for participation at most shows. Competition is usually keen.

Boys and girls compete together in the following classes: Novice Junior, ten years old but under thirteen, who have won two or less first places in AKC point shows; Open Junior, ten years old but under thirteen, who have won three or more first-place wins; Novice Senior, thirteen but under seventeen, who has won two or less first places in a Novice class; Open Senior, thirteen but under seventeen, who has won three or more first places. The Junior who wins eight or more first-place wins at sanctioned AKC shows during a given year becomes eligible to compete in Junior Showmanship classes at the annual Westminster Show.

To enter Junior Showmanship, the blank entry on the back of the official entry must be used. The information required includes: class, name of junior handler, birth date, address, city, state, zip code, and, if not the dog's owner, the relationship between the junior handler and the dog's owner.

In Junior Showmanship it is the *handler,* not the dog, who is judged. The junior is not allowed to take grooming tools in the ring. The junior handler must not only be able to handle the Lhasa well, but must be prepared to answer questions concerning the history of the breed as well as the structure, care, and grooming of Lhasas.

It takes a great deal of skill to handle a Lhasa Apso effectively in the Junior Showmanship ring, and junior handlers with Lhasas are rising above the prejudices which have appeared to exist concerning small dogs in this competition. To show a Lhasa well, the junior handler should be involved in his training. In fact, it is my firm belief that a junior handler should not be allowed to show any dog for which he has not been responsible for training and showing.

Dress is quite important in the Junior Showmanship ring. Girls are expected to be clad in skirts, neat tops, stockings, and appropriate shoes; boys are expected to be dressed in slacks, sports jackets, and neat shirts.

Lori Dolanch, twelve, is shown winning first in novice division with Kachina Palatala Kambu. Photo by Ashbey.

Below:
Carole McFague is shown handling Ch. McFague's Bo-Jan-Gulls to a junior handling win in 1978. Photo by Ashbey.

OBEDIENCE

Lhasas can do well in the obedience ring. However, this is an activity which you and your Lhasa will not enter until both of you have mastered the exercises as mentioned under training, Chapter 10. In the ring you must follow the judge's instructions and work as a team. Scores are based on a perfect score of two hundred. Errors cause points to be deducted from your score. One hundred and seventy points are needed to qualify. Three qualifying scores, or "legs," are required for the title "Companion Dog," or DC. Qualifying scores must be earned in each of three shows under three different judges.

The classes which you enter at a show are determined by the handler's obedience experience and the titles the Lhasa has acquired. The Novice class is entered in search of a CD (Companion Dog) title.

Section A is for the novice who has never shown in obedience before and who has not handled any dog to an obedience title. Section B is for the experienced handler who has previously handled a dog to its CD or other obedience title.

Open class enables you to qualify a Lhasa for its Companion Dog Excellence (CDX), and it also has A and B sections. More training is necessary for this class as the exercises are more difficult. A Lhasa may also earn a Utility Dog (UD) and a Tracking Dog (TD) and a Tracking Dog Excellence (TDX) and an obedience championship. While Lhasas are capable of obtaining these latter three awards, very few trainers attempt them. Past records reveal that at least four Lhasa Apsos have earned their UD awards. These include: Americal Sandar UD, Ching Ching Choti UD, Mee-Tu of Charmel UD, and Haywood's Alana Pansette UD.

Ch. Innsbrook's Patrician O'Sulan and his daughter (right). Patrick is sired by Ch. Orlane's Inimitable ROM, out of Ch. Innsbrook's Scarlet Lady. Owners, Suzette Michele and Marlene D. Kimbrall.

13

PUBLICITY AND PHOTOGRAPHY

If you have never advertised an animal, placing your first ad may seem traumatic. You may tend to put off advertising, to question its viability, and to wonder what it can do for you. Advertising is really sending out a message to the world about your Lhasas. If you plan to take your breeding program seriously, then advertise your Lhasas and let the "world" know what you are doing.

The first step is the decision to advertise; the second is deciding how to advertise. To help you determine this, study the breed magazine ads. Note the ads which you like: the placement, the words, the print, the pictures. The third step is to determine how much you wish to spend and how often you plan to advertise. Rates are printed in the magazines.

If your Lhasa has done any winning, you may have show photos available. If not, and you are at least a semiskilled photographer, you could take your own or find a local photographer to take one. You will notice that most of the photos tell about a win, but you can use a different type of shot, one which concentrates on something special about your Lhasa.

The last thing to remember at this point is that you do not have to prepare the ad layout if you prefer not to do so. The magazine staff will prepare the ad from your directions.

ADVERTISING PLAN

Perhaps the best way to advertise is to start small and build. There are two ways. Take a kennel card ad which gives the name of your kennel, address, telephone number, perhaps a brief philosophy ("Temperament Our By-Word"), stud service, or puppies. The second way, if you have a litter of puppies, is to advertise in the litter listings.

One thing to remember is not to expect the world to beat a path to your doorway as a result of your ad. Gradually you will get inquiries, but your breed specialty magazines have a limited, specialized audience. But people do read and remember. People do come up to you at shows and do have an idea who you are if you phone them.

If your Lhasa has done some winning, use one of your show photos in an ad, which doesn't have to be a full page. Start with a quarter or a half page and later take a full page. You may, in fact, constantly alter the size of your ad unless you have a contract. Pictures help people to visualize your Lhasas and thus are important in an ad.

Watch for special rates: stud issues, bitch issues, owner-handler issues, puppy issues, special win columns.

Advertising your Lhasa may pay unexpected dividends. Yes, you may sell puppies or dogs, especially if the stud or bitch is a great winner. You may gain stud services. But in addition, your ads make you and your Lhasas known. Thus doors of friendship and other opportunities may be opened.

Free Advertising

If you watch the all-breed magazines, occasionally an announcement will be made that their supply of pictures for Lhasas has been exhausted. They usually request show pictures with vital information, and most will return the photo to you after it has been used if you follow instructions and label it properly on the back.

What to Use in Your Ad

You may have an unusual symbol which you desire to be used in your ads. These illustrations give a custom touch. Usually if it is done in black on white, it will reproduce well. Art should be done fairly close to the size you intend it to be used. Sketches or lettering of noncopyrighted material may be "borrowed," or you may find something in the "clip art" or "press on" material available from your printer.

Also, you may specify a special type. If you are in question, go to a book or stationery store, or a drug store carrying such supplies, and look at the dry-transfer letters. Decide which style you like.

Should you choose to have your picture appear in other than a rectangular shape, that is, in a circle, an oval, or a heart, tell the publisher what you desire in your instructions. *Never cut the picture.*

When sending off photos, be sure that your name, address, phone number, and dog's name are on the back of the picture. Do not write on the photo itself, but rather use a label which can be applied to the photo, or use a rubber stamp. If these things are not available, never write on the back of the photo with a ball-point pen as it tends to damage the picture on the reverse side. Instead, use a felt-tip pen.

Be sure to include all pertinent information in your copy also.

PHOTOGRAPHING YOUR LHASA

Photographing your Lhasa can be fun and most rewarding, but it can also be very challenging. You will, of course, need a camera, fast film, and extra lights if you are taking pictures indoors. If you own a movie camera, you may use that light. Or you could get an inexpensive reflector and use that. Another thing which I have seen used to reflect light is a white silk umbrella, which diffuses the light for a softer picture.

Probably the first thing you must determine is your purpose for taking photographs. You may be taking photos because you maintain memory albums of important things in your life. The photos may be for records of your breeding program, for advertising purposes, or for sending to a prospective buyer. On the other hand, you might be entering a contest. Your purpose for taking the photos may determine how you take them.

Record of Your Lhasa's Life

Often we just snap pictures of a Lhasa's activities or of a Lhasa's growth from puppyhood through adulthood. These are pictures which will probably not be reproduced, and thus top quality is not essential. But, you will want good pictures and could therefore use some of the techniques which follow.

Since photos taken as a record of your breeding program will probably not be reproduced, quality will not be essential. However, you will certainly want your photos to record heads and body structures. These records will show your breeding results and progress. Your photos will need to be clear and precise. Thus some of the techniques should also aid you.

Advertising Photos

When you publicize your dogs, you want to emphasize what is outstanding about your Lhasas. First you must determine if you wish to underscore temperament, coat, head, body structure, fronts, or gaits. Your picture should be planned to emphasize strengths.

When a photo is to be sent to a prospective buyer, the picture must adequately show your Lhasa. A black-and-white photo will certainly emphasize structure. But buyers are often color conscious. To obtain a quick color photo, use a Polaroid. An inexpensive Polaroid will accomplish what you desire, especially with the new color film which more accurately depicts color.

Photo Contests

Photography contests such as those run by breed or all-breed magazines, the AKC *Gazette,* and other sponsors usually provide a theme or frame of reference for your photos. If they do not, establish your own. Determine how you can achieve this theme. Remember, too, that you must abide by the rules of the contest.

In this case your restrictions are also governed by whether or not you do your own processing. Judicious printing of any negative can enhance a photo.

Photography courses are sometimes offered which will instruct you on many aspects, including processing. Your own darkroom can be created without too great an expense if you do not go overboard on equipment. This is not a viable expense unless you are a serious camera "bug."

TECHNIQUES

There are a variety of techniques which can help you improve your photos. For instance, when you are photographing small dogs such as Lhasas, the angle at which the photo is taken can be quite important as it can either distort or enhance the dog. Thus, as nearly as possible the camera lens should be level with the Lhasa whether the Lhasa is on a table, the floor, or the ground.

Cameras today have various markings on the sites. For instance, my 35mm has a small yellow square outlined in the center of the viewfinder which is directed on the dog. The focus of the picture is then directly on the dog in the photo, and not on what is around him.

Try to photograph your Lhasa from his eye level as this will prevent distortion. With a Lhasa, do

Three lovely ladies (left to right): Green Pond's Bow Bay CDX, Green Pond's Ani CD, and Green Pond's Golden Glow. Breeder-owner, Miriam Krum. Photo by Newell.

143

not aim your camera down. This is a mistake made by many photographers, including professional dog-show photographers. The perspective will be distorted, and your Lhasa will appear very short legged and large bodied. Conversely, if you angle your camera up at the Lhasa, your Lhasa may appear long legged and small bodied. Moreover, check the head angle, as this also can be affected. The muzzle may be distorted and look very long or very short if it is angled too much either up or down. As you sight the head, the nose angle should line up so that the tip is not much below the lower eyelid; in fact, it should be just about level.

The angle at which your Lhasa is standing can also make a difference. Do not have the rear closer to the camera unless you wish to elongate your Lhasa. A three-quarter front view is often a good angle to photograph. The front will be placed about four inches closer to the camera than the rear.

If your Lhasa has large eyes, close-set eyes, or a long muzzle, do not take head-on shots. A profile or three-quarter shot would be better. Keep all these things in mind as you are taking your photographs.

The setting for the photograph can also be vital. Your Lhasa will usually be revealed best against a plain background of a contrasting color. If the wall is covered with scenic or striped paper, you might use closed drapes as the background. If you have a folding screen, you might use it or your movie screen. The white screen, the wall, or the folding screen could be covered with a pastel sheet or a piece of fabric. You could use a plain afghan or blanket, or even a woven Indian rug, as a background piece. Another item which could be used is an upholstered loveseat or chair. This item works well with puppies.

Outdoor shots of Lhasas should be taken on flat surfaces or on well-cut grass, as long grass and uneven surfaces would tend to interfere with the photo of the dog. As a background, use a good-sized pine tree, evergreen, stockade fence, or a brick or stone wall. You might also pose the Lhasa on the wall. Oriental-type garden statuary make interesting figures in a picture also.

Personality Shots

If personality is what you wish to reveal, take a head-study photograph. Background can be vital for this shot as you want nothing to detract from the Lhasa. Use a plain background: light for a dark dog (never blue, as it swallows the Lhasa; a pink or mint green might be most effective); darker for a light-colored dog.

The dark dog is usually more difficult to photograph, making judicious lighting essential. For any color, sunlight filtering through trees can be used to highlight a head. You can also use reflector lamps indoors for highlighting. In addition, consider sunlight coming through a window as a highlighter. You will have to observe the highlighting on your Lhasa to select the best angle. The flash on your camera is insufficient when used alone. Without

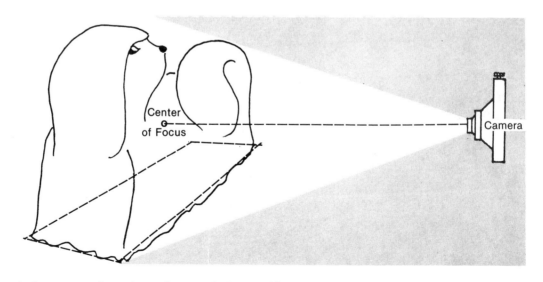

A three-quarter front view makes a good photographic pose. Camera should be at dog's level.

144

highlighting, you may get more detail by overexposing the photo by one or two f/stops.

Head studies necessitate effective grooming. Use a sterile eye wash to clarify eyes. Remove any signs of discharge from the eyes. If there is staining on the facial coat, use cornstarch and peroxide to remove them (see Grooming). Head shots, as they usually are close-ups, will reveal coat quality; so the coat should be clean and well groomed.

As you take these shots, vary both camera and light angles. Determine whether or not you desire a shadow effect, which is controlled both by the Lhasa's distance from a lighted background and the reflection of light.

Use bait, a squeaky toy, or have someone else call the dog's name in order to get variety in expression. In addition, take as many shots as you can so that you have a choice of shots.

One of my favorite head shots is one of Rumpie with the log wall forming a simple, but interesting contrast to his coat and with the morning sun shining through the window highlighting the white

A 1000-year-old breed against a 150-year-old log cabin wall.

markings in his apricot coat. Since the picture is a black and white, the emphasis is on lines and expression rather than color.

Structure

To obtain a picture that reveals structure, at least one handler will be needed if the person is to be in the picture, and perhaps two or three handlers will be needed to get a picture of the Lhasa alone in show pose. Structure photos are usually posed as in show photos.

The background material should be kept at a minimum so as not to detract from the Lhasa. The handler's clothes also are vital and should enhance rather than detract from the dog. Wear light clothes with a dark dog (but never light blue), and clothes in shades darker than the light dog. Avoid large and bold patterns and stripes. If the picture is in color, be sure the colors complement the Lhasa's coat. For instance, do not wear purple or magenta with a red Lhasa.

If you wish to emphasize a good front, aim the front toward the camera in a three-quarter shot. This is also true if your Lhasa has an exceptionally beautiful head with proper eye set. This is not a good shot for the Lhasa with a long muzzle or close-set eyes. It also should not be used unless the Lhasa has good head furnishings. The three-quarter shot will shorten the back length.

Placement and grooming of the tail can also affect the results. Because a Lhasa's tail should balance the head, there should be some arch to the tail. Instead of having a hand in view weighting down the tail, hide the hand off to one side. If you wish to shorten the back or if you wish to emphasize a beautiful, exceptionally furnished tail, allow it to fan over the back. However, if you desire a balanced look, groom the tail to look smooth, collected, and long.

Take a wide variety of shots, especially if you are using a 35mm camera. If you don't want the expense of having them all printed, order a proof sheet.

Once your prints are available for study, examine them carefully and note which ones provide the best pictures of your Lhasa. Use that knowledge in future shots. Don't be afraid to experiment with your camera and your Lhasa. Some of your best photos may result from the unexpected shots.

145

Ch. Tabu's Kiss Me Kate. Sired by Ch. Zijuh Seng Tru ROM ex BIS Am. Bda. Ch. Kinderland's Tonka ROM. Breeder-owner, Carolyn Herbel. Photo by Gilbert.

146

SO YOU WANT TO BREED

Before you decide to breed Lhasa Apsos, even just one litter, consider all that is involved. The facts start with zoning laws and extend to the sale of puppies. The choice of being a breeder of Lhasa Apsos is a serious one. This is a breed, after all, which needs more coat care than some other breeds. Moreover, in many areas it is not yet a well-known breed. Consequently, when you are considering whether or not to breed, remember the care involved, think of the expenses, consider the time, and examine your potential market.

Examine the zoning codes for your area. Some residential codes either prevent the establishment of kennels or place stringent restrictions on them. Here in New York State, three or more dogs constitutes a kennel. Consequently, before you take the breeding step, be sure that you can legally do so in your present location. This could prevent later heartbreak or legal battles.

In addition to zoning codes, check the requirements for use permits, purebred dog permits, kennel licenses, etc. If you must apply for a use permit, do not apply only for today's Lhasas, but project how many you might someday have. Using that number might prevent further aggravations with your planning board.

HOUSING

The next aspect to consider is the housing of your Lhasas. Ample space may be important, and the amount of space needed will be determined by the number of Lhasas which you have. Lhasas may not be mutual friends and thus may need to be separated. Even if you have only two or three, if they do not get along, you must have room to separate them to prevent problems. If you have more than three, the very number may pose a problem.

Breeders cope with this problem in a variety of ways. Almost all have had or have Lhasas who roam the house, and almost all have an area for their Lhasas. Dorothy Cohen (Karma Lhasa Apsos) mentioned that they moved to a new home which had a room for the Lhasas. Some people put on additions; some people use basement family rooms with "walk-out" doors. Some people do as I did and give up a room for them.

My Lhasa living room is 15 × 23 feet and holds fifteen large sleeping crates and nine 3 × 3-foot exercise pens. There are three large windows for light. The floor is covered with linoleum. Another small room is used for grooming. Outside there is a large fenced-in area in which the Lhasas play.

As Lhasas are house dogs, raising them in kennels can adversely affect their temperaments. They need constant contact with life in the home. For this reason you must have space in your home for them to sleep and perhaps to put raised exercise pens for them, especially if you have very many, and if they are being shown.

ECONOMIC FACTORS

The economics of breeding Lhasas can become involved because of the hidden costs. When I started, one breeder told me that she figured her costs in this manner: the sale of puppy #1 = the stud fee; of puppy #2 = veterinary costs and food costs; of puppy #3 = advertising and miscellaneous costs. Her average litter size was four to five puppies. Then there is always the unexpected: the extra visit to the vet, a bad selling season for companion puppies, or a very small or very large litter.

The cost of equipment must be considered. Your Lhasas need sleeping places. The price of pet beds at the present time varies according to type and style, and these may be practical for from one to three Lhasas, but if you have more, other arrangements must be considered. You may need some type of stackable units, which also vary in price and which can be very expensive.

When one is starting out with limited funds, I personally prefer fiberglass air crates because these allow the needed flexibility. For the first few years my Lhasas slept in #200 air crates. Each had his own. Air crates are very stackable and easily moved; they can be shifted around when rearrang-

ing the Lhasa living room. One can easily be pulled out for cleaning, which can be done in a stationary tub. In addition, for puppies who are being prepared for shipment or who are being house trained, #100 air crates, which I use for shipping and motorhome travel, fit easily into the arrangement. The air crates are easily cleaned and sterilized. Moreover, the price of the air crates is reasonable, and they can be purchased as needed. But the new breeder needs to fit these costs into his/her economic plan.

Recently, I was quite lucky to be able to purchase professional stack crates such as used in veterinary offices and pet stores. Since these were second-hand, but in excellent shape, I was able to purchase them at less than one-fourth of the original price. Watch for sales, check ads in magazines and the *Match Show Bulletin,* spread the word around that you are in the market, and you may get lucky.

The benefit of using these stack crates instead of air crates is that the pans beneath the grates can be removed without opening the doors, and there is plenty of room for a Lhasa to move around in the 24 × 24-inch area. A sick dog could be kept in one. My Lhasas sleep in them at night.

Ch. Gin Sing Yoshi Su, foundation bitch for Joan Paul's Gin-Jo Kennels.

The next items to be considered are exercise (x-) pens or puppy play pens. Exercise pens come in folding sections 2 feet wide by two, three, or four feet high and fold out to make a pen at least four feet square. Puppy pens are usually 3 feet square and include a top cover and a raised wire mesh floor with a pan that can be used below the floor or inside it for whelping. I have tried breeding with and without pens, but I much prefer puppy play pens for hygenic reasons. These are used with the Lhasas starting about the puppies' fourth week. Exercise pens can be quite an expense.

The puppy pens are also valuable if you should be showing your Lhasa. These can be used in lieu of public exercise pens and lessen the chances of picking up diseases or parasites. Also, when the ground is wet, raised pens help to keep the Lhasa's coat clean, dry, and neat. These raised pens also provide the Lhasas with a type of isometric exercise which keeps their muscles firm and taut.

Other items of equipment which you will need include a sturdy grooming table and a professional drier – stand type preferred.

Your library will also need to be developed: paper tracts and hardcover books. A library is essential because you need handy information for breeding and knowledge about Lhasas. A book for emergency health care is a necessity. Subscriptions to breed magazines are invaluable.

Another economic aspect is food. If you have not already done so, you might check out distributors of your favorite brand of dog food. Usually the cost at the distributors is cheaper than other sources. And remember, you may have to provide young puppies with formula.

Veterinarian costs are another item to be considered. Be sure to know whether or not you must pay on receipt of services, especially in emergency situations. Ask about breeder discounts, or kennel discounts. At the very least there will be an Oxitocin shot after each whelping, and there will be puppy shots to be considered. So medical funds are necessary.

If you are breeding your bitch and do not own the stud which you plan to use, there is the stud fee to be considered. If there is not a suitable stud in your area, your bitch will have to be shipped for breeding, which will mean extra transportation costs. The choice of a stud then requires a substantial outlay.

Fiberglass airline crates provide security at home and at the show, and are necessary for shipping.

A raised-floor pen is a necessity for showing and raising puppies. One with a top is preferable.

Included with economic aspects are kennel help and personal time. If yours is a family operation, this may not be too much of a problem. Of course, children do grow up and leave home. There are times when all of us can use help. This is a problem each of us must work out. Keep in mind that good kennel help may not be easy to locate and will cost something. In addition to help, there is your personal time to consider. Breeding requires much time and many sacrifices. When whelping time approaches, your time is not your own. You may have to sacrifice social activities. Thus, if social life is important to you, a breeder's life may not be for you. Puppies, too, require much of your attention. You must be prepared not only to give up your social life, but also in emergencies be able to take time off from your employment.

Thus, economic aspects, whether they involve money or time, become very important in your decision about becoming a breeder. When I started out, Lynn Lowy of Marlo Lhasas advised me that it took about eight years to establish a Lhasa kennel. It takes time to gain experience, to develop your own line, and to establish a reputation. Consequently, be prepared to subsidize your venture for some time.

SELECTING YOUR BREEDING STOCK

If you are to breed in a practical manner, certain basic information is necessary. A knowledge of inbreeding, linebreeding, and outcrossing is needed. (These factors are discussed in a later chapter.) Knowing the breed standard is essential. In addition, some understanding of genetics is important.

You need to evaluate your own stock in an unprejudiced manner. You may need to seek help from an honest friend. Personally, I find it beneficial to get this help from someone who is knowledgeable about Lhasas, but who is involved with another breed and has no "axe to grind." For me, this person breeds another nonsporting breed, has had Lhasas in her home, is a match show judge and is very knowledgeable about breeding.

The evaluation of your own stock is vital so that you recognize the faults which you wish to eliminate and the good points you prefer to perpetuate.

Pedigrees

Pedigree research can be vital to your breeding program. But to be helpful, names need to be visual. It is necessary to know about the actual dog.

While pictures can provide a visual concept, these pictures unfortunately do not give us all the information which we need. For example, pictures did not do the famous BIS Ch. Kyi-Chu Friar Tuck justice. His breeder Ruth Smith and his owner-handler Bob Sharp will tell us that movement was vital to his overall picture. Pictures, unless a "scale" is involved, do not tell us how tall nor how long a dog is. Pictures do not provide coat texture and often, either because of the angle at which they were taken or because of corrective touches, do not give true pictures of the dogs. Moreover, no picture can provide temperament.

Thus, it is a difficult job to research pedigrees. But it is an important one. Luckily for me, some of the old magazines have provided some good mental images of Lhasas in my line. Also, many of the important breeders of the 1960s and 1970s

Ch. Kimrick's Jeh Sah Cah, WB at Westminster, 1969, foundation bitch for Taglha. Owner, Jane Browning.

150

have shared material about their top Lhasas. Perhaps some day this information will also be published.

Your Brood Bitch

Usually a breeder starts with a brood bitch, and that may be the best path for you. If you are purchasing a bitch, choose the very best that you can afford. While many breeders are showing their bitches to their championships, this is not absolutely necessary. Moreover, at this point I cannot recommend that you purchase a finished bitch champion, as they do not always make either the best or the most productive brood bitches. Age and previous breeding record should be examined.

Your bitch should have no major structural faults and should possess a good temperament. Evaluate her objectively and thoroughly. List both virtues and faults carefully. Then select her stud with those facts in mind. For example, if your bitch could be faulted on her bite, select a stud with a good bite and full dentition and who tends to produce these qualities. Consider other faults in the same manner.

Another factor to examine is color. Should your bitch be a light color—sandy, gold, light red, or white—check the colors in the three generations behind her. Some say that it is only a tale, but many experienced breeders stress the need for black in their program in order to maintain pigment and depth of color. That black should be in the three generations directly behind your bitch. If it is not there, then you should check carefully the male of your choice for color background. Even with a black in the background (i.e., within three generations), pigment problems and faded colors still may result.

Choosing a Sire

The stud which you choose should complement your bitch. For this reason, do not wait until your

BIS Am. Can. Ch. Arborhill's Rapso Dieh is a stud that appears in many pedigrees. Owner, Janet Whitman, Ja-Ma Lhasas.

151

bitch comes in heat to choose your stud. Stud pedigrees must be checked for linebreeding, inbreeding, or outcrossing information. Then studs need to be examined for faults and your choices narrowed. The stud should be strong in areas where your bitch has faults. Again, this requires expenditure of your time.

Once your stud choice is made, and if you do not own the stud, contact the owner in order to make preliminary arrangements. This should include the stud fee and its payment. Also, the stud owner might not think that the breeding is viable or the stud might not be available, either of which would necessitate another choice. If arrangements can be made, then a knowledge of the stud's whereabouts at the time the bitch is expected to be in heat, especially if the stud is on the show trail, can be vital.

It may be necessary to fly your bitch to the stud. Check the airlines for flight information and cost. Also, make certain how early flight reservations must be made and whether or not the airline carries animals on weekends. Another factor which must be considered is weather: too hot or too cold weather may present a problem when transporting dogs. During the summer of 1980 I found it necessary to drive one of my bitches to Ohio to meet the stud's owner and then to Kentucky to pick her up. The temperatures were so high during the time, that she was unable to be flown either direction.

RESPONSIBILITIES

You are responsible for finding homes for your puppies, unless you plan to keep the whole litter. "Cull" sounds like such a harsh word, but it is necessary to determine early which puppies will be placed as companion Lhasas and which have show potential. You may need the help of your knowledgeable friend to do this.

Involved with the sale of puppies is advertising. Advertising can be a costly aspect of breeding and involves your time.

Also included in the sale is the matching of a puppy to a new owner. This can be important.

Your emotions are also involved in breeding. Sending a bitch to be bred can be stressful, especially when that bitch is a vital part of your life. Selling puppies can also be stressful. Losing a

puppy or two, or even a whole litter, to illness or for other reasons can also be a great strain. You must be prepared to face these aspects.

So you have decided that you are going to be a breeder of Lhasa Apsos. Now *responsibility* is a key word. Do not breed your bitch for the sake of having her have the experience, nor that your children need to be a part of that experience. *If you do not intend to be seriously involved, do not breed.* Avoid using a local stud just because he is readily available. Use the local stud if he fits your breeding program. Learn something about your breed.

As you learn about Lhasas, study the Standard and consider it a guideline. Remove your rose colored glasses and study your bitch. Know her good points and her bad points. Know her pedigree. Choose her stud with those facts in mind. The stud and the bitch should complement each other.

Study, knowledge, and planning should help you avoid indiscriminate breeding.

There are breeders who breed only to make money. They breed indiscriminately and sell at reduced prices. These breeders rarely use studs other than their own, which rarely have been shown in the breed rings. Temperament, size, and standard mean little to them. These people flood the pet market and supply pet stores. They do not know restraint.

As I write this, a law is in the process of being drafted in New York State of importance to us. This law is being prepared to prevent the sale of puppies in retail stores. Should this become a reality, it should be for the good of all dogs.

OUTLINE FOR SUCCESS

Your conception of the ideal Lhasa will be the controlling factor as you outline your plans for breeding and will therefore be your goal. Perhaps an aspect which needs to be kept in mind is that we must live with the Lhasas we produce; so we must be very conscious of temperament. In addition, a beautiful Lhasa coat can cover both good and bad; so the structure of the Lhasa must be kept in mind.

We must also remember that what is winning in the ring may or may not be the ideal Lhasa which fits our Standard, albeit the dog may be in vogue that year. Since our Standard has remained quite constant since its original conception in 1934 with only a few changes, your conception of that Standard should be an important factor in your outline.

It will be necessary then for you to evaluate carefully any stock that you own. List those aspects of each stud and bitch which you wish to retain in your Lhasas; i.e., Bitch D has proper coat texture, proper tail carriage, good eye, good bite. Also consider those aspects which need improvement; i.e., Bitch D could be cobbier and have more leg. In choosing the stud to be used with Bitch D, these latter points would be kept in mind.

Keep notes describing certain Lhasas and keep pedigrees in your file. Stud and bitch issues of breed magazines can be invaluable when searching for a proper stud to use with your bitch or to purchase a bitch to add to your breeding program.

While establishing your plan, also consider how large a kennel you desire, with how many dogs you desire to cope, and how many litters you plan for a given year. In addition, consider the financial investment involved and include that aspect in your overall plan.

Records

Complete and accurate records are very important. The records help you to understand the facts concerning your Lhasas and to evaluate them.

Keeping records can be tedious and time consuming. It is a good idea to have a collection spot for materials until you can get at them on that proverbial rainy day. The difficult thing to know is what materials to keep and what records to maintain.

One method is to purchase a show log which has owner records, show records, breeding records, medical records, and expense records. These show logs are available in handy loose-leaf notebooks or spiral notebooks. They can be very helpful to the novice.

Another method is to maintain a folder for each Lhasa you own. Such things as registration papers, pedigrees, vaccination certificates, health records, show records, and breeding records can be kept there.

Ch. Lori Shan Mona Lisa. Owners, Jackie Hamilton and Lorraine Shannon.

Still a third method is to have a pedigree file, a health folder, a breeding folder, and so forth, which include all the dogs and bitches in your kennel.

In addition to these methods, a second set of records can be valuable at shows when approached for puppies or stud service, and that is a photo album which includes vital statistics for your dogs.

There are two other types of records which you should keep. One of these will be your kennel expense records. This should include a complete breakdown of all expenses involved with your kennel. It should be set up to include daily expenses each month, major expenses, travel expenses, advertising expenses, etc.

The other record should be kept at the end of each year and the beginning of the next. At the beginning of each year a projection of what you hope to accomplish—bitches to be bred, Lhasas to be finished, major kennel improvements, etc.—should be recorded. At year's end you can determine how well you have done as you prepare a brief survey of your accomplishments (and failures) for that year. When you complete that summation, prepare a projection for the next year. These projections and summations provide a guideline for your program.

These latter two types of records—financial and projection/summation—can be very important if you declare your kennel as a business. The IRS may request to see them.

Evaluation

Evaluation for the breeder is continuing and ongoing. There are breeding stock, litters, and overall results to be evaluated.

Culling your litters is a part of your evaluation. Do not rely solely on your own judgment. Find someone who will be very truthful in helping with this project. But don't rule out intuition either. You may have a request for a show prospect. This dog or bitch needs to have certain attributes to win in the ring. You need to separate the show prospects from the companion prospects.

One thing that is obvious in young puppies, sans their future coats, is bone structure. Measure leg bones, and back bones. Use a protractor to check lay-back and angulation. Note tail set. Check the line-up of the jaws. Check for any notable defects. Make decisions as to which Lhasas will be kept and which sold at each cull. If there is a questionable health or structure problem, rely on your vet's advice. Seriously consider selling companion puppies on neutering contracts.

Then, after evaluating your litter, consider whether or not it brought you closer to achieving your goal. You know now the faults and good points

Ch. Queen's Tarakot. This lovely bitch was owned by Jewel Queen, who bequeathed her to Doris Marquez, Dormar Lhasas.

Ch. Taglha Pokhara of Nottoway, dam of several champions. Breeder-owner, Jane Browning.

154

which resulted from the breeding and must determine at what point you are in your plan. You can determine if you have been successful in either eliminating a fault or in passing on good assets.

The most important aspect of a breeding Lhasa is that it produce quality offspring, not its performance in the ring. Perhaps one of the best examples of such a producer is Ch. Chen Nyun-Ti ROM. While he did not become the famous winner that his son Kori did, he produced exceptionally well and has more than twenty champions to his credit. Evaluation of your bitches and studs should include their offspring.

As a breeder you are also responsible for the puppies resulting from your breeding program. Included in your evaluation should be the placement record of these puppies. As a responsible breeder you will probably use sales contracts and screen buyers in order to control pet population and to assure that your Lhasas are getting good homes. You should also determine whether you yourself are raising too many.

To Be or Not to Be

After each annual evaluation, you must reassess your overall plan and goals. To be or not to be a successful breeder will be the end result.

Remember—it will take time to achieve your goals. There are few shortcuts.

Am. Can. Ch. Orlane's Good As Gold (Ch. Quetzal Feyla of Kyi-Chu ex Ch. Kai-Sang Flame), BOB Westminster 1967, Top Terrier in Canada 1967. Owner, Dorothy Kendall. Photo by Ritter.

155

Am. Can. Ch. Krisna Kam-Tora of Sunji with Ch. Krisna Talika, age ten weeks. Owner, Wendy Harper. Photo by Langdon.

15

THE CREATIVE
ART OF BREEDING

Many variables form the breeding scene: genetic inheritance, breeding practices, breeding stock, whelping, nurseries, and markets. All of these must be considered if one is to be a good breeder of Lhasa Apsos.

A knowledge of heredity and genetics could be vital to the successful breeding program. The seeds for this knowledge were sown and reached fruition during the nineteenth century, and from those fruits molecular genetics is rapidly developing. The nineteenth century was dominated by Charles Darwin and his theories about evolution and heredity, and in his shadow is found the work of Gregor Mendel. The at least eight references to Mendel's work between 1866 and 1900 indicate that it was not "lost," but rather was not accepted as it did not fit the recognized observations on inheritance then.[1] It was only after his death that the value of Mendel's work was realized. The writings of twentieth-century geneticists have provided a synthesis of the works of both Darwin and Mendel.

Genetics, especially Mendelian genetics, has never been my cup of tea, probably because I have never felt myself to be science oriented. Moreover, the genetic jargon, the language used, can be most confusing, and the terms are often little remembered by lay people. In addition, the simplicity of Mendel's basic principles gives way to a confusing number of aspects when applied to Lhasa Apsos. The reason for this is that "most characters are controlled by a number of genes acting together and modifying each other's activities, and so simple ratios will not be observed when their inheritance is studied, although each separate gene is inherited in a Mendelian fashion."[2]

---

[1] Richard E. Leakey (ed.), *The Illustrated Origin of Species by Charles Darwin,* New York, 1979, p. 23.
[2] Leakey, *Ibid.*

During the last thirty years, knowledge of genes—their chemical nature, their replication, their influence on the characteristics of organisms, and on their regulation of living-cell activities—has been vastly expanded. Knowingly or not, our breeding programs are formed on Darwin's ideas of evolution and heredity and Mendel's three basic principles, plus these subsequent refinements.

"In dogs there are almost unlimited inherited factors and combination of factors," wrote Lloyd C. Brackett. "The complexity of all these influencing factors is such that any attempt to use the Mendelian theory in the breeding of dogs is, for all practical purposes, out of the question."[3] This is very true, but the advent of molecular genetics, while it adds complexity to the genetic picture, also clarifies our understanding of it. One thing must be remembered: genetics is not a static entity, but is evermore a spiral of information about the living body.

CELLS

All living organisms are composed of cells. In animals these cells usually are round, square, rectangular, egg shaped, tree shaped, or long, thin, and pointed. The shape of each cell is determined by its purpose.

Near the center of each cell is formed the nucleus, the control center which directs the cell's activities. Each cell has its own set of chromosomes, which are strands of chromatin consisting of deoxyribonucleic acid (DNA) and proteins. Every living thing's heredity is determined by DNA, which makes a Lhasa Apso give birth to a Lhasa Apso instead of a Great Dane or a cat. DNA determines thousands of characteristics. The chromosomes are shaped like rods and multiply by division when a cell divides to make two new reproductive cells in a process called meiosis. In each cell of a Lhasa there are thirty-nine pairs of chromosomes, or a total of seventy-eight chromosomes.

Each cell contains thousands of genes, each of which is arranged in a regular space in single file on a specific chromosome. These genes are responsible for all inherited traits. Some genes are dominant (D) and others recessive (d).

FACTORS OF HEREDITY

Chromosomes carrying genetic factors exist in both the bitch and the stud. These chromosomes are found in the nucleus of each cell which possesses pairs of chromosomes carrying complementary sets of genes. The genes located on the string of each matching (homologous) pair of chromosomes are coded for the same characters (bite, angulation, etc.). Each gene on one of the pair has a "sister" gene on the other member of the pair. Just as two human sisters may or may not be identical, these gene sisters may or may not be identical; they control the same characters but do not necessarily produce the same effects on that character. That is, the one may be a dominant expression and the other a recessive.[4]

The reproductive process is an orderly affair. The first step is meiosis, the process of cell division during which the gametes, the special sexual reproductive cells, are formed in both the male and the female. This process starts with the chromosomes pairing off and assuming a side-by-side position. At this point chromosomes may break off and switch with the other half of the pair, a process known as "crossing over." Crossing over accounts for a reassortment of genetic material and for variations in offspring. However, the closer together two genes are in the line on the chromosome lessens their chance of being separated, and these genes will usually be inherited together, which is called "linkage."[5]

The next step of meiosis, the reduction division, is the formation of the gamete containing one-half of each pair of chromosomes. The egg (gamete) from the female is fertilized by the sperm (gamete) from the male, and this union provides a cell with thirty-nine pairs of chromosomes, and that cell develops into the embryo.[6]

It is possible for an offspring to inherit an identical gene from each parent. Such a gene is said to be homozygous. When the inherited gene from one

---

[3]Lloyd C. Brackett, "Planned Breeding," *Dog World Magazine,* Westchester, Illinois, 1961, p. 25.

[4]Leakey, p. 25.
[5]*Ibid.,* p. 24.
[6]*Ibid.*

parent differs from that of the other, the pair is said to be heterozygous. In this latter case the dominant gene is usually expressed, while the recessive gene remains in the background until such time as it randomly pairs with the same recessive gene in some future offspring.

Thus, fifty percent of the genetic makeup of an offspring comes from the sire, fifty percent from the dam. One gene for each trait from the bitch pairs with one gene for each same trait from the stud.

Usually, if the genes from both parents are alike for the same quality (for example, full dentition), then that quality shall be expressed. It is now known, however, that the recombining process, the cross over, which takes place during meiosis makes it possible for pups to have characteristics very different from each of its parents, which is especially true when Prapsos result from the union of two Lhasa Apsos. Prapsos will be discussed later in this chapter. It must be noted that this recombining quality, the crossing over which occurs with a pair of chromosomes, extends the possibilities of gene variations and appears to make genetics a giant guessing game.

GENETICS

When discussing basic genetics, there are some terms which are essential for understanding. A *gene* is a unit of inheritance, the smallest, individual unit of heredity. An *allele* may be any of several forms of a specific gene at a given point on the chromosome. A *chromosome* is the slender "thread" in the nucleus along which the genes are "strung." *Homozygous* means possessing two doses of the same allele of a given gene. *Heterozygous* means having two different alleles of a given gene.[7]

---

[7] William T. Keeton, *Biological Science,* New York, 1972, pp. 841–854.

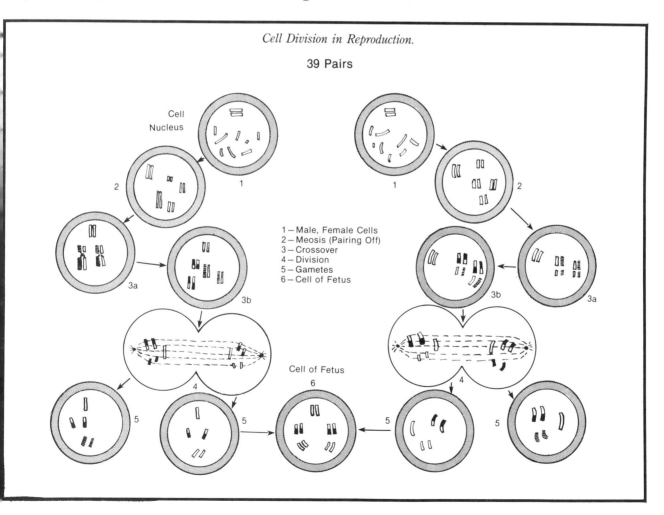

Cell Division in Reproduction.

39 Pairs

Cell Nucleus

1 — Male, Female Cells
2 — Meosis (Pairing Off)
3 — Crossover
4 — Division
5 — Gametes
6 — Cell of Fetus

Cell of Fetus

The offspring (in our case a Lhasa pup) inherits one-half of each pair of chromosomes from its dam and the other half from its sire. Along those chromosomes the genes are strung not unlike a string of pearls. Each gene has a specific place in the line-up. However, the gene expression, or allele, of one chromosome may or may not match that of the other member of the chromosome pair. Moreover, one form of the gene, or allele, may be dominant while the other is recessive. Dominant alleles are written in capitals (DD), while recessive alleles are written in lowercase letters (dd).

Genes do not just exist in two allelic forms, but "may exist in any number of different allelic forms. Of course, under normal circumstances, the maximum number of different alleles for each gene that any individual may possess is two, because he has only two doses of each gene. But many other alleles may be present in the population to which he belongs."[8] This explains some of the varieties which result in the matings of even two seemingly similar Lhasas, even when linebreeding or inbreeding.

The crossing over of chromosomes, the random reorganizing of chromosomes during meiosis, creates genetic variation. Each offspring receives from its parents some combination of the genes possessed by each parent. Another random event which can occur is gene mutation, which produces a novel or new and different gene. Mutations are the sources of new genes and new variations of gene combinations and are also the seeds of evolution. Exposure to radiation (ultraviolet, X ray, gamma rays, or neutrons) and to a host of unrelated chemical compounds can increase the rate of mutations. These factors either "react with DNA bases or interfere with DNA replication."[9]

These mutations can be either deleterious or beneficial. Deleterious mutations cause a reduced fitness among offspring and can also be lethal. These genes are weeded out by natural selection. Certainly a Lhasa carrying a deleterious gene should not be used for breeding.

The beneficial mutations which occasionally occur enhance fitness. It has only been since 1953, when James Watson and Francis Crick announced the "discovery" of DNA (deoxyribonucleic acid, the chemical structure of the gene), that a true understanding of what occurs in the formation of mutants has become possible.

Mr. Leakey describes the DNA as follows: "The genetic message of the DNA is contained in the sequence of bases: three bases taken together code for an amino acid. Thus the string of bases is translated into a string of amino acids, that is, a protein. Occasionally there is a mistake in the replication [copy] of DNA and one base is substituted for another, a base is lost, or one is added. These mistakes are known as mutations."[10]

---

[9]David A. Hopwood, "The Genetic Programming of Industrial Microorganisms," *Scientific American* (Vol. 245, No. 3), September 1981, p. 93.
[10]Leakey, p. 26.

---

[8]Keeton, p. 481.

Male and Female Chromosomes.

2 "X" Chromosomes

"X" Chromosome

"Y" Chromosome

Cell

Cell

Nucleus

Nucleus

Site of sex-linked gene; none on "Y" chromosome

Molecular genetics has provided us with two precise implications. First, the genetic code seems to be universal. The second is the Central Dogma of molecular genetics: that all genetic information flows only from the DNA outwards. This means that the "function of genes is to code for protein assembly. Properly speaking, there are no genes for eye colour [sic] or seed shape; these are merely phenotypic consequences of that protein coded for by the particular gene. The proteins themselves generally act as enzymes: substances which control chemical reactions in the body."[11]

Perhaps at this point it should be stressed that Lhasas, as a breed, from their conception in the years B.C. (before the Birth of Christ) through the nineteenth century, could be considered a "small (restricted) population," not unlike the groups of Amish in Pennsylvania, as the Lhasas were for the most part not only restricted to Tibet, but also to being bred by the Lamaist Buddhist monks or Tibetan aristocracy. Moreover, from the 1930s to the 1960s the Lhasa population in the United States generally was restricted to a small group or community of Lhasas. In cases of small populations, chance can cause a change in gene frequencies, the order in which genes appear. In such small "communities," chance produces "genetic drift," or a random change in genetic frequencies. Thus, the smaller the community, the greater is the effect of the drift when genetic disorders may be caused by recessive genes. These are more apparent in small, self-contained breeding groups.

Genetic disorders, such as those which cause debilitating and lethal kidney disease, or which cause serious stifle problems, or which might be the cause of Prapsos, are the physical manifestations of genetic drift in a small population. Another manifestation of genetic drift is allometric growth; that is, the rates of growth of separate parts differ. Allometric growth might describe the fact that the jaws in Lhasas grow at different rates—upper jaw to lower, from individual Lhasa to individual Lhasa, and from one line of Lhasas to another.

Darwin and today's biologists underscore that natural selection acts on the individual only. Thus, in multiple-birth litters this would explain why a deleterious character would be apparent only in one, or perhaps two puppies.

Even as this is being written, new breakthroughs involving our understanding of genetics are being announced. It is now possible to locate specific chromosomes which are the causes of specific defects. If a gene located in a precise place on the sixth chromosome can be involved in mental illness and can be so specified, it must only be a matter of time before all genes will be able to be so identified. The length of that time will be determined by funds for research and the difficulty of unlocking further secrets of genetics.

Since 1973 the science of genetics has been making giant strides. That year it was announced that "new techniques were developed that make it possible (in principle) to transfer genes from any source into any microorganism. These techniques of genetic engineering are powerful laboratory tools for revealing the structure and function of genes."[12] Biologists are using recombinant-DNA techniques in industry, and they are able to clone almost any desired gene, such as in the making of insulin. Cells are being used to create animal-feed supplements which are protein rich.

What all this means is that in time breeders will be able to eliminate specific deleterious characteristics by very scientific methods. What a long way knowledge about genetics has come during a relatively short time: from the mystery of evolution and Mendelian genetics to molecular genetics. It is in the latter that the answers to the mysteries of breeding lie.

Sex-Linked Characters

In our Lhasa Apsos, the sex of each is determined by a pair of unlike chromosomes, "X" the larger and "Y" the smaller. The bitches inherit two X chromosomes and the studs an X and a Y. The Y chromosome carries few genes, but the X chromosome may carry recessive or dominant genes.[13] Because rare recessive genes tend to be paired with dominant genes on the other X chromosome, these are rarely expressed in bitches. On the other hand, as the rare recessive gene is not found on the Y chromosome and therefore cannot be masked, the males will express the character of the recessive gene.

[11]*Ibid.*, p. 28.

[12]Hopwood, p. 91.
[13]Leakey, p. 24.

However, genes which determine the development of sexual organs are autosomal, or genes other than sex genes, and are present in both dogs and bitches. The different phenotypic expressions in bitches and in studs indicate that these are sex limited. Thus, a monorchid phenotypic would not be sex linked.

Dominant and Recessive Lhasa Characteristics

As far back as 1975 Dr. Catherine Marley, M.D., a Lhasa breeder, stated that much work needs to be done in the genetics of Lhasa Apsos. Now, just as then, we need to know how the dominant and recessive characters behave. Of course, a major problem in our research would be that many traits are controlled by multiple genes.

A breeder must note that in one generation a dominant characteristic can be bred out, and that a recessive trait can be fixed, but that recessive trait will be difficult to eliminate. Inbreeding and linebreeding tend to maintain dominants. Outcrossing can bring in undesired recessives; for that reason, experienced breeders outcross rarely. Recessives may take as much as six generations of breeding to eliminate. To do this, all breeding must be done to known homozygous dominants.[14]

But the problem of determining dominants and recessives remains. The narrow skull, according to general beliefs for most breeds, is a recessive trait. However, if a Lhasa with a broad skull from a line known for broad skulls is bred to one with a narrow skull, the result seems to be a narrow skull, which if bred back to a linebred broad skull, results in a broad skull. Thus, until more research is available, it perhaps is better not to comment. We need to know much more in this area. We need to share information and observations.

COLOR GENETICS

Of importance is the fact that Lhasas, unlike many breeds, have not been bred true to color, i.e.,

consistently blacks to blacks to produce blacks, golds to golds to produce golds. Thus, many Lhasas do not breed true for coat color even when bred to Lhasas of like coat color. Such Lhasas would be termed heterozygous for coat color.

You could work a Punnett Square, devised by Punnett to utilize Mendel's laws, as I did for a stud and a bitch by including all available knowledge on colors from their offspring and from their ancestors. To fulfill the whole range, the bitch would need to whelp sixty-four puppies. Then, when she did whelp, one puppy had a coat color not on the chart. So sometimes it is like pushing the unmarked button on a slot machine and getting a surprise each time. Perhaps that is how Lhasas got the name "Jelly Bean" dogs. Many breeders, including some long-time breeders, reported the same results. In fact, Mary Smart Carter labels her litters as baskets full of colored Easter eggs.

Breeding for the rare colors, the apricots and the blues, sometimes provides surprises. Neither color appears to be dominant. When bred to other colors, those litters about which I know have turned up an apricot or blue in a ratio of about 3:1 (3 others: 1 apricot/blue) when one of the parents was either an apricot or a blue. However, in the cases of apricot-red-gold breedings, the ratio was about 2:4 (2 apricot: 4 others) in litters of six or seven. (A true apricot, by the way, has no black showing at the part.)

Periodically using a black with the very light colors is recommended for retaining black pigment and for avoiding the faded-color syndrome. Each time a black is used with a "color," though, confusion as to resulting colors may be deepened.

One aspect which may have led to the confusion in colors has been breeding practices which emphasize conformation with disregard to color. However, a survey of American kennels has revealed that some kennels, once they have obtained other qualities, are doing some breeding for color consistency.

One other factor about Lhasa coat color should be mentioned. Coat colors tend to change throughout the Lhasas' lifetimes. Some Lhasas (apricots, true blacks, and blues) tend to be born that color and stay that color. Some puppies are born deep shades, such as Irish-setter red, which for some stay and which for some lighten substantially. Some are born black and may take a year or two,

---

[14]Catherine Avery Marley M.D., "Genetics," Part III, *The Lhasa Apso Reporter* (Volume 1, Number 5), February/March 1975, pp. 2–4.

or even three, to turn grey. Light-gold, light-red, or cream-colored pups may be born with dark overlays which grow out, leaving solid-colored dogs.

Often the amount of sunlight affects the coat. While it may cause one Lhasa's coat to lighten, it may also cause another to darken. If you look closely at the coats of many of the light-colored Lhasas, you will see very subtle shadings. Thus, determining the genetics of Lhasa coat colors is a very intricate matter.

PRAPSOS

Occasionally, there is an "odd" occurrence during whelpings. It is not restricted to Lhasa Apsos, but occurs in other breeds as well. This is the whelping of a smooth coat, or as the Australians call them, a Prapso.

When the first Prapsos occurred, it must have been quite a shock for the breeders involved. Most tried to keep these puppies a secret, but the news leaked out. It does appear to have been a worldwide phenomenon which occurred after World War II. The Prapsos were not restricted to one line of Lhasas, but seemed to affect many.

The Australian breeders took "the bull by the horns" and determined to find the cause, if possible. Mrs. Joan Beard started searching for information both in Australia and overseas. All identification of material was kept confidential, and the informaton was forwarded to CHART, an organiza-

tion in England which researches animal abnormalities. Geneticists worked on the charts prepared by this organization.

Facts about Prapsos started to become apparent. Test matings ruled out straight dominant or recessive genes. CHART's report indicated that the cause was quantitative characteristics.[15] This type of inheritance results from the interaction of numerous genes affecting each other in differing degrees. Although much additional research has turned up new knowledge about genetics, no recent information on this problem has been located.

Since the passing of alleles to offspring is accomplished in a random manner, there are several possible explanations for the results of quantitative characteristics. One is the inheritance of mutations, genes whose chemical structures have been slightly altered or changed. These mutations could have been spontaneous in nature, or they could have been caused by exposure to either chemicals or to radiation. During the period when many of these Prapsos occurred, new pesticides such as DDT were quite popular. Now it is known that these may cause gene defects.

Another possibility is that there may have been a protein shift in that one of the amino acid bases of those genes which order coats. This chemical

---

[15]Joan Beard, *Asian Breeds Bulletin,* Sydney, Australia, May 1970, pp. 4, 5.

Prapso puppy.

Three Prapsos from a litter of five.

Normal puppies from same litter.

163

change might then have changed a gene or genes which in some way affect coat characteristics.

This small bit of genetic knowledge may help breeders to do a better job until the exact gene on the exact chromosome may be located. There is, for instance, no reason to rule good Lhasas out of breeding programs because Prapsos have been produced. However, they must be used with care. Such breedings should not be repeated. The bitch owner should use judicious care in subsequent breedings. Most bitches that produced Prapsos when bred to one sire did not when bred to others.

Much responsibility lies with the owner of a stud that has produced Prapsos, as a stud can sire many more puppies than one bitch can produce. The owner of the stud should keep accurate records, should examine carefully the pedigrees of bitches to be bred, and should the potential of Prapsos be present, either refuse the breeding or clearly explain the potential to the bitch's owner. Such a stud will be able to produce his many good characteristics if care and discretion are practiced.

Prapsos have several characteristics which are apparent quite early. One aspect is muzzle hair. On a Lhasa puppy it grows like a chrysanthemum's petals, spreading out using the nose as a focal point. The muzzle hair on the Prapsos is smooth. In the coats of the Prapsos there will be shiny, stiff hairs which are like coarse guard hairs. The Prapsos may have no hair between the pads, a distinguishing factor of Lhasa Apsos, and may have hare feet, a sparse head fall, no feathering on the fronts of the legs, and abruptly short coats. It is also said Prapsos cut their primary (baby) teeth by four to

four and one-half weeks, when the average Lhasa may be just starting to cut his.

There are several factors to remember: *avoid repeat breedings of those resulting in Prapsos; sell Prapsos as pets on neutering contracts; keep complete records; and use discretion.*

USING GENETICS

One thing must be kept in mind: the perfect Lhasa has yet to be bred. To breed better Lhasas, we must carefully study our sires and our dams. Consider the positive and the negative aspects of each Lhasa and then never double on a fault. When breeding, common knowledge tells us that if a dam has short legs, the stud chosen should have normal legs.

If you are very familiar with the sire and the dam of a particular Lhasa, you can conjecture as to some of the genes which the dog inherited. In addition, an examination of the offspring of this same dog may reveal some recessive genes carried. By careful examination of the dogs and bitches involved in breeding programs, and by searching out information on those Lhasas not owned, it is possible to increase our knowledge about our studs and dams. There are numerous sources from which information may be obtained. Old breed magazines and ALAC stud issues are good sources. Look for articles on specific dogs. The owners of these Lhasas may be willing to tell you about them. Remember that in all cases when you are discussing particular Lhasas to use tact, integrity, and discretion. The knowledge gained can lead to better overall breeding programs.

Ch. Oro's Bani Leu (by BIS Ch. Arborhill's Rapso-Dieh ex Ginseng Gander of Oro). Breeder-owners, Etta and Harold Orenstein, M.D.

164

There is a formula available in two versions, which will be combined below, which advises us of the influence of family inheritance upon genes. The parents contribute one-half of all genes: 25 percent dam and 25 percent sire. The four grandparents contribute one-fourth (25 percent) of the total, or one-sixteenth each. The eight great-grandparents contribute among them one-eighth (12.5 percent) or one-sixty-fourth each. The next generation contributes 6.25 percent, divided equally by sixteen great-great grandparents. The prior generation of thirty-two members contribute 3.125 percent. The breakdown continues in this manner. What is important, as Lloyd C. Brackett informs us, is that grandparents or great-grandparents appearing only once in a pedigree have very little influence.[16] When an individual appears more than once, his influence is increased accordingly.

When we are aware of the percentages of genes inherited from various parents and grandparents, and when we use the knowledge about these Lhasas to breed for better Lhasas, we are using genetics.

The day of the computer is at hand, and perhaps the use of a computer in genetics will become valuable. But to do this we would need a vast knowledge not only of our own breeding program, but of all the Lhasas in their backgrounds. Since it may take from six to ten generations to eradicate a recessive, that would encompass a vast amount of information. We would have to be exceedingly observant and keep extensive records on each Lhasa and each litter.

Consequently, for the time being it may be best to combine a general knowledge of genetics with common sense to produce your Best In Show Lhasa. A good rule of thumb is to never breed two Lhasas with the same major fault. The bitch and the stud should complement each other.

[16]Brackett, p. 25.

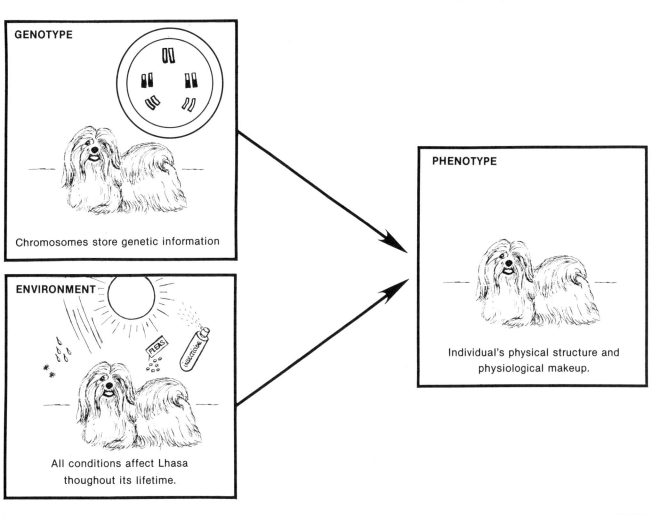

GENOTYPE

Chromosomes store genetic information

ENVIRONMENT

All conditions affect Lhasa thoughout its lifetime.

PHENOTYPE

Individual's physical structure and physiological makeup.

Inherited factors may also be affected by environment. Consequently, it must be stressed that the expression of the gene depends both on the other genes present (genetic environment) and on the physical environment. Genes are potentialities. Factors such as temperature, sunlight, humidity, or diet can greatly influence the realization of potential.

BREEDING BY PLAN

A true professional breeder makes an art of breeding. A frame of reference with which the breeder intends to gain the quality of Lhasa Apso desired is determined. Each one of us hopes to be the one whose dogs produce a "Kham," a "Tibet," a "Tuck," or a "Kori."

This is not an easy task. It takes time and experience. There will be both joy and heartache along the way. But remember, although a perfect Lhasa Apso is an ideal and not a reality, it is the goal of the professional breeder.

The professional breeder is one who makes a creative art of breeding, not for numbers, but for quality. A professional breeder may breed one or a dozen litters in a year, depending on the kennel size, but he does not run a "puppy mill."

Thus, if you desire to be a professional and create through your plans and breeding program the best Lhasas, you must have a frame of reference and an overall plan. Perhaps the first step in any breeding plan is to establish a frame of reference for desired results, and then determine how to reach that goal. There may be several paths to follow.

Remember, the actual preparation for breeding starts with good health practices for your Lhasas. Evaluate your Lhasas and determine the areas needing improvements—bites, coats, movement. Also, determine the good points which you desire to keep. Then determine how you will retain the virtues while improving the faults.

At this point it is advantageous to know as much as possible about your bitch's pedigree. If you know from which of her ancestors the faults and virtues

BIS Am. Can. Ch. San Jo's Shazam, bred and owned by Marianne Nixon. Sired by San Jo's Shenanigan ROM ex Ch. San Jo's The Prune Pit. Photo by Roberts.

BIS Ch. Qua-La-Ti's Makara, the youngest Lhasa in history to win BIS (at fourteen months). Breeder, Nancy Coglianese. Owners, Eva and Darlene Schlatter.

166

ppear to derive, it will help you to determine your pproach: inbreed, linebreed, or outcross.

Hopefully your choice will be influenced by the esire to improve your line. The choice should not e the number-one Lhasa stud just because he has famous name and it will look good on a pedigree. he potential of a stud or a dam, regardless of its ody type, depends upon genetic background. Both re and dam are important in the results. Do reiember that all sex-linked genes come from the am, not the sire, and that the dam provides the nvironment for fetal development. Therefore, her ealth is vital.

nbreeding

The breeding of closely related Lhasas is called ibreeding. The American Kennel Club defines inreeding as the breeding of closely related dogs— arent to progeny, brother to sister. One factor is pparent and that is with inbreeding you will find iajor faults or major virtues in a hurry. Perhaps should be underscored that no faults nor virtues

caused by recessive genes can turn up except those already hidden in the gene banks of the dogs involved. In other words, inbreeding *itself does not cause* faults or deformities, as the potential is inherent in the Lhasas involved. Inbreeding brings faults and virtues into the open because it concentrates the gene pool.

One of the most outstanding results of this type of breeding would be the great BIS Am. Can. Bda. Mex. Int. Ch. Kyi-Chu Friar Tuck, the result of a mother-to-son mating:

                    Ch. Hamilton Jimpa
          Ch. Quetzal's Feyla of Kyi-Chu
                    Ch. Colarlies Miss Shandha
BIS Ch. Kyi-Chu Friar Tuck
                    Ch. Colarlies Shan Bangalor
          Ch. Colarlies Miss Shandha
                    Miradel's Ming Fu Chia C.D.

Inbreeding can be a powerful tool. It will "fix" desirable genes by making them homozygous. When it uncovers undesirable genes, it is also providing necessary information for the breeder. Prepotency, which is dependent on homozygosity, will be developed. Remember, though, that a Lhasa may be prepotent for both desirable and undesirable traits.

Outcrossing

Outcrossing occurs when Lhasas of completely different lines are mated. These Lhasas will have no related ancestors in at least the first five generations. The purpose behind outcrossing should be to eliminate a fault or to gain a virtue.

The first generation of an outcross may be outstanding. However, subsequent outcrosses often do not produce Lhasas of the same quality. Outcrossed litters are more inconsistent in type. Moreover, outcrossed studs and dams may or may not produce puppies of similar phenotype.

An example of an "outcross" pedigree follows. True outcrosses are of totally unrelated dogs, but this is extremely difficult in a breed like Lhasas. Behind the eight great-grandparents in this pedigree are many of the same Hamilton dogs.

nt. Mex. Am. Ch. Ginseng's Lotta Class in Mexico City · reeder-owner, Tom C. Meador, Jr.

167

Outcrossing is most successful when a breeder does one outcross to gain a specific quality not available in his own line, and then returns to the basic line. It may also be successful when the individual dogs outcrossed are very consistent in type.

Ch. Yeti's Paper Tiger
Ch. Rimar's Rumpelstiltskin
Ch. Arborhill's Lho-Lha of Rimar
Ch. Sharpettes Rumpie Dil Dox
Ch. Chen Korum Ti
Tabu's Tinker Toy
Ch. Kinderland's Tonka
Can. Ch. Kachina RM Sabu Tecumseh
Ch. Kyi-Chu Friar Tuck
Ch. Eastcroft's Woodsedge Tuckim
Kyi-Chu Cinde of Sharbet
Kachinas Mysty Shadow Lakota
Woodsedge Smoky Khyi
Kachina Beryl Shalimar
Ebony Crystal

Linebreeding

By dictionary definition, linebreeding is breeding within one line (family) of Lhasas in order to develop desired favorable characteristics. Related individuals are bred, but not as close as brother, sister, or parent.

For example, bitch A was bred by stud B, resulting in bitch C, who is an outcross. When considering the breeding of C, it was decided to line breed. Upon evaluation, it was determined that the stud should be related to her sire and that he should be prepotent for good bite and a shorter back. Relatives of B were evaluated for these qualities, plus that the stud be typey and have a good temperament, qualities not to be lost. Ultimately, stud D was found. There were thirty-eight mutually related Lhasas in their five-generation pedigrees, and by stroke of luck, some were even related to the bitch's dam. From this breeding bitch E was retained, and she too will be linebred.

One factor about linebreeding that can be important is the predictability of results. Using the long and detailed pedigree can be very valuable for the linebreeder, as the origin of body shape, bite, gait, temperament, etc., can be determined. The pedigree provides information on the gene pool with which the linebreeder is working.

Judicious linebreeding in which careful attention to desired traits is practiced can result in prepotency.

Kachina RD Tauy-Jones. Photo by Ashbey.

Pedigree of a linebred Lhasa. A study of the picture pedigree behind this Lhasa on the following pages reveals a remarkable continuity of type, and is an example of the kind of picture study every breeder should try to compile on their foundation stock.

Sire: Am. Can. Ch. Sharpette's Rumpie Dil Dox.

```
                                                              BIS Ch. Chen Korum-Ti ROM*
                                                     ┌Ch. Kyi-Chu Chaos
                                                     │         Ch. Kyi-Chu Inshalla C.D.
                                           ┌Ch. Yeti's Paper Tiger ROM
                                           │         │         Ch. Pan Chen Tonka Sonan ROM*
                                           │         └Ginger Lee Ruby ROM
                                           │                   Bzan-Po's Pandora of Yin Hi I.Q.
                                ┌BIS Ch. Rimar's Rumpelstiltskin ROM
                                │          │                   Ch. Kyi-Chu Kaliph Nor
                                │          │         ┌Ch. Cherryshores Bah Bieh Boi ROM
                                │          │         │         Ch. Cherryshores Mah Dahm
                                │          └Ch. Arborhill's Lho-Lha of Rimar ROM
                                │                    │         Ch. Kham of Norbulingka ROM
                                │                    └Ch. Arborhill's Lhana**
                                │                              Ch. Arborhill's Karoling Karolyn ROM
                      ┌Am. Can. Ch. Sharpette's Rumpie Dil DOX
                      │         │                   Ch. Chen Makalu of Dzunger
                      │         │         ┌Ch. Chen Nyun-Ti ROM
                      │         │         │         Licos Gia La
                      │         │ ┌BIS Ch. Chen Korum-Ti ROM*
                      │         │ │       │         Ch. Panda Bear Sing of Kyi-Chu
                      │         │ │       └Ch. Chen Karakorum
                      │         │ │                 Ch. Kyi-Chu Kara Nor
                      │         └Tabu's Tinker Toy***
                      │                              Karma Tharpa
                      │                    ┌BIS Ch. Tibet of Cornwallis ROM+
                      │                    │         Ch. Licos Cheti La
                      │                    └BIS Ch. Kinderland's Tonka ROM+++
                      │                              BIS Ch. Kham of Norbulingka ROM
                      │                    └Ch. Kinderland's Sang-Po**
                      │                              Ch'ha-Ya-Chi
                      │
Am. Can. Ch. Kachina RD Tauy-Jones
                      │
                      │                              Hamilton Toradga
                      │                    ┌Ch. Zijuh Seng Tru ROM
                      │                    │         Ch. Hamilton Shim Tru
                      │         ┌Ch. Tabu's King of Hearts ROM++
                      │         │          │         BIS Ch. Tibet of Cornwallis ROM+
                      │         │          └BIS Ch. Kinderland's Tonka ROM+++
                      │         │                    Ch. Kinderland's Sang-Po ROM**
                      │ ┌BIS Ch. Rimar's J. G. King Richard
                      │ │       │                    BIS Ch. Kham of Norbulingka ROM
                      │ │       │         ┌Ch. Linkhor BHU of Norbulingka**
                      │ │       │         │         Can. Ch. Luigi's Tonka of Lingkhor
                      │ │       └Ch. Rimar's Tipit ROM
                      │ │                 │         Ch. Karnes Khambo**
                      │ │                 └Rondelay Lama of Zen-Ma
                      │ │                           Ch. Rondelay Lhama Kutra
                      └Can. Ch. Sharpette Munday's Dolly Lama
                                │                   Ch. Chen Makalu of Dzunger
                                │         ┌Ch. Chen Nyun-Ti ROM
                                │         │         Licos Gia La
                                │ ┌BIS Ch. Chen Korum-Ti ROM*
                                │ │       │         Ch. Panda Bear Sing of Kyi-Chu
                                │ │       └Ch. Chen Karakorum
                                │ │                 Ch. Kyi-Chu Kara Nor
                                └Am. Can. Ch. Tabu's Hello Dolly***
                                          │         Karma Tharpa
                                          ┌Ch. Tibet of Cornwallis ROM+
                                          │         Ch. Licos Cheti La
                                          └BIS Ch. Kinderland's Tonka ROM+++
                                                    BIS Ch. Kham of Norbulingka ROM
                                          └Ch. Kinderland's Sang-Po**
                                                    Ch'Ha-Ya-Chi
```

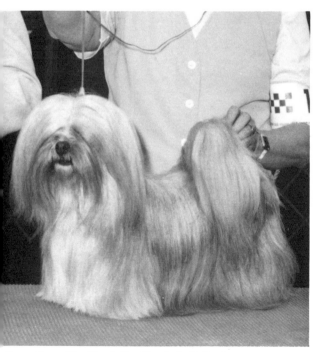

Dam: Can. Ch. Sharpette Munday's Dolly Lama.

Paternal grandsire, BIS Ch. Rimar's Rumpelstiltskin ROM.

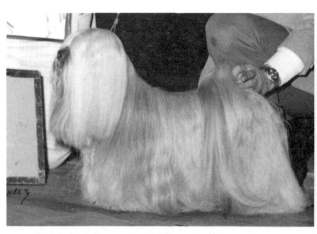

Maternal grandsire, BIS Ch. Rimar's J. G. King Richard.

Maternal granddam, Am. Can. Ch. Tabu's Hello Dolly (litter sister to Tabu's Tinker Toy, paternal granddam).

Great grandsire, maternal, Ch. Tabu's King of Hearts ROM.

Great great grandsire, paternal and maternal, Ch. Chen Nyun-Ti ROM, winner of the Jimpa Award as outstanding producer. He sired both BIS Ch. Chen Korum-Ti ROM who won the Jimpa award four times and of multiple group winning Ch. Chen Krisna Nor ROM who won it five times. Breeder-owner, Pat Chenoweth.

170

Great granddam, maternal, Ch. Rimar's Tipit ROM.

Ch. Chen Korum-Ti, paternal great grandsire.

Great granddam, paternal, Ch. Arborhill's Lho-Lha of Rimar ROM.

Great great grandsire, paternal and maternal, BIS Ch. Tibet of Cornwallis ROM.

Great great great grandsire, paternal and maternal, BIS Ch. Kham of Norbulingka ROM. Kham was a top winner during the 1960's, winning five Best in Show awards. Breeder-owner, Phyllis Marcy.

171

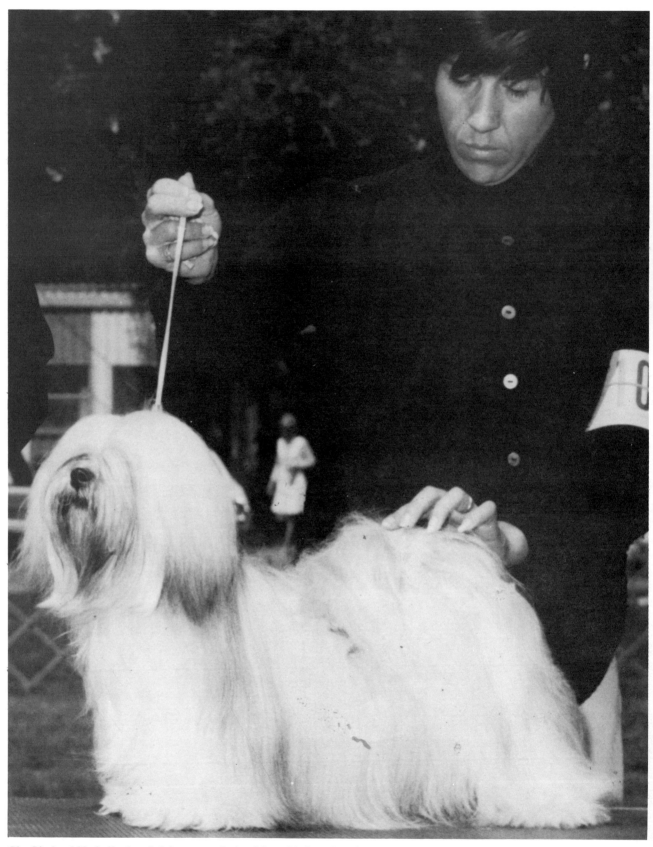

Ch. Gindy of Norbulingka, tied for top-producing Lhasa bitch to date, is found in many pedigrees. Breeder, Phyllis Marcy. Owner, Norman and Carolyn Herbel.

16

THE BROOD BITCH

There is a wide variance in the maturation and the readiness for breeding among Lhasa Apsos. The earliest age for the onset of estrus (heat) is about five months and the latest is about thirteen months. A bitch should not be bred before she is at least a year old. Lhasas are a long-lived breed and take a somewhat longer time in reaching full maturity. For this reason, Lhasas also have a longer breeding life than most breeds. Although a healthy bitch in good condition can whelp a litter at eight or nine (and some have done so even later), the general consensus is that bitches should not be bred after they are six years of age.

BREEDING PATTERNS

It is very important that a bitch be in good health during pregnancy and whelping, as the degree of her health can certainly be reflected in the quality and health of her puppies. Thus, I do not believe in breeding before the second or third season, and I do not believe in breeding the bitch every season nor, except in rare circumstances, two out of three seasons. A good bitch can be bred once a year until she is six years old and, in some cases if she is in exceptionally good health, until she is eight years old. This means that she could have from six to eight litters during her prime years. If she is used for breeding only until she is six, or if she is shown to her championship and then has only five or six litters, surely that is plenty. It is my opinion that only the greedy breed a bitch more than once a year, unless there are special circumstances which are not a regular event.

Every veterinarian in the many areas in which I have lived has stressed that breeding in every other heat is the best program. Whelping and pregnancy are really quite stressful, and a bitch needs plenty of time to recover. Overbreeding not only can debilitate the bitch, but it can produce poor offspring or even the loss of the offspring at a very young age. Some breeders will breed bitches twice in a row. This is really feasible only when a bitch has a very small litter of one or two puppies, which indicates there may not have been such a strain on her as would result from a larger litter. The practical reason for breeding twice in a row might be to change a breeding pattern; that is, for example, to switch from winter to summer litters.

Accurate records should be kept on breedings: dates bred, dates whelped, factors about whelping, number of offspring, problems, and sales.

CONDITIONING

Daily exercise is an important aspect of conditioning. This could consist of a good brisk walk or running in the yard. Good muscle tone can make whelping easier for the bitch. This daily routine should continue throughout the pregnancy, as it will help maintain muscle tone. The exercise a bitch gets in a raised exercise pen also aids in toning muscles—it tends to have the effect of isometric exercise. This is helpful during the stormy winter day in the north and during rainstorms anywhere.

Diet is an important factor. Our Lhasas should always be kept on well-balanced diets which include about twenty-seven percent usable protein. The bitch should not be overweight when bred, as the extra weight will tend to put added stress on the heart and other organs. Do not wait for her to be bred to give her such things as cottage cheese, liver (in very small amounts), chicken gizzards or hearts. These can be given periodically with the kibble so that she is somewhat accustomed to them before being pregnant.

PRELIMINARY VETERINARY VISIT

A potential brood bitch should have a thorough physical exam prior to breeding. Your veterinarian will examine the bitch to determine her ability to whelp puppies and to be bred. Do not wait until after there have been problems breeding her—have the examination first. If your bitch is unable to whelp normally, or even to be bred, you should know beforehand. In addition, your bitch should have a brucellosis test and be given any necessary

shots such as rabies or distemper. Many stud dog owners require a brucellosis test prior to breeding as a precaution. It would be rare for a virgin bitch to have brucellosis. However, it is possible for a brood bitch to have contracted it during a previous breeding.

Breeding stock should be checked annually for brucella canis. If a stud stands for breeding frequently, he should be checked more frequently. The brucellosis test is one of the first to be suggested in cases of reproductive failure.

The bacteria causing brucella canis was discovered in 1966 at Cornell University by Dr. Leland Carmichael. The disease causes spontaneous abortions, whelping failures, dead puppies, or weak puppies which may die in one to three days. It may be responsible for a poor conception rate, testicular atrophy, lymphadenitis, and epididymitis. Females abort after the forty-fourth day of gestation. Abortions or failure to whelp may occur in one to three pregnancies, but the bitch may subsequently have a normal pregnancy and whelping. The infection is spread from contact with vaginal discharges, sheath discharges, aborted fetuses and placental tissue, and urine. It is usually transmitted during breeding as a venereal disease.

Symptoms vary per dog. Some adults show few signs, perhaps only a lassitude or a lack of energy. Males may have swollen testes and scrotum, scrotal dermatitis, a decreased sperm count, and testicular atrophy. The female may have vaginitis and a brownish-green discharge for two to sixteen weeks.

Identification and care for this disease are very important. So for your own protection, request the test. Also, it is your prerogative to ask if the stud also has had a recent test. Many stud owners will request that your bitch have been tested within six weeks prior to the projected breeding date. You may request the same of the stud.

The disease is difficult to treat and isolation from other breeding animals is required. Affected animals are often sterile even if the infection is cured. The common practice has been to remove affected dogs from a breeding kennel. Sometimes they are destroyed, and sometimes the bitch is spayed and

---

[1]Dan Johns, DVM, "Brucella Canis A Canine Venereal Disease," *Lhasa Tales* 4, 11 (February 1976), p. 25.

the stud is neutered; then they are placed in a non-breeding environment, as they may carry the disease. At this point there is no positive cure and no immunization. However, as this disease is under research at veterinary research schools the world over, and as progress is being made, at any time a breakthrough may occur. Thus, it would be wise to check with a nearby research veterinary university for the latest information before taking any drastic action.

ONSET OF ESTRUS

Most bitches experience their first estrus (heat) periods between five and seven months of age. It is possible to miss this first heat, as it may be very short and there may be minimal physical evidence such as swelling or bleeding. That a puppy bitch is in heat may be discovered by accident as, for instance, when tiny blood spots may be found on clothes or bedding. Some bitches do not experience this first heat until they are eight or nine months old. Therefore, do not be overly concerned if your Lhasa bitch appears to be late in experiencing this first heat.

Signs that a bitch is coming in heat may appear anywhere from five to thirty days in advance of the onset of estrus. She may be restless, unusually playful with male Lhasas, or may "ride" another female. A few bitches will lift their legs when urinating. There should be some swelling of the vulva, although it may be minimal on some bitches, even when ready to be bred. The vulva will have a soft appearance.

The size of the vulva pre-estrus does not indicate a bitch's ability to be bred. This size varies from bitch to bitch. The vulva will usually increase greatly when the bitch is "in season." Should you possess a male Lhasa, he may indicate to you by his reactions or signals when a bitch is coming in season and even when that bitch is ready to be bred. When I notice my Lhasa male taking up a position in front of the door to the Lhasa living room, I know that one of the girls is coming in heat. Males may also mark their territory by lifting their legs and depositing a small amount of urine in various spots. The studs will be testy with each other in a way that they are not when none of the bitches are in heat.

BIS Ch. Hamilton Torma with America's Torma Lu, whelped in 1959 when Torma was seven years of age.

It is not recommended that a bitch be bred during her first season, especially when under a year old. At this point the bitch is simply not socially ready for breeding, just as a twelve-year-old girl is not. A Lhasa bitch needs time to grow up; consequently, do not rush her too much. Breeding during the second or third season is sufficiently early to start her breeding career.

When your Lhasa bitch is in estrus, do not let her run freely. Exercise her in a protected area under human supervision. Do not allow her to consort with the males in the home or in the kennel. Do not *isolate* her, but do segregate her. Isolation could adversely affect her joyous personality. If necessary, use the sprays or sanitary belts available at pet supply houses to protect her. Usually, keeping her in an enclosed raised exercise pen will work well.

THE ESTRUS PERIOD

The estrus period is divided into three parts: proestrus, true estrus, and metestrus.

It is important to notice the onset of the bitch's proestrus period. Lhasa bitches are usually exceptionally clean so you may not notice much blood

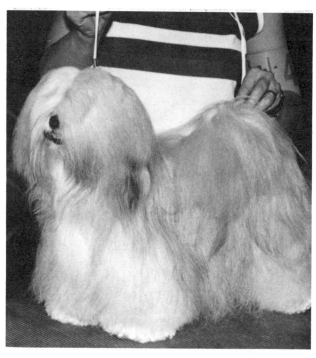

Group winning Ch. Kyi-Chu Inshalla C.D. was said by Ruth Smith to be "the epitome of feminine elegance and style." Photo by Petrulis.

176

unless during a heavy flow period. For this reason daily checks of any bitch due in heat are necessary. Should the bitch be suspected "in" and should there be no physical signs, gently insert a sterile swab into the vaginal lips. It will reveal blood if she is in proestrus.

The discharge at onset is a bright, clear red. Within several days the shade of red may deepen somewhat—perhaps several degrees. This color will continue until shortly before the end of proestrus, when the color will gradually become a pale pink and then a yellowish straw color. The amount of discharge at first is light, then becomes quite heavy during the deeper shade of red, then gradually decreases.

The amount of discharge varies greatly from bitch to bitch. It may be a very small amount, or slight, in any bitch, but especially in the very young, unbred bitch. There could be no sign of discharge at all, as happens in some cases, or the discharge could be quite heavy.

Young bitches in first heat may not be as thorough in cleaning the area as the more mature bitch, but again this depends upon the bitch. Sometimes the flow may be so great that even the mature bitch will have trouble coping. It is wise to check the vaginal area at least once a day. If there is an excess of dark blood caked on the area, cleanse with sterile water or a mild douche solution. This will aid in preventing infections. The prevention of infections is very important in a brood bitch.

The length of proestrus varies from bitch to bitch, and it may even vary from heat to heat for a given bitch. Therefore, the keeping of records on each bitch is essential. This stage could be very short, as few as four days. For instance, one bitch came in heat on Saturday with no prewarning signs. On Monday the vet examined her for her health certificate and prepared a "vaginal smear" which indicated she was just about ready for mating. She was shipped on Tuesday and bred on Wednesday.

The average bitch remains in this stage from eight to ten days; for some bitches this stage may last up to twenty days. Some bitches will stand for breeding the eighth to tenth days, although for the majority twelve or fourteen seems to be about right. A few bitches will not stand before the twentieth or twenty-first days, but this is not unusual as the heat period for most Lhasa bitches extends twenty-one to thirty-six days overall.

When the discharge lessens, the bitch often becomes very playful with the stud. Gradually the vulva will soften and the bitch will stand for breeding. During this receptive period, the true estrus, care should be taken that the bitch be in contact with no stud except that one chosen as sire for her litter. The onset of the stage, the true estrus, may be signaled by flagging; that is, when the bitch is patted on her rump, her tail will immediately switch firmly to the opposite side. Flagging indicates readiness, but the degree of readiness varies from bitch to bitch. This receptive period can last as little as a few hours or a day or as long as a week.

The optimum breeding period is at the time the egg cells (ova) are discharged from the bitch's ovaries into the oviduct near the end of the receptive phase, or estrus. This is the time when conception can occur. Not only will conception have a higher percentage of success, but also larger litters can result as more eggs will be fertilized by the sperm. To be sure of breeding at this optimum breeding time, the use of the vaginal smear technique is valuable. This will be discussed later.

While the bitch may continue to be attractive to the males for a few days or for a week or more after breeding, she will repulse their advances during the third stage, metestrus. She should be continuously segregated, even during this period. An easy means of segregating her is to keep her in a raised exercise pen with the cover hooked.

THE VAGINAL SMEAR TECHNIQUE

Vaginal smears help to take the guesswork out of breeding, reveal infections in bitches, and increase the conception rate. Since vaginal smear slides need to be made daily for the best results, it will be less expensive, take less traveling, and possibly even be more accurate if you do them yourself. It is not a difficult procedure.

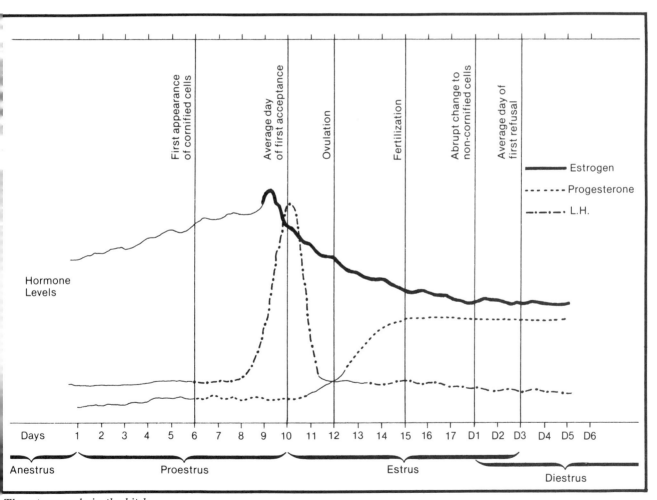

The estrous cycle in the bitch.

To aid you in doing your own slides, Jerry Watson's excellent article "Breeding by Vaginal Smears" has been included in Appendix A.

The use of this method has been helpful to me in many ways, especially with the varieties of breeding patterns among Lhasa Apso bitches. Very often the bitches vary from one estrus period to the next. Sometimes it seems an inordinate length of time before a bitch is ready to be bred. The smears tell us that we haven't missed her estrus. They also can alert us to low-grade infections which may explain why a bitch has missed. These low-grade infections are usually caused by some type of vaginitis which, if treated in time, may not prevent the bitch from being bred. The smears also tell us if the bitch does not ovulate. If this occurs more than once, hormone therapy may be indicated.

REPRODUCTIVE PROBLEMS

The major cause of infertility is breeding at the wrong time. As each bitch has her own cycle, keep accurate records. These records can aid in future heats. Use the vaginal smear method for determining the optimum breeding time.

Breeding only once is another cause because it increases the possibility of insufficient sperm. Breeding two or three successive days usually proves more productive.

Hormone, anatomical, thyroid, or other problems could cause an infertile mating. The male may have marginal fertility, and in such cases it is important that the bitch be at her fertility peak.

Another reason could be improper socialization for the bitch, which may make it impossible for her to have a natural mating. Temperament can make a difference.

It is interesting that wild animals, including dogs, usually come in heat only once a year. Domesticated animals, including dogs, come in heat more often, usually twice a year. There are Lhasa bitches, even though the breed has been domesticated from the beginning, who come in heat only once a year. Some come in every seven to nine months. Occasionally one may miss a cycle or two. This type of problem can cause a temporary delay in a breeding program. Why these skipped cycles occur is not really known.

A serious problem for the breeder is the typey well-conformed bitch, perhaps a champion, who never comes into heat. This problem may be congenital or acquired. Hormone treatments are available, but the degree of success has been erratic, cost is prohibitive, and the resulting puppies may perpetuate an hereditary problem.

Another problem affecting fertility is hypothyroidism, which is caused by a lack of the hormone thyroxine. Some signs of this include obesity, heat seeking, skin disease, lethargy, intestinal disorders and infertility. Adequate tests are available, and tables such as thyroxine replace the missing hormones. Reading these tests must be done carefully. The Lhasa bitch whose reading is in the low normal range may be having a fertility problem indicated by missing breedings or by absorption of puppies between the thirtieth and forty-fifth days. Bitches suffering from a low normal thyroid may show several symptoms: hot spots during estrus, a good coat but very scant undercoat, irritability. One solution has been to put such bitches on .2 mg. thyroxine. This treatment has sometimes resulted in healthy litters. The thyroxine not only aided in the conception and the whelping of healthy litters, but also seemed to stimulate coat improvement in the bitches, eliminated the hot-spot problem during estrus, and improved temperament.

Acute metritis, pyometra, and endometritis are bacterial infections which affect fertility. Endometritis is a leading cause of infertility, and it appears to have no symptoms aside from that of infertility. To determine if this is the cause of infertility, cultures must be made during heat. The disease is treated with antibiotics for about a week. Some bitches may need periodic treatment, especially when bred.

Pyometra and metritis may be acute or chronic. Since these are usually associated with brood bitches, the subjects are discussed following whelping.

TOXINS AND BREEDING PROBLEMS

It is essential that, if we are to breed the best possible Lhasas, our Lhasas are kept as free as possible of toxins. Recent studies on humans and animals are showing that environmental and industrial chemicals can cause insecticide poisoning, birth defects, and infertility.

In the August–September 1978 issue of *The Lhasa Apso Reporter* there is a letter from Jean Raymond and Art Tashnek, M.D., entitled "An Open Letter – Of Warning" which was written after their experience with insecticide poisoning which involved one of their Lhasas. "It seems *spectracide* and *Sevin* work in a similar way on the cholinesterase system but in a slightly different way. The symptoms are dependent on the amount of chemical absorbed by each dog – mild degree causes nausea, vomiting, muscular twitching. Moderate degree causes muscular twitching, paralysis of varying degrees and for variable periods of time. Severe degree – paralysis and death. Dogs cannot breathe."[2]

The major difficulty is the actual diagnosis of insecticide poisoning. For Raymond and Tashnek the problem developed in their efforts to control fleas to which one of their Lhasas was allergic. They sprayed their yard with *spectracide* and dusted the kennel, pens, and dogs with *Sevin*. Another of their Lhasas reacted to this and developed a partial paralysis. They wrote that "there is definitely a greater danger when *spectracide* and *Sevin* are used at the same time or close together. The same thing can occur with either chemical alone."[3]

In cases such as this, the awareness of insecticide poisoning is clear and sharp because of the resulting allergic reaction. But insecticide poisoning can be much more subtle and the effects not immediately recognized.

Earlier studies involving birth defects and infertility have been concerned with the dams' (mothers') contributions to whelping/pregnancy problems. More recently studies have examined the sires' roles in such mishaps. The studies have found that both dams and sires are involved in chemical-related birth problems.

Lhasas may come in contact with chemicals in various ways: kennel cleaning and antiseptic substances, insecticides, grooming materials, and chemicals used to stimulate coat growth. Since bitches used for breeding are usually kept in a home or kennel situation, we must be concerned with products used in those situations. But our concern must not stop with the bitches; it must involve seriously the choice of studs. George Payton, in an article in *The Lhasa Apso Reporter,* mentioned the uses of coat-growth stimulants such as arsenic which are occurring in our breed. Such uses must be considered because they can cause problems. According to Dr. John McLeod, "almost any kind

---

[2]p. 6.
[3]*Ibid.*

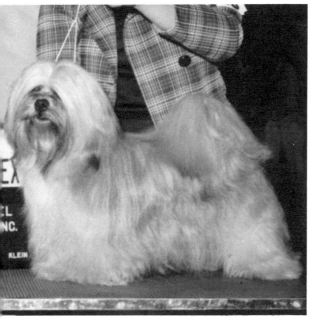

Thea," Am. Can. Ch. Khabachen Kasha's Thetis. Breeder-o-owner, Marlene Annunziata with Carol Strong, Bihar.

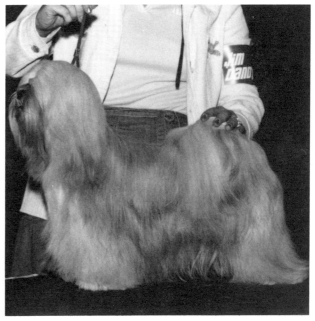

Orlane's Brandywine is the dam of BIS Eng. BIS Am. Ch. Orlane's Intrepid. Breeder-owner, Dorothy Kendall.

of noxious chemical, if taken in enough quantity, will affect the testes."[4]

The male reproductive tract has been compared to "a garbage disposal system" by Dr. Leonard Nelson. Chemical substances, such as lead and cadmium, "may collect there for future elimination. This collection of chemical substances has been found toxic to sperm."[5]

Many chemicals have been found to affect the reproductive system. The pesticide dibromochloropropane (DBCB), for instance, causes infertility. The pesticide carbaryl (*Sevin*) and tobacco smoke are known to have the potential of interfering with the normal development of sperm. *Tris,* a flame chemical retardant chemical and a close chemical relative of DBCB, has been found to damage the genetic material of cells. DDT, polychlorophenois, and hexachlorobenzene are other potentially harmful chemicals. Should the Lhasas inhale marijuana smoke or have contact with the pesticide *Kepone,* lead, or radiation, their sperm may also be damaged.[6]

Infertility may be a problem at the moment with a given stud, but better infertility than abnormal sperm. The abnormal sperm damage may be inherited. Dr. Andrew Wyrobek stated, as a result of his studies with mice, that "animals treated with chemicals that cause sperm defects tend to father offspring that have chromosomal abnormalities or

that produce abnormal sperm too, suggesting that sperm damage can be inherited."[7]

Miscarriages and stillbirths (and absorption?) can also be caused by exposure to contaminants such as nitrous oxide, lead arsenic, cigarette smoke, marijuana smoke, and DBCB. The latter is also known to cause cancer.

Consequently, the products and substances used around our Lhasas, including our smoking habits, should be carefully examined. Instructions on products used for ridding areas of fleas and other similar problems should be followed to the letter. Precautions should be taken with cleaning materials. Those things, such as carbaryl, which have been proven to cause either malformed sperm, birth defects, or miscarriages should not be used in contact with our Lhasas. In addition, we should question all chemicals, such as the new internal flea-control chemicals, as to what harm they can do to our Lhasas and to their proposed progeny.

CHOICE OF STUD

Once you have chosen your approach (linebreed, inbreed, or outcross), your next move is to select an appropriate stud. Remember that the stud chosen should complement the bitch.

If you choose to inbreed, your choices are limited to sire, to progeny, or to a litter mate. Evaluate each potential and project the outcome as you make your choice. Be sure to include all known variables, bad as well as good. First, evaluate your bitch

---

[4]Jane E. Brody, "Sperm Found Especially Vulnerable to Environment," *The New York Times,* March 10, 1981, C1.
[5]*Ibid.*
[6]*Ibid.,* C1, C3.

[7]*Ibid.,* C3.

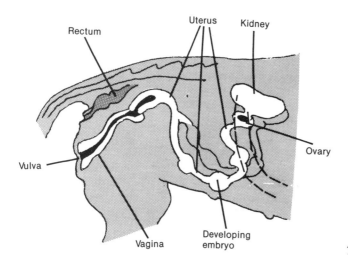

The reproductive system in the bitch.

Know which virtues you wish to keep and which faults you wish to improve. It might be wise to contact the owner of the bitch's dam to see what litter brothers are available and to ask her suggestions. A discussion should also be held with the owner of the sire to determine interest in such a breeding. If the bitch has offspring, your records should indicate what is available. Inbreeding should be used with judicious care. It can be very helpful in establishing consistency in breeding. Once that has been established, inbreeding can then be used to maintain quality.

Should you wish to outcross, you will have unlimited choices. In this case choose several alternatives, as for one reason or another, your choice of stud may not be available. To aid you in selecting the right stud, use the ALAC yearbooks and ads in the breed magazines, each of which will include pedigrees for many of the Lhasas included. Names, addresses, and telephone numbers will also be available. Be sure that each of your choices possesses something which you wish to gain, such as a good bite, strong rear, good front, good tail set. If possible, see the Lhasa in question. Contact your number-one choice first. Be prepared to supply adequate information about your bitch.

Linebreeding also can offer many variables. Again your choice should complement the bitch. Prepotent sires have often been either inbred or linebred, a fact which should help in making your choice of stud for linebreeding. The stud should be linebred. One often recommended approach is to breed the bitch to her maternal grandsire, providing he has the qualities the bitch needs. In linebreeding, both Lhasas should be closely related to one outstanding Lhasa whose type is very desired.

Contact the owner of the stud of your choice, supply details about the bitch, and give your purpose for desiring the breeding. A responsible breeder will help you decide if the stud in question should complement your bitch.

Fees

Once your stud has been selected and his owner agrees, a discussion of the financial options should take place. You should clearly understand what is involved: stud fees and terms for paying, what constitutes a litter and terms for rebreeding, shipping costs, health certificates and examinations required.

Each stud owner sets his/her own stud fees and the requirements for paying. These stud fees may be advertised or may be set by private treaty. Some stud owners require the entire fee in advance; some take fifty percent at breeding and fifty percent at whelping. Usually the litter registration papers will not be signed until the stud fee has been received in full. Occasionally the stud owner will take a puppy in lieu of all or part of the stud fee. Usually this puppy will be the number-one pick of the litter. This must be stated in the contract.

Since there are no refunds, be sure that you have a breedable bitch. Also, make certain how many puppies constitute a litter and what considerations are involved should a rebreeding be necessary. If the breeding doesn't take, a repeat breeding is usually permitted. Make sure that this is stated in writing. Stud owners sometimes include other specific restrictions such as that no puppies from a union with his or her stud can be sold in any manner to a pet store or wholesaler of dogs.

Secondly, if your bitch has been bred previously and/or if she is on a regular heat cycle (such as every six months for the average twenty-one days), you may be able to advise the stud owner about the date you expect the bitch to be in heat and also about her approximate breeding time. Any information about your bitch which you can give the stud's owner will probably facilitate the actual breeding experience. If your bitch eats a special diet, eats certain amounts, is on medication, or has any special needs, you should advise the stud owner. When feasible, send the bitch's food. I like to measure it in daily amounts, with any additives, and put it in baggies. I also send the canned dog food which is to be added. Of course, when shipping by air, this isn't possible. But if arrangements are made in advance, food could easily be shipped to those areas served by United Parcel Service (UPS) within a few days, and it could be timed to coincide with her arrival. This is necessary only if the bitch eats food different from what is available at the stud's kennel. Some kennels also charge board for the bitch during her stay, which will usually be at least a week, and may also charge for other miscellaneous services such as airport pickup.

Remember that your bitch visits the stud. All travel/shipping expenses are yours. If your bitch is to be shipped, the next step is to check the airlines about flight arrangements. It is helpful to know flight schedules, as one flight may be more convenient than another for a stud owner to meet. Check the cost not only for the flight, but also for an air crate if you do not own one. Most Lhasa bitches can be shipped in a #100 air crate. It is wise to pick up the crate well in advance so that your bitch can become accustomed to it and so that you can have it well labeled.

I prefer to stencil my crates in case of lost labels. On the front I usually put the bitch's call name. At the back of the top I stencil my kennel name, address, and phone number. When shipping, I secure destination labels in two places, top and back, one of which should survive. Tape a plastic bag with the copy of the health certificate and rabies certificate to the top of the crate. Since one airline threw away certificates, I now send only copies. I also include a "BITCH IN HEAT" label which could prevent an accidental breeding. On the handle I secure an old show lead in case she must be exercised. On the back of the crate I secure a portion of kibble for feeding in case of emergency. Inside the crate I include a favorite safe toy, to aid her in relaxing and to prevent boredom. Make sure that the small plastic water dish is in place on the door. Do not fill, as it will only spill.

One of my bitches didn't get put on the next flight and sat in an airport for seventeen hours while the airline was searching for her. Her call name on her crate aided in her identification, and she was relaxed as she amused herself with the toy. She arrived at her destination none the worse for wear.

Final Arrangements

If all your homework has been completed in advance, two or three phone calls will complete your arrangements when your bitch comes in heat. If your bitch is flying, call your veterinarian for an appointment to obtain the necessary health certificate for your bitch. At this point you may wish to have a vaginal smear done to determine the stage of heat and the approximate breeding day, if you have not already done so yourself.

The second call would be to the airlines for flight reservations if the bitch is flying. Be sure to note flight number(s), departure time, arrival time, and if there is a flight change. If possible, ship your bitch early enough so that she has a couple of days in which to adjust before the mating.

Third, call the stud owner. Identify yourself and your bitch. Give all the details: flight number, arrival time and departure time, airports and airlines involved.

Fourth (I think that this is important also), bathe and groom your bitch. Trim her nails and clip away any excessively long hair in the vaginal area. You want your bitch to make a good impression.

Fifth, send her on her way with kind and loving words. Call the stud owner after she is airborne to confirm her departure. Request that the stud owner call you "collect" to confirm her arrival.

Sixth, relax and wait for news of her breeding and her subsequent arrival home.

THE WAITING PERIOD

During the approximately fifty-eight to sixty-three-day waiting period, there are a number of things which can and should be accomplished.

Your lady in waiting needs an adequate diet so that neither she nor her puppies will suffer any adverse effects. Maintain her normal diet pattern, using the same basic kibble, but supplementing it with small amounts of liver, cottage cheese, cooked chicken parts, and eggs. If you are not already doing so, include a daily teaspoon of brewer's yeast and, if your veterinarian recommends one, a good, balanced vitamin/mineral supplement.

During the first four weeks of pregnancy your expectant bitch may eat the amount which she always has, except that the appetites of many Lhasa bitches will decrease for a week or two shortly after being bred. Consequently, during this period maintain a steady diet and observe the amount the bitch eats. Some bitches will even experience morning sickness, or daily nausea. It is good to remember that if the bitch goes off her food, cooked rice or cooked barley in place of the kibble may stimulate her appetite. Barley water may help the nausea. For this reason the water from the cooked barley should be saved and given to the bitch for drinking water.

During the third or fourth week, her appetite should return to normal. Now start adding supplements, if you are not already doing so. In addition to her regular ration of a high-quality, complete kibble, several times a week add a tablespoon of small-curd cottage cheese, a good source of calcium and phosphorus. (If the bitch suffered eclampsia after a previous litter, my feeding program would include a daily supplement of cottage cheese.) My feeding plan alternates cottage cheese with very small amounts of cooked liver (not more than a level tablespoon) or a heaping tablespoon of chopped chicken gizzards and hearts. Once or twice a week a beaten egg yolk is added. Raw egg seems to help maintain the bitch's coat. Occasionally an egg, mixed with a tablespoon of milk, is scrambled and added to her food.

During the fifth or sixth week, the bitch's appetite may start to increase. Rather than increase her daily meal, give her a supplementary meal. Since my Lhasas are fed at my family's dinner time, the pregnant and nursing bitches receive their additional meal at breakfast. The first few days this meal may be about one-quarter the amount of the regular meal. Then it is increased to one-half.

About a week, perhaps even ten days, before the bitch is due to whelp, her appetite will probably decrease. The meal for which I cut back the amounts when the bitch's appetite lessens is the larger of the two. Cutbacks and increases are always made in the amounts of the kibble, not in the supplements.

During the pregnancy period my bitches are also introduced to ice cream; a tablespoon or two will do. After whelping, some bitches tend to refuse food for a short period, but often they will eat ice cream. Thus, I like them to be familiar with it in advance. Another product which can be used is *Pro-Magic,* a powdered cottage cheese which is an excellent source of protein, containing a long list of essential amino acids. However, I restrict the use of this to ½ teaspoon several times a week for all my Lhasas. Another tempter for the finicky eater could be Chinese vegetables, which all of my Lhasas dearly love.

Remember, an adequate diet based on a good kibble with food supplements which add proteins, calciums, and phosphorus naturally will help the bitch and her puppies be as healthy as possible.

PREGNANCY CHECKS

From about the twenty-fifth to thirtieth day post-breeding your veterinarian may be able to palpate your bitch and give an estimate as to how many puppies she will whelp. The puppies feel like small nodules at this point. Sometimes the count will be quite accurate. The point of palpation, however, is to determine if the bitch is indeed pregnant.

X rays should, of course, be used with grave discrimination. The bitch cannot be X-rayed before the forty-fifth day without endangering the fetuses. Usually a veterinarian will only X-ray a bitch which might have problems whelping, perhaps because of her size or because she had problems with a previous litter. Or some other warning signs might signal a problem to a veterinarian. But a good veterinarian will not X-ray unnecessarily.

Ch. Tulku's Shades of Magic, foundation stud at Milarepa. (Sired by Ch. Milbryan Kim Ly Shim ex Licos Kargan La.) Breeder-owner, Mary Carter; co-owner, Janet Krissel.

183

BIS Can. BIS Am. Ch. Balrene Chia Pao, "Augie," top Canadian Lhasa for several years. He had 13 BIS awards and over 100 group placements, and was the sire of 20 champions. Owner, Dr. Ellen Brown. Photo by Streeter's.

184

17

THE STUD DOG

Standing a Lhasa at stud is not easy. From research to contract to training the stud to perform, there are many responsibilities. The stud owner meets all sorts of people, takes care of many Lhasa bitches, keeps the books, and pays the bills.

THE STUD AND HIS COSTS

Whether the stud is of your own raising or purchased, you have expended money. But just obtaining your Lhasa stud is not the end of expenses. A good Lhasa Apso will probably be shown to his championship. The costs here can be extensive, even if you show him yourself. There are entry fees, possibly handling fees, and travel fees. Moreover, these fees always seem to be increasing. Entry fees at this writing vary from $12 to $24. A dog must have fifteen points for his championship, including two majors. In projecting the cost for finishing this dog, the approximate least and the approximate most will be considered.

Case one: The dog finishes in one weekend with three five-point majors, owner handled. Entry costs would be about $42. Expenses for going to the shows and eating would be not less than $100. Thus it would cost the owner about $150 to finish this dog, a very rare dream.

Case one A: The dog finishes in one weekend with three five-point majors, but with a professional handler. The handlers' charges vary from $35 to $60, with $50 being a good average. In this case it would cost about $195, plus board, to finish the dog. Still a dream.

Case two: This is a good Lhasa in keen competition, and it takes fifty shows to finish him. Entries are $700; minimum costs are $2,500. It costs $3,200 to finish the dog.

Case two A: It takes fifty shows with a professional handler. The cost is $3,900.

It often occurs that a dog may need one elusive point to finish. Sometimes this seems to take forever. On the other hand, the dog may need a difficult-to-find major. Many entries may be made at which shows the dog will be pulled for lack of majors. Consequently, the stud may cost up to $3,900 to finish, he may have cost $500 or more to purchase, and he has to be fed and cared for. So investment in a champion stud could be from $1,000 to $5,000. These costs do not include the advertising charges. Full-page black-and-white ads are costly. If you advertise six times, your bill could be $400 to $600, plus the price of the pictures.

No matter how one looks at it, to invest in a champion stud requires considerable monetary outlay.

STUD OWNER'S RESPONSIBILITIES

The stud owner has a variety of responsibilities. First and foremost, the background of the stud needs to be understood.

The ancestors of the stud need to be known. The pedigree thus becomes both a guide and, ultimately, a blueprint for breeding. The research can involve much "digging." I wade through old magazines, bulletins, and newsletters searching for information. I have talked with people and have corresponded with people, and after five years am still finding out facts about the dogs behind mine. Now I am at the point where I can say that the bite came from . . ., the color from . . ., etc. That pedigree provides mental images. As a stud owner, that is my responsibility.

Knowing my Lhasa can aid me in being honest and objective with the owners of the bitches. Knowing only his background, however, is not enough. Records have to be kept of his offspring. I need to know what type of puppies he sires, their faults and virtues. I need to know what he can offer to complement any given bitch. This is part of the honest and objective package that is part of his stud service.

Yes, a lot of money is invested in a stud. It would be nice to regain it in stud fees, but. . . . I firmly

---

(KENNEL NAME/ADDRESS)
(PHONE NUMBER)

BETWEEN _____ *(name of bitch owner)* _____ and _____ *(name of stud owner)* _____

STUD: _____ REG. # _____

DAM: _____ REG. # _____

OWNED BY: _____

ADDRESS: _____

STUD FEE _____ CONDITIONS: _____

_____

CONDITIONS OF SERVICE

1. No fee refunded in whole or in part.
2. A guarantee of actual mating (tie) only is made and not of pregnancy.
3. If bitch fails to be in whelp, the owner must give me notice not later than fifty days after the mating. In such cases a return service will be given to the same stud without charge at the NEXT heat. Owner of the bitch shall pay all express and shipping charges.
4. If stud is unavailable for any reason, stud owner has the right to mate the bitch with another stud, of choice, unless the parties mutually agree on a second choice. This applies only to a repeat breeding.
5. If bitch changes ownership, right of full return service is at stud owner's option. In order to be assured of pregnancy condition, the right to see and examine the bitch is granted.
6. Two live puppies constitute a litter.

DATE _____

_____
OWNER OF THE STUD

DATE _____

_____
OWNER OF DAM
(PREPARE IN DUPLICATE, ONE COPY TO EACH OWNER.)

Sample contract for stud service.

feel that a reasonable fee based on a stud's producing ability is the only viable way to go. A high fee may keep away good bitches because a good bitch and a full purse don't always go hand in hand. Too high a fee might restrict services to full purses but not the very best bitches. I think, too, that location does influence stud fees.

For the benefit of all, a written stud contract spelling out the details, the responsibilities of each owner, and the fees is the responsibility of the stud owner.

In addition to all this, there is a responsibility to the bitch to be bred. If she flies in, she must be picked up promptly at the airport. Thus, if a flight simply is very inconvenient, almost impossible, to be met, tell the bitch's owner so that congenial arrangements can be accomplished.

For instance, when I talked with the stud owner to whom I was shipping one of my bitches, I discovered that Wednesday was a really bad day, but that on Thursday her household help would be there, making it convenient for her to meet the only flight on which the bitch could fly from our area. Since she was being shipped in plenty of time, the day's difference would not hurt. Moreover, the stud owner could more easily pick her up. So it is the responsibility of the stud owner to let the bitch's owner know of complications in scheduling.

While the bitch is visiting, it is the stud owner's responsibility to give her good care: food, place to sleep, exercise, and attention. The stud owner should ask about the bitch's feeding requirements.

The bitch's coat should be kept in reasonable condition. Time and scheduling sometimes prevent bathing, but she should be sent home at least brushed out.

The stud owner may also have to be responsible for shipping the bitch home. (Of course, all shipping costs are borne by the owner of the bitch.) This, of course, entails another trip to the airport, and a phone call to alert the bitch's owner of flight details.

In addition to all of these responsibilities, the stud owner has another: the stud. He must be kept in good health and free of parasites, must have his innoculations and brucellosis tests, and must be groomed and clean.

Ch. Licos Omorfo La, "Murphy," one of the outstanding Lhasas of the early 1970s. Owner, Grace Licos. Photo by Ludwig.

Stud Fees

These may seem high to the uninitiated who may think that there is about an hour's work involved, and that on the part of the stud. On an hourly basis, the fees are, in reality, very reasonable, if not downright cheap. In fact, in relationship to stud fees for some other species, such as Arabian horses, stud fees for Lhasa Apsos may indeed be too low.

The range of fees is approximately as follows:

$150	for unproven stud;
	for unshown stud;
	for pointed, but unfinished stud.
$150–200:	for proven stud, unfinished;
	for unproven champion.
$200–350	for champion, proven producer of quality get.

TRAINING THE YOUNG STUD

The stud must have confidence in the person handling the breeding. While he is a puppy, do not correct your male for sexual behavior. This is the period in which he develops his interest in the opposite sex and is learning the techniques. He will play in a sexual manner long before he is mature enough to produce puppies. Should such actions be disturbing to your for any reason, quietly pick the puppy up and put him in his crate or his pen with something else to distract him. Never say "No!"

However, from five months of age on, keep a close eye on him. One famous mating took place with a five-month-old male. Others have bred at seven months, and several of my studs have bred and produced puppies well before they were a year old. In fact, I have heard that to use a stud once before he reached that year mark often improves ring performance.

But do not hurry the young stud. If he is not interested, he may be a bit too young. Lhasa studs do mature at different rates. One may do well at nine months and another at two years.

The choice of his first bitch is very important. The most important factor is that the bitch is experienced. A young dog who is on the show trail may be assertive enough to accept a bitch whether he knows her well or not. On the other hand, with a young stud who has been kept at home or who is not at all aggressive, the choice of a bitch that he knows might be better.

It is important that this first breeding go well. Consequently, the temperament of the bitch is important. One that snaps, that repulses, or that is a tease may be disconcerting to the young male.

Try to have a treat ready to give each when the breeding is completed. Do exercise both Lhasas in advance. If they are not exercised, they will perhaps be uncomfortable, and they may not tie.

Choose a quiet, undisturbed area, use the same place every time, if possible, and use the least possible help. My choice is the grooming room, which works just fine. There is both the floor and the table to use. Most of our breeding takes place there; the kitchen, the fenced-in yard, and the outside x-pen have been used as well.

For instance, an owner brought a bitch who was said to be ready THEN. Well, nothing happened in the breeding area. So I put them into the outside pen in the shade of a big Aspen, the owner left, and, you guessed it, before she got to the corner the Lhasas were tied! I had some fun getting over the 4-foot pen.

I have a mat for the studs to use. The first time I do endeavor to have the breeding take place on the mat, under my supervision, and while I am holding the bitch. If you are doing the breeding alone, and often that is the best way, a good method is to put the stud in a corner and back your bitch into him. Or, sit on the floor, your legs in a V, bitch over one thigh and under your arm, enabling you to keep her secure and your hands free to assist the stud if necessary. Use a phrase that you will repeat in future breedings, such as "Do your work."

Praise the male frequently. Be careful about touching him as it may "put him off," but sometimes he'll need some guidance. When the tie has been accomplished, and it may surprise him a bit the first time, praise him. Some studs will of their own accord lift their bodies off the bitches. Some may turn completely back to back. Others prefer not to and may lie at an angle or stand at an angle. If the stud does not get off of his own accord, gently lift the front half off the bitch and then very carefully lift a hind leg over the bitch's back. The stud may then of his own accord move into a comfortable position. Or you can slowly turn him back to back with the bitch.

Speak to the dog reassuringly during the tie. Most ties will last from ten to twenty-five minutes, but some may be as short as two and some as long as forty-five.

When the tie is over, praise the stud and the bitch. Give them treats. Allow them a few minutes for "loving." Make sure that the penis has retracted properly into the sheath. Allow them to exercise briefly, and then put the bitch in a quiet place.

Acquaintance Period

My personal preference is that a bitch arrive here a couple days in advance so that she and the stud become acquainted and so that she can adjust to strange surroundings. Breedings seem to go more easily when the Lhasas are not strangers.

I usually allow them some play time together, and I often put them in adjoining x-pens and side-by-side crates. A good stud will often have little loving habits such as "kissing" a bitch's ears, which encourages her relaxation.

To Determine a Bitch's Readiness

Usually, when the bitch is ready to be bred, the color of her discharge has turned to a very, very pale pink or clear color. This may happen any time from the fourth to the twenty-first day, although the extremes are unusual. Hopefully, the owner of the bitch will supply some information about the heat periods of the bitch.

Another sign of readiness is flagging. If you observe the bitch flinging her tail to one side when near the male or when you pat her rump, she is probably ready to breed.

The smear technique is fairly accurate. To do this, make a series over a period of days rather than just one. When the slide fills with "clumped, nucleiless cells," the bitch is ready for breeding (see Appendix).

Problems

To prevent problems, I suggest that if possible the vet dilate the bitch before she leaves on her trip, perhaps when the health certificate is obtained. Occasionally a bitch has a vagina that is too small or tissue within the vagina which prevents breeding. This should be known, as artificial insemination may be necessary if the decision is to breed such a bitch.

A major problem in breeding could be height differences. Usually an experienced stud will cope, but sometimes even he will have a problem. If the bitch is obviously taller, or if she holds herself tall, and if the stud has a deep chest, there may be problems. Put something smooth, a rolled towel or a piece of foam padding, under the end of the rug on which the male stands. It should be just enough to raise his rear legs sufficiently for him to do his work. Conversely, it may be necessary to raise the bitch's rear legs if she is considerably shorter than he, although this isn't usually a major problem.

Multiple BIS Ch. Everglo's Spark of Gold, left behind a heritage of 44 champion offspring to date. Thanks to the foresight of Dorothy Kendall, his owner, his sperm went into the sperm bank. Photo by Olsen.

There are times when the stud may have a problem entering the vagina; if so, a bit of *KY Jelly* may help. Use a sterile plastic glove, or even a baggie, in which you insert the finger easiest for you to use, cover with the jelly, and insert gently into the vagina. For any other problems which may become apparent, seek the advice of your vet.

Supervision

Do not allow a dog to mate a bitch unsupervised and, if possible, without your holding the bitch. Some few bitches will refuse to stand when held, but most are not upset by it. It is better if you do the holding because the stud trusts you. An owner might let go at the wrong time.

Notes

It is a good idea to keep a record of the conditions each stud likes. It may make future stud work easier for both of you. Things to note would be reception of bitch, position he likes the bitch to be in, how much he will allow you to help, actions he does not like, and his reception of others in the breeding area.

ARTIFICIAL INSEMINATION

Artificial insemination is an alternative that should be done only under extenuating circumstances such as when injury to the stud dog prevents his participation, or when a bitch is too small or will not stand for breeding, or when either male or female has a mild inflamation which could be irritated by breeding. Sometimes a bitch will show a mild staph or strep in a prebreeding culture, but no pathogenic bacteria that should affect her fertility. Artificial insemination prevents the spread of unwanted bacteria to the stud.

Artificial insemination, AI, should be done under veterinary supervision as the AKC requires a form signed by a veterinarian to accompany the litter registration. Since a veterinarian's fee is also involved, the owner of the bitch must be contacted and must give permission for her to be bred artificially.

No studies regarding the percentage of success from artificial breedings appear to have been published at this writing, but discussions with breeders reveals that when AI is done by persons knowledgeable and experienced in the correct techniques, the conception rate is high. Technique has much to do with success. Among horse breeders, for example, some people have up to ninety-nine percent success, and others have very little.

Artificial insemination is a two-person job. One must hold the bitch while the other collects the semen and inseminates the bitch. The crux of the matter is collecting semen from the stud. With some studs this is no problem, but others get upset by having a veterinarian handle them, or by having a strange person present while they are being ejaculated. If you have a popular stud dog you may want to train him to accept this as a normal procedure.

It is easier to collect a stud when a bitch in heat is present. To prevent him from mounting, grasp

BIS Ch. Taglha Kambu at home.
Owner, Jane Browning.

190

the penis firmly, but not tightly, with your thumb and forefinger resting behind the Cowper's glands (the pea-sized bulbs on each side at the base of the penis). Pull the sheath back of the glands, to allow room for them to swell and to prevent discomfort. This distention of the bulb indicates sexual arousal. The male will push against your hand. As he does so, place the collection vial in front of the penis so the ejaculate enters the vial. The first part of the ejaculate is clear and contains no sperm. The second, sperm-rich portion is milky in appearance. A last, and final, portion is somewhat clearer and is nature's method of mobilizing the sperm, flushing them up the vagina of the bitch.

The sperm should be kept warm by holding your hand over the base of the vial. Insemination must take place immediately after collection. Your veterinarian can work with you to teach you to do the actual insemination or to assist him in his office. He can also provide you with the insemination equipment.

Frozen Semen

Recently the AKC adopted rules for registering litters produced by using frozen canine semen for artificial insemination. These rules involve extensive record keeping to prevent registration errors. The collectors, the owners of donor dogs, the breeders, and the agencies storing the semen are involved in the record keeping.

The semen owner, the bitch owner, and the veterinarian involved in the insemination process are required to submit certificates to support the application for registration of a frozen-semen-produced litter.

This rule will make it possible to preserve semen of some excellent studs in order to maintain certain qualities. The semen of the great "Sparky," BIS Ch. Everglo's Spark of Gold, owned by Dorothy Kendall, was collected and frozen a number of years ago by Dr. Seeger. At some near future date we may see a new "Sparky" son in the ring.

BIS Ch. Tibet of Cornwallis ROM, all-time top Lhasa sire with 48 champions to date. Breeder, Paul Williams. Co-owned by Keke Blumberg and Carolyn Herbel, and later owned solely by Carolyn.

191

BIS Am. Bda. Ch. Kinderland's Tonka ROM holds the Best in Show record for Lhasa bitches with four BIS titles. Owners, Mr. and Mrs. Norman Herbel. Photo by Gilbert.

18

THE MATERNITY WARD

As whelping time draws near, your observations of your brood bitch should sharpen. In fact, starting not later than her fifty-eighth day of pregnancy, it would be wise to plan your schedule around her. Since many Lhasa bitches whelp early according to the whelping calendar, it is not advisable to leave her alone for any length of time the week that she is due.

It may be helpful to know what day of gestation her previous litters were whelped. The whelping date is determined by the bitch, and may vary from one litter to the next, although a bitch tends to show a recurring pattern. However, we have observed that litters sired by a certain stud usually arrive on the fifty-eighth day. This is probably due to the fact that this sire will not breed a bitch until she is close to ovulating, or on the optimum breeding day. A number of these bitches whelped litters sired by other studs which were whelped at sixty-one or sixty-two days. It is also interesting to note that this sire has two sons that have sired litters whelped on the fifty-eighth day.

Although many Lhasas are free whelpers, the unexpected may happen. A puppy may be caught in the track, thus causing problems. Your presence could prevent the loss of puppies and possibly your bitch, even if your only assistance is to take her to a clinic.

About two weeks prior to whelping date (about the forty-ninth day), take your bitch's temperature to determine her normal range. It should vary between 100 and 102° F. Keep a temperature chart starting with this reading. Begin taking her temperature morning and night and recording it. Should her temperature rise over 102.5° F, she should be checked immediately by your veterinarian to be sure there is no infection. What you expect to see is a gradual drop the week before whelping to around 100°F and then an abrupt drop to between 98° and 99°F which will indicate that whelping is imminent, usually within twelve hours.

THE WHELPING BOX

Decide ahead of time where you want the bitch to whelp. It should be in a relatively quiet and draft-free area where you can keep an eye on her, but where she won't be disturbed by daily activities or by non-family members coming and going. A quiet corner in your kitchen or family room is good. My own choice is a 4-foot-square closet off my kitchen. The door has been removed and a low barrier installed. The bitch can keep an eye on everything, but is secluded from curious eyes and drafts.

There are numerous inexpensive ways to create a whelping box. You can obtain plans and build a wooden one, you can buy one already made, or you can use a corrugated cardboard box. An area 20 × 30 inches is adequate. My own favorite is a #200 air crate. The bottom half, with the doorway blocked, makes a good whelping box. There is more than adequate room for the dam and her new puppies as they arrive. The crate is easily cleaned and sterilized.

Just outside the whelping crate I place a small round crocheted bed for the bitch, which she will usually occupy after the third day except when nursing and caring for her puppies.

A second alternative is to turn the top half of the crate upside down and fasten it to the bottom in the doorway. Turn the kennel heating pad on and direct the heat lamp into the half for the puppies. The dam can lie in the cooler half. As the puppies start to move around, they can sleep in one half and eat, play, and exercise in the other. The dam will then move to a bed just outside the crate-whelping box.

The whelping box should be disinfected. Pad the bottom with newspapers. Cover these with a section of old sheet. It is not good for the puppies to be directly on the newspapers because the ink tends to rub off on them. I prefer to cover the newspapers with old sheets rather than towels because the puppies cannot catch their claws in the sheets, which also dry more quickly when washed. Never use indoor–outdoor carpeting, as the combination of urine and chemicals in the carpet may cause burns severe enough to be lethal to puppies and cause severe discomfort for the dam.

Put the box into position. Locate a heat lamp or a bulb in a reflector over it. In the bottom of the box I use a kennel heating pad which is turned on when the bitch starts to whelp. Test the lamp with the heating pad on to be sure that it will heat the box to 80–85° F. Check the setting so that the proper setting is known in advance.

In addition, prepare a small box for the newborn puppies in case you have to remove those already born while a new one is whelped. But keep in mind that some bitches get very disturbed if you remove

TEMPERATURE CHART FOR WHELPING BITCH

Date Oct.	Time	Temperature	Comments
15	10:00 p.m.	100.4	
16	11:30 p.m.	100.4	
17	10:30 p.m.	100.0	
18	2:00 p.m.	100.2	
	10:00 p.m.	100.4	
19	5:30 a.m.	100.4	
	6:00 p.m.	100.4	
	12:00 m	100.4	
20	5:30 a.m.	100.0	
	5:00 p.m.	100.8	
	10:00 p.m.	100.4	
	12:00 m	100.4	
21	5:30 a.m.	100.4	
	6:45 a.m.	100.0	
	3:30 p.m.	99.4	
	5:30 p.m.	99.2	Face has developed tight, pinched look.
	7:30 p.m.	99.2	Felt occasional small contraction.
	9:30 p.m.	98.4	**Bitch has "bottomed-out."
	11:30 p.m.	98.4	
22	3:30 a.m.	98.8	
	5:30 a.m.	98.8	Bitch panting.
	7:30 a.m.	99.0	Now in obvious discomfort. Felt pup moving.
	8:00 a.m.		Gradually panting harder. Doesn't want me out of her sight.
	12:30 p.m.	98.8	
	2:30 p.m.		Hard labor. First puppy arrived shortly after.

194

WHELPING CHART

Date bred	Date due to whelp	Date bred	Date due to whelp	Date bred	Date due to whelp	Date bred	Date due to whelp	Date bred	Date due to whelp	Date bred	Date due to whelp	Date bred	Date due to whelp	Date bred	Date due to whelp	Date bred	Date due to whelp	Date bred	Date due to whelp	Date bred	Date due to whelp	Date bred	Date due to whelp
January	March	February	April	March	May	April	June	May	July	June	August	July	September	August	October	September	November	October	December	November	January	December	February
1	5	1	5	1	3	1	3	1	3	1	3	1	2	1	3	1	3	1	3	1	3	1	2
2	6	2	6	2	4	2	4	2	4	2	4	2	3	2	4	2	4	2	4	2	4	2	3
3	7	3	7	3	5	3	5	3	5	3	5	3	4	3	5	3	5	3	5	3	5	3	4
4	8	4	8	4	6	4	6	4	6	4	6	4	5	4	6	4	6	4	6	4	6	4	5
5	9	5	9	5	7	5	7	5	7	5	7	5	6	5	7	5	7	5	7	5	7	5	6
6	10	6	10	6	8	6	8	6	8	6	8	6	7	6	8	6	8	6	8	6	8	6	7
7	11	7	11	7	9	7	9	7	9	7	9	7	8	7	9	7	9	7	9	7	9	7	8
8	12	8	12	8	10	8	10	8	10	8	10	8	9	8	10	8	10	8	10	8	10	8	9
9	13	9	13	9	11	9	11	9	11	9	11	9	10	9	11	9	11	9	11	9	11	9	10
10	14	10	14	10	12	10	12	10	12	10	12	10	11	10	12	10	12	10	12	10	12	10	11
11	15	11	15	11	13	11	13	11	13	11	13	11	12	11	13	11	13	11	13	11	13	11	12
12	16	12	16	12	14	12	14	12	14	12	14	12	13	12	14	12	14	12	14	12	14	12	13
13	17	13	17	13	15	13	15	13	15	13	15	13	14	13	15	13	15	13	15	13	15	13	14
14	18	14	18	14	16	14	16	14	16	14	16	14	15	14	16	14	16	14	16	14	16	14	15
15	19	15	19	15	17	15	17	15	17	15	17	15	16	15	17	15	17	15	17	15	17	15	16
16	20	16	20	16	18	16	18	16	18	16	18	16	17	16	18	16	18	16	18	16	18	16	17
17	21	17	21	17	19	17	19	17	19	17	19	17	18	17	19	17	19	17	19	17	19	17	18
18	22	18	22	18	20	18	20	18	20	18	20	18	19	18	20	18	20	18	20	18	20	18	19
19	23	19	23	19	21	19	21	19	21	19	21	19	20	19	21	19	21	19	21	19	21	19	20
20	24	20	24	20	22	20	22	20	22	20	22	20	21	20	22	20	22	20	22	20	22	20	21
21	25	21	25	21	23	21	23	21	23	21	23	21	22	21	23	21	23	21	23	21	23	21	22
22	26	22	26	22	24	22	24	22	24	22	24	22	23	22	24	22	24	22	24	22	24	22	23
23	27	23	27	23	25	23	25	23	25	23	25	23	24	23	25	23	25	23	25	23	25	23	24
24	28	24	28	24	26	24	26	24	26	24	26	24	25	24	26	24	26	24	26	24	26	24	25
25	29	25	29	25	27	25	27	25	27	25	27	25	26	25	27	25	27	25	27	25	27	25	26
26	30	26	30	26	28	26	28	26	28	26	28	26	27	26	28	26	28	26	28	26	28	26	27
27	31	27	May 1	27	29	27	29	27	29	27	29	27	28	27	29	27	29	27	29	27	29	27	28
28	Apr. 1	28	2	28	30	28	30	28	30	28	30	28	29	28	30	28	30	28	30	28	30	28	Mar. 1
29	2			29	31	29	July 1	29	31	29	31	29	30	29	31	29	Dec. 1	29	31	29	31	29	2
30	3			30	June 1	30	2	30	Aug. 1	30	Sep. 1	30	Oct. 1	30	Nov. 1	30	2	30	Jan. 1	30	Feb. 1	30	3
31	4			31	2			31	2			31	2	31	2			31	2			31	4

their puppies and may even delay the delivery of the next one until the puppies are returned to them.

Allow your bitch to use the whelping box starting about the fifty-first day. She will nest and get accustomed to the box. If the weather is mild, it will not be necessary to heat the box until the puppies are whelped. However, if it is quite cold and damp, turn the heating pad on at a low setting. Too high a temperature may disturb a bitch at this time.

THE WHELPING KIT

A small box or basket in which you keep whelping supplies can be very helpful. Mine contains:
- a rectal thermometer
- vaseline or KY Jelly
- a small notebook and pen
- thread or dental floss for tying cords
- peroxide or iodine for disinfecting navels
- hemostats

In addition, have ready in a convenient spot next to the whelping box a good supply of newspapers, towels, washcloth, several pieces of sheet or blanket for bedding, a baby or household scale, plastic garbage bag, plastic or rubber gloves, surgical disinfectant soap, and a roll of soft paper towels.

A puppy kit is also handy. In it you may put syringes or small baby bottles or a tube feeding kit, *Esbilac,* and liquid or dry glucose. Do not wait until you need the glucose as it may be difficult to locate. You may also want to keep a recipe and supplies for making your own formula in your puppy kit.

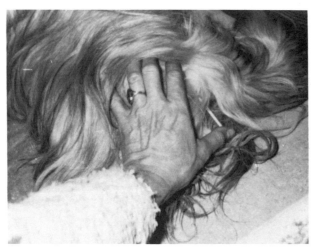

Take the bitch's temperature twice daily using a rectal thermometer.

196

PREPARATIONS

On or about her fifty-fourth day of pregnancy, bathe and groom your bitch. At this point, trim hair in the vicinity of the vagina and also around the nipples. If this bitch is not being shown, then also clip down the belly coat. There is no reason to clip the top coat which, if clipped, will take a very long time to regrow.

I would suggest recombing or rebrushing the bitch's coat the following day in order to remove hair loosened by the bath.

Between the fifty-fourth and fifty-seventh day, contact your veterinarian's office to see if he or she will be available during the expected whelping period, especially if the period includes a Sunday or a normal day off. If your vet will not be available, ask for recommendations for a substitute vet. If you are an experienced breeder, your vet may provide the Oxitocin shot for you to give.

It is best to have all the above information in case of problems. Minutes may be critical, or you may live some distance from your vet. Sometimes contact by phone can avoid an unnecessary trip. But if you need a vet, knowledge of his whereabouts can be vital.

PRELABOR

There are several symptoms which indicate a bitch is in prelabor. She may be uneasy and restless, and she may look for a hiding place. Some bitches will dig holes in the yard, perhaps under bushes. Some bitches will "root" under beds and in closets. Thus, this is a good time to confine her to an area around the whelping box. Provide plenty of papers for her to scratch and tear to satisfy her nesting instincts.

A Lhasa bitch may go through such actions for several days, even a week, prior to whelping, but each day these actions will become more intense. For other bitches these actions commence within twenty-four hours of whelping. In either case, the periods of stress during which nesting activity occurs will be alternated by periods of rest. Some bitches will sleep a great deal.

This prelabor period may also be indicated by a reduction in appetite. The bitch may eat only half of her usual portion.

Remember to check the bitch's temperature morning and evening. Her normal temperature should be between 101–102° F. A temperature which rises over 102° F would warrant a call to your veterinarian. What you are watching for is a drop in her temperature, which will bottom out between 98 and 99° F. This low point will vary from bitch to bitch. Some will drop to 98° F, while others may not go below 99.1° F.

This latter stage of prelabor, the start of which is indicated by the drop in temperature, will last from six to twenty-four hours. The usual pattern is for the first puppy to arrive between six and twelve hours after the temperature bottoms out. If a bitch shows obvious signs of prelabor and a temperature drop, but does not go into hard labor within twenty-four hours, she should be checked by a veterinarian.

If a greenish or reddish discharge appears BEFORE the first puppy is born, there may be a placental breakdown, which spells trouble for the bitch. Check with your veterinarian immediately if such a sign appears.

TRUE LABOR

This stage is characterized by purposeful straining. The bitch may lie in a prone position or may act as though she is trying to have a bowel movement. This straining may go on for some time, which may seem interminable as you wait. Do note the time, as the straining should not continue over two hours without the birth of a puppy. If you place your hand on the abdominal area, you should feel the force of the contractions. If two hours of hard contractions go by without the appearance of a puppy, contact your veterinarian for advice.

Within two hours after the labor pains commence, if all is normal, a sac somewhat like a greenish bubble will protrude from the vulva. Sometimes the sac will appear, disappear briefly, then reappear. A few forceful contractions will usually force out the puppy plus the afterbirth or placental membrane.

The puppy may arrive either head first or feet first; the latter is called a "breech birth." Do not be surprised by breech births. Many breeders have indicated that about fifty percent of Lhasa puppies arrive by breech birth. After each puppy arrives, expect to see some greenish and/or bloody discharge, which is normal just after the whelping of a puppy.

The assumption is made here that all puppies are arriving easily and without problems. Problems will be covered later.

Once the puppy has emerged from the birth canal, it is best that you remove the sac from the puppy and clear the air passage. The sac should be removed from the head down. It may be easiest for you to accomplish this while the puppy is lying next to its dam, although some like to gently pick the puppy up. Slit the sac by gently tearing it near the face or head, and work it off, much as you would a glove. Open the mouth of the puppy and carefully remove any mucous with a soft cloth. The puppy may be starting to wiggle.

I do not recommend letting the bitch eat the afterbirth. Animals in the wild hid the afterbirth to protect their newborn from predators. Should the bitch eat the afterbirth, she may develop diarrhea or may vomit.

The next step is to tie the umbilical cord. Grasp the cord and milk any blood in it back toward the puppy. Using a sturdy cord—size 50 thread, dental floss, or buttonhole twist—tie the cord about one inch from the abdominal wall. Use a simple square knot. Cut the cord one-half inch below the knot using sterile scissors, or tear it apart with your fingers. Discard the placenta. Dab the cord with corn starch, peroxide, or iodine to end the bleeding.

Now dry the puppy with a very soft, pliable paper towel. Cradle the puppy in the cloth and use the edges to rub the puppy briskly, but gently, to dry it. Note its sex, weigh it, and then put it close to its dam. Place it at a teat to see if it will nurse. The dam will probably lick it briskly. All of this will be accomplished in a matter of a very few minutes. While you may feel awkward at first, your skills will grow and your speed will increase.

When the puppy is back with its dam, take a minute to note your records: time of birth, sex, weight, color, markings, breech or head first, pertinent observations.

Rest Stage

The rest period starts immediately after the first puppy is born. During the rest period the bitch will clean the puppy thoroughly. She may even appear to sleep for a brief period. The length of the rest period will depend on the readiness of the next puppy to whelp. The rest period will last from a few minutes to about an hour and a half.

Repetition

The labor and rest stages will be repeated until the bitch is through whelping. There should be from minutes to no more than two hours between each puppy. When she is whelping a subsequent puppy, remove the newborn puppies only if it does not disturb the bitch. Otherwise, keep them with the bitch but under close surveillance. When she is through whelping, the bitch will cuddle down with her puppies, and at this point her abdomen will be spongy and flacid.

With a little experience you may be able to palpate the abdomen to determine whether any puppies are left. Keep in mind, however, that sometimes, because of its position, you may not feel a puppy. Thus, if you have any questions, contact your veterinarian.

It is difficult to state the average size of a Lhasa Apso litter, as litter sizes range from one to eleven. Many litters of which I know have numbered from four to six, but many have only one or two, and others have seven or eight. One piece of information which may help you estimate potential litter size is the size of litters whelped by the bitch's dam. The physical size of the bitch is no indication of the number of puppies in a litter. Some small bitches have only one or two; however, I know of one 9-inch bitch weighing about 10 pounds, who had six, and another approximately the same size who had litters of nine and eleven. In order for the bitch to produce a maximum size litter, it is important that she be bred on the optimum day.

Indications of Problems

It is quite important that you be aware of potential whelping problems. One of these indicators is too much time either in hard labor or between puppies. A good rule of thumb is a maximum of two hours in either case. If that amount of time elapses with no birth, call your veterinarian for advice THEN, not later, especially if this is a first litter.

Your records become valuable when there are indications of problems. While it is normal for bitches to have puppies within two hours, and usually less, your bitch may have a different pattern which would be indicated by your records. Should she digress from her normal pattern, contact your veterinarian.

198

The vaginal opening starts to dilate.

A puppy arrives enclosed in the sac.

Remove the sac from the puppy's head.

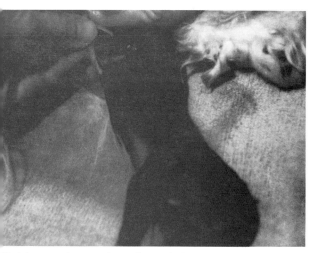

Finish removing sac from the pup's body.

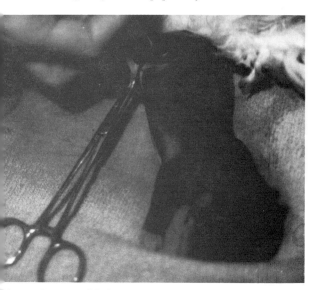

Clamp placenta with hemostat.

Tie the placenta with strong cord.

Another problem would be a puppy caught in the birth canal and which cannot be dislodged. For instance, a puppy can be in a breech position, but instead of the legs being in their normal position, they may be stretched out on either side of the head. The cervix just may not give enough for the puppy to pass. In such cases a quick visit to the veterinarian is in order. He might decide that a cesarean section is in order to save the other puppies and perhaps the bitch herself.

An excessive amount of red blood during the delivery may also be indicative of a problem. In such cases call your veterinarian for advice.

Removing a Puppy from the Birth Canal

There are numerous reasons why a bitch may not expel a puppy completely. When this happens, as midwife you will have to help the puppy on its way. Work as quickly and as smoothly as you can. Since the puppy and its sac will be rather slippery, use a soft paper towel or washcloth for gripping the puppy. PULL VERY GENTLY. If the bitch is still having contractions, try to work with them. If she is not, pull gently and steadily until the puppy is clear of the vulva. TRY TO GENTLY PULL AT ABOUT A 45-DEGREE ANGLE DOWNWARD FROM THE DAM'S BODY, working with the curvature of her body. Putting a lubricant such as KY Jelly or vitamin E oil in the vulva area to ease the delivery of the puppy is another help.

Occasionally a puppy will arrive sans sac or with sac punctured. Be gentle. Use the paper towel for easier grip and remove the puppy from the canal. Be sure to clean up such a pup well as it may be covered with an ugly green mucous-type material.

The most difficult will be the puppy in breech position, especially when a foreleg is aside the head. It may be necessary to gently turn the pup from side to side in order to dislodge it. Use a smooth wrist action to do this; do not jerk the pup.

Another problem will be the puppy encased in two, three, or four sacs. While this is not a usual problem, the survey of breeders indicated that double sacs were not unknown by the experienced breeder. Several noted puppies encased in triple sacs, something which has been occurring in recent years. My own experience includes one puppy born within four sacs. Sometimes these multiple sacs will be difficult to break. Perservere and work

199

as quickly as possible. Endeavor to get the head free from all of the sacs and to remove mucous from the mouth before trying to remove the sacs completely. The causes of such multiple sacs are not known at this point.

No matter how squeamish you might be, you will find that you can do the necessary actions. It may mean the difference between live and dead puppies and even a live or dead bitch. The secret is to keep your mind focused on saving the puppy and the dam and to be gentle but firm. If this is your first experience, it may be a good idea to have someone with you who has whelping experience, preferably with Lhasas.

Be sure that the paper towels which you choose are soft, flexible, and strong. Stiff paper towels simply will not do. Paper toweling is preferable to other toweling because they are inexpensive and disposable, and easy to have in quantity.

Removing an Attached Placenta

When the placenta to which the puppy's cord is attached remains inside the dam, you will have to separate the puppy from the dam. Gently grasp the puppy with your left hand. Take the cord with your right hand and pull carefully, being careful to no put pressure on the puppy's navel. To just pull the puppy and the placenta away from the dam, putting pressure on the puppy's navel, would create an um bilical hernia. Therefore, keep the tension betwee your hand and the dam, never on the umbilical cor where it joins the puppy at the navel. Pull gently but firmly, until the placenta and the afterbirth are clear of the birth canal. Then complete the car of the puppy in the usual manner.

If you experience a problem in freeing th placenta, clamp the cord with a hemostat so it can not recede into the bitch, and cut or tear the cor to free the puppy. Tie the cord in the usual manner

Reviving a Puppy

Occasionally puppies will, for one reason o another, seem not to breathe or to have an audibl heartbeat when removed from the sac. There ar several revival techniques which you can use. First

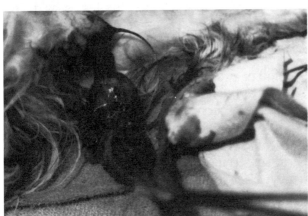

Left: Clamp placenta near the bitch with a hemostat. Cut cord one inch from where you tied it with cord.

Below left: Remove afterbirth gently by pulling with the hemostat. Dispose of it.

Below right: A breech birth—tail and rear legs are first.

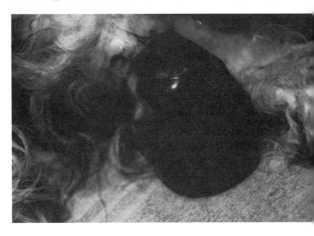

200

be sure the puppy's mouth and nostrils are cleared of mucous.

The simplest of these techniques is shock: a drop of whiskey or brandy is put on the tip of the puppy's tongue; then, the puppy is rubbed briskly with a terry cloth washcloth or towel.

The second method, also a simple one, is to immerse the puppy's body into a small basin of warm water, keeping the head out, of course, or to hold the puppy under a faucet from which comes warm water. The purpose is to raise the puppy's body temperature. Alternate the warm water with a brisk toweling.

The third method, slinging, is more difficult to describe, but not difficult to perform. It is like flicking a thermometer to send the mercury down. Hold the puppy face down, head on your fingers, thumb over the body, in your right hand. Cover the puppy with your left hand to prevent its slipping. Bend the elbow, bringing the hand to shoulder height; then flick downward quickly and hard, as you would the thermometer: straighten the elbow and snap the wrist in one combined movement, bringing the arm straight down. Repeat several times if necessary.

There are other methods. Some people have used smelling salts and others have used mouth-to-mouth resuscitation. Don't give up too easily. It may take ten or fifteen minutes of stimulation to get a puppy to breathe normally.

Before your puppies are whelped, consider which method you will use in an emergency.

CESAREAN SECTION

Your veterinarian may deem it necessary to perform a cesarean section either as a preplanned event or as an emergency. If this is a planned event, the bitch probably should have no food or water for about twelve hours preceding the operation. If it is done on an emergency basis, it will be necessary to recall the food and the liquid intake of the bitch during the previous twelve hours, and it may be necessary to empty her stomach.

The procedures of the cesarean are, of course, the veterinarian's prerogative. It is possible that you will be allowed to take the bitch and her puppies home as soon as she is satisfactorily out of danger. To prevent the stress which causes shock and hypoglycemia, keep both the puppies and the bitch warm. Use a preheated box or air crate to take them home.

After surgery the dam will feel the effects of the anesthetic for several hours. She will not yet be experiencing pain and should, therefore, have her maternal instincts encouraged by contact with her puppies. She will lick them and will probably remove the threads from their cords. She may be disturbed by the fact that the puppies may not nurse at this time.

The bitch may have a cough and a raspy bark, the aftereffect of the anesthetic. These should disappear within a few days. Keep water within her reach; she will desire it from four to six hours after surgery. She may also be offered glucose or honey. Continue to offer her glucose or honey each hour.

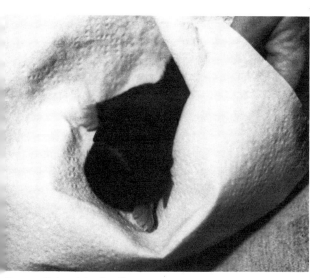

Use a soft towel to dry the puppy.

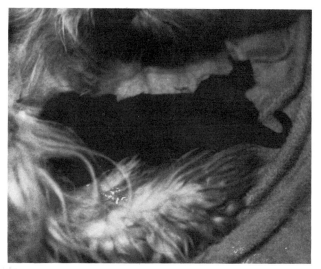

Place puppy at the dam's teat.

Her need to urinate may be signaled by fussing, crying, or barking. She will need help at first. Lift her gently to the papers beside the whelping box and hold her while she urinates. She may even have accidents within her box. Be sure to keep her bed dry and change it as needed. It is important to keep her warm and dry to prevent heat loss.

Allow her to use the papers about every two hours with your help until she can manage on her own. It is important that she be moving on her own within eight to twelve hours, as this aids in preventing pneumonia. If she is reluctant to walk, encourage her to do so by taking her a short distance away from her puppies.

Food, such as rice or barley and broiled ground beef, should be offered in small amounts and quite often. You could also tempt her with ice cream, cottage cheese, yogurt, or liver in small amounts. Within a few days she should be eating normally.

Her stitches will remain up to fourteen days and should be checked regularly for danger signals — redness and drainage. These signals indicate infection. Should they appear, contact your veterinarian immediately for prompt care for the bitch.

Care of Puppies Delivered by Cesarean Section

The puppies' breathing will probably have been depressed by the anesthetic; therefore, the puppies should be moved and touched, even fondled a bit, in order to stimulate their breathing. Approximately four to six hours after birth, you should start feeding the puppies per your veterinarian's instructions. You may tube feed, or you may use the syringe, which I prefer.

During the first twenty-four hours each puppy should get about 2 cc's of formula every two to three hours and 2 cc's plus as each gets hungrier. Allow the bitch to burp and to clean them if she will. After twenty-four hours start the puppies nursing on the bitch. If the milk supply is available, or when it becomes available, the puppies will nurse contentedly. Weigh the puppies regularly to be sure that they are gaining weight.

Consideration, love, and understanding are important for the dam during this period.

UTERINE INFECTIONS

One major problem for bitches can be uterine infections, which include acute metritis, chronic metritis, or pyometra. These can strike any bitch of breedable age. Research is ongoing concerning these infections, and new medications are being developed.

Acute Metritis

This disease usually runs its course in one week, but if the disease is untreated, the bitch will die. Symptoms include a 103–104° F temperature; a listless and dull attitude with no interest in her puppies; dehydration; a reddish, odoriferous vaginal discharge. The next development will be an enlarged uterus and a tender abdomen. Subsequently, severe abdominal pain, indicating the danger of a uterine rupture and peritonitis, will develop.

The causes are numerous, and the actual cause of a given case of acute metritis may be unknown: improper use of equipment, inept help, the introduction of pathogenic bacteria into the genital tract, and abortion.

Often factors in the bitch's background may indicate the potentiality of acute metritis. She may have chronic metritis or some other low-grade infection; she may have suffered previous abortions, stillborn puppies, or an abnormal discharge. It is quite important that the veterinarian examine the bitch before and after whelping and that she be given Oxytocin or other uterine stimulant to clear out any retained matter, and antibiotics to prevent infection.

Early medical care can be effective. The prognosis will be good for the bitch who is interested in her puppies, is not dehydrated, and is only slightly depressed. The prognosis is poor for the bitch who is dehydrated, has abdominal tenderness, seems very depressed, and who neglects her puppies. Early diagnosis is essential. If you suspect a problem, have the bitch checked immediately. It is better to be wrong and safe, than sorry.

The treatment includes controlling the infection with antibiotics, the elimination of diseased tissues, and hand raising the puppies. This latter is necessary because of the potentiality of toxic milk which could give the puppies septicemia.

If the bitch shows no response to medical treatments and severe infection continues, a hysterectomy would probably be the answer. However, prior to doing a hysterectomy, be sure the latest developments in treating the disease have been checked. Often there are new medications in the process of development which have not yet been released, or which have just become available. So it is wise to check all alternatives with a veterinarian specialist or college of veterinary medicine before radical surgery.

Chronic Metritis

The indications of this disease are abortion, stillbirths, or weak puppies. The symptom is a slight vaginal discharge. The obvious symptoms occur only when the bitch is bred. The diagnosis is made by a microscopic exam of a vaginal smear. Treatment is with antibiotics. Should the bitch whelp a live litter, both the bitch and the puppies must be treated with antibiotics.

Pyrometra

This usually affects bitches six years and older. However, several breeders reported cases in younger bitches. The infection occurs one to twelve weeks after estrus, and its primary cause is endocrine disturbance. The symptoms include listlessness, a slight vaginal discharge, and increased water consumption and urination.

The bitch then develops a high temperature, a copious brownish-red discharge, and appears to be seriously ill. In order for the situation to be cured, the cervix must remain open so that the infection drains. Should the cervix close, the uterus will enlarge and fill with pus, and death can result in a very short time.

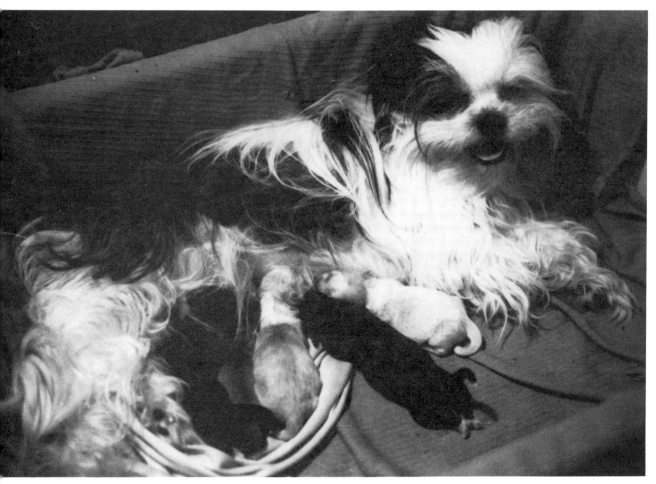

When whelping has been completed, the bitch will "cuddle down" with her newborn puppies.

Treatment must be immediate and concentrated. While some veterinarians feel that hysterectomy is the only answer, many feel that today it should be used only as a last resort in valuable young bitches. Some success has been achieved by the use of cervical catheterization, uterine incision, and antibiotics. The uterus is flushed out thoroughly, a drainage tube is installed, and the antibiotics are given to fight the infection. A "collar" such as an Elizabethan collar or one made of a rolled towel must be used to prevent the bitch from chewing on the tube. Some sources suggest performing hysterectomies on bitches eight years and older whose breeding times are over in order to protect them from pyometra. Recent experiments have reported successful treatment with the use of prostaglandin.

Mary Smart Carter, Milarepa Lhasa Apsos, wrote that this problem is being investigated at the University of Minnesota Veterinary College. When one of her bitches experienced metritis recently, her veterinarian contacted Minnesota. As a result, Prostin Fz Alpha, an Upjohn product also known as Prostaglandin injectable for mares, was tried with very good results. This drug at this writing is still being tested for dogs, although it has been released for other animals.

Eclampsia

Some Lhasa dams suffer eclampsia (milk fever), which is a calcium deficiency. This may occur about three weeks after whelping, and it may occur in dams who have had no problems with previous litters, as well as in first-time whelpers. The symptoms are nervousness, whimpering, spasms, and a stiff, unsteady gait. If you notice what may be signs of eclampsia, it is important to get your dam to the veterinarian as soon as possible, as it is vital to restore her calcium balance with injections.

While the dam is nursing her puppies for the first two or three weeks after whelping, she will need two or three times her normal food intake. Proper diet may help prevent eclampsia. Since milk products and milk are good sources of calcium and phosphorus, offer them in some form. Bone meal or calcium tablets may be used when the bitch is known to have problems with eclampsia.

The weaning process should start by the third week. This will take the strain off the bitch. In cases of eclampsia it may be necessary to wean completely at this time rather than to wean gradually. This will depend upon the severity of the dam's condition.

POST-WHELPING CHECKS

The Bitch

When all puppies appear to have been delivered, there has been no straining for several hours, and bitch and puppies have settled down to rest and eat, you should examine the bitch again. Check to make sure there is no copious or foul-colored discharge from the vulva. Palpating the abdomen may reveal a retained puppy. Sometimes the uterus contracts so tightly it feels like a lump, possibly a puppy. In any case, if you are uncertain, you should take the bitch to your veterinarian for examinations.

From five to twenty-four hours after delivery of the last puppy, your veterinarian may recommend an Oxytocin shot to help contract the bitch's uterus and expel any retained puppy or placental material. Experience has shown that the sooner the bitch receives the Oxytocin injection, the better. The bitch may also need antibiotics to prevent uterine infection, especially if she had an infection during previous pregnancies.

The Puppies

Weigh each puppy after birth and then morning and night for the first week or two. Accurate birth weight is important for several reasons. First, the weight of each puppy provides a basis for determining weight gain or loss. A lack of weight gain indicates that a problem may be developing. The puppies should each gain from ½ to 1 ounce daily. Second, the record provides you with an indication of the size of future puppies which your bitch may whelp.

Next, determine that each puppy is able to suck effectively. It is most important that each puppy nurse adequately during the first forty-eight hours. The colostrum (first milk produced by the dam (after whelping) includes antibodies that provide immunity from various diseases.

Within twenty-four hours the puppies should be checked for abnormalities such as cleft palate, harelip, and other deformities. A cleft palate is a congenital fissure or groove in the palate or roof of the mouth. The opening allows air and fluid to go from the mouth into the nasal cavity, and prevents a puppy from nursing normally. A harelip is a cleft lip—a lip with an obvious fissure. Puppies with severe birth defects should be euthanized by your veterinarian. Some abnormalities are acquired; some are hereditary.

Note any birth abnormalities on your records. If they occur in numbers, or repeatedly, or are hereditary, you should seriously reconsider your breeding stock and breeding program.

A healthy puppy is a joy to see. Its skin will have a firm feel once it has dried. If you pick up the skin between your thumb and forefinger, it will quickly go back into place when released. The membranes of the mouth and nose should be a warm pink. Do not be concerned if the pigment of the nose is pink at birth, as it gradually turns black.

The healthy puppy cries very little. If it is hungry and its dam is not in the box it may fuss, much as a baby does when hungry. When the mother is present, the hungry puppy will make a strong effort to get to a teat. The smallest puppy in one of my litters, a three-ounce puppy, was at his dam within minutes after birth and pushed so hard that his back feet were actually under him, supporting him as he nursed.

Puppies should nurse within two hours after birth. If the litter is very large, probably more than six puppies, the weaker puppies may need to be assisted to nurse every hour. If the puppies are too weak to nurse efficiently, or if the dam has insufficient milk, the puppies should be fed with a bottle, syringe, or tube.

SUPPLEMENTAL FEEDING

Puppies sometimes need to be supplemented because they are too weak to nurse, because there are too many puppies, because some may not be gaining weight, or because the bitch is unable to nurse them. They can be fed by bottle, tube, or syringe.

The bottle has the advantage of encouraging the sucking reflex. If you decide to use this method, get a premature baby nipple, which is softer. Prop the puppy in position and insert the nipple.

If you have several puppies that require around-the-clock feeding for an extended period, you could gavage or tube feed. Your veterinarian can supply you with the equipment and teach you how to insert the stomach tube. It is very important that this tube be correctly inserted because if improperly inserted the puppy can die of pneumonia if formula gets into the lungs.

Ch. Licos Cheti La, dam of the breed's top sire, BIS Ch. Tibet of Cornwallis ROM. Breeder, Mrs. John Licos. Owners, Carolyn and Norman Herbel.

Ch. Pon Go's Ton-Kha took BOS at Westminster in 1972. Breeder-owner, Edmund R. Sledzik. Photo by Klein.

An eccentric tip (offset) 6 cc or a 3 cc needleless syringe (or an eye dropper) can be used. Gently ease the mixture into the puppy's mouth, and if it is necessary, encourage him to swallow. Feed slowly. The puppy will suck on the tube much as he would on the nipple and will turn away when full. Feed slowly, as a puppy can choke from aspirating formula into the lungs.

The formula which I use is:

- 1 can evaporated milk
- 1½ can boiled water
- 1 egg yolk
- ½ tsp. powdered yeast (increase to 1 tsp. at 2 weeks)
- ¼ tsp. corn syrup (optional)
- ⅛ tsp. ascorbic acid (optional)

Warm the formula until it is lukewarm and test by putting a drop on your wrist. It should feel warm, but not hot.

The formula can be stored in the refrigerator. You can also purchase ready mixed or powdered bitch's milk substitutes from your veterinarian or pet supply outlet.

A small, weak puppy may take only about 1 cc of formula. It is better to feed small amounts often than to overload a puppy's digestive system. Weak puppies should be fed every two hours. Strong, healthy puppies that have been taken off the bitch, or puppies that are being supplemented because the litter is large, can be fed every four hours.

An easy way to figure the amount of supplement needed is to determine the total caloric requirement of the puppy and divide that by the number of feedings. All formulas provide approximately 1 calorie per cc of formula. An eight-ounce puppy during the first week requires 30 calories per day; a four-ounce puppy requires fifteen calories per day. Divide the total calories by the number of feedings to get the amount per feeding. For example, a four-ounce puppy fed every two hours would get 15 cc divided by twelve feedings, or 1¼ cc. An eight-ounce puppy supplemented every four hours would get 30 cc divided by six feedings, or 5 cc per meal.

POST-WHELPING CARE

It is very necessary to keep Lhasa puppies in a quite warm area (80° to 85° F). A newborn puppy's body temperature is 96° to 97° F. It is at these temperatures that viruses flourish. Thus, as a preventative, keep the puppy quite warm in order to raise its body temperature above the viral invasion level.

Keep the puppies at 80° to 85° F for at least two weeks, and perhaps three, using a combination of a kennel heating pad and a heat lamp. The kennel heating pad maintains a warm surface on which the puppies may lie. The heat lamp can be focused so as to keep the air around the puppies sufficiently warm to keep their body temperatures up. The lamp can be adjusted up and down in height to maintain the desired temperature. It is a good idea to keep a thermometer at the puppies' level to have an accurate measurement of the temperature.

Then gradually lower the temperature to 72° F during the fourth week. These temperatures should be maintained regardless of the weather. The bitch may not like it so warm and will often lie outside the puppies' box after the third day except when nursing, cleaning, or loving them.

Most Lhasa bitches are excellent dams and need little or no encouragement to care for their puppies. However, as a precaution, observe the bitch's relationship with her puppies. Breeders tell of bitches who have rejected or destroyed their puppies, although such cases appear to be rare. If signs of rejection are apparent, or if a bitch is neglectful, or if she is very rough with the puppies (even pushing them from her), remove the puppies from the dam, keep them in a warm box (temperature about 85° F), and watch them carefully when you place them with the dam to nurse. In such cases do not leave the puppies alone with the dam.

The causes for these reactions seem uncertain. Some breeders report that rejection and destruction occurred after a particularly difficult delivery. Others report no apparent reasons. Some reported dams who were subsequently discovered to have infections and were perhaps in pain. It may happen once and never again. It may happen after a bitch has had several litters and has been a good dam. It could be caused by a dietary deficiency.

Some dams are quite possessive of their puppies. This is especially true with a first litter and less so with subsequent litters. The possessive dams often have to be encouraged to eat and even carried to an exercise area. Most dams will keep a close watch over their puppies and will be reluctant to leave the whelping area for about three days.

Thereafter they will leave the puppies for short periods which will gradually lengthen. Thus, when weaning begins, it is not a great shock to the dams.

If you bottle feed and the puppy is sucking strongly, you can let the puppy nurse as long as he wants or until his tummy feels full and tight to touch. Do not let a hungry puppy overeat at first.

Once the puppies have been fed, return them to their dam. She will usually clean them immediately and stimulate their abdomens so that they will urinate and defecate on their own. It is better for the dam to do this if she is able. However, if the bitch cannot or will not stimulate and clean the puppies, you must do it for her. Use a small, soft washcloth dipped in warm water which is squeezed out. Gently stroke the puppy's abdomen, from navel to tail.

FEEDING THE DAM

The dam may refuse food immediately after whelping. Be sure to provide her with fresh water. Try giving her warm broth.

If the bitch is still refusing to eat twenty-four hours after whelping, tempt her with ice cream, cottage cheese, plain yogurt, or rice and barley with broiled beef. Her appetite will usually increase in ratio to the puppies' increased intake. Once she is back on solid food, feed her two or three small meals daily, decreasing the number of meals again when weaning begins. Be sure to keep fresh water available at all times. She will need a good ration high in protein, and your veterinarian will probably recommend a vitamin supplement or regular protein supplements during lactation.

Should there appear to be a lack of milk you can try giving the bitch a small amount of beer. About 3 cc of beer three times daily for a few days should be sufficient to stimulate the milk supply. (It is used for this purpose in human nursing mothers, too.) Try feeding it in a dish, or fill a 3 cc syringe and squirt it into her mouth.

RECORDS

Keep accurate records for each dam and litter. Note the bitch's estrus periods, the duration, the dates on which she is bred and on which she whelped. Note the facts about whelping: behavior prior to whelping, length of delivery time, types of birth (head first or breech), and any other pertinent factors. Record the number and weight and sex of each puppy. If there are problems such as infection, note these plus any treatment given. These records may be invaluable in future whelpings.

When the puppies are a week or two old, if all are doing well, prepare and mail your litter registration form. It must be signed by the owner of the stud before it is sent to AKC. You will receive a "blue slip" for each puppy, which must subsequently be filed to obtain an individual registration form with the name of the puppy and the new owners.

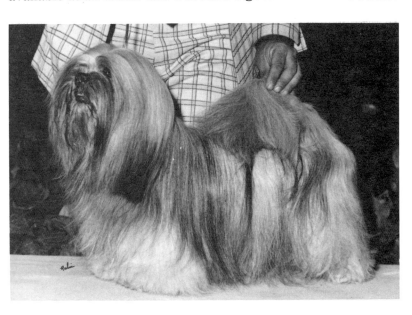

Dormar's Touch of Endrehea is the granddaughter of Ch. Queen's Endrehea. Breeder-owner, Doris Marquez. Photo by Rubin.

207

A grizzle-colored Lhasa puppy. Photo by Rosenkoetter.

19

PUPPY LOVE

The first forty-eight days of life for any litter of puppies are vitally important. Nice, plump, active puppies are a joy to see, but no matter how healthy they may seem to be, danger is ever present. It is essential that they receive warmth, food, and affection.

Lhasa Apso puppies may weigh from 3 to 8 ounces at birth, although the average weight is close to 6 ounces. There will be few as small as 3 ounces, and a fully formed 3-ounce puppy is not premature. In fact, they will usually double their weights in five to six days. Of course, because they are tiny, they will need close supervision to be sure that they are nursing sufficiently. These small puppies will nurse more often than the larger ones.

Birth size is usually not indicative of adult size in Lhasas. The smallest puppy may turn out to be the biggest adult, while conversely, the largest puppy may turn out to be the smallest adult.

At this point I should repeat a warning—avoid using indoor–outdoor carpeting with puppies. The chemical reaction of urine on the chemically formulated or treated carpet may severely burn the puppies. These burns can be lethal. Waxed linoleum or any slippery surface may also cause problems and will possibly affect gait. Puppies cannot get enough traction to propel themselves to the bitch. Weak puppies may get separated from the heat source and chilled. From birth, puppies need a surface with which their little paws can make a gripping contact, such as old flannel, percale, or muslin sheets which may be changed and washed daily. This surface will facilitate easier movement from the beginning.

THE FIRST TWENTY-ONE DAYS

So very much happens during these three weeks. First, the puppies should be kept at a temperature of at least 85° F.

During the first three weeks of the puppies' lives, their body temperatures are low—about 95–97° F. Viruses flourish at this temperature. Consequently, the puppies must be kept in an environment warm enough to elevate their body temperatures in order to prevent viruses from invading their bodies. One of the most virulent viruses during this period is herpes, which is one major cause of viremia.

Weigh each puppy every day, morning and night, until the puppy doubles its birth weight. If a puppy doesn't gain or if it loses weight, immediately start supplemental feedings until its weight gain is again consistent. The puppies should be each gaining from about ½ to 1 ounce daily. If there are no other problems when supplemental feedings become necessary, it usually only takes a few meals to get the puppy back on track.

Take advantage of the weighing to give each puppy personal attention. Talk to it, pat it, and gently rub its back. Hold it against your face or neck. Take time to examine it. Even put the puppy on its back and scratch its tummy. At first spend only a couple of minutes with each puppy, as you may find its dam getting anxious. Gradually extend the time.

When the puppies are about a week old, one friend's son tucks a puppy inside his shirt and walks around with it there. He does this each day after school and on weekends. These puppies are some of the best adjusted I have seen. Daily contact with the puppies is very important.

The puppies will be moving around considerably. Though they will be sleeping much of the time, each day they will move around more. About the tenth day, their eyes will open. An occasional puppy will start opening his eyes about the seventh day, and some will not open their eyes until about the fourteenth day after whelping. The eyes do not open all at once. First there will appear to be a slight crack which widens gradually. During this time the puppy will also begin hearing. Lhasas have very sensitive hearing. Dogs have three semicircular canals filled with fluid in their ears, and like humans, the balance of the dogs is affected by these canals. The sense organs are within the cochleae.

As this period moves along, the puppies will tend to sleep in one area where the sheet-blanket is and will crawl to the other end where the papers are to make their first stabs at playing and later to exercise.

After the fourteenth day you may start weaning them if you wish, although healthier puppies usually result if you wait until they are three weeks old. Take the weaning process very slowly, and feed only once a day at this point. I find that a baby rice cereal gruel, thin at first and gradually thick-

PUPPY WEIGHT CHART

No.	Sex	Description	11	12	13	14	15	16	6 pm	17	18	19	20	21
									Date (in December), Weight (in ounces)					
1	Male	Gold/wht. shawl	5	5	5	6	6	6	7	7½	8	8	9	*10
2	Female	Wht./spt. head/tail	6	6	6	6	7	7	8	8	9	9	10	11
3	Female	Wht./dark parti	4	5	5	5	5½	5½	6½	7	*8	8	9	10
4	Female	Gold/wht.	6	6	6	6	7	7	8	9	9	10	10½	11
5	Male	Gold/wht. ch. blk. mask	6	6	6	6	6½	7	8	9	10	10½	11	*12
6	Female	All Gold	5	5	5	5	6	6	7	8	8	9	9½	*10
7	Male	Wht./gold parti	6	6½	6½	7	8	8	9	10	10	11	*12	13

ened, works best for weaning. I use reconstituted dehydrated milk for liquid. The first few days, take one puppy at a time before he nurses, and put him by a low container of food. Individual plastic hamburger-patty containers are ideal for the food at this point. You may have to gently push the puppy's face to the food, and it may take a couple of days before each one eats freely. As each one finishes, wipe the excess food off its face with a damp cloth. Baths, unless absolutely necessary, are dangerous at this age because the puppy may chill afterward. This is especially true during very cold weather. The dam will usually keep them quite clean.

During this whole period, check each puppy to be sure that he is urinating and defecating without problem. Watch that the anal area does not "wax" over; that is, get stuck with fecal matter. The bitch usually takes good care of the puppies during this period, and she seems to know just how much and how long to stimulate the puppies. It is really better that this be a natural act; therefore, do not stimulate the puppies to "go" unless there appear to be problems, as you could establish a habit. If there appears to be excessive hair around the anal opening (the stool may stick to it), take a small scissors and very carefully trim the hair for about ¼ to ½ inch around the anal opening.

Sometime between fourteen and twenty-one days you should see some efforts toward play. The puppies will roll around, play with their paws in the air, and look around solemnly. Remember that each litter and each puppy develops at his own pace.

During this period there will be changes in each puppy's appearance. For instance, angulation is ap-

parent at birth. However, within hours the puppy starts to fill out, and as he fills out, angulation is hidden. At first the puppy will curl up, much as in the womb, but as he grows and if he is sufficiently warm, he often will sprawl with his front legs forward and his rear legs straight out behind. In fact, he will look like a tadpole as he sleeps in this position.

Puppies will huddle together for warmth when they feel cold, but when they are kept in a warm temperature, they will sleep sprawled out. When the temperature in their whelping box is lowered after fourteen days, they will start huddling again.

The puppy's chest will seem flat to the touch until the puppy starts getting up on its legs. At that point the ribs and the chest will shape up. The time at which this occurs will vary. I have had puppies getting on their feet as early as fourteen days, but I find that most puppies can be expected to make an effort to get on their feet about the twenty-first day.

The most apparent physical change besides growth will be in the head. When a Lhasa puppy is born, his head has an odd, squashed look as the muzzle is not shaped and seems to come from the forehead. During the first week the head gradually shapes up. By the time he is three weeks old, the muzzle placement is quite apparent and should be level with or just barely below the lower eyelid. The muzzle should come out level and straight and should not slope. Between the second and third weeks, as the muzzle forms, the chrysanthemum growth of hair on the face becomes noticeable.

Eight puppies by BIS Ch. Yojimbo Orion ex Ch. Kykee Rum Poppy. Breeder, Jeanne Holsapple.

Usually the pigment on the nose and paws will be pinkish, even on a dark puppy, when he is whelped. However, occasionally one will be born with black pigment. The nose leather will start to darken within hours, but the degree of darkening will vary from puppy to puppy. Some puppies will have black noses within forty-eight hours, and for some the time will be longer. Usually the noses will be black by the fourteenth day. However, if the puppy's coat is very light in color, do not panic. Sometimes the black pigment on a puppy with a light colored or white coat will take a long time to develop. Such a puppy will usually develop a dark nose and dark eye rims, but it is not unusual for a light colored or white coated Lhasa to have pink or natural colored pads with white toenails.

A change in coat will be noticed quite early, with some definite growth by the twenty-first day. The white hair often seems to grow faster than that of other colors, and the hair growth will vary from puppy to puppy.

FOURTH WEEK

During the fourth week start weaning the puppies if you have not already done so. If you have started, increase the puppies' meals to two a day, morning and night, and thicken the gruel until it is the consistency of paste; feed the puppies as a group. Crockery feeding bowls about 2½ inches high become useful at this point. The gradual weaning process is beneficial to both the puppies and the dam, who now can be out of the pen a good portion of the day.

Sometime during this week, I move my puppies from the whelping pen to a 4-foot-square raised puppy exercise pen, or play pen, in the corner of the kitchen by two windows. This pen improves the sanitary conditions, prevents contact with parasites which could be in stools, and makes it much easier to clean up after the puppies. The raised pen has another advantage in that the puppies often seem to housebreak easier. When out of the pen they search for a piece of paper, however small, on which to "go."

The pen is in a draft-free corner, but is where there is stimulation for socialization and acquaintance with the outside world, vital for Lhasa puppies. It is not unusual to see the puppies watching the birds on the fence or in the feeder or the Brittanies in their pens. Put various types of toys in the pen for play. Use small squeaky toys, old socks, nylons, or pieces of panty hose (knotted), tubes from paper towels or toilet paper, and small rubber balls about 2 to 3 inches in diameter. Playing stimulates motor development.

Since the puppies now are group eating, they tend to get more food on their coats. Thus, this is a good time to introduce them to baths. Which method you use depends upon the amount of time which you are able to spend on them. I prefer to do them individually so that I spend time with each. However, if other plans interfere, I will do them as a group.

I like to wash them in my "dog" tub because the sides prevent any chance of falling. During the cold weather the room is first warmed up; then the tub is filled with about 2 to 3 inches of lukewarm water. I dilute the shampoo just as for adult dogs (see chapter on grooming), but 4 cups of diluted shampoo will wash four puppies. I set the puppy in the tub and, with a plastic cup, gently pour water over the puppy until the coat is soaked. Then I pour about 1 cup diluted shampoo over it. (Use neither flea shampoo nor dip at this age as both are hazardous to the puppy, the other puppies, and to the dam.) Use your fingers to be sure that all the food is out of the coat, and use a cup to dip up and pour the diluted shampoo and water over the coat numerous times. Wash the puppy's face with an old soft washcloth. Then rinse the puppy's coat with

Mom and dad with a litter of four-week-olds.

a gentle spray, cuddle in a towel to take off excess moisture, and place on the grooming table under the drier for a few minutes. Comb the coat as it dries.

Should I be pressed for time, I'll pop the puppy into a wire crate lined with towels and with a small drier aimed in. I add puppies as I get them washed and towel blotted. Once all are washed, I comb (starting with the first) and check for complete dryness. This is also a good time to clip nails—cut the tips only.

During the fourth week, a puppy's motor development will be very apparent. He will be unsteady on his legs at first, but he will develop his walking skill quite quickly. He will play by "biting" his tail and his own legs, and he will start playing with the other puppies in the same manner. The play will be quite gentle at first, but becomes rougher as the week progresses. At first the play periods will be very short, sandwiched between naps. Gradually the play periods will lengthen.

At this period the puppy will exhibit early signs of teething as he "gums" his legs or tail, another puppy, or even a small toy. If he hasn't already done so (some do by the twenty-first day), he will find his voice and start making little growl noises and even little barks. Sometimes a puppy is quite surprised by his voice and will look around to see where the noise is coming from. He will now become aware of noises and actions outside the whelping area.

Socialization can start under careful adult supervision. There should be no excessive, rough, nor extensive handling. A puppy can be tickled or played with gently for a short period of time.

At this point the puppies will often sleep lined up side by side. They will be growing rapidly, but their growth rates will vary. The puppy who is the

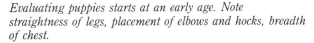

Evaluating puppies starts at an early age. Note straightness of legs, placement of elbows and hocks, breadth of chest.

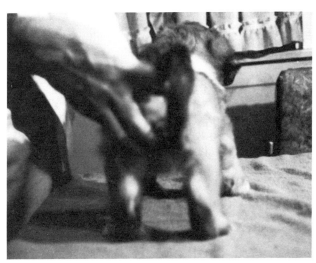

213

smallest at this point may end up the largest when full grown. By the end of the week the puppies should weigh between 1½ to 2½ pounds.

FIFTH WEEK

The weaning process should now be on the last stage. Increase the puppies' meals to three a day. Add softened puppy chow to the gruel; add just a little at first and then increase the amount gradually until the meal is completely puppy chow. To soften the chow, place the desired amount in a bowl and cover with water; allow to soak until the water is absorbed. During this last step allow the bitch to nurse the puppies and to nuzzle and to play with them once a day. She won't want to nurse them too much because their teeth will be erupting. But this method will enable her milk to dry up gradually and will spare her unnecessary discomfort. However, she should still be in contact with her puppies. She can supervise them from outside the play pen.

Evaluate your puppies at this point. Those faults which may make a difference between a show dog and a companion dog may well be apparent: bites (especially undershot), back length, ear set, pigment, eye color. Do not judge on leg balance because the legs should still be in the process of growing at this point.

For a few minutes each day, or every other day, stand the puppy on a grooming table to begin table training. This should be very brief. If you like, allow the puppy to drag a tie, loosely tied around the neck, around on the floor. This prepares for lead training.

During this fifth week also start being aware of excessive shyness or hyperactivity. Such puppies need plenty of fondling. Avoid quick actions or rough play, and keep voices soft. Extra human contact will help. Again, someone could carry the puppy close to his body for that extra contact and for body heat.

The puppy will continue to grow rapidly and will weight between 2 and 3 pounds by the end of the week. There will be more coat growth, and the puppies will start to get their teddy bear look. It may be necessary to clip long toenails again.

214

SIX TO EIGHT WEEKS

At this time the puppies should be completely weaned. Allow the dam to visit them briefly, but do not allow the puppies to nurse. If the puppies are not already on puppy chow, shift them gradually from the gruel to the chow, or make the final step. Also, keep a bowl of dry puppy chow in their pen for teething. Another thing that puppies like to chew on is small dog biscuits.

After the very last nursing by the puppies, apply camphorated oil to the breasts of the dam. This oil will aid the drying up of the milk. But do not allow the dam to be with her puppies while she has the camphorated oil on her. Once she appears to have no more milk, bathe and groom her. Then start allowing the bitch to play with her puppies again. She will teach them and will act as their intermediary into the adult Lhasa world. This is an aspect often neglected, but it seems important in the adjustment of those puppies who remain and who are destined for the ring. Moreover, some studs can also aid in this transition process.

Continue the "neck-tie" experience. This will gradually get the puppy accustomed to a lead. Lead training can be done between six and nine weeks. My best successes resulted from using a figure-eight harness. Some puppies may be very resistant to walking on martingale or show lead. It was this reaction which encouraged me to return to using

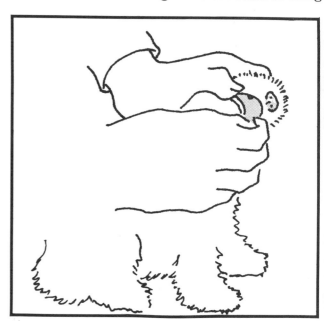

Examine the bite. Note the jaw position. Illustration by Shirley Lennox.

the harness. The harness can be put on alone at first. The puppy may be given time to get used to it, and the puppy's coat will not be damaged by the harness. Use a fine snap lead. As opposed to a lead around the neck, this method usually finds the puppies walking on lead very quickly. Once they are walking well, the shift can be made to a martingale lead and later to a show lead. Never use collars on Lhasas as collars tend to mat the hair. The figure-eight harnesses do not appear to damage the coats and can be left on while you put the puppy outside periodically for housebreaking. However, do not leave the harness on for more than a couple hours at a time.

Continue table training. Encourage the puppy both to lie down for grooming and to stand in show pose. Gradually increase the table time. You may start baiting on the table and training the puppy for mouth examination. This latter may be done by using gravy or something tasty. Rub it on the lips and gently open.

As soon as the puppy will walk on harness or lead, start bait training. But remember one thing: the puppy which walks looking for bait can be spoiling its gait and appearance. Do encourage the puppy to be aware of you and to occasionally look at you, but baiting should be done only when the puppy is stopped and you desire alertness in pose.

Four-week-old puppy is introduced to toy.

Give the puppy the treat when he stops and stands with four feet on the ground, but never if he jumps. Make this exercise fun and praise often. There is one other factor to keep in mind and that is that some puppies will not bait until they are older, even until two years old.

By three months most puppies will be performing on lead. Do not be too upset with your late starter, however. Some just are. At least one Lhasa puppy did not walk on lead until she was nine months old.

EIGHT TO TEN WEEKS

Some say that this is a bad psychological time for puppies to leave home and that those who do have difficulties with house training and in adjusting to new surroundings. Thus, do not be in a hurry to push your puppies out of the door.

However, I have both purchased and sold puppies within this time period which not only adjusted well, but did no crying at night and house trained easily.

The answer probably depends on several things: the breed of puppy, the individual puppy, the new home and new family, and its experiences prior to the change.

The puppies continue to grow rapidly during this time. Their weight gain should be gradual and in proportion to their structures. Do not allow a puppy to become too heavy as this weight might affect his legs.

Now is the time to start evaluating a young puppy. From the front, note the straightness of legs, the placement of the elbows, and the breadth of chest. From the side, note the topline, the tail set, and the stance. From the rear, note the straightness of the legs, the position of the hocks, and the closeness of the legs. This examination should be accomplished both with the puppy moving freely and with the puppy on a table. It is difficult to evaluate a young puppy without help, and the person who aids you should be knowledgeable.

Now is the time to examine the puppy's bite and to note the jaw position. The puppy which has either an undershot or overshot bite at this age should be designated as a pet puppy. Those with tight scissors and tight reverse scissors bites should be examined again at a later age. Even the level

215

bite must be checked later. Obviously crooked legs, cowhocks or sickle hocks, blue eyes, and liver-colored noses also indicate a pet-quality puppy. These faults do not make a puppy less lovable, but merely mean that it should not be sold for show potential or as breeding stock.

INNOCULATIONS

There are varying attitudes toward inoculations. It is a subject each breeder must analyze in cooperation with his or her veterinarian.

A measles vaccine for distemper may be given at six weeks, with a permanent DHL being given at twelve or sixteen weeks. The vaccine for canine distemper, hepatitis, parainfluenza, and leptospirosis may be given at younger than nine weeks, but if so given, must be repeated every three to four weeks until the puppy is twelve weeks or older. One manufacturer suggests that the first dose be given at nine weeks and a second three weeks later to provide a higher level of immunity against canine parainfluenza.

Opinions differ on parvo vaccine. This was discussed with a veterinarian–researcher at a major manufacturer. His suggestion is that parvocine not be given until the puppy is eight or nine weeks old, and then every three to four weeks until the puppies are sixteen weeks old.

Puppies receive natural immunity from their dams for many diseases. This immunity lasts for varying lengths of time. For instance, about 85 percent of all puppies lose their passive immunity to canine distemper by the time they are nine weeks old, at which time the vaccine will become effective if given. One reason for vaccinating puppies at this age is to establish immunity before they are exposed. This kind of immunization plan has reduced the incidence of communicable diseases.

No puppy should leave you without having the DHL and the first parvo shot. If the puppy leaves at eight weeks, it should then be given its second DHL and second parvo shot by the new owner's veterinarian.

The first rabies shot is usually given at six months. However, the state or province to which

Below left: Am. Can. Ch. Ahisma A. Tantras wins a puppy match at the start of his show career. Owner, B. Steele.

Lhasa six to eight weeks of age.

a puppy may be being shipped could have specific rabies shot requirements. Your veterinarian will have that information. Also, boosters are required in all states and provinces, and these requirements vary in different areas; some require yearly boosters and some accept three-year boosters. The requirements vary according to the incidence of rabies in each area.

NEW OWNERS

The conscientious breeder will want to know something about the owners-to-be. Their familiarity with dogs and with Lhasas in particular is important, but do not rule out those who have never had a pet dog. They may have desired pet dogs for a long time, but were prevented by situations beyond their control. Be interested in why they want a dog, their physical environment, size of family, etc. Reasons for wanting a puppy may influence the choice of puppy.

When people come to my house, they must pass the "Rumpie test." Rumpie's reaction to them can tell me much about them. Since Rumpie is normally an outgoing and friendly Lhasa, albeit reserved with strangers until he "sizes them up," his reactions which reflect his intuitive opinions of them are important. He senses their care, love, and interest in dogs. Moreover, during conversations, facts often come out which more than justify his reactions. You, too, may have a Lhasa who is an instinctive and accurate judge of people. Use the talent to your advantage. After all, that ability is a part of a Lhasa's heritage.

Provide each new owner with written care instructions or a care phamphlet. Should you not be able to have such things printed, have the instructions typed or handwritten in a very legible manner, dry copy them, and encase in a theme folder. Keep your master for making future copies. These care phamphlets are more than worth the time involved in preparing them. The new owners gain a sense of security from them. Also, include instructions for contacting you should there be problems. For instance, new owners sometimes have problems coping with puppies who are blowing coats and return for grooming help.

Always advise new owners of the value of air crates, which help to give the puppy a sense of security in that the crate becomes his "den," and which can be used in house training. Also, crates are the safest method for traveling and provide the puppy, young, or older Lhasa with a sense of security in a strange place.

Four little darlings: Young bitches bred by Mary Carter and owned by Mrs. Alton G. Marshall with the Marshall's daughter, Sarah, left, and a classmate.

217

Am. Can. Ch. Krisna Kam-Tora of Sunji was top-winning bitch on the west coast for two years, a multiple group placer, and dam of a champion. Owner, Wendy Harper.

218

20

PUPPY ILLNESS

A bouncing, happy, healthy puppy is a joyful sight. Even though we breeders struggle to keep our whelping areas and our Lhasa living areas as sanitary as possible (using products such as *Clorox* and *Odokleen*) in order to prevent the existence and spread of viruses, diseases, and parasites, illnesses still occur.

There are numerous signs of trouble for the very young puppy and the somewhat older puppy. If you are weighing your young puppies daily, and if you find one who is not gaining or who loses weight, this is a sign of trouble. Nursing ineffectiveness also can be a sign; check to see how the puppy sucks on your finger. Crying or whimpering are vocal signs. A puppy off by itself, isolated, is another. Skin that is cold and clammy is a symptom, and muscle limpness is another. Diarrhea is still another trouble sign.

Keep a watchful eye on the large puppy. This puppy, which may weigh about 8 ounces at birth, may dehydrate more quickly than the smaller ones. The dehydration may indicate a serious problem. If the larger puppy starts to lose weight, contact your veterinarian for advice immediately. If you cannot reach your veterinarian, be careful about giving supplemental formula. It might be better to use non-carbonated *Gatorade* (which contains electrolytes), distilled water, or boiled water. Veterinarians are prescribing *Gatorade* to prevent dehydration, and it has been used with very small puppies. Instant *Gatorade* mix can be purchased in the grocery store. Use 1 cc to 3 cc, depending on the size and the age of the puppy, until you can discuss the problem with your veterinarian. Usually it does not take much to reverse dehydration, and that reversal may be vital to the puppy's life.

Once the puppies are weaned, there are also signs which indicate problems. A puppy may not join in play with the others, or eat with them, or may seem to sleep too much. The puppy may have diarrhea or excessive mucous in his stool. The puppy may even vomit or pass roundworms in his stool. The puppy may feel excessively warm and be running a temperature. His eyes may have a glazed appearance, and his coat may lack lustre. Often he will not cry, even when in pain, although in some cases there may be whimpering.

All of these factors may be the symptoms of an ill puppy requiring special care.

WEIGHT GAIN

A Lhasa Apso puppy should double its birth weight by the time it is ten days old; i.e., if it weighs 6 ounces at birth, it should weigh 12 ounces at ten days. My experience has revealed that the smaller the puppy, the sooner it doubles its weight. Thus, my 3-ounce Laddie weighed 6 ounces by the seventh day. Puppies should gain from ½ to 1 ounce per day.

A puppy should not gain too much, however. Obesity could prevent walking and cause problems with the bones in the legs. Moreover, swimmers are usually heavy puppies.

If the puppy is not gaining, is not crying, and there is nothing apparently wrong, try giving it some formula every other feeding. A weight gain should be noticed within twenty-four hours. If the puppy is very fussy or appears to have something wrong with it, a visit to the veterinarian is in order to determine the problem. Do not allow the puppy to get chilled in transit. Use a lined box for the puppy; if necessary, fill a hot-water bottle, wrap it in a towel, and put it in with the puppy.

SICK PUPPY'S TEMPERATURE

A very young sick puppy's temperature may not be measureable on your thermometer, as it may be below 96° F—as low as 78 to 83° F. If this is the case, warm the puppy slowly. One way to do this is by putting the puppy next to your own body, which acts as a heater. If a heating pad, a heat lamp, or even an incubator is used, turn the puppy frequently.

DO NOT GIVE THE PUPPY FORMULA. Use a 5-percent glucose or sugar water solution—1 teaspoon of sugar or *Karo* syrup to 1 ounce of water. Give five drops by medicine dropper every half hour. This will give the puppy needed energy.

Dehydration is another problem. This can come on very rapidly, especially when the puppy is under a heat source. Thus, water or *Gatorade* is a necessity. *Gatorade* has been found to be effective in off-setting dehydration. If you use water, use cooled boiled water. Use about 1 cc every hour for a small puppy and more for an older, bigger puppy.

Our veterinarians, when treating a sick puppy, will provide fluids to prevent dehydration, will combat hypoglycemia, and will raise the puppy's temperature. If it is possible, get the puppy to your veterinarian as soon as possible so that you know what you are fighting.

FADING PUPPIES

After all the planning, there can be nothing more disheartening than to lose the puppies. One manner in which they are lost is by the Fading Puppy Syndrome, a term which covers a broad spectrum of puppy diseases which occur during the first fourteen days of life. To prevent this, it is very important that the dam receive adequate nutrition during pregnancy. A primary cause of the fading puppy syndrome is that the puppy is born malnourished. It is usually too weak to be able to nurse in an effective manner. These puppies will need to be hand fed at least part of the time.

Another cause of the fading puppy syndrome is a lack of adequate lactation. In this case supplemental feedings are essential. It might help to give the dam about 3 cc's of beer several times daily.

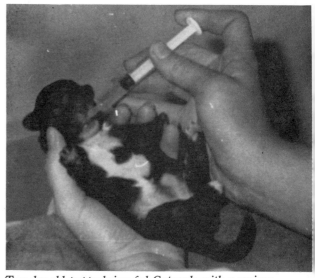

Two-day-old puppy being fed Gatorade with a syringe.

220

The beer will probably not only stimulate the supply, but may also improve the quality of her milk. Two to three doses daily should be sufficient.

An environment which simply isn't warm enough is another cause of fading puppy syndrome. Keep the temperature at 85–90° F for one week; then lower it to between 80–85° F for two weeks.

The source might also be a combination of any or all of the causes. It is important that supplemental feedings start shortly after birth, within a matter of hours, and that weight checks be made frequently. Moreover, the puppies must be kept warm to avoid chilling.

VIRUSES, BACTERIA, AND PARASITES WHICH ATTACK PUPPIES

There are many viruses which attack puppies: canine distemper, infectious hepatitus, canine herpes virus, canine adenovirus type 1, canine adenovirus type 2, rotavirus, canine parainfluenza, reovirus, canine coronavirus, parvo virus.

Bacteria which cause infections in puppies include: brucella canis, escherichia coli, staphylococci, pseudomonas, streptococci.

Among the parasites which affect puppies are roundworm, hookworm, whipworm, and coccidiosis.

Puppy Viremia

Viremia is a broad term which indicates the presence of a virus in the blood. While the common cause of viremia is the herpes virus, there is always the chance that another virus, such as parvo, could cause it. Canine herpes is similar to Herpes Simplex, the form which causes cold sores in humans. Herpes itself is an extensive subject about which much is still unknown.

Puppy viremia causes a high rate of fatalities when contracted during the first three to five weeks of life. The puppies may contract this disease as they pass through the vagina of a bitch who has contracted herpes less than a month before whelping. Cleansing the bitch's vagina or using a douche prior to whelping may be a helpful preventative. Some veterinarians recommend douching with *Furacin*. Your veterinarian should be able to suggest other precautionary measures.

Puppies may contract herpes from infected littermates or other adult dogs and thus develop puppy viremia. Consequently, keeping the puppies segregated from other dogs might be another preventative.

The high susceptibility rate for newborn puppies appears to be caused by their low body temperatures during the first three weeks, as the herpes virus flourishes in temperatures of 94–97° F. Therefore, keeping the puppies quite warm, at about 85–90° F, for a full three weeks is advisable.

The first symptom in an infant is a soft, green, odorless bowel movement. But a conscientious bitch may prevent this symptom from being seen. The puppies may vomit or retch as the disease progresses. The first symptom which I noticed was a refusal to nurse. Until that point my puppies were seemingly healthy and gaining weight. Then breathing difficulties became apparent. The puppies next began to cry. According to some, the puppies cry continuously and piteously. My own experience found the puppies whimpering on an intermittent basis. According to most research, once the puppies start to cry, hemorrhaging has probably started and survival is doubtful.

The biggest problem is diagnosing the disease because the symptoms are so similar to those of other puppy diseases. Moreover, there is very little time in which to diagnose (the afflicted puppy usually dies within twenty-four hours).

At this point there is only one effective treatment, and it may not be foolproof. It is what I call "the heat treatment." The puppies are kept in a high environmental temperature for twenty-four hours in order to raise their body temperatures above 97° F, this higher temperature being detrimental to the virus.

During the first three hours, the puppies are kept in a 100° F temperature and are given *Gatorade* (uncarbonated) every fifteen minutes to one-half hour in order to prevent dehydration. The puppies, whether newborn or three weeks old, will need about 3 cc's per hour. The most efficient way we found to give the *Gatorade* was with a scaled syringe. An eye dropper could also be used. During the following twenty-one hours, the temperature needs to be maintained between 90–95° F, and the *Gatorade* given at least once every hour.

During the first three hours the puppies will cry continuously and try to escape the heat. Throughout the last twenty-one hours they will sleep most of the time. It is very important that they receive the *Gatorade* on a regular schedule.

To create a kind of incubator on short notice presents a challenge. A #200 air crate works well. A kennel heating pad, small size, with a thermostat should be placed over the existing false bottom. A heat lamp may be directed in from the top. It should be situated so that either the lamp or the crate bottom can be raised or lowered as needed. A thermometer must be kept where it is readily visible at all times. If necessary, a sheet, light blanket, or a large towel can be used to make a tent over the crate bottom. Do not forget to block the doorway. Use masking tape and cardboard.

Be prepared to lose sleep, as you will be constantly giving one puppy or another *Gatorade* to prevent dehydration. Survival through the treatment is a good indication that the puppy/puppies will live. Puppies that were crying before the treatment started and that survive may develop chronic kidney disease during the first year. Moreover, once viremia is diagnosed in one puppy, all the other puppies, both littermates of the ill puppy and any other puppies, must be "heat treated" as a preventative. It is possible that some may not have contracted it, but that chance cannot be taken.

This problem, herpes and puppy viremia, is usually self-limiting according to many sources. However, occasionally herpes can be a recurrent problem. Should this occur, a gamma globulin serum can be prepared from the blood of the dogs who have recovered from herpes. This can be given as an immunizing agent to newborn puppies.

Recent research indicates that puppies may be able to obtain canine herpes virus within the uterus from bitches who in a previous pregnancy transmitted CHV to newborn puppies in a natural manner. In such a case involving an Afghan bitch, an examination of the subsequent puppies revealed characteristic herpes lesions in the fetal placenta. This case was reported by Hashimoto, Hirai, Okada, and Fujimoto. Their description was as follows: "The placenta was congested, was dark red, and was poorly developed. Several grayish white foci (chief sites of infection) were beneath the allantochorionic (afterbirth) membrane on the fetal side and the cut surface of the placental Labyrinth. The size of the lesions varied from military to rice grain; sometimes, the lesions formed zonal structures 2 to 3 mm wide."[1]

In this case five puppies were stillborn and of the other two, one died within twenty-four hours, the second at twenty-two days. The autopsies revealed "a few petechial (minute spot) hemorrhages on the cut surface of the kidneys, adrenal glands, and thymus in the stillborn pups. In the pup that survived for 22 days, a relatively large number of subcapsular cysts were in the kidneys."[2]

I have repeatedly been assured that this disease is usually self-limiting in small kennels. The adults rarely exhibit any signs of herpes infection and are immune after recovery. By the time symptoms appear, it is usually too late to save the puppies.

Herpes raises many questions in a breeder's mind. A blood test is now available to check immunity, but it would be more helpful if vaccines were available to prevent outbreaks and if knowledge concerning the spread and prevention of herpes were readily available. None of these are available at this time. However, once a puppy has been diagnosed as having viremia which may have been caused by a herpes infection, a blood test can be given the bitch prior to rebreeding to determine her titer level.

Since there is no quick way to know that puppies have viremia, the whole litter must be treated as though it does. But in my mind, prevention is worth much more than cure and will prevent more heartache. Thus, keeping the puppies warm in 85–90° F temperatures and using a good cleansing agent on the bitch's vagina at whelping time may be the best preventatives we have now.

Puppy Septicemia

This disease strikes puppies between four to forty days of age. The cause is either streptococcus, staphylococcus, escherichia, or pseudomonas bacteria. The dam of the puppy often has metritis or mastitis. The symptoms are crying, distention of the abdomen, diarrhea, and rapid respiration. Death often occurs within eighteen hours. The pup-

---

[1]"Pathology of the Placenta and Newborn Pups with Suspected Intrauterine Infection of Canine Herpesvirus," *American Journal of Veterinary Research,* Vol. 40, No. 9, p. 1236.

[2]*Ibid.*

pies become ill one after the other. Three conditions—hypothermia, hypoglycemia, and dehydration—become apparent and must be counteracted as soon as possible if the puppes are to be saved.

The puppy's body temperature may fall to 78 to 94° F, and it must be raised slowly. An environmental temperature of 85 to 90° F with a humidity of 55 to 60 percent is used to raise the puppy's body temperature to normal. During this period the puppy must be turned frequently and gently massaged to stimulate circulation. This is important so that the puppy's body heats within as well as on the surface. Use an infant's rectal thermometor to monitor the puppy's temperature.

Glucose therapy is used to avert hypoglycemia. Give the puppy about 1 to 2 cc's of a 5- to 15-percent glucose-water solution orally every half hour. This dosage should be gradually increased to 4 to 6 cc's as the puppy improves. Do not feed formula at this time, as it may cause an intestinal blockage.

If the puppy's condition is very serious, the veterinarian may administer subcutaneous hydrating solutions. Another solution with which to fight dehydration is *Gatorade:* 1 cc every hour.

Viral Enteritis

Viral enteritis in puppies can prove fatal. There are several forms which are attacking our dogs. Corona virus is one of these and is responsible for several infectious diseases, including gastroenteritis. Parvo virus was added to the list of viruses in 1978. A reo-like virus, or rotavirus, has been found to be the cause of death in some puppies where neither parvo nor corona were located.

Enteritis refers to inflammation of the intestine. Corona and parvo attack cells in the intestinal tract. Vomiting, diarrhea, fever, and bleeding are symptoms. Symptoms of corona virus include an orangish feces with a foul odor containing some blood and a lot of mucous.

Parvo virus may invade the bone marrow and cause a drop in the white-blood-cell count. This, of course, is a sign that a dog has parvo virus. Vomiting is the first symptom of parvo, followed by diarrhea. Puppies four to eight weeks old often die from heart failure caused by parvo virus infection. Rotavirus has similar symptoms to the others: vomiting and diarrhea.

Clorox in a 1:30 solution used in cleaning is one agent which kills parvo virus.

There is a strange virus-type disease which is attacking puppies from four weeks to three months of age. Tests and autopsies have ruled out parvo, corona, rota, distemper, and leptospirosis, at least so far, but the symptoms are similar and it strikes quickly. Sometimes the diagnosis has been parvo, but autopsies find that that is probaby not the cause. The first symptoms are lassitude, diarrhea, dehydration, and muscular weakness. All of these may not be apparent. What is important is to stop the diarrhea and the dehydration. Give the puppy up to 24 cc of *Gatorade,* in 3 cc doses, and get the puppy to the veterinarian. The usual treatment involves injections of fluid under the skin and intravenous feeding. Puppies caught early and treated in this manner have survived.

If you are a breeder, you should discuss with your veterinarian in advance how you should cope in an emergency sickness, especially what steps to take and what medications to give. He may provide you with an emergency prescription drug to have on hand. Veterinarians have products in which they are confident and which they will recommend.

If you need to give first-aid treatment because your veterinarian is temporarily unavailable, continue the *Gatorade* (about 12 cc's every hour to prevent dehydration) and give what you have on hand to control diarrhea. You could give one teaspoon of *Kaopectate.* One breeder has had great success with liquid *Bactrovet* and has saved puppies as ill as those previously lost. Since this can be kept on hand for use with adults also, *Bactrovet* can be valuable in other emergencies. Several breeders have been given *Eisol M* by their veterinarians (use the dose recommended by your veterinarian). If you do as I do, keep diarrhea medication supplied by my veterinarian with you when traveling to shows (use *Neo-darbazine*); according to my veterinarian, one *Neo-darbazine* or one diapect with neomycin can be given under emergency conditions. BUT GET THE PUPPY/PUPPIES TO THE VETERINARIAN AS QUICKLY AS POSSIBLE; AND DO NOT GIVE DIARRHEA MEDICATION ONCE THE DIARRHEA STOPS. You will constipate the puppy.

It is important to tempt their appetites. Cook up some rice, or barley, and mix about half and half with regular food, or if the puppy seems to have no appetite, use plain rice with a tablespoon or two of broiled beef – broil until cooked through but not brown and crispy, then blot on paper towels to remove any excess grease. If the puppy will not eat any of this, try: ⅛ cup of *Foal-Lac* (seems to work better than *Espilac*), ¼ cup of water, ½ teaspoon of brewers' yeast powder, ⅛ teaspoon of ascorbic acid, one drop of vitamin E oil, ½ teaspoon of white *Karo* syrup or honey; shake this thoroughly. Use a syringe to feed to the puppy. If the puppy is small, about 3 cc's at a time will be best. Repeat every couple hours until the puppy starts eating on its own. This formula, or one of which you know, gives the puppy the energy to keep living until on the road to recovery. You could use concentrated formulas available from veterinary supply houses or from your local veterinarian. *Espilac* and *Foal-Lac* are both commercially prepared formulas.

Whatever the disease is, and it appears to be some form of enteritis, its incubation period appears to be forty-eight hours or less and travels – who knows how.

Umbilical Infection

Staphylococcus or streptococcus, either of which could contaminate the whelping area, is probably the cause of umbilical infection. The pup will cry, bloat, and become dehydrated and often hypothermic. Inspection will reveal a distended abdomen, bluish discoloration in the flanks, and a small spot of pus on the navel. Antibiotics and supportive care are essential or the puppy will die within twelve to eighteen hours. The puppy must be taken to the veterinarian as quickly as possible.

Toxic Milk Syndrome

Symptoms of toxic milk syndrome are diarrhea, green stools, a raw protruding rectum, and excessive moisture around the lips. Affected puppies cry and exhibit bloating.

If there is a slightly pink or almost clear discharge on the vulva and surrounding hair of the bitch, the problem may be in her uterus. Toxic substances in her milk result from debris and fluids from the placenta which were retained in the uterus. The bitch must be treated for twenty-four to forty-eight hours so that she eliminates the toxins. While this is being accomplished, the puppies must be fed formula. Once the toxins are gone, the puppies can be returned to their dam for nursing.

Puppy Strangles

This situation involves a skin condition on the muzzle which develops about age four or five weeks. The eyes and ears are next to be infected, after which the lymph glands swell, giving the appearance of mumps. The cause is staphylococcus. It is possible for the puppy to develop an allergic reaction to staph. If treatment is started early and is thorough, it can be successful, although there can be scarring on the muzzle.

Hemorrhagic Syndrome

Hemorrhaging because of a low clotting ability can cause death in puppies up to three days old, the period during which they have only minor production of prothrombin, a plasma protein. Prothrombin, produced in the liver, combines with vitamin K to control the clotting of blood.

Symptoms are lethargy, weakness, and a declining condition. Lesions on the lips and the tongue indicate hemorrhage. Treatment involves giving vitamin K to all the puppies in the litter.

Parasites

Roundworms, hookworms, whipworms, and coccidia are the common parasites which may affect puppies. Symptoms of worms include: distended abdomen, diarrhea, vomiting, presence of worms or mucous in the stool. Pale gums are a symptom of hookworm.

Although a dam may test clear of roundworms, she may carry them encysted in her muscles. The roundworms are activated by hormones about the fortieth day of pregnancy and infect the fetuses. The young puppies then start passing eggs or even worms shortly after they are three weeks old. Puppies should be wormed at this young age only under the direction of your veterinarian.

224

By the way, water bugs may carry the round-worm eggs, deposit them on the dogs' dishes, and start a new cycle. If water bugs are a problem, place the legs of the raised exercise pen in bowls of a solution which will kill the waterbugs. The use of raised exercise pens, in addition to helping to prevent roundworms, will also help in preventing whipworms and hookworms, as the Lhasas do not come in contact with the stools nor the ground containing the eggs or larvae.

Coccidiosis is stimulated by stress. It is a protozoan infection which may be caused by a change in environment, a change of diet, or the development of a cold. Coccidiosis is said to be passed by a carrier bitch and usually occurs in a kennel situation.

While some people may not like the idea, Lhasas exercised in raised play pens seem to be freer of parasites than those exercised on the ground daily. Many breeders have commented on this benefit gained from the raised exercise pens. Cleanliness in the whelping and puppy pens is extremely important.

Distemper

Distemper produces the same symptoms as parvo virus. Prior to World War II it was a dreaded disease, but the development of a vaccine which controls by preventing the disease has been a blessing. In many areas distemper has virtually been eliminated.

THE SWIMMER PROBLEM

Perhaps you have heard of a swimmer. Possibly you have had one among one of your litters. The swimmer becomes a frustration for the breeder, who sees a plump, healthy puppy doing nothing. This puppy does not participate with his littermates who try to play on wobbly legs or to get to the dam on those legs. Instead the swimmer moves very little, which is backward or forward by pushing himself with his legs spread-eagled.

The evidence of this condition appears at about two weeks of age when the puppies should start trying to walk. Usually the Lhasa Apso puppies which are swimmers are fat, or heavy-boned, or fat and heavy-boned. The weight seems to prevent the puppies from getting their feet under their bodies and then pushing their bodies up on their legs. Two reasons are put forth: lack of initial strength and lack of motivation. The sprawling puppy develops a flattened rib cage and holds his legs stretched at right angles to his body. He may move by pawing and by using his head and neck as levers. Unless the problem is corrected, the puppy may die from a collapse of the chest cavity.

Sometimes the first sign which is observable in very young puppies is the gradual flattening of the chest. Elaine Erganbright wrote that "pneumonia can easily set in with a reduced lung capacity, so I have given ¼ cc of Combiotic and ½ cc of Vitamin E in the thigh muscles. Dr. Burkhardt had called it a form of 'white muscle disease' which is a term

Can. Ch. Ralda's Tangerine Tornado as a puppy (by Can. Ch. Ralda's Apple Cider Man ex Kuku La Creme Puff). Owner, Arlene Dartt.

BIS Ch. Tiffany's Qua-La-Ti ROM, sire of 10 champions. Owner, Nancy Coglianese. Photo by Booth.

used for a similar condition in larger livestock. If the swimming condition is not observed until about the third week, the puppy is generally strong enough to be given 1 cc of Vitamin E in the thigh muscle. The Vitamin E injections are then continued on any size puppy either twice weekly or once weekly depending on the puppy's condition."[3]

Dr. Ben E. Sheffy, a canine nutrition expert at the Cornell University's James A. Baker Institute for animal health, reported that vitamin E deficiency in dogs can cause puppy weakness and disability as well as "damage to the eye and visual acuity, and can also lead to muscular lesions, . . . and reproductive problems."[4]

The problem appears to be environmental rather than hereditary, is preventable, and may be helped when it becomes apparent.

Be sure that the bitch is in good health and is providing the puppies with ample nourishment. When the puppies are whelped, start checking their development. Early recognition that problems are developing can assure early success in treatment.

A good preventative measure is providing the whelping box with a floor surface which provides traction for the puppies. This can be done by using washable and rough surfaces for bedding such as towels, blankets, mattress pads, or sheets. Terry cloth presents a problem because the puppies tend to catch their little toenails in it. Newspaper is acceptable under the sheeting for absorbent purposes, but newspaper by itself is bad for small puppies because the puppies tend to slip and slide on it. The materials used should provide the traction necessary for the development of balance and movement. Be very careful of carpeting, especially indoor–outdoor carpeting which causes chemical burns after urine contacts it. Looped carpeting also can trap toenails.

The only child and the large puppy are good candidates to be swimmers. The only child has no competition for the milk supply and may grow fatter by the day. The large puppy may have his favorite nipple and uses his strength to utilize it. Such puppies may be placed on diets by controlling the intake of food and by early weaning.

---

[3]Elaine P. Erganbright, "Vitamin E Deficiency," *Dog World,* May 1978, p. 81.

[4]"Dog World Round Up of Science Briefs," *Dog World,* October 1981, p. 8.

The fat swimmer puppy should be examined by your veterinarian. There are a number of treatment methods from which the veterinarian can choose. Shots of vitamin E and selenium and of calcium have produced good results. The veterinarian may choose to physically involve a change: i.e., the puppy's legs are taped together under the body, putting the legs into proper position. This procedure tends to mold the rib cage back into its normal rounded shape. The results of this method can be surveyed within one to two weeks.

Exercise would be another choice for combating this problem. The puppy's chest may be massaged and his legs manipulated. At this young age, a puppy's bones are very pliable and may easily be misshapen, but they may also be reshaped with relative ease for the same reason. Such treatments should be prescribed by your veterinarian and done under his supervision.

Water can be used effectively to correct this problem also. Put the puppy in a basin of water four or five times daily. Submerge the puppy to midchest, cupping the rib cage in your hands and allowing the legs to dangle. Move the puppy back and forth in the water, simulating swimming. This act will encourage the puppy to use his legs.

Dysplasia is a danger for those dogs whose condition is not diagnosed and treated at an early age.

Thus, to have a happy, healthy dog, follow good nutritional practices, provide footing material for whelping boxes, seek prompt help when a swimmer problem emerges, and faithfully follow the diagnosis.

EMERGENCY KIT

All breeders should have on hand an emergency kit for treating puppies who suddenly become ill, until these puppies can visit a veterinarian. There are times when the breeder just cannot reach the veterinarian, as during a bad storm, when such a kit may be vital. Staple items which can be kept on hand are an infant thermometer; peroxide for cleaning it and wounds; a small hot- or cold-water bag; heating pad and/or heating lamp; a medication for diarrhea—*Kaopectate, Bisol M, Bactrovet, Amforol, Neo-Darbazine,* or whatever your veterinarian recommends; instant *Gatorade* (each package mixed with distilled water will make two quarts); *Livotonic;* and perhaps *Chloromycetin palmitate;* and a notebook with care instructions and notes from previous experiences.

Such kits may be vital. Here in the north a blizzard can effectively prevent reaching a veterinarian, as could a tornado, a flood, or an ice storm. It seems as though it is always at such times that puppies or adults become ill. If the telephones are usable, your veterinarian may provide instructions. Should the lines be down, your notes and common sense will be a help.

If you take some of the dog magazines, you might note specific care articles on 3-by-5-inch cards and file them appropriately in a file box. Notes on your own experiences and those of friends could be included.

One other item which is very handy to have in a storm emergency is a generator, which is valuable in an emergency involving power outage to provide a source of power for keeping the puppies warm. A sterno heater for heating water to fill the hot-water bottle will also help. If you have no hot-water bottle, fill a small glass jar with the water (put a silver spoon into the jar to prevent break-age while filling), wrap the jar in a towel, and put near the puppy.

Advance preparations for emergencies can be vital for the breeder. We all have that feeling that it won't happen to us. But we never know when it will. Emergencies often seem to occur at the most inopportune times. Be prepared.

SOURCES

"The Fading Syndrome, Septicemia and other puppy diseases." Gaines Progress, Summer 1980.

Ronald Harling, D. V. M., Barre Center, New York.

Lowell Lyons, D. V. M., Ottawa, Kansas.

Dr. J. E. Mosier, "Puppy Diseases Involving Litter Problems," *Lhasa Tales* (Vol. 6, No. 7), November 1977, pp. 16–18, 24.

"New Findings on Puppy Viral Diseases," *Dog World,* January 1980, pp. 20–21, 77, 91, 129.

"Science and the Dog," *Dog World* (Vol. 65, No. 4), April 1980, p. 7.

Erwin Small, D. V. M., M. S., "The First 18 Days—Do Or Die," *Lhasa Tales* (Vol. 6, No. 9), January 1978, pp. 10, 12, 14.

An eight-week-old litter sired by Am. Can. Ch. Chen Krisna Nor ROM, out of Cordova Sin-Sa ROM. Photo by Chenoweth.

Am. Can. Ch. Bara's Flickering Ember. "Porky" is foundation stud for Ma-Lee's Lhasa Apsos. Owner, Marilyn Lisciandro.

228

21

CREATIVE SALESMANSHIP

Salesmanship may be truly a "creative art," one which will be practical to know if you raise Lhasa Apsos. It would be nice if you could keep every puppy that is whelped, but that isn't practical. The necessary selling aspects include timing, business trends, advertising, reaching prospects, approach, and avoiding panic. Your Lhasas have a built-in appeal which will work only if they have people on which to practice.

Timing is not always something on which you can plan, as your Lhasa bitch has to be bred when she comes into heat. However, you may select which heat for breeding, as a potential whelping date might interfere with other plans such as vacations. Puppies whelped in September would be old enough to be sold at Christmas. Of course, many breeders will tell you that a new puppy should not go into the hubbub of the Christmas holidays, which is probably very true. March puppies would be ready for June, at school's end when some people like to purchase puppies, and June puppies are ready for September, when vacations are over and school is beginning. Your timing will be dictated by both your bitch and your market area.

Business trends vary. Probably recessions and depressions affect the "dog business," as money is tighter during such times. Thus, it might be well to survey the trends before breeding too extensively. Also, certain breeds sell better than others in certain areas. For instance, working dogs and sporting breeds will probably be in more demand in rural areas. On the other hand, small dogs such as Lhasas will be in demand as house dogs in suburban and metropolitan areas. But many people with large farms also own Lhasas. In order to determine the breeds of dogs on the market in your area, you might also check out the retail stores for dogs. Another source of information might be a local dog club. Thus, survey the situation before getting too involved and know where best to advertise.

Reaching sales prospects may be accomplished in a number of ways: advertising—in newspapers, shopping papers, dog magazines, and general publications; personal contacts—casual in social or business situations, dog shows, signs, pet supply stores, veterinarians' offices, printed literature, mailing lists, and referrals.

Preparation for the sale of your puppies should start at the time of mating. At this time, if you wish information about the prospective litter to reach magazines in time to be of benefit to you, send out litter announcement ads. You also may determine your overall method of advertising. In addition to this, pedigrees can be prepared and duplicated so that a copy can be given to each new owner or sent to prospective buyers. Other enclosures such as price lists and kennel brochures may be prepared in advance.

ADVERTISING

We are daily bombarded by advertising, which has become a way of life. Thus, to advertise effectively, ads must be clear, succinct, and attractive. Ads must attract attention.

Your ads may include the following information: sire, dam, special factors such as outstanding temperament or color, Lhasas free of diseases, registration, inoculations, "housebroken," show trained, ages, telephone number. Avoid crowding your ad with useless adjectives such as "cute," "loveable," and "beautiful." Use the space for precise descriptions or precise information. If possible, avoid including the price in your ad. In addition to advertising puppies, this information applies to older Lhasas for sale, and for stud service.

The next thing to consider is where to advertise, how much to spend, and how often. As a breeder you should set aside a sum for advertising. When you are starting out, this sum may seem a disproportionate percentage of your gross income. Gradually this percentage should be reduced; although what you spend will not necessarily be less, your gross income will probably increase. A goal to aim for is 10 percent of gross income for advertising and for publicity.

Remember that advertising reaches people in a manner which is often residual. People may recall up to 20 percent of what they read and 30 percent of what is pictured. However, if you tell them the good points of your Lhasa, they may recall up to 60 percent. It is essential that any advertising stress truthfully the good points of your Lhasa.

Magazines

Lhasa Apso breed magazines have litter announcement columns in which to place ads at a minimum cost. These announcements should be simple: names of sire and dam; expected whelping date or date whelped; if the latter, number of pups, sex, and colors; kennel name; your name, address, and phone number.

To announce an expected litter, such ads should be sent in almost immediately after the breeding, as the ads must reach the magazines about two months in advance of printing. This ad would be published coincidently with the whelping of the litter. On the other hand, the ads may be sent after the whelping, but these ads will not appear until the puppies are at least two months old, or when you will be ready to sell at least some of them.

Litter announcements may also be included in comments in an ad for either the sire or the dam. Ads in breed magazines often have long-term residual effects, as the magazines are kept by many breeders as resources. Also, these magazines are sent overseas, thus extending the market.

Rather than making a one-time big splash with a full-page ad, it might be better to use a smaller ad on a regular basis in order to keep your kennel name current. Quarter-page and half-page ads can be quite effective. Contracts for these on a regular basis can usually be had at a slightly reduced cost per ad. Then occasionally run a full-page ad when you have something special to put forth. Of course, when funds are plentiful, a full-page ad could be used.

All-breed magazines reach a wide audience, especially if the magazines have national circulation. These magazines are read by breeders and fanciers of many breeds. In addition, many of them are available on news and magazine stands from which they may be picked up by the casually interested, albeit prospective buyers. These magazines are often kept to be used as resources, and in this manner the ads have an extended residual effect, often many months after publication.

Ads must be submitted two months in advance of publication. The cost of such an ad is usually on a per-word basis, with a minimum set-up cost, in the classified section. Also available are breed display ads which are rated by the unit, the minimum unit being 1 column inch. Special rates apply for both types when contracts are made for repetition over several months to a year.

Include all pertinent information in the classified ad: sire, dam, kennel name, address, telephone number, expected whelping date, or whelping date, with sexes and colors. The breed display ads may contain a small cut of one of your Lhasas, kennel name, address, telephone number, and a brief announcement. One word of caution: be prepared to refuse collect calls.

Miscellaneous Publications

It is possible to use other types of publications to advertise those Lhasa puppies which are for sale. Club magazines, bulletins, and newsletters often have space for advertising. This type is aimed at people with common interests, as are those such as *The Match Show Bulletin*. The costs for ads in these publications are usually minimal and even free in some cases. These ads will be brief: kennel name, address, telephone numbers, breed, puppies for sale, or stud service.

Another type of magazine in which you might advertise is the so-called society publication:

Puppies at Kachina.

specific city magazines: *Town and Country, Country Gentlemen,* and the *Smithsonian* are examples of magazines which may be found in the homes of people desirous of Lhasas. Ads in these magazines may cost more and should be planned carefully to give an attractive, yet succinct appearance. Do not mention price. The residual effect from such magazines should be good. Also, such magazines are often found in beauty shops, barber shops, and doctors' and dentists' offices where the ad could be seen by the casual viewer, albeit potential customer.

Newspapers and Shopping Papers

The effect of advertising in these publications depends upon your area. A first step might be to check with other breeders in your area as to which papers give the best results. Ads in newspapers may be very inexpensive if your puppies sell very quickly but, on the other hand, also may be very expensive if the ads must run for any extended period. There are no residual effects. When you contact a newspaper be sure to check for special rates for multiple days, e.g., a weekend rate, a three-day rate, a seven-day rate, or a ten-day rate. Take advantage of these offers when you can.

Your ad should provide only pertinent information which includes breed, good points such as temperament, whether or not housebroken, shots, AKC registered, and telephone number. Do not include address unless you are willing to have people drop in unannounced, and especially if someone is not always at home. This lends itself to break-ins. Avoid mentioning the sex of puppies, as some breeders have been receiving some perverted telephone calls. Also, unless required by the type of ad, avoid giving prices, which also should not be given out over the telephone, a fact which will be discussed under telephone calls.

Breeders in our area have found ads in the local newspapers at times to be ineffective, and therefore expensive, perhaps because of the price requirements or the market, but that ads in cities located about 70 miles from your home are very effective. So consider advertising in other papers in nearby cities.

Some people have had good luck advertising in the small weekly newspapers and in weekly shopping papers. This type, of course, has a restricted circulation, which indicates just how many people your ad may reach. Again the amount of information printed should be specific and limited. However, such ads are usually quite inexpensive. You would need to determine whether the classified ad will be sufficient or whether a block—column-inch type—ad would be more effective in your area.

Keep an accurate record of these ads: dates run, the costs, the days on which you get responses, the number of responses, the number of visits, the number of Lhasas sold. One breeder tells me that she spends the price of one companion puppy on her newspaper ads. Thus, the returns from such ads indicate that the ads may be quite expensive. The records may also indicate the days on which you may expect no telephone calls, and they may also indicate the best time of the year to advertise in your area. These records are both valuable and informative.

Pet Supply Stores

These stores are often a good source of prospective pet owners. Many pet supply stores keep breeders' directories for referrals and have bulletin boards for announcements. Ask about them.

Usually the referral forms will be prepared with blanks to be filled in with the desired information: breed, kennel name, your name, address, telephone number, organizational memberships, names of studs for stud service, whelping dates, sex, color, prices. You could request that only your telephone number be given out.

A small attractive sign may be prepared for the bulletin board. Use a picture and give pertinent information. Include telephone number, but not address.

Stop-In Shops and Services

Laundromats, small shops, grooming shops, post offices, and veterinarian offices often have bulletin boards for announcements. Small signs, such as those used for pet supply stores, will suffice. Do not include address, but stress calling by telephone. Some veterinarians maintain breeders' directories or notebooks in which you can put a kennel card. These are used for referrals. Again, stress calling by telephone.

232

PERSONAL CONTACT

Personal contact selling includes a variety of methods, such as face-to-face, printed literature, mailing lists, good will, and correspondence. Always remember that the image which you present of yourself and your Lhasa in person can stimulate both interest and disinterest. Thus, common courtesy and deportment are important. Your printed literature—your stationery, business cards, and stud cards—also speak for you, as do the letters which you write. Neatness and legibility say a great deal. Thus, it is important to make an effort to make a good impression, or "to put your best foot forward."

Face-to-Face Contact—Contacts with people who may one day be interested in purchasing Lhasa puppies may occur in many places, some of which might seem unlikely to you. Such encounters may occur at social occasions, at places of employment, at doctors' or dentists' offices, at sporting events, at dog shows and matches, at organization meetings, and while shopping.

Should anyone express an interest in obtaining a Lhasa, whether now or in the future, give them one of your business cards. Also, these people often may pass on the information to others. This is a relatively inexpensive manner in which to advertise your dogs.

Obvious places where you will possibly meet prospective buyers are at dog shows and dog matches. Spectators often are interested in the dogs because they desire to purchase one. Other breeders may be interested in stud service or a show prospect for their own kennels. Then, too, breeders of other breeds may be looking for a second breed. Thus, a show or match may be an excellent place for such contacts.

Remember two things, however: if someone approaches you about your Lhasas, ALWAYS be polite, no matter how rushed you are. If you can't talk while grooming or if you must get to the ring, request in a nice manner that they return to your grooming area after the showing of Lhasas is completed, and give them your business card or a brochure on your Lhasas until you can talk with them. (Keep some handy in your tack box.)

Printed Literature—Printed literature through which you make personal contact includes your stationery letterheads, envelopes, stud cards, business cards, and kennel brochures and folders. Stud cards, business cards, and kennel brochures may be kept in your tack box or brief case for momentary dispersal. Such items can also be sent through the mail to prospective clients.

To prospective buyers, attractive printed stationery presents a favorable picture of you—that you are reliable, have pride in your Lhasas, and are businesslike. Impressions are often lasting.

Business cards should be clearly printed. You may use a picture or a sketch of one of your Lhasas. Choose an attractive lettering pattern for your kennel name, your name, mailing address, and telephone number. Stud cards will have basically the same information on the front side, including a picture. On the opposite side a three-generation pedigree of your stud will be printed.

Kennel brochures or folders include a brief history of your kennel, show records and brief background sketches of your Lhasas, feeding and training suggestions, grooming hints, and brief pedigrees of studs. The information which a novice Lhasa owner needs should be included. Pictures will enhance the brochures.

Mailing Lists—A breeder should maintain a mailing file. There are several methods of doing this: 3- × 5-inch cards, spiral or looseleaf notebooks, or an address book. Either one or two files could be compiled. A joint file could have an indication of prospective buyers, prospective stud service users, and actual customers. The use of two files, one for prospective stud service or Lhasa purchasers and one for actual clients, may be more desirous. Of course, you must find time in your busy schedule to update these files.

Good Will—Satisfied old and new customers may both come back to purchase a second or third Lhasa or may spread the word to friends and acquaintances about you and your Lhasas. Once you are an established breeder, this will be a strong source of your sales.

Correspondence Selling—On receipt of a letter of inquiry, answer promptly (within two or three days). The prospect may well have written to several breeders. The first one to answer satisfactorily will get the sale.

In advance, prepare brochures or leaflets about your kennel and printed lists of available Lhasas. These can be printed, typed, or mimeographed. Have pictures ready or use a Polaroid camera to provide them.

Do not misrepresent your Lhasas, offer deals, or sell bargains. Sell your dogs emphasizing their good points, temperament, color, size, and health. Do advise when the Lhasas would be available and when you could ship them.

Your kennel brochure or leaflet should include background information about your kennel and your Lhasas. This should provide the client with an overview of your program, your breeding philosophy, your bloodlines, and your general type of Lhasa. It may include information on the care of Lhasas.

Puppies and children—a natural combination, and good for the puppies' socialization.

A list of Lhasas for sale with prices and brief descriptions may expedite the sale. This may be printed by a local enterprise quite inexpensively, and it may even include photographs. You might instead use copies of ads featuring the Lhasa or Lhasas for sale (or at stud), which would include pictures and pedigrees. Magazine ads copy quite well. Another valuable item to have on hand are pedigrees for all the Lhasas, including new ones, which you have for sale. These can be included with letters and pictures, and thus letters need not be too extensive.

Your letter should first thank the correspondent for inquiring about your Lhasas. The letter should be pertinent, precise, and of reasonable length. It should provide information in response to the inquiry and either advise about available Lhasas or refer to enclosed list. Do take time to include shipping information and cost. Also, ask the customer to supply you with some details about themselves to avoid placing a Lhasa in an inappropriate home or a puppy mill. In addition, you might encourage the prospect to call you collect (most of them won't), but this would provide you with an opportunity not only to talk about your Lhasas, but also to "size up" the prospective buyer.

Do not fail to answer all correspondence whether or not you have a Lhasa available, for to do so would be rude. Common courtesy indicates a response. If the inquiry is not clear regarding the request for a Lhasa, i.e., the type—show or companion, etc.—advise of what you have, enclose your brochure, and request clarification.

When you are dealing by correspondence with people who live a great distance from you, do not hesitate to use other contacts to find out something about the people. Such an inquiry could prevent heartache over one of your Lhasas and monetary loss.

SETTING PRICES

To determine an adequate price for your Lhasa puppies, there are several steps which you may take. Evaluate your puppies. Check the prices of Lhasa puppies with reputable breeders within a 50- to 100-mile radius, with area pet stores, and with members of your breed club.

Normally you should not charge less than your stud fee. Remember that there are many expenses involved in properly raising puppies—stud fees, transportation costs, veterinarian fees, food costs, and advertising costs. Even when you own and use your own champion stud, you must consider a stud fee, as it surely cost you something to own and to finish the stud.

Should you be selling your puppies at eight weeks of age (and I do not recommend selling them at less and there is a federal law which prevents shipping them at less than eight weeks of age), your choice is to sell them at pet prices. It is difficult to evaluate puppies with certainty at eight weeks or less, although the very experienced breeder may make some good educated guesses. You will be able to spot the obvious faults such as poor pigmentation, extremes in bites, excessive body length, poor tail sets, perhaps bow legs, and Prapsos. In our area members of our breed club set the price for pet (companion) puppies, and nonmembers who use our studs are encouraged to use this price also. Pet Lhasa puppies are sold in area pet stores for considerably higher prices. Thus, the buyer saves money when buying from the breeder. It would behoove the breeder to check local prices.

A puppy with a major fault may be sold with a refund given when proof of neutering is provided. In this latter situation, registration papers would be withheld until proof of neutering is received. The idea of a refund seems to encourage people to neuter Lhasas which you feel should not be bred. Moreover, according to Pamela Mathews, AKC administrative assistant, "If a seller feels that a dog, for one reason or another, should not be used for breeding purposes and if the dog is not neutered, the dog should be sold without papers. Our Rules do provide that a written agreement between the buyer and seller, properly signed and executed to the effect that a dog is being sold with the understanding that no AKC registration papers are to be furnished, will be honored."[1] But remember that the neutered dog cannot produce Lhasas at all.

If you keep your Lhasa puppies until they are ten to twelve weeks old, you can better evaluate them. Fronts and rears can be examined with more

---

[1]"On Withholding AKC Papers," *The Lhasa Apso Reporter* (Vol. 8, No. 4), December-January 1982, p. 62.

surety of judgment. Bites will still be adjusting, but the overbite may be leveling out, or the undershot may be more obvious. Topline and coat quality will be more evident.

The three- to four-month-old Lhasa should start to give the appearance of being balanced. Remember that a Lhasa with a good pedigree and which is of good quality can be used as a brood bitch or stud whether or not it reaches the ring.

From five months on, it is easier to evaluate the young Lhasa because it has adult teeth, most of its growth, and some of its adult coat. At this point the gait of the Lhasa should be very apparent, and the head type should be determinable.

Prices have been relatively stable over the past ten years, but it should be remembered that prices vary some from area to area. Those factors, then, which must be considered in the selling of Lhasas and their prices are: the pedigree, the quality, the age, and the apparent condition of a given Lhasa. Consideration should also be given to the Lhasa with generations of champions behind him, especially best-in-show or outstanding producer champions, as that Lhasa might be considered to have more potential and thus draw a higher fee.

DEFERRED PAYMENT SELLING

Because the prices for Lhasa Apsos may be somewhat higher than a prospective purchaser can easily pay at one time, determine in advance a deferred payment plan acceptable to you. In such

Ch. Ja-Ma Fancee Footwork, "Footsie," foundation bitch at Ja-Ma at thirteen months. Breeder-owners, Janet and Marv Whitman.

cases a simple sales contract is essential, as it protects both the seller and the purchaser.

In preparing for deferred payment, determine a down payment – one-third of the purchase price is reasonable. Then indicate a date each month on which a subsequent payment shall be received and insist that it be received on time. Also, determine the amount of the payment.

Registration papers are provided to the purchaser upon receipt of the final payment. Retention of these papers is essential for the seller's protection. Even if the Lhasa is registered in a co-ownership, the papers should go to the seller–owner. This information should be included in the contract. In this latter case, the buyer receives the papers in sole ownership upon completion of payment.

TELEPHONE CALLS

Decide in advance just how you will deal with telephone inquiries. This is especially important if several people will be answering your telephone. It is best if only one or possibly two people discuss the puppies for sale. Therefore, place a pad and pen or pencil near the phone for writing down all information from the calls. With the pad and pen also place those questions which you want answered and the information which you will give out. This helps in times of confusion.

Ask the children NOT to give out ANY information, but instead to call the person handling the sales to come to the telephone. If that person is not available, have whoever answers the telephone carefully write down the caller's name and telephone number and advise the caller that you will return the call when you return and about what time that will be. If you are to be gone for any extended length of time, advise your children, the baby sitter, or other person answering the phone approximately what time you can be expected to recall. AT FIRST, NO INFORMATION SHOULD BE GIVEN OUT EXCEPT THAT YOU HAVE LHASAS FOR SALE.

Upon receiving a call, first ask for and record the caller's name, address, and telephone number. Callers unwilling to give this information are unworthy of your time. If possible, for your records, find out which ad source was used. Make notes on answers given you and keep your record. After all, if you cannot provide the potential customer with a Lhasa puppy immediately, you may be able to do so in the future.

Next, find out whether the caller wants a companion puppy or a show prospect. The caller may have a color or sex preference. Emphasize that either sex will make a good house pet.

If feasible, during the discussion find out more about the caller's situation: rural or city home, apartment or single dwelling, number of people in the family, ages of the children, fenced-in yard, Lhasa knowledge, previous dog experience, present dog members in the family, other pets, swimming pool or decorative garden pool.

At this point, give out only that information which will encourage the caller to make an appointment to see your Lhasas—such facts as the backgrounds of the sire and the dam, temperaments, and colors. Avoid giving prices. People who can afford your Lhasas may be put off by the price tag, as they have a false or unrealistic impression concerning the prices of good companion Lhasas. Once they see the Lhasas, they may be "hooked," and the price will not be an obstruction.

Set an appointment date and time. Allow sufficient time to prepare the puppy for viewing—bathing and grooming. Be sure the time and the date allow sufficient time for the prospective customer to view the puppy and for discussion.

If the customer does not keep the appointment, call to find out why.

VISIT FROM THE PROSPECTIVE BUYER

In order to prevent "accidents," do not feed your puppies just before the buyers arrive. Provide a pen in which your puppies can be easily viewed and place any puppies which you do not want on view in another room before the prospective buyers arrive.

When the prospective buyers arrive, make them comfortable. Do not prejudge the buyers by their appearances. Some, who have little money and who want to put their best foot forward, will be dressed "to the nines." On the other hand, others will dress down. There is one affluent gentleman who tells about wearing his oldest clothes and driving his most disreputable car to the veterinarian's in order to receive a lesser charge for services. Appearances can be deceiving.

Have brief discussions with the potential buyers to determine what type Lhasas they wish, what purposes they have, and any other necessary information so that they make the best choices. For instance, a timid puppy should not be placed in a home with boisterous children. Also, these are your opportunities to evaluate the buyers. If you feel that they will not provide a puppy with a good home, then nicely discourage them.

Remember that if they desire a companion puppy, present only pet prospects for viewing, and present these one at a time. Too many puppies may only confuse the issue. Conversely, if the purchaser wants a puppy with show potential, present only those puppies, one at a time. Never show the pick of the litter if it has been promised, and do not show any puppies for which you may already have deposits. If the pick of the litter has not been promised, hold it until last so that if you should be "stuck" with a puppy, it is one which you may show or use for breeding. Also, many people wanting show or breeding Lhasas may buy an older puppy or young dog whose potential is more readily seen.

Once a puppy has been chosen, if it should need a bath or a trip to the vet, offer to deliver the puppy. At this point take a substantial deposit and consider it firm. When you deliver the puppy, you will have a chance to survey the situation. If it should not be acceptable to you, refund the deposit and return home with your puppy. The right buyer has a habit of showing up.

ETHICS OF SELLING

Whether in personal contact, advertising, or correspondence, do not misrepresent your Lhasas. Never guarantee a Lhasa to finish. Should you feel strongly about a given Lhasa, state that this show prospect may finish if both properly conditioned and properly handled with no adverse events occurring. Moreover, qualify statements about a well-structured Lhasa puppy or adult with phrases such as "no apparent faults at this age."

It is neither fair to the puppies nor ethical to sell puppies at too young an age. Eight weeks is the absolute minimum, and ten to twelve weeks would be better for the companion prospect, providing you have the time to properly socialize and train during these formative early weeks. Puppies cannot be left in the kennel to "grow up" and then be expected to adjust as family house pets. Lhasas with show potential should be at least three to four months old. A copy of the puppy's pedigree should be provided at sale time. The litter registration certificate may be given at the time of purchase when an in-full cash payment is made. In cases of payment by check, it is both reasonable and wise to withhold the registration certificate until the check has cleared the bank. Partial payment conditions are discussed in this chapter under deferred payments, but the same provisos for transferring certificates would prevail.

It is suggested that a reasonable amount of time be given the purchaser to have a veterinarian examine the Lhasa after purchase. While some veterinarians may still give health certificates for selling, many no longer do so. The reason given is the danger of being held liable.

The replacement of puppies can reasonably be considered under certain circumstances: the puppy develops a disease within ten days of purchase; the puppy is later determined to be dysplastic; the show puppy develops a fault which could cause a problem for the exhibitor. It should be determined that the fault, such as a damaged coat, was not caused by the exhibitor. Replacements should be made at your discretion and only after reasonable examination of the circumstances.

Evaluate your puppies and be honest about them. Avoid misrepresenting them. Try to be fair to the purchasers without being taken advantage of by them. Try to place your puppies in good homes.

Contract Selling

Sometimes it is advantageous to use contracts when selling your Lhasa puppies, as when deferred payments are involved or when you have a companion puppy which for some reason you absolutely do not wish used for breeding.

In the cases of deferred payments, the agreed-upon provisos protect both the seller and the purchaser. If the purchaser defaults on payments, the seller has a tool with which to reclaim the Lhasa in question. The purchaser also can be sure that registration papers are provided when his payments are completed.

SAMPLE SALES CONTRACTS

NEUTERING/SPAYING:

Kennel Name/Address
Sales Agreement

Between _____ (your name) _____ and _____ (purchaser's name and address) _____.
_____ is hereafter referred to as the "Purchaser." _____
is hereafter referred to as the "Seller."
This dog is identified as follows: _____ (Kennel) _____ Lhasa Apso _____ (name) _____ whelped
_____ (date) _____. Registered with _____ Kennel Club. Reg. # _____.

1) The purchaser agrees to the purchase of the above dog under the terms which follow, and to provide a responsible home, medical attention when necessary, and will assume complete financial responsibility for such.

2) The purchaser agrees to pay to the seller $_____. This shall be paid as follows:

_____ .

3) This Lhasa Apso shall be neutered/spayed by age _____, date _____ by a reputable licensed veterinarian.

4) When this Lhasa Apso is neutered/spayed and the appropriate forms or copies thereof as obtained from the veterinarian are provided the seller, the registration papers will be provided to the purchaser within one week after receipt of the neutering/spaying papers.

Date _____

_____
Purchaser

Contract #_____

_____
Seller

A companion puppy not to be used for breeding may be sold on a neutering or spaying contract and registration papers withheld until proof of neutering or spaying from a reputable veterinarian has been received.

When selling a show or breeding prospect, the contract can include requirements for showing a dog or bitch or breeding restrictions or restrictions on the sale of puppies from a bitch or stud. For instance, a show prospect may be sold, but in co-ownership until the Lhasa obtains its championship. A bitch might be sold with restrictions as to the selection of the stud for a potential litter, especially if a puppy (or puppies) is part of the payment. Moreover, restrictions on the sale of puppies to purveyors of puppies to retail stores or directly to retail stores for the purpose of resale may be included with the notation of a sufficient fine for so doing plus the reclaiming of the bitch or stud to prevent such acts.

PUPPY KITS

Puppy kits are usually very much appreciated by those who purchase Lhasa puppies, especially the novice owner who may have some sense of insecurity. Included in a puppy kit are: a pedigree, a care pamphlet, a shot record, a small package of puppy chow (enough for two days), some puppy biscuits. Optional things which may be included are: phamphlets on training, worming, care, etc., put out by food and pharmaceutical concerns; a chew bone; a toy; a fine, inexpensive show lead (a collar and lead in one which is ideal for a Lhasa). What is included is up to the breeder, of course. The leads, for instance, are not always easy to come by. In this area we also may, if we are registered, give a puppy a gift certificate to be used at the pet supply store. The gift certificate entitles the owner who takes his puppy to the store a collar, a 2-pound sample of dog food, and a chew bone.

SHOW PROSPECT:

Kennel Name/Address
Sales Agreement

Between _____ (your name) _____ and ____ (purchaser's name and address) ____
_____ is hereafter referred to as the "Purchaser." _____
is hereafter referred to as the "Seller."
This dog is identified as follows: ____(Kennel)____ Lhasa Apso ____(sex)____ whelped ____(date)____.
Registered with the _____ Kennel Club as ____(registered name)____.
Individual Registration #_____. Litter Registration #_____.

1) The purchaser agrees to the purchase of the above dog under the terms which follow, and to provide a responsible home, medical attention when necessary, and will assume complete financial responsibility for such.

2) The purchaser agrees to pay the seller $_____. This shall be paid as follows:

   _____.

3) It is also understood that the seller will be notified BEFORE any disposal of the dog is made and given first option to the dog for the amount being offered for. The seller will also be notified in the event of the loss or death of the above dog.

4) The purchaser agrees to use this dog at stud only on registered bitches; i.e., registered with a recognized group such as the AKC (American Kennel Club) or CKC (Canadian Kennel Club).

5) This dog will not be used at stud on any bitches owned by anyone who wholesales dogs or sells dogs to pet shops.

6) No puppies from this stud may be sold to any wholesaler of dogs, pet shops, or any person known to deal in the resale of purebred dogs.

7) If there is a violation of this agreement involving the use of this dog at stud, the seller will have the option of being compensated in the amount of $1000 damages and/or reclaiming the dog without charge.

Date _____

_____
purchaser

Contract #_____

_____
seller

The phamphlet includes feeding and grooming instructions, suggestions about housebreaking, the values of using a crate, and an invitation to call the seller if problems arise. It may also give some historical background on the breed and information about the breeder and the Lhasas the breeder owns. The phamphlet attempts to answer those questions which a new owner may have.

Puppy kits are an example of good will and cost little to prepare.

CO-OWNERSHIP OF SHOW PROSPECT

Kennel Name/Address
Sales Agreement

Between _____ (your name) _____ and _____ (purchaser's name and address) _____
_____ is hereafter referred to as the "Purchaser." _____
is hereafter referred to as the "Seller." This Lhasa Apso is identified as follows: Name _____.
Whelped _____. AKC Reg. #_____. CKC Reg. #_____.

1) The purchaser agrees to the purchase of the above Lhasa Apso under the terms which follow, and to provide a responsible home, medical attention when necessary, and will assume complete financial responsibility for such.

2) The purchaser agrees to pay the seller $_____. This shall be paid as follows:

_____ .

3) Co-ownership of _____ (dog's name) _____ shall be received by the Purchaser upon the completed payment of the monetary fee.

4) This dog, _____ (name) _____, shall be co-owned until the publication of his American championship in the Gazette or receipt of his championship certificate. At this point the purchaser shall receive sole ownership of the dog. The Seller will retain life-time stud rights on this dog for use with bitches owned or co-owned by her/him.

5) The purchaser will be responsible for all entry fees, handling costs, and any other cost involved in showing this dog. The seller shall choose the handler for this dog.

6) The purchaser shall notify the seller of any change of address as long as this dog can be used at stud.

7) If the ownership on this dog must change hands for any reason, the seller must be notified and given first refusal of purchase. If the seller declines to purchase the dog, the contract must be fulfilled by the new owner.

8) Failure to comply with any of the agreed upon terms will result in the immediate repossession of the dog by the seller at no charge.

9) No puppies sired by this dog may be sold to any wholesaler of dogs, pet shops, or any person known to deal in the resale of purebred dogs.

10) Any additions or changes to this contract will be in writing and signed by all parties. No verbal agreements shall alter this contract.

11) The purchaser may advertise this dog, using the names of his sire: _____ and of his dam: _____; in reputable breed or all-breed magazines.

Date _____

_____
purchaser

Contract #_____

_____
seller

The lovely Ch. Queen's Endrehea, bred and owned by Jewel Queen, was bequeathed on Jewel's death to Doris Marquez.

22

PROVIDING
FOR YOUR LHASA BY WILL

A major concern for me, and I am sure for many others, is providing protection for my Lhasas in case of the unexpected. My research had not provided me with any material which my lawyer found satisfactory. Therein often lies a problem. Thus, I am most appreciative of the help of Charles Steele (Doctor of Jurisprudence) who provided the following material for me in his outline "Preparation of information to submit to your lawyer for drafting of a will providing for your dogs."

THE LAW AND THE PROBLEM

Not only is the law of each state different, but even within a state there will be no single form to cover every situation.

Although your lawyer knows the laws and the practices of your state, he does not know your facts. Consequently, you must investigate, make tentative factual choices, and inform him of the information.

Live Animal Gifts

A gift of a live animal, whether during your lifetime or afterwards, is different from and much more complex than the gift of an inanimate object.

The gift of any of your Lhasas involves several important factors: a proposed recipient who wants him, who will care for him, and who is physically situated and has the means to do so. These factors are important if your Lhasa is to have a comfortable life. If the proposed recipient does not have the means to care for the Lhasa, then you must either provide the means or eliminate that person as a possible recipient.

Recipients

Consider your potential recipients, talk to them, and determine whether your conjecture was correct, not forgetting the four main factors: *desire, care, situation,* and *finances.* Be prepared for the fact that your proposed recipient may have a wide variety of questions, some of which you may not be able to answer.

Any such possibilities should thoroughly be discussed. Details concerning care for the Lhasas should be covered. In addition, details concerning the recipients' freedom to care for, to handle, and to dispose of should these situations arise should be considered, including their right to neuter, sell, give away, or put a dog to sleep. Costs also must be discussed. The recipient must be made aware of costs involving transportation, temporary care or kenneling, veterinarian fees, and those of daily care. If these costs are of substantial concern to the recipient, eliminate that person from your list unless you have the means to be made available for the purpose. It would be a good idea to prepare a list of potential problems before talking to potential recipients of your Lhasas.

It is not necessary to make a final selection as to the recipient or recipients so long as you receive an affirmative answer from the possible recipient. If possible, investigate two or more potential recipients.

Of vital importance to your discussion with each recipient is the number of your Lhasas each would be willing to take, the specific ones presently in your kennel, and any later puppies or purchases. An understanding on your part as to who specifically will take your unidentified dogs, or a limited number of specific dogs, is important.

Prepare a thorough memorandum of any of these conversations for discussion with your lawyer.

Once you have determined acceptable recipients for all of your dogs, it is time to prepare the following memorandum:

a) The recipient, if any, with address and phone number, who will take all of your dogs, and the name and the AKC number of each Lhasa.

b) The names and pertinent information of recipients, if any, who will take a limited number of unidentified dogs or specific dogs by name and list by each name the name of the Lhasa and the AKC number of those to go to each recipient.

c) List the names and pertinent recipients of possible unidentified dogs.

d) List the names of possible alternative recipients and the names of Lhasas and AKC numbers to go to each and the conditions triggering such receipt (e.g., the primary recipient is unable to accept the Lhasas).

e) List the conditions under which each possible recipient will take the Lhasas if willingness to do so is conditional on particular facts, such as location of abode.

f) List financial commitments which you may have made to a possible recipient in connection with dog care.

This should be done in dollar amount in total and by time period. Do not tie yourself down to a particular method (e.g., outright gift by will, trust, insurance policy, annuity, etc. – assuming you have the financial means to do so) as your lawyer may have suggestions concerning the method.

Remember, if a possible recipient expects money or other financial help to care for your Lhasas and you either don't have it or don't wish to give it, forget that recipient. In addition, you should list any special authorization requested by recipients (such as right to neuter, sell, give away, or put to sleep) or any restrictions you desire to impose and to which the recipients will agree.

Insufficient Acceptable Recipients

Should you not be able to find acceptable recipients for all of your present Lhasas, and potential future ones, then you must do further investigation and some soul searching. Examine your situation in a realistic manner to determine if you possess the financial means to provide for the maintenance of your Lhasas as you desire and the funds you wish to devote to that purpose.

Should you have both the means and the desire, note this fact and discuss the amount and type of economic aid so that you may discuss with your

242

lawyer the technical legal devices to accomplish that end.

There are several alternatives. Should there be an acceptable boarding kennel, an outright gift in exchange for permanent care is a possibility. Remember, however, that times may change. On the other hand, if you do not know of an acceptable kennel or prefer to have someone oversee the kennel, a trust is preferable. You may want or be required to use an individual trustee. Corporate trustees usually will not accept small trusts. You will have to ascertain the minimum amount your bank or trust company will accept.

If you do not have the means to allow for the care of your Lhasas, you should plan to have someone be responsible for your dogs from your death until a designated person finds a home for them by gift, by sale, or by either. The person responsible for placing your Lhasas in homes should be authorized to kennel your Lhasas at an acceptable place, and all expenses involved in their care be charged against your estate. In addition, delineate the powers of the individual responsible for your Lhasas. Moreover, if euthanasia is contemplated as a last resort should the designated person be unable to place them within the period for which minimum funds will provide for them, you should specify both the fact and the conditions. As an alternative to euthanasia you might prefer a humane society or another agency to take over the care and disposal.

VISITING YOUR LAWYER

Only after you have done your homework, as previously described, will you be ready to talk to your lawyer, who will give you his views and will provide suggestions relative to your will in the light of that information. Your lawyer will advise you on the methods of achieving your desires under given circumstances. You will have to decide what you want to do after considering all the possibilities: legal, financial, availability of recipients, and so on.

Inter Vivos Gift or Will

There is an alternative to providing for your Lhasas in your will and that is choosing a co-owner *with a right of survivorship* now. Such a gift is called an *inter vivos* gift, or gift during lifetime, and only you may desire to make your contemplated recipient or recipients co-owners.

Your lawyer can advise you whether or not such a co-ownership is recognized in your state and, if so, the words necessary to create it. In addition, the AKC registration certificate must be filled out and filed. Moreover, if special words are required, as they are in many states, a supplemental memorandum signed by the parties involved is necessary because the AKC form does not provide for them.

An inter vivos gift is *for "always"* unless the recipient is later willing to give his or her interest back to you or unless the memorandum of gift also provided for return of that interest under certain circumstances.

Your lawyer will be able to advise whether such a provision vitiates the effect of the gift under the law of your state.

The choice between inter vivos gift and will must be based both on the advice which you receive from your lawyer and on the extent to which you are prepared to give up control.

The instrument of transfer may also provide for who kennels the dog now, who shows it, who advertises it, and who controls it. Your lawyer can advise whether this detail is necessary or whether merely indicating that you control all except takeover at death is sufficient.

Moreover, even though you dispose of your Lhasa by inter vivos gift of a co-ownership interest, you should plan to provide for all your Lhasas in your will. Periodically, as conditions change, you should revise your will. This should be done not merely because of your Lhasas, but also because of general desirability, as your lawyer will undoubtedly explain. Each time you make a change or plan to make a change in your will relative to your Lhasas, you should go through this drill before you go to your lawyer and have this same material available for him.

When we truly care for our Lhasas, we must be concerned enough to make arrangements for their lives in case of our unexpected demise. The string of fate has a way sometimes of notifying us of this impending event, but sometimes gives us no notice at all.

Our duties lay in protecting our beloved Lhasas now.

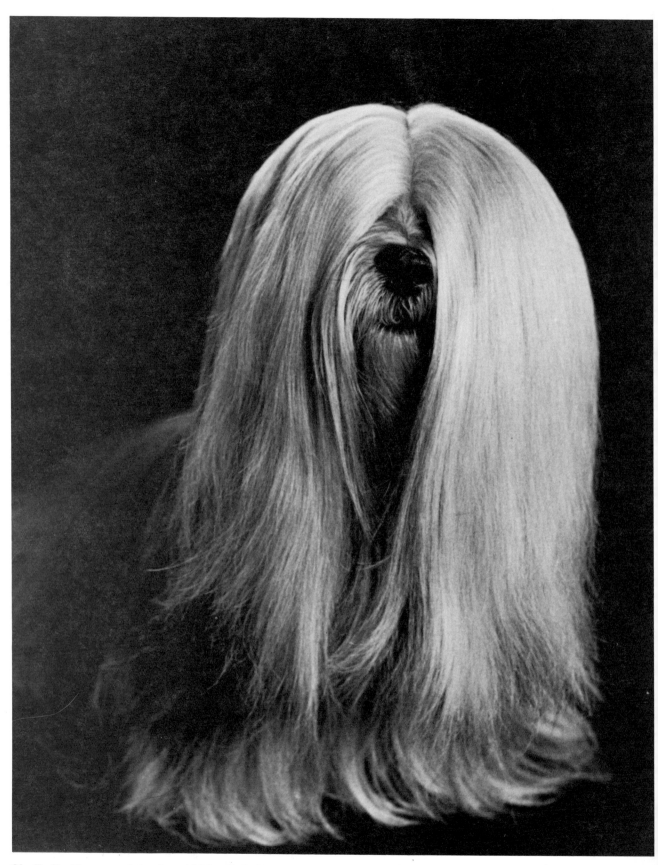

Ch. Taglha Kusu reveals her beautiful headfall. She is the dam of several champions. Owner, Jane Browning.

23

TIME AND THE LHASA APSO

Although the Lhasa Apso is a very old breed, little information about the breed is found in old records or books. Indeed, the Lhasa Apso has been recorded in England since 1900 only, in Canada since the 1920s, and in the United States since the early 1930s. The breed originated in Tibet, a land long hidden from the rest of the world and often, as it is now, governed by China. Tibet's isolation was a major factor in the lack of knowledge about Lhasa Apsos. The religion then, as now, was Buddhism, or a form of Buddhism, and any mention of these long-haired dogs during the early period was often entwined with stories of Buddhism. To understand the relationship of Lhasas and their oriental owners, and also to understand the mystery which surrounds this breed, one needs to understand some facets of Buddhism.

TIBETAN BUDDHISM

Tibetan Buddhism is distinctive from all other forms of Buddhism. Buddha lived and developed Buddhism during 5 B.C. in India; as his disciples traveled, his religious beliefs spread out and were accepted by other oriental countries. Will Durant mentions that Buddhist missionaries were sent from India to Tibet shortly after the death of King Ashoha, about 250 B.C.;[1] so it is possible that Buddhism reached some portions of Tibet at that time.

It must be remembered that during this era there must only have been pocket communities among the Himalayan mountains, whose heights and steepness prevented easy communication between communities and countries. Consequently, the Buddhist missionaries may have reached only a few of the isolated communities.

---

[1]*Our Oriental Heritage,* New York, 1954, p. 249.

Bon

The native religion of Tibet was Bon, a very magical religion which gave many aspects of life mythical powers. Thübten Jigme Norbu, brother to the Dalai Lama, tells us in *Tibet* that Bon is still practiced in many parts of Tibet and that one cannot understand present-day Tibetans and their practice of Buddhism without understanding Bon.[2]

Bon appears to be (to have been) a type of native worship—a recognition of a supreme power and the need to have a good relationship with that power.[3] There is a strong parallel between the Bon religion of the Tibetans and the religious worship of the Hopi Indians of America, even to the sand paintings which each create. Like many early religions, there was much ritual involved in Bon. The Bon also believed that by using proper discipline man could develop supernormal powers.[4]

During 7 A.D., Srontsan Gampo, the king of Tibet, had two wives—one Indian and one Chinese—both Buddhists. Their influence caused him to reject Bon and embrace Buddhism; consequently he vitally encouraged Buddhism in Tibet.

Lamaism

Lamaism, the form of Buddhism practiced in Tibet, is quite symbolistic, with religious rituals and other aspects similar to the color and drama found in the Catholic Church.[5] Tibetan Buddhism is a blend of shamanism, tantrism, and Indian Madhyamika, all various forms of oriental Buddhism. The term Lamaism is, in fact, erroneous, but the use of the term for Tibetan Buddhism has developed and has become established. Various sects of Buddhist monks established themselves under different masters in the isolated communities of Tibet. These flourishing institutions gained both religious and temporal powers in their areas, and then they became involved in intense rivalries and struggles with neighboring lamaseries.

Gelugpa

One of these sects was the Gelugpa, or Yellow Hats, so named because of the color of their head gear. Both the Dalai Lama and the Panchen Lama are members of this group.[6] By the eleventh century the Gelugpa were quite prominent, and from the eleventh to the seventeenth centuries, rivalry between the monasteries developed. The rivalry was not concerned as much with Buddhist interpretation as with temporal power.

During the seventeenth century the Gelugpa requested the aid of the Mongol chieftain Güühri Khan in its struggle for power with the Karma-pa sect. The Mongols defeated the Gtsang forces of Karma-pa, and subsequently made a religious gift of Tibet for the Dalai Lama. The various "reincarnated" Dalai Lamas ruled in Tibet from 1642 until forced to flee the Chinese in 1959.[7]

Dalai Lama

The Dalai Lama is known as the "living Buddha" and was a "god-king," an ancient type of human ruler. The word "lama," or Bla-ma as it is in Tibetan, means spiritual one, and in Tibetan Buddhism the lama is a spiritual leader. In its true sense lama should be applied only to the heads of monasteries or great teachers, but it is now used as a sign of respect for any monk or priest.[8]

The Dalai Lama was both a spiritual and a temporal leader. The lamaseries in Tibet were controlled by abbots of aristocratic background who were both free to marry and to bequeath wealth and possessions to their sons. The monks, who practiced celibacy, often doubled as warriors during the period from the eleventh to the seventeenth centuries when the monasteries were in constant struggle for power and were involved in the intrigues surfacing between groups.

The monks were also involved in translating the works of Buddha and in preparing the many religious texts. They produced the Kanjur,[9] and it was within these sacred writings that the references to the little long-coated dogs, our Lhasa Apsos, were found.

---

[2]and Colin M. Turnbull, New York, 1968, p. 119.

[3]*Ibid.,* p. 121.

[4]Norbu, p. 147.

[5]Durant, pp. 594–595.

[6]*The New Encyclopaedia of Britannica* (Vol. 3), Chicago, 1974, pp. 378–399.

[7]*Ibid.,* pp. 388–411.

[8]H. G. Wells, *The Outline of History,* New York, 1930, p. 392.

[9]Britannica, pp. 388–411.

BUDDHISM AND THE LHASA APSO

The conception of the Lhasa Apso, presumed to be one of the oldest breeds of dogs in the world and dating back prior to 800 A.D., may have concurred with the advent of Buddhism in Tibet around 632 A.D. or earlier.

The Buddhist faith of the Tibetans provides an understanding of their relationship with their dogs. Buddhism allows the dog a soul and thus permits a close relationship with man. "Buddhists, indeed, recognize no essential differences, on spiritual grounds, between dog and man. . . . In the Buddhist cycle the spirit of man commonly passes into the form of a dog."[10]

The Lamaist branch of Buddhism had been encouraged by the Manchus, conquerors of Tibet in 1645. One result of the Manchus' rule over the Tibetans was their contact with the small favorite dog of the Tibetans. Pairs of these dogs, today called Lhasa Apsos, were sent in tribute to the Chinese emperors.

The little long-coated dog, a variety she called Tibetan, was the favorite of the Empress Dowager Tzu Hsi, known to her subjects as "Old Buddha." She is said "to have encouraged the comparison of her lion-dogs to the spirit-lions of Buddha, with a view of attracting to herself . . . more of the prestige rendered to the Lamaist Buddha by the might of his supernatural supporters."[11] The picture of a lion-dog, as found in the *Imperial Dog Book*, does indeed appear to be a Lhasa Apso.

The true Lamaist lion "is a mountain spirit, having powers of instantaneous projection through space, visible or invisible at will, and similarly capable of infinite magnification or reduction of size."[12] This sacred spirit-lion is associated with the lion-dog, and the lion-dog, many believe, was bred to resemble the spirit-lion. Through fable and superstition the spirit-lion symbol became a visible sign of the power of the Buddhist faith. By this means the Lamaists, according to Collier, impressed the realism of Buddhism upon an isolated people.[13] This is apparent even in Tibetan sacred writings, as the following shows:

> In the West there was a Buddha named Manjusri (the Chinese Wenshu) who was always accompanied by a small 'hah-pah (pet) dog and who traveled the four continents as a simple priest. On his travels he one day met a Taoist who begged him to obtain an audience with Manjusri. The Buddha invited the Taoist to accompany him to his home. When the Taoist had taken tea and rice, he again requested the Buddha to secure for him a vision of Manjusri Buddha. The Buddha told him that he must observe his vows with great strictness and that the Manjusri would then be manifested to him. On this the Taoist, bursting with anger, cried vehemently, "I am indeed keeping my vows. If not, why should I have come hither to see the Buddha?" Then said the Buddha, "If this be verily so, look up into the sky." The Taoist raised his head and perceived in the sky a glow of five-coloured lights together with clouds of five colours. In the heavens he saw the 'hah-pah dog transformed into a mighty lion with Buddha riding upon his back. The Taoist had affinity with Buddha in a previous incarnation, and consequently was enabled to see the true Buddha.[14]

There are other references to the spirit-lion in the Lama Gospels, such as this one:

> The lion is the King of Beasts. Its power of increase is without limit. Similarly it may diminish (at will) and become like unto a dog. Even so is the anger of man. He who keepeth his anger in subjection shall be free of calamity, but woe of him that shall fail to bridle his wrath shall be even as the boundless increase in size of the lion. Through the lion's form therefore is the nature of anger known unto man.[15]

THE CHINESE INFLUENCE

Thus it was that when the Dalai Lama visited the Manchu Emperor in Peking in 1653, the popularity and desire for the small lion-dog, now known as the Lhasa Apso, was enhanced. The members of the royal Manchu court, already having an affection for dogs, wished to obtain these delightful religious symbols. Collier tells us that "the Tibetan grand lamas encouraged this similitude. According to Chinese authorities they [Tibetan Lamas] originated the Manchu dynasty name, basing it upon the name of Manjusri Buddha, the Chinese Wen

[10]V. W. F. Collier, *Dogs of China & Japan in Nature and Art*, New York, N.D., p. 38.
[11]*Ibid.*, pp. 151–152.
[12]*Ibid.*, p. 97.

[13]*Ibid.*, p. 100.
[14]*Ibid.*, pp. 101–102.
[15]*Ibid.*, p. 103.

Shu, who is always represented in Chinese sacred literature as riding upon a lion. "According to report handed down by the ancients, the Manchu power was strengthened from the time in sending state dispatches the Tibetans honoured the Manjusri Emperors by calling them the Man Chu Hsi Li (Manjusri) Emperors, which name in the Buddhist Gospels denotes Wen Shu Buddha.' "[16]

While the Lhasa Apso may have been seen by those rare travelers who succeeded in reaching Tibet prior to 1800, there may have been other reasons for its comparative scarcity and dog lovers' lack of knowledge concerning its existence. Its religious significance—that is, its somewhat lion-like appearance and association with the lamas—may be one reason. Another may have been the difficulty in breeding them outside of Tibet, and perhaps even in Tibet.

Old Buddha, the Empress Dowager, had her favorite long-coated dog, Tibetan, but she "was not successful in breeding this somewhat delicate race."[17] The Tibetan dogs at the royal court were

---

[16]*Ibid.*, p. 148.
[17]*Ibid.*, p. 152.

Madam Ailine, an early Lhasa.

248

susceptible to pneumonia and required more care than the usual Pekingese.[18] It is known that the Dalai Lama presented the Empress Dowager with several of the small Tibetan lion-dogs, our Lhasa Apsos, in 1908. These were the last "presents" of this nature. Foreigners who saw these dogs said that the lion-dogs were similar to those existing in Peking for at least forty years prior to 1908.[19]

Collier has documented materials concerning a number of careful breeding programs which existed in China during this period. From that information it could be conjectured that such programs could also have existed in Tibet. Among those breeding programs mentioned by Collier was that of the wife of Emperor Tao Kuang. During his reign careful breeding programs resulted in eight distinctive varieties of the "lion-dogs of Tibet." Some of the differences involved only color or length of coat. Subsequently the Empress Dowager Tzu Hsi (Old Buddha) and the Eastern Empress had nearly one hundred of these dogs in their kennels.[20]

The Empress Dowager's breeding program was concerned with developing symmetrical markings, and she was against breeding for abnormal or artificial modifications of body form, a fad among the palace eunuchs.[21] The Empress bred not only for symmetrical markings—a white spot on the forehead and a symmetrical saddle mark on the back—but also for color. She avoided breeding for bowed legs, very short noses, or for protruding tongues.[22]

The Chinese also considered three colors to be important: apricot, liver, and black. Apricot varied from golden-yellow to a rich orange-red shading into yellow. The apricot shades were the most highly prized. A dog possessing this golden glossy coat would be forgiven by the Chinese for weaknesses in other areas. These dogs were honored with the title "Chin Ssu Ha-pah," the rank of the chief button of the mandarin rank, or, as the symbol of our top-ranking athletic teams, number one.[23] It is noted that dogs of this color were not seen in

---

[18]*Ibid.*, p. 86.
[19]*Ibid.*, p. 182.
[20]*Ibid.*, p. 151.
[21]*Ibid.*, p. 53.
[22]*Ibid.*, p. 152.
[23]*Ibid.*, p. 160.

China after about 1860.[24] If one could make an educated guess, the preference for the apricot-golds here in the Western World may have stemmed from the Chinese preference.

Parti-color dogs were known as "flowered" dogs. Tortoise-shell coats ranked first and were followed by yellow and white, liver and white, and black and white. It has been noted that certain clans and families specialized in breeding certain colors and markings.[25]

The origin of the Chinese lion-dog appears to be closely connected with that of the Lhasa Terrier, or Lhasa Apso, and to the repeated subjugation of Tibet by the Chinese. The Chinese lion-dog, or Shih-Tzu Kou, was an appellation applied to all long-coated dogs, large or small, foreign or native. In Tibet, according to Ramsay, such dogs were called "lags K'yi," or hand dogs.

That the Tibetans should have selected their small lion dogs, and in accordance with the universal custom should have sent them as curiosities and presents to the Manchu scholar Emperors Ch'ien Lung, K'ang Hsi, and other sovereigns, as a flattering reminder of the Lamaist association of the Dynastic name of Manjusri, the god of learning, habitually accompanied by a small pet dog capable of being transformed into a mighty lion as his steed, seems perfectly natural. There is evidence that the compliment was acted on in the spirit in which it was given, for the palace eunuchs state that the Emperors were continually followed by their small dogs, and that their entrance to audiences was often announced by the barking of the accompanying dogs—a signal for all servants to hide themselves, or at least to avert their faces.[26]

Another to describe a lion-dog was Dr. Lochart, who did so in 1867. His description follows:

There is a kind from the Western Foreign (country), low, small, clean, and cunning, with which you can play; it is called "ha-pa dog." How the breed came to be produced or originated in Thibet [sic] it is impossible even to conjecture. As the Tibetans resembled the Chinese in counteracting the cold by increase in the amount of clothing worn and not by heating the living-rooms, the production of long-coated dogs was natural to the climate. Short-coated dogs would have had but small chance of survival. The association of Manjusri Buddha with a small pet dog, which on occasions was apt to be changed into a lion, may have suggested to the devotees of Lamaism the idea of breeding miniature lions as something

of a pious duty, a means of acquiring merit, as well as an indirect strengthening of their creed. The Lamaists themselves say that their Tibetan lion-dogs are bred to resemble lions, and they, like the Chinese, appear to be willing to call any shaggy coated dog a lion-dog.[27]

The description of the Tibetan lion-dogs found in Peking during the early 1900s gives a variety of sizes—some the size of the common "Pekingese," but usually somewhat larger.

There are many stories about the lion-dogs, including this one from 1131 A.D., during the reign of the Emperor Kan Tsung, the Southern Sung Dynasty, as recorded by magistrate Dei Yen Cheng, Hauchow, Kiangsu:

In a lonely temple twenty li from the city dwelt a priest and his one servant. He had two pets: a cat, upon which he lavished much care, and a dog which was well-known on account of its being a lion-dog. It happened one day that, during the absence of the servant, who had been sent to buy salt, the temple was entered by a robber, who murdered the priest and got away. He was silently followed by the dog to his retreat whence, after two days, he made for the city, still followed by the dog. Upon reaching a frequented place the dog attacked him and would not be beaten off. When at last he gained the city, the dog again attacked him, barking furiously. The dog was recognized as belonging to the priest, and the vehemence of its attacks was such that the murderer was questioned on the point, and failing to give a satisfactory

[27]*Ibid.,* p. 183.

Antique oriental figurine with Lhasa.

[24]*Ibid.,* p. 168.
[25]*Ibid.,* p. 161.
[26]*Ibid.,* p. 181.

249

explanation, was apprehended and, by the dog's guidance, taken to the temple. There the priest's body was found, guarded by the cat. The murderer was taken to the city, tried by the magistrate and executed on full confession of his guilt.[28]

THE PLACE OF THE LHASA IN THE TIBETAN HOUSEHOLD

All classes in Tibet prized the dog as a useful animal and punished severely anyone who killed a dog.

"The compensation for a good house-dog is 37 rupees, for a dakpyi or mastiff 25 rupees, and for a common dog 12 rupees. The importance of the house-dog to the Tibetans is shown by a further remark by Das: "When a thief steals a lock or key or a watch-dog from a house his offense will be tantamount to stealing the contents of the house or store to which these belonged. The stealing of a lock or key or a dog is the same as robbing the treasure which they guard."

These customs may be connected with the ancient religious Beliefs found in the Zend Avesta: "Who-so-ever shall smite either a shepherd's dog, or a housedog, or a vagrant dog or a hunting-dog, his soul when passing to the other world, shall fly amid howling and fiercer pursuing than does the sheep when the wolf rushes upon it in the lofty forest. . . . If a man shall smite a shepherd's dog so that it becomes unfit for work, if he shall cut off its ear or its paw, and there-upon a thief or wolf break in and carry away sheep from the fold, without the dog giving any warning, the man shall pay for the lost sheep, and he shall pay for the wound of the dog as for willful wounding. If a man shall smite a house-dog so that it becomes unfit for work . . . and thereupon a thief or a wolf break in . . . the man shall pay for the lost goods, and he shall pay for the wound of the dog."[29]

Thus it was that the Tibetan lion-dog was revered in the home and in the monastery. Tradition states that the lion-dog, or Lhasa Apso, was a companion to the Lamas, and this custom persists in Scotland where Tibetan Lamas and monks share their exile with their Lhasas.

UPDATING THE TIBETAN LHASA APSO STORY

Most of the monasteries in Tibet where Lhasas are said to have originated have been deserted. Ac-

---

[28]*Ibid.,* p. 184.
[29]*Ibid.,* pp. 86–87.

250

cording to those who have visited Tibet, the fortresses surrounding the monasteries have been destroyed by the Chinese, but the monasteries still stand. There are perhaps four still occupied. At one of these, at Sera, the Lamas have expressed great pleasure that for the first time in many years two or three boys have joined them as acolytes. The lower floors of the Potala are still open as a museum. Harrer, on his early extended visit to Tibet, saw many prayer wheels, that important symbol of Lamaism, had counted up to eight hundred of them at Chung Rivoche, and the prayer wheels are still in evidence at Dharmsala. Throughout their visit in Tibet the Kaelbers saw none of the well-known prayer wheels in evidence.

Much of Tibet is still without the physical amenities of civilization, as there is a lack of plumbing facilities in many areas. Unlike pre-Chinese days when visitors stayed in private homes, visitors are now put up in army barracks and are served common Tibetan food, including buttered tea. Transportation throughout the country from one settled area to another is usually by jeep-type vehicles.

No Lhasas were seen in Tibet, at least no Lhasas which could be so identified. The dogs which were seen all appeared to be of the "Heinz 57" variety. There are perhaps a few Lhasas in the homes. One of the Tibetan guides mentioned owning one to the Kaelbers. It was said that there may be as many as three in the vicinity of Lhasa and perhaps thirty in all of Tibet.

The largest number of Lhasas in the Orient have been seen in Dharmsala and in Darjeeling. On a previous trip which included Darjeeling on the itinerary, the Kaelbers saw many Lhasas exercised on the flat roofs of the homes as a safety precaution against the tigers. They saw no dogs in the Chinese cities.

In 1951 the Dalai Lama fled the overtaking of Tibet by the Chinese communists. Subsequently, the Dalai Lama and his followers took up abode in Dharmsala, India, which Lenore Rosselot visited. In her report contributed to *The Lhasa Bulletin* in March 1973, the following is found.

In Dharmsala one probably sees more Lhasa Apsos than in any other Tibetan community. The people are proud when they own a pure-bred dog and they treasure the animal. The Lhasas are not generally bred for color and therefore most colors are in evidence. There are many red dogs, gray dogs and the usual mixture of spotted dogs. The people tend to favor smaller dogs, but here again there is no great effort to control breeding. Proper veterinarian care is unavailable to the Tibetans, so the dogs cannot always be kept to standards westerners would seek. Also the extremes of weather do make it difficult to always keep dogs in good coat, but a Lhasa in a Tibetan family is a special pet and truly loved by all.[30]

Thus, the Lhasa Apso continues to play a part in the lives of the Tibetans as they live in exile. Some of the Panchan Lama's "dreams" for his Tibetan people—airfields, for example—have come about in a way which would have saddened him. It is now possible to fly in, thus avoiding the long, hazardous mule and yak trip. When the 14th Dalai Lama will be returning to Tibet is unknown.

Since 1959 the Dalai Lama has been located in Dharmsala, India, where his present home is high on a mountain top.

One can search and search for references to Lhasas in books which are about Tibet or refer to Tibet. Over one hundred and fifty such books were perused in university libraries and rare book collections within a 100-mile area. Some books were simply not available. After four years of this searching, treasure-loaded boxes arrived from Mary Carter of Texas. Among the treasures was *Nowhere Else in the World,* the story of Gordon Enders who possessed the "Passport to Heaven."

Gordon Enders spent his youth in India, where his father taught, and it was then that his interest in and knowledge of Tibet was nurtured. It was this that subsequently led to his friendship with the Panchan Lama. It was at his first appointment with the Panchan Lama that he observed the following:

> There was a straight-backed Grand Rapids chair in a corner beside the bookcase, which had struck my eye as soon as I entered the room. On it was resting a huge yellow-silk affair, which looked like a mammoth tea cozy—a fur-lined hood, open in the front, on top of a padded cushion. Under the hood were two tiny "lion

---

[30]"Dharmsala," *The Lhasa Bulletin,* March 1973, pp. 16–20.

Left: A Lhasa sired by Lhasa-Litsi, bred by Mrs. A. C. Dudley and owned by Mrs. May Ingmire.

Below: Early Lhasas owned by Mrs. W. D. S. Browning.

dogs," of a Tibetan breed which is much like the well-known Pekingese.

These dogs have an important religious significance in Lamaism and are always kept in personal attendance upon the great incarnations. They are the rarest breed in the world, being exclusively a palace dog in their native Tibet. As the living symbols of a legend, they recall the occasion when Buddha was befriended by lions when lost in a forest. Tibetan monks, never having seen a lion, had tried by breeding and cross-breeding several types of small dogs to create an animal which would look like a miniature of their conception of the King of Beasts. After hundreds of years of experimentation, they produced this diminutive "Fu-kao" (Buddha dog). Having created the breed, they reserved it for the Grand Lamas as one of the badges of the holy office. Every Fu-kao had a white spot on his forehead, and a white "saddle" marking over the loins, symbolic of the seat on which the Buddha sat when his lions took him from place to place.

The Panchan's pair of lion dogs accompanied him everywhere. The supervision of their care was one of the principal duties of Lo, religious prime minister and high priest. Each of the two dogs had its own retinue of servants.

At Lo's invitation—which was a most unusual one—I went over to the chair and tried to make friends with the little canine royalties. The male dog, a white and tan, consented to let me scratch his ears and indicated his pleasure by wagging a feathered tail, which fluttered amusingly in its tight little backward curl. But the fe-

male, which was jet black, gave me an experimental sniff and then retreated with unfriendly scowls into the shadow of her hooded refuge. She would have none of me—one smell was enough.

Research By Others

Among the many clippings and articles about Lhasa Apsos which were sent by Mary Carter was one entitled "The Grandest of Great Dams, Champion Hamilton Karma," by Dorothy Cohen. The following excerpt is from that article.

Most everyone that becomes interested in Lhasas simultaneously becomes interested in the history of the breed. Very little was found out by those few people that have been in Tibet. The Hon. Mrs. Eric Bailey wrote an article, "Dogs From the Roof of the World." Describing all the breeds they had encountered during the 7 years Colonel Bailey was Political Officer for Tibet— 1921 to 1928 [sic]. . . . Tibetan dogs have been in England since the late 1800's. Pictures and articles dated 1895 in "The Ladies' Kennel Journal" and 1902 in "The Illustrated Kennel News," shows [sic] some excellent specimens, but also some variation in size, and type. [sic] . . .

Probably the most extensive research into the old history of the breed is found in Virginia Leitchs [sic], "The Maltese Dog," where she claims the Lhasa or Tibetan terrier more closely resembles the Maltese than any other breed and believes them to be of common origin. Effigies of these Tibetan dogs have been found dating as far back as 2000 B.C.

Mrs. Beard's article, "A Brief History of the Tibetan Apso" tells of frescoes found of two sizes of Tibetan dogs; one the size of a donkey and the other, a mere 10 inches high thought to be those of the mastiff and the Apsos. These would be dated prior to 322 B.C.

The dog geneology chart shows the Apso as the first descendent from the first domesticated wild dog.

With this much as evidence, we have proof that the Tibetan Lhasa Apso or Lhassa Terrier as it was originally called and spelled is a very old breed. [sic]

Lhasas waiting for the judge at the Cheltenham show in England, 1933.

LHASAS OUTSIDE OF TIBET

There are no specific records of Lhasa Apsos outside of Tibet, India, or China until about 1900. However, pet dogs in paintings and writings do resemble them. For example, in a biography by Nancy Mitford, the dog pictured with Madame de Pompador is generaly considered to be a Lhasa Apso. A sketch drawn by Beatrix Potter in 1885 is of a very Lhasa-type dog. Also, some small Chinese figurines with Lhasa-type dogs found their way to American what-not shelves.

Introduction of Lhasas into England

In 1901 Miss Marjorie Wild obtained her first Lhasa (then known as Lhasa Terrier) from the Hon. Mrs. McLaren Morrison, who brought the Lhasas back from Darjeeling, India. This black and white parti color led her into a seventy-year breeding career.

The first Lhasa champion, from 1908–1911, was Ch. Rupso, imported from Shigatse, Tibet, in 1907. When Rupso died in 1917, his body was presented to the British Museum.

World War I caused difficulties for dog breeders, and the Lhasa "Terrier" breed almost became extinct. The first Tibetan dogs which arrived in England were usually classified as Lhasa Terriers. In C. Sudyam Cutting's book, his Lhasa Apso, named Apso, is classified as a Lhasa Terrier. In

Satru, a famous Lhasa of the 1930s in England owned by Mr. William Hally.

1935, they were registered as Lhasa Terriers. "The name, by the way, was first registered outside Tibet by Lieutenant-Colonel and Mrs. Bailey, who introduced them to England."[31] Actually, they reintroduced the Lhasa Apsos, as the original Lhasas were decimated by diseases such as distemper and the war which disrupted breeding programs. It wasn't until 1928 that a resurgence in the breed occurred. At that time the Col. and Hon. Mrs. Eric Bailey returned from India with seven Lhasas.

Shortly after 1921 Mrs. Bailey received two Lhasas from Colonel Kennedy of the Indian Medical Service who had been given them by the Commander-In-Chief of Tibet. These first two Lhasas were known as Sangtru and Apso. She bred from those two Lhasas until 1924 when she obtained other Lhasa stock. She borrowed "Demon," a bitch, from a Tibetan officer to do so. When the Baileys returned to England in 1928, they took with them five golden descendents of Sangtru and Apso — Taktru, Droma, Tsitru, Pema, and Litsi — as well as Demon and Lhasa, a grey and white male.[32]

The pictures in Walter Hutchinson's book give evidence to the growth of interest in the Lhasas in the 1930s. Pictured are: Satru (bred by Mrs. Bailey) and Sona (by Mrs. A. C. Dudley) owned by M. Wild and who were Best of Breed and Best of Opposite Sex at the Ladies' Kennel Association Show, May 1934; Lung-Fu-SSu and Tang owned by Mrs. E. M. Hutchins; Chantru owned by Lady Freda Valentine; seven Lhasas presented at the Cheltenham Show in 1933; Taktru and Droma, Mrs. A. C. Dudley; one owned by Mrs. May Ingonire; Hibon and Yangtze, Mrs. W. D. S. Brownrigg; Aislaby Chen-Joe Singhi, Mrs. Geoffrey Hayes; and a variety of others.

According to Hutchinson, the dogs purchased by Mrs. M. Hutchins and Mrs. W. D. S. Brownrigg in Peking were originally registered as Apsos, "but in 1934 they officially separated from Apso, on recognition by the English Kennel Club as a seperate breed," Shih Tzu.[33]

[31]Suydam Cutting, *The Fire Ox and Other Years,* London, 1947, p. 221.

[32]Walter Hutchinson, *Hutchinson's Dog Encyclopaedia,* London, Vol. II, (no date), p. 1144.

[33]*Ibid.,* p. 1819.

FIRST REGISTERED AKC LHASAS

The American Kennel Club Breed Standard was approved on April 9, 1935, and the first Lhasas were registered on May 1, 1935. These first Lhasas were registered as Lhasa Terriers and were a part of the Terrier Group. Lhasas were registered as Lhasa Terriers until January 1945 when the first Lhasa Apsos were recorded in the AKC Stud Book. Lhasas were shown in the Terrier Group until January 1, 1956, when they were moved to the Non-Sporting Group.

The first Lhasa to be registered on May 1, 1935, was Empress of Kokonor, #987979, and the second was Tarzan of Kokonor, #987980. Both of these Lhasas were bred by M. Torrible of Canada and were owned by Bruce Heathcote. Empress of Kokonor was whelped August 28, 1933; her sire was Chang Daw and her dam was Ching Ming. She was cream colored with a little black on her ears. Tarzan of Kokonor was whelped September 5, 1933; his sire was Taikoo of Kokonor and his dam was Dinkie. Tarzan was white with black markings. The sire and dam of both Chang Daw and Ching Ming were Taikoo of Kokonor and Dinkie.

Mrs. Margaret Torrible lived in Victoria, British Columbia, Canada. Her husband was a Canadian diplomat stationed in China during the 1920s and 1930s. From there he sent his wife a number of Lhasas, known then as Lhasa Terriers. At that time, as far as it can be determined, Mrs. Torrible was the only Lhasa breeder on the American continent. The Ashby family managed her Kokonor Kennels and looked after the Lhasas. During the depression in the 1930s many of the Lhasas were sold, including Tarzan, the adored pet of the Ashby children, whose fee was $500. Many Kokonor Lhasas were sent to the United States.

Tarzan's name can be found behind Miradel's Que Tee. It is said that Tarzan spent the last years of his life in Victoria, B.C. According to Peg Bishop, a little old lady appeared outside a Lhasa ring and told her that Tarzan had lived with her at the end and had died about 1955. He would have been about twenty-one at the time.

Peg also tells us that Tarzan appeared in at least one movie. Bob Ashby said that at a movie matinee their dog was suddenly on the screen, "and in one voice the family called out, 'Tarzan.' "[34]

THE CUTTINGS AND LHASA APSOS

Among the first Lhasas in the United States were those received as gifts by Mr. and Mrs. C. Suydam Cutting from the 13th Dalai Lama. Cutting made a number of trips to Tibet—1930, 1935, 1937—and these journeys were recorded in *The Fire Ox and Other Years*. One of the dogs presented to him is pictured in that book opposite page 245. Cutting carried on a correspondence with the Dalai Lama following his 1930 trip. The following was from the Dalai Lama, who sent him a pair of Apsos: "I am sending you two dogs by way of Kalimpong. Please take great care of them when you receive them. Dated 7th of the 1st Tibetan month of the Water Bird Year [1933]."[35] The Dalai Lama died that same year.

These first two Lhasas were the black-and-white parti-color male Taikee and the raw-silk-colored bitch Dinkie. A short time later, three more arrived. In 1937, Mrs. Cutting accompanied her husband on the third trip to Lhasa. At one stop along the difficult journey Mrs. Cutting "picked out a very good black-and-white Apso dog."[36] At Gyantsee the Cuttings viewed three beautiful jet-black Lhasa Apsos at the Office of Rai Sahib Wangdi. In Lhasa, the Cuttings visited the Regent, Re-ting Po gya tsap Rimpochi, supreme ruler of Tibet after the death of the 13th Dalai Lama, for pictures and tea.

Fred Huyler, Hamilton Farms kennel superintendent with Chs. Le and Phema, who earned their American titles after arriving from Tibet in 1950. Photo courtesy of Mary Carter.

[34]Ann-Marie Adderley, May 4, 1981.
[35]Cutting, p. 178.
[36]*Ibid.,* p. 189.

"At parting, the ruler told my wife he would send her a pair of Apso dogs, which greatly delighted her. I had received five of these dogs from the late Dalai Lama and started to breed them successfully in New Jersey. They are a pure Tibetan breed, usually golden, blue-grey, or black; to describe them, I can only say that if a Pekinese [sic] were mated with a Yorkshire Terrier, the offspring would look like a first cousin of the Apso."[37]

"The Regent kept his promise, and the last day we received two golden Apsos, the dogs so much admired by the Tibetans."[38] On their trip home through Tibet there was plenty of milk for the Lhasas, a male and a female. "The dogs rode well, especially Tsing Tu, the female, who bounced miraculously on my wife's saddle mile after mile. A mile and a half from every stop they would race ahead chasing marmots, which would squeal at the edge of their holes, waiting till the dogs were on them before ducking in."[39]

In 1936, Hamilton Lhasas were recorded in the March studbook. The list included Hamilton Bidgy, an imported sandy and light-slate bitch; Hamilton Tsaring, an imported golden dog, and their offspring—whelped 1/10/33 Hamilton Tashi (d); whelped 7/26/35 Hamilton Drepung (d), Hamilton Khampa (d), Hamilton Lhun Po (d), Hamilton Padmeh (d), Hamilton Rimpochi (b), Hamilton Sera (d)—and Hamilton Sarong, a lovely sandy-colored imported dog.

In 1950, Le and Phema traveled from Tibet to join the Cuttings as gifts of the 14th Dalai Lama. "They are worth a lot of money to us," Fred Huyler, Hamilton Farms kennel superintendent, said on their arrival, "because they are new blood. It isn't like going out and getting dogs in this country with our own blood lines. First we will breed them separately. Then we might breed them together to get an original family."[40]

Both Le and Phema became American champions. Unfortunately, Ch. Phema never bred, but she did live to be fifteen. Ch. Le sired several puppies and lived to the age of eighteen.

---

[37]"Hamilton Farms Kennels," "The Lhasa Bulletin," December 1972, p. 13.
[38]*Ibid.*, p. 221.
[39]*Ibid.*, p. 241.
[40]*Ibid.*, p. 243.

The Lhasas obtained from Tibet became the foundation dogs in the extensive breeding program of the famed Hamilton Farms and are found in the pedigrees of Lhasas throughout the world. They also found their ways into many prominent homes. Lhasas were still very rare during the 1940s and 1950s. They were difficult to be found, and even when found, were difficult to purchase. However, a few prominent people managed to obtain Lhasas from Hamilton Farms. One, Hamilton Xanar, became a Hollywood movie dog. Hamilton Towasg was obtained by Errol Flynn. Lily Pons, the opera star, purchased a bitch, Hamilton Aksa.

Thus Lhasa Apsos became, in a manner of speaking, status symbols. Those who saw them often fell in love with them and waited several years to obtain one.

MING KENNELS

Judge Frank T. Lloyd, Jr., owned Ming Kennels in Merchantville, New Jersey, where he began raising Lhasas in 1943, after obtaining his first two Lhasas. Ch. Ming Loo, out of Ch. Ming Lu, was Judge Lloyd's first champion, and she produced five champions—all her offspring in two litters. Ch. Ming Lu (sire: Ming Tai; dam: Tai Ho) was whelped August 23, 1943, and was bred by William N. Hatch who had purchased the sire and the dam from Holly Heath Kennels, Mrs. Harvey Hall, of Shanghai, China.

Another of Judge Lloyd's Lhasas, Ch. Ming Changnopa, was the first of his breed to win the Terrier Group, in which Lhasas first participated before becoming a part of the Non-Sporting Group. Other Lhasas owned and bred by Dr. Lloyd were Ch. Ming Tongo, Ming Tsarong, and Wu Tai, sire of the famed Ch. Ming Tali II. Ruth Smith, Kyi-Chu Lhasas, has commented on the excellence of Judge Lloyd's kennels and on the apparent happiness of his Lhasas.

For a number of years the only Lhasa Apsos appearing in shows were from the Hamilton or the Ming kennels. From them, plus some other imports, came the foundation dogs of most of the well-known Lhasa kennels today.

Ch. Marlo's Ice Cream Man O'Rimmon. Breeder, Lynn Lowy. Co-owners, Lynn Lowy and Kathy Hammond. Photo by Yuhl.

24

LHASA KENNELS

The quality and distinctness of any breed depends upon the integrity of the breeders, and this is very true for the Lhasa Apso. Since the advent of the Lhasa in the United States in the early 1930s, conscientious breeders have been selecting the best Lhasas available to them for breeding. In addition, these breeders have also been breeding with the special unique qualities of the breed in mind: the facial expression, the size, the structure, and the beauty.

As one compares today's Lhasa Apsos with pictures of those of fifty years ago, one can see a remarkable similarity. Of course, we must remember that this breed has been in existence over a thousand years, and since Lhasas were bred in relatively small areas, the gene pool certainly must have been somewhat restricted and thus concentrated on the qualities which we find today.

Those of us breeding today certainly owe much to the early breeders for the quality and consistency of our present Lhasas.

KENNELS 1933–1960s

Let us first touch on some of the kennels which have left an impression on our breed. If the majority of American pedigrees are researched thoroughly, Hamilton Lhasas will often be found somewhere in the background. Mr. and Mrs. C. Suydam Cutting established Lhasa Apsos in 1933 at **Hamilton Farms,** their world-reknowned kennel, in Gladstone, New Jersey. One of the best-known Lhasas from this kennel was Ch. Hamilton Tatsienlu, who is found in the pedigrees of many Lhasas.

One of the earliest of the California breeders was Daisy Ellen Frazier, a dog breeder who emigrated from England. During the early 1940s she established the **Lost Horizon Kennel** in Hayward, California. Her original Lhasas were Rudok Tu-Fan and Shatra of Tu-Fan. Daisy's

foundation stock also included two Hamilton line Lhasas: Ch. Hamilton Zinga, male, and Hamilton Kala, female.

On the East Coast Dr. Lloyd established **Ming Kennel** in New Jersey in 1943. That kennel was known for the outstanding atmosphere—clean, relaxed, and happy—in which the Lhasas were raised. Ming Lhasas were known for their excellent temperaments, which they tended to pass on to their offspring. An outstanding Lhasa Apso from Ming was Ch. Ming Tali II C.D., who appears in many pedigrees. This great Lhasa was the foundation stud for **Miradel Kennel,** 1947, owned by Eloris and L. R. Liebman of California.

Another well-known early California kennel was **Las Sa Gre,** 1945, owned by Mrs. Dorothy Sabine Grey at Encintas, California. Lhasas from her kennel found in many pedigrees include Las Sa Gre, Ch. Fardale Fu Ssi, Ch. Fu La Simpatica, and Ch. Manchado Dorado. Las Sa Gre Lhasas were also known for their temperaments and for their outstanding showmanship and were prepotent for these characteristics, as were their offspring.

Ch. Knolwood's Most Happy Fella. Owner, Marion Knowlton.

Chig Kennel was established in 1954 at Mountainside, New Jersey, by Anna and Robert Griffing. Their Ch. Ming Toy Nola (Ch. Ming Changnopa X America's Chia Yang), the first Lhasa ever to win a Non-Sporting Group in the East, was Best of Opposite Sex in 1962 at Westminster when she was about eight years old. At least two of her offspring also became champions, Ch. Chig Chig and Ch. Chig Jo Mo.

October 26, 1957, is the milestone date on which the first Lhasa Apso in history went Best in Show. That Lhasa was BIS Ch. Hamilton Torma, a 16-pound, deep red-gold bitch, who was handled by Mitch Wooten at the Twin Cities' Kennel Club Show in Yuba City, California. This first Best in Show was earned under judge Maurice Baker. In 1953, her owner, Mrs. Marie Stillman, had purchased the year-old Lhasa from the Cuttings, and thus Americal Lhasas came to be.

Torma was shown only seventy-three times, garnering Best of Breed sixty times, Best of Opposite Sex twelve times, Reserve once, thirty-five Group placings, and one Best in Show. Her record included a 1957 BOB and a Group II at Westminster. Torma is often seen pictured with Mrs. Randolph Scott, Marie Stillman's daughter.

Torma was an excellent producer. Her son, Ch. America's Torma Lu, owned by Dorothy Benitez of New Jersey and Florida, took Best of Breed and a Group IV in 1965 at Westminster. Her daughter, Ch. America's Rika, became one of the foundation bitches at **Licos** and produced BIS Ch. Licos Kulu La, the second Lhasa Apso to win Best in Show, who was owned and bred by Grace Licos.

Marie Stillman and Grace Licos, contemporary Californians, were both very influential in Lhasadom.

BIS Ch. Licos Kulu La, said to be the epitome of Lhasas, was whelped on May 19, 1956. His sire was Ch. America's Leng Kong and his dam Ch. America's Rika. This red-gold with sable overlay Lhasa was noted for his coat, his conformation, and his movement. At maturity he was 10 inches tall and weighed 15½ pounds. He finished his championship at thirteen months of age under the guidance of Porter Washington. He was campaigned for Grace Licos by Maxine Beam only during 1961 and captured four of his Best in Shows that year, plus nineteen firsts.

Hamilton Farms Lhasas were all purchased in 1962 by Mrs. Dorothy Cohen, who carried on the Cuttings' breeding program under the Karma prefix. Many more outstanding Lhasas were produced before Mrs. Cohen died March 30, 1977, and many kennels today are still breeding the Hamilton-Karma line.

Lui Gi Kennel was originally established in Palo Alto, California, by Mrs. Albertram McFadden, who combined English bloodlines with Hamilton. Her stock included the first English Lhasa Apso import, Ch. Chumpa of Fuzzyhurst, whose grandson was Ch. Lui-Gi's So Nan, a black and white parti-color. Another from her breeding was Ch. Lui Gi's Shigatzoo, who sired the third Lhasa Apso bitch to win Best in Show, BIS Am. Can. Mex. Ch. San Saba Chi Chi Jimi, owned and bred by Mrs. B. K. Scott of Texas.

During the late 1950s and the early 1960s numerous other kennels were established. Among these was **Arborhill,** a kennel owned by Sharon and Robert Binkowski in Michigan. The Arborhill prefix is found in many pedigrees. BIS Ch. Arborhill's Rapso Dieh and BIS Ch. Arborhill's Rah-Kieh will be among those reflected in numerous pedigrees.

In Florida, Mrs. Winifred E. Drake established **Drax Kennels.** Her foundation sire, Ch. Colarlies Shan Bangalor, produced a total of seventeen champions. Mrs. Drake obtained Shan Bangalor from Ruth Smith of Kyi Chu, who started her kennel under the Colarlies prefix.

Glen Pines Kennel was founded in California by Mr. and Mrs. Glen Bagley. Their foundation stud dog was Ch. Shangri-La Rajan of Glen Pines, who sired Ch. Joli Grumpa of Glen Pines.

In January 1963, a small Lhasa joined the Collies and the Westies at **Crest-O-Lake Kennels,** owned by Blossom Dillon. That first Lhasa was Green Diamond Decidedly, "Debbie," an eighteen-month-old grizzle-colored bitch, who whelped five litters (a total of twenty-two puppies). In 1965 Marja Dalpho Karmo, a gold-and-white parti, became the foundation stud for Crest-O-Lake Lhasas. Like many Lhasas, "Henry" really didn't like shows, but was almost unbeatable if he decided to show, and he finished his title in 1967. Peggy Haas, a very lovely lady handler of Plainfield, Illinois, showed and finished a number of Blossom Dillon's Lhasas,

including Ch. Crest-O-Lake Pretti Plez and Ch. Crest-O-Lake Hed-Dee.

Cherryshores was another kennel located in the Midwest. Multiple-group winner Ch. Cherryshores Bah Bieh Boi, behind so many Lhasas, was noted for his bright orange-gold coat. Bobby was bred by Elaine Bassett. During his brief show career he was owned by Victor Cohen. His last owner was Norma Borzenski. Bobby was a fine producer of twenty-six AKC champions, including Best in Show winners, and as a producer was prepotent for an outgoing personality and an even temperament.

Another well-known California kennel, established by Ruth Doty and Marilyn Sorci, was **Shangri-La Lhasa Apsos.** Their foundation stock included Ch. Tenzing of Lost Horizons, Lynchaven's Tangla, and Ch. Hamilton Achok. Down from them came Ch. Shangri La Sho George, found in many pedigrees.

Ch. Taylor's Ming of Miradel.

259

John Partanen established **Rinpoche Lhasa Apsos** in San Francisco, California, and his breeding program was later carried on by his daughter Alice. Well-known Lhasas from that program include Ch. Kham Te-Ran Rinpoche C.D., Ch. Tashi Rinpoche, Ch. Kepa Rinpoche, and Rincan of Telea, the latter being found in many pedigrees as he was sire of the famed Ch. Colarlie's Shan Bangalor ROM.

Bea Loob created another well-known kennel, **Zijuh Lhasa Apsos,** in Napa, California. One of the best known from her breeding was Ch. Zijuh Seng Tru ROM, found in many pedigrees. Others from her breeding program are Ch. Zijuh Tsam, Ch. Zijuh Thori, Ch. Zijuh Jinda, and Ch. Zijuh Cha La.

Onnie Martin was the guiding hand behind the famed **Pandan Lhasa Apsos** of Chico, California. Outstanding among her foundation stock was Ch. Zijuh Seng Tru, ROM, sire of many famous Lhasas. Mrs. Martin's Parade of Champions started with Ch. Pandan Lhamo C.D., with whom she fell in love as a cute eight-week-old puppy. Lhamo and Onnie were introduced to dog shows when Lhamo was six months and one week old, a show career which began with a three-point major. The Martins bred only a few litters a year, but always with their plan in mind.

Shar Bo Kennel was established at Danville, California, by Sharon Rouse, whose breeding program included BIS Ch. Shar Bo Zijuh Zer Khan ROM and BIS Ch. Shar Bo Topguy (an outstanding black Lhasa), and Int. Ch. Sharbo Tsan Chu.

Paul Williams was owner of **Cornwallis Kennel** in Pennsylvania from whence came the reknowned BIS Ch. Tibet of Cornwallis and BIS Am. Can. Bda. Ch. Ku Ka Boh of Pickwick.

Dzong Lhasa Apso Kennel was established in Kathleen, Georgia, by Mrs. Beverly Garrison. One of Mrs. Garrison's outstanding Lhasas was Ch. Colarlie's Miss Shandha ROM, bred by Ruth Smith of Kyi Chu. Notable among the Dzong Lhasas were Ch. Quetzal Fun Tu of Kyi Chu ROM, Ch. Dzong Firelight ROM, Dzong Sassy Cookie ROM, and Ch. Dzong Bamboo Pete.

River Ridge, Louisiana, is the home of **Dandi Lhasa Apsos,** established by Mrs. Diane R. Dansereau. Foundation dogs were Ch. Sugarplum's Number One Son and Ch. Crest O Lake Kin Go.

Darno Kennel is located in Illinois and was established by Norma C. Mileham. She obtained her first Lhasas from Lillian Stittig. Her foundation stud was Darno Kesang Tru, a grandson of Ch. Hamilton Tatsienlu. Her first bitch was Stittig's Lucknow Deimar, a great granddaughter of Ch. Le. Their first homebred champion was Ch. Darno Be Mieh of Maraja. One of her outstanding producers was Darno Su Lin of Maraja whom she received from Jane Bunse as a five-month-old. BIS Ch. Luty Tony of Darno spent most of his short life at Darno and sired three litters to carry on in his spirit.

Some other kennels who made their marks, but who have either cut back or have discontinued breeding programs, are **Dunklehaven, Shyr Lyz,** and **Sharpette. Dunklehaven** is owned by Elsie and Jim Dunkle of Ohio. Their Dunklehaven prefix is found on many pedigrees of good Lhasas. Outstanding among their Lhasas are Ch. Dunklehaven Rai Zen, Ch. Dunklehaven Red Victor, Ch. Dunklehaven Bianca, Am. Can. Ch. Shoot's Dunklehaven Curly Ho. Jim is an artist whose cartoon characters provided messages for their children when they were growing up. Among those characters was Dil Dox from whom Rumpie Dil Dox acquired his name.

Another recent retiree from the breeding scene is Mrs. Shirley Scott of **Shyr-Lyz,** a former Michigan Kennel. Some of the outstanding Shyr-Lyz Lhasas include Ch. Shyr-Lyz Shi-Zango, Ch. Shyr-Lyz Ko Shan, Ch. Shyr-Lyz Fabulous Flirt, and Ch. Shyr-Lyz Shama Shama.

Robert Sharp earned the appellation "Mr. Lhasa Apso" by handling many of the top Lhasas and by finishing many champion Lhasas during the 1960s and 1970s. He loves these "little dogs with the big dogs' personalities." His first three Lhasas were all bitches. He obtained his first parti-color from Mrs. McFadden, with whom he corresponded. Then he received a small blue-grey grizzle livewire, named Kyi-Chu Lohni, from Ruth Smith. He said, "I could hardly wait for her to turn six months—the day she did, she was winners bitch and went on to finish her American championship undefeated before she was seven months of age. Probably one of my greatest thrills was finishing and then owning Ch Kyi Chu Friar Tuck, whom at eight years of age still had that air and flair for the show ring." Tuck who never lost that special flair throughout his lifetime, won over three hundred BOB's, thirteen

BIS's approximately one hundred Group I's, and two American Lhasa Specialty Shows, and also achieved his Bermudian, Canadian, and Mexican Championships.

Bob also handled the great BIS Ch. Chen Korum-Ti ROM, bred and owned by Pat Chenoweth, during his outstanding career, and the beautiful bitch, BIS Ch. Kinderland's Tonka ROM, bred by Ellen Lonigro and owned by Carolyn Herbel. At one time Bob owned over eighty Lhasas, he whelped more than fifty litters, and he owned more than thirty champions. Mr. Sharp is now an AKC judge.

Another figure of note during the 1960s and 1970s was Ann Hoffman of **Tal-Hi Lhasas,** Waverly, New York. Among the outstanding Lhasas at Tal-Hi were Ch. Kasha's Tsonya of Tal-Hi, Ch. Tal-Hi Pre-Ti Celeste, and Ch. Tal-Hi Kori Ti-Ko.

Keke Blumberg established **Potala** in 1964. Her breeding program started with Ch. Keke's T'Chin T'Chin. Another of her foundation bitches was BIS Am. Can. Ch. Kyi Chu Shara ROM, who gained her Best in Show at the Camden County Kennel Club Show in December 1966. Shara thus became the second Lhasa bitch to take a Best in Show. Shara (Ch. Karma Kanjur X Ch. Kyi Chu Kira C.D.) was obtained from Ruth Smith. Keke purchased BIS Ch. Tibet of Cornwallis ROM as a young dog from Paul Williams and gave a co-ownership to Carolyn Herbel who handled Potala Lhasas. Later she sold Carolyn full ownership. The lists of outstanding Lhasas for **Potala** includes: Ch. Keke's Bamboo ROM, BIS Ch.

Potala Keke's Yum Yum, Ch. Potala Keke's Zin Zin ROM, BIS Ch. Potala Keke's Zintora, Ch. Potala Keke's Tomba Tu ROM, and Ch. Potala Keke's Adromeda.

Lhasadom lost two prominent breeders in 1981—Winifred Barton and Maria Asperu—and in early 1982 a third—Ruth Smith.

Winifred Barton died after a long bout with cancer on April 15, 1981. She and Jim Barton purchased their first Lhasa as a pet, but that Lhasa became Ch. Tai-Ping Tien Kuo, a foundation bitch for Jawin.

Maria Asperu came to Hialeah, Florida, from Cuba with the ascension to power of Castro. There she established **Tsung Lhasa Apso Kennel.** During the years her Lhasas were shown extensively, and her kennel probably listed more champions than any other. She purchased some Lhasas from prominent kennels and those which she became outstanding in the show ring and as producers, and in addition, her kennel produced many more. Among her champions were: BIS Ch. Karma Frosty Knight O Everglo ROM, Ch. Daktayl Tsung, BIS Ch. Shar Bo's Zijuh Zer Khan ROM, BIS Ch. Banji Bang Bang Tsung, Ch. Azabache Hen Tsung, Ch. Karma Rus Tilopa, Ch. Karma Cordova Tsung, BIS Ch. Drax Ne Ma Me ROM, Ch. Tabu's Chubby Checkers, and Ch. Kwan Ting Tsung. Miss Asperu's love and concern for her Lhasas was revealed by her foresight in preparing for their care after her death.

The kennel with one of the longest active breeding records was **Kyi-Chu** (1956-1982), owned by Ruth Smith of Boise, Idaho, whose Lhasas are world renown and who are still making their marks. Ruth's first Lhasa was Miradel's Ming Fu Chia C.D., whose outstanding eight champions included Ch. Colarlie's Miss Shandha ROM, Ch. Colarlie's Dokki C.D., Ch. Colarlie's Hui Ling, and Ch. Kyi Chu Yum Yum. Shandha also produced eight champions, of which one was Ch. Kyi Chu Kira, who produced nine champions. Of course, one of Shandha's offspring turned out to be one of the most famous Lhasas of all time—Ch. Kyi-Chu Friar Tuck ROM.

The death of Ruth Smith in January 1982 was a shock to many. She was an outstanding and honest breeder. She willingly and freely shared information. As Pat Chenoweth said: "For some of us she was a conscience."

Ch. Hamilton Chang Tang.

There have been many who have left their marks in some manner. Three other outstanding breeders established their kennels shortly after Ruth Smith: Georgia Palmer, Gloria Fowler, and Patricia Chenoweth. In December of 1956 Glenflo's Girja, Josie, a six-month-old, black and white parti-color bitch arrived at the Palmer's from Eloris Liebman, and **Ruffway** was started. Georgia Palmer started a breeding program which has lasted over thirty years and which has included among its famous Lhasas Ch. Ruffway Marpa ROM, BIS Ch. Ruffway Mashaka, and BIS Ch. Ruffway Patra Pololing.

Gloria Fowler's first Lhasa, a cream colored bitch, Kai Sang Tzi-Ren of Miradel came from Delores Lieberman. Kai Sang was the dam of Kai Sang's Clown of Everglo. "I discontinued the Clow line," Gloria said, "because there was too much controversy over the imports." Now most of her Lhasas are down from Ch. Licos Chu-lung La and three bitches—Ch. Kyima of Everglo, Karma Sha-Do of Everglo, and Ruffway Phari.

Pitti-Sing, bred by Ruth Smith, became the first foundation bitch of **Chen,** which has produced some great champions, including BIS Am. Bda. Mex. Col. Ch. Chen Korum-Ti ROM, number one Lhasa for three years in the early 70s; Ch. Chen Nyun-Ti ROM, an outstanding stud; and Ch. Chen Krisna Nor ROM, still winning at age 12½. These three great Lhasas and about 20 more were lost in the fire which destroyed the Chenoweth's home in November 1984. Pat is working with the survivors.

Marianne Nixon established **San Jo** Kennel in 1960. She has been helped in her endeavors by her daughter Leslie Ann Engen. The present day San Jo Lhasas descend primarily from Ch. Gyal Kham-Nag of San Jo ROM and Am. Can. Ch. Kyi Chu Kissami. San Jo has had an outstanding record which includes over fifty champions, ALAC Grand Futurity champions, and a number of BIS Lhasas, including an outstanding bitch, BIS Ch. San Jo's Hussel Bussel ROM.

Norbulingka Kennels, reg., came to be in 1961. Phyllis Marcy has bred many outstanding Lhasas, including four BOB winners at Westminster. In 1973, BIS Ch. Kham of Norbulingka ROM was the number one ROM producer on ALAC's list.

The story of **Orlane,** Dorothy Joan Kendall, and BIS Ch. Everglo's Spark of Gold ROM is familiar to most. The Orlane prefix is found on many dogs world wide.

Joyce Hadden, **Tn Hi** (1966), Carolyn and Norman Herbel, **Tabu** (1967) and Steve Campbell, **Rimar** (1968) are still actively involved with Lhasas, as are Wendy Harper, **Krisna** (1968); Lorraine Shannon, **Lori Shan** (1968), Cassandra de la Rosa, **Suntroy** (1969); Jane Browning, **Taglha** (1969), and Marion Knowlton, **Knolwood** (1969). These people have long been involved with Lhasas.

During the 70s and 80s Lhasa Kennels proliferated. Some are still with us; many have gone by the wayside. Space limitations prevent discussing all of them.

APPENDIX A

BREEDING BY VAGINAL SMEARS

by Jerry L. Watson

Most Bulldog breeders will concede that the conception rate is low among our bitches. I believe that this low conception rate is due in part to the fact that many Bulldog bitches ovulate abnormally, i.e., other than between the tenth and thirteenth days. By using vaginal smears, one can easily detect optimum breeding time in the bitch. I have bred bitches as early as the fifth day of their seasons and as late as the twentieth day using vaginal smears, and conception occurred. I know of incidences where the bitch was bred even later. The bitches that ovulate early will often continue to discharge and remain in heat for several weeks. It has been my experience that these bitches are not receptive to the male at breeding time unless they are older bitches. Older bitches will often be receptive for a week or longer before they are ready to breed. Also, I have found from experience that bitches rarely conceive on the same day from one litter to the next litter.

As an example, one of my own bitches was bred on the eighth and ninth days of her cycle for her first litter; the thirteenth and fourteenth days for her second litter; and on the fifth day for her third and final litter.

If there is any Bulldog breeder (or other breeders for that matter) that never has problems with his bitches conceiving, vaginal smears can still be beneficial. Not only do vaginal smears indicate when to breed, but just as importantly, when not to breed. If one has two or more bitches that came in heat at approximately the same time and only one desired stud dog, one can easily determine which bitch is more advanced and breed that bitch first. I have bred as many as three bitches back to back to the same stud, i.e., on three consecutive days, and each bitch conceived. Had I bred them in any other order, conception might not have

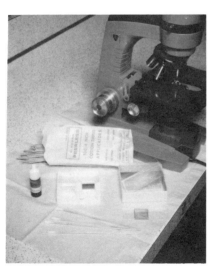

Fig. 1

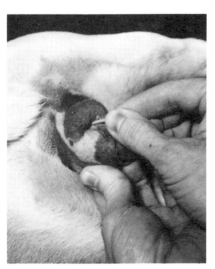

Fig. 2

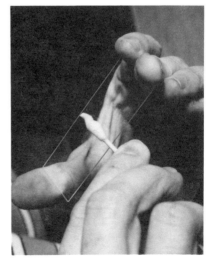

Fig. 3

occurred; however, this is purely an academic question, since the sought after conception occurred in each. Early examination of the vaginal smear can often detect an infection. If a breeder wished to ship a bitch, he might change his mind if such an infection shows up. However, some bitches still conceive with an infection, and I will discuss this later.

In order to do smears, the breeder needs first of all a microscope. I would recommend a microscope that has at least one low power magnification (100×) and at least one high power (400×). A microscope with a variation of these powers might do just as well. One needs the low power to examine the overall view of the smear and the high power for close examination. In addition, one needs microscopic slides, slide covers, long cotton swabs (not regular Q-Tips), and new methylene blue stain (Heartworm Diagnostic Stain by Pittman-Moore is the same or similar). These supplies can easily be obtained from your Veterinarian and are shown in Figure 1.

To take the smear, clean the external genitalia of the bitch. Spread open the vulva and insert the swab past the vestibule well into the vagina (under the base of the tail). Rotate the swab gently before withdrawing it (Figure 2). "Roll" the smear firmly onto a clean slide as in Figure 3. (One complete roll is sufficient). Put a drop of new methylene blue stain on the slide cover (Figure 4) and invert the cover onto the smear (Figure 5). Using this method of staining, the smear must be examined immediately as deterioration begins within a few minutes. There are other methods of collecting and staining the smear, but the above method is simple and very satisfactory for the breeder.

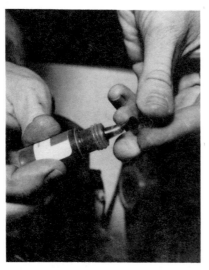

Fig. 4

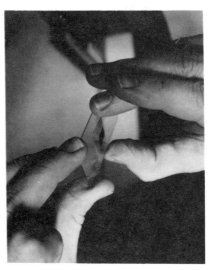

Fig. 5

With the onset of proestrus (the first sign of heat) the estrogen level begins to rise in the bitch and continues through estrus (receptive stage). Vaginal smears measure the estrogen level, and the bitch ovulates at estrogen peak,[1] provided there are ova to ovulate. Ova are not fertilizable immediately following ovulation,[2] and there is a time lag between actual ovulation and vaginal cellular response. The purpose of this article is to pin-point *optimum breed-* *ing time,* not ovulation per se.

With the increase of estrogen levels in the bitch, the cells from the vaginal smear progress from non-cornified cells (normal, rounded cells) to cornified cells (dead, flat-sided cells).[3] With the disappearance of estrogen, the non-cornified cells return, and the bitches [sic] goes out of heat (metestrus). There are four main types of cells, with variations of each type, seen in the vaginal smear. First, there is the parabasal cell – non-cornified cell with a large nucleus (see slide A). Next, there is the intermediate cell – cornified or partially cornified cell with a smaller nucleus than the parabasal cell (see slide B). Next, the superficial cell – cornified cell, with a very small nucleus or a nucleus that appears to be dividing. (See slide C). Finally, there is an anuclear cell – a cornified cell with no nucleus (see slide D). These four types of cells appear roughly in the above stated order, i.e., *parabasal, intermediate, superficial, anuclear.* Optimum breeding time occurs when practically all the cells in the smear are cornified anuclear cells. However, there are other conditions necessary for conception to occur. After the height of estrogen effect, i.e. full cornification of cells without nuclei, the cells in the smear return to all parabasal cells within twenty-four hours, or in some bitches the change gradually occurs over several days before the entire smear reverts to parabasal cells. White blood cells may or may not be present at this time.

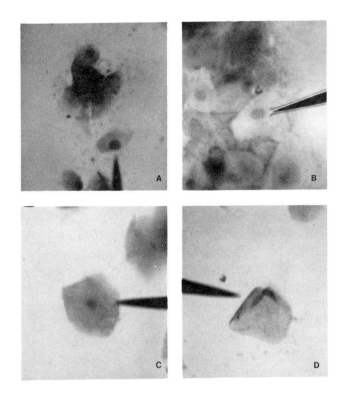

In slide E, *the pointer is on a leukocyte (white blood cell). There are several types of leukocytes, but this type, the neutrophill, is seen most often in the vaginal smear. The other types are very similar in appearance and very easily distinguishable. Leukocytes may be present in proestrus and again when the bitch is "out" (out for optimum breeding time, possibly still receptive); but there are no leukocytes present at optimum breeding time. Erythrocytes (red blood cells) may or may not be present throughout the cycle and have little or no effect on reading the smear. Red blood cells are very small compared to white blood cells and usually are not visible using the new methylene blue stain. Therefore, don't worry about red blood cells.*

Slide F *is the smear of a bitch that has been out of heat for approximately four months. Notice the round cells and large nuclei. White blood cells are also present. The next seven slides (G–M) are representative of the estrus cycle of one given bitch. All but the last two slides (L and M) are taken on low magnification (100×) in order to give an over-all view of the smear. The discussion of the slides is as follows:*

Slide G – *This slide was taken on approximately the third day after the first sign of heat. The cells are under the influence of estrogran and are beginning to cornify. (Note the difference between this slide and slide F.) Notice the "trashy" background of cellular debris and the frayed edges of cells. As the smear progresses toward optimum breeding time, this "trashy" background will clear up and the edges of the cells will be very sharpe (sic) and well-defined.*

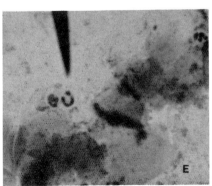

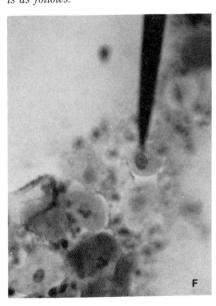

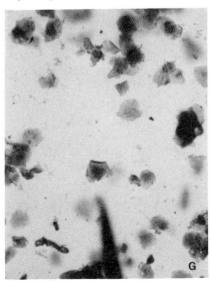

265

If there is an unusually large number of white blood cells present in proestrus or anytime during the cycle, the bitch probably has an infection even though her smears may look fairly normal during the optimum breeding time. However, usually when a bitch has an infection, neutophils and intermediate or parabasal type cells appear at an inappropriate time.[4] The clustering effect of anuclear cells does not appear; therefore, success by using vaginal smears is limited. When the bitch goes "out" however, the smear reverts back to normal. The bitch should then be bred immediately and infused with a solution of Gentocin and saline approximately twelve hours later. The bitch may not conceive, but breed her anyway. Slide N shows a bitch with an infection. Notice that some of the cells are anuclear but abnormally round and notice the abundance of white blood cells. This bitch developed a discharge a couple of weeks after artificial insemination and was diagnosed as having some type of vaginitis by her owner's vet. She did not conceive.

Notes to the Breeder

1. Learn to do smears yourself. Many veterinarians lack experience in doing smears and most veterinarians do not have the time. Vaginal smears should be done daily for best results. It is impossible to accurately predict what the smear will look like the next day and each bitch is different. I have bred several bitches that had only one day of smears that indicated optimum breeding, and the very next day they were "out." You do not know if you have bred correctly until the bitch goes "out."

2. Be patient and don't breed too early. It's better to breed late than early. The object is to breed just before the bitch goes "out," i.e., the return of round cells with large nuclei and white blood cells. If you should miss "optimum breeding time," it is not too late to breed immediately when the bitch goes out, but the bitch might not be receptive. If you plan to breed more than once, breed on consecutive days. Vaginal smears take the guess-

Slide H—*This is the smear taken several days after slide G. Notice that the cells are beginning to "cluster." This "clustering" effect is very important and indicates a "healthy" smear. Close examination of this smear under high power magnification will show that the cornified cells still contain a nucleus.*

Slide I—*This smear was taken the next day after slide H. The "clustering effect" is continuing and the cells are beginning to become anuclear. Notice that some of the anuclear cells appear almost as perpendicular lines. Notice the background is almost clear. Close examination will reveal cells with nuclei.*

Slide J—*Taken the following day. If one plans to breed more than once, I would recommend breding (sic) here. Notice the large cluster. I categorically state that even though all the cells in a bitch's smear are anuclear and all other signs are good, the bitch will not conceive unless this "clustering" effect takes place. (However, there is usually an exception to every rule, so breed anyway.) A few nuclei can be seen on the fringes of this cluster, but the vast majority are anuclear. Large clusters do not stain well and may appear almost void of color. A very good smear, but . . .*

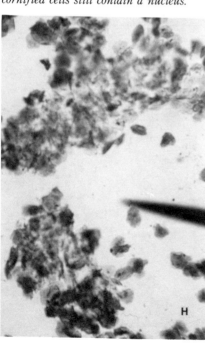

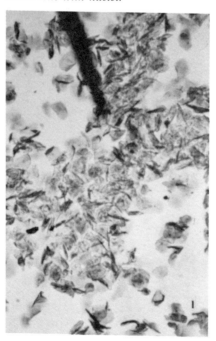

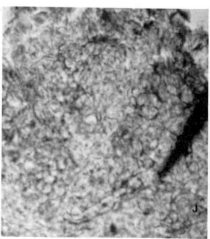

work out of breeding. Some bitches seem to go up and down in estrogenic effect, so wait them out, and don't breed too early or you will have to continue breeding.

3. The purpose of this article has been to pinpoint optimum breeding time and to minimize technical language for the breeder. Vaginal smears are no panacea for all out breeding problems, but they do guarantee that the bitch is bred at her best time and the rest is up to her.

Acknowledgements

Many thanks to Dr. Andy Suber, D. V. M. for his continued support and assistance through the years. Also, many thanks to Gary Kightlinger for his advice on microphotography.

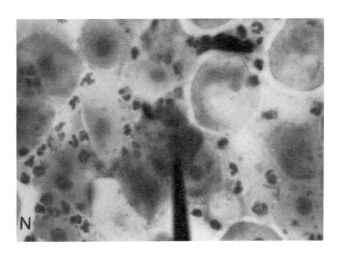

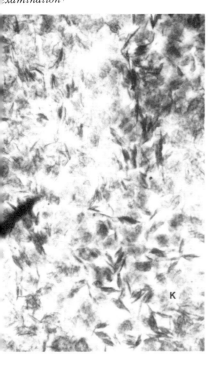

Slide K – *Taken the following day is better. Notice that the field as seen through the eyepiece on low power, and close examination*

Slide L – *Close examination under high power shows that practically all cells are anuclear. This is the height of estrogen effect.* **Breed here!**

Slide M – *Taken twenty-four hours later. As you can see the estrogen effect is over and the round cells with large nuclei are back as well as the trashy background. No white blood cells are present in this particular smear, but the noncornified cells indicate the bitch is "out." If you bred the bitch the day before, you hit it right on the nose. (Compare Slide M to Slide F).*

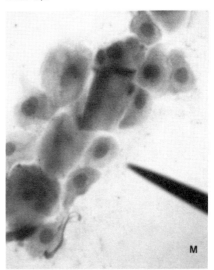

References

[1] V. M. Shille, D. V. M. and G. H. Stabenfeldt, D. V. M., Ph.D., "The Estrous Cycle of the Bitch," Canine Practice July-August 1974:34.

[2] Ibid. 31.
[3] Ibid. 32.
[4] Jeffie Fisher Roszel, "Genital Cytology of the Bitch," Scope XIX, No. 1, 1975, 9.

INDEX